PERSISTENCE OF FOLLY

signale
modern german letters, cultures, and thought

Series editor: Peter Uwe Hohendahl, Cornell University

Signale: Modern German Letters, Cultures, and Thought publishes new English-language books in literary studies, criticism, cultural studies, and intellectual history pertaining to the German-speaking world, as well as translations of important German-language works. *Signale* construes "modern" in the broadest terms: the series covers topics ranging from the early modern period to the present. *Signale* books are published under a joint imprint of Cornell University Press and Cornell University Library in electronic and print formats. Please see http://signale.cornell.edu/.

PERSISTENCE OF FOLLY

On the Origins of
German Dramatic Literature

JOEL B. LANDE

A Signale Book

CORNELL UNIVERSITY PRESS AND CORNELL UNIVERSITY LIBRARY
ITHACA AND LONDON

Cornell University Press and Cornell University Library gratefully acknowledge the College of Arts & Sciences, Cornell University, for support of the Signale series. Publication has also been made possible by the generous support of the University Committee on Research in the Humanities and Social Sciences (UCRHSS), Princeton University.

First published 2018 by Cornell University Press and Cornell University Library

Printed in the United States of America

Library of Congress Cataloging-in-Publication Data

Names: Lande, Joel B., author.
Title: Persistence of folly : on the origins of German dramatic literature / Joel B. Lande.
Description: Ithaca, NY : Cornell University Press and Cornell University Library, 2018. | Series: Signale : modern German letters, cultures, and thought | Includes bibliographical references and index.
Identifiers: LCCN 2018021945 (print) | LCCN 2018022513 (ebook) | ISBN 9781501727139 (epub/mobi) | ISBN 9781501727122 (pdf) | ISBN 9781501727108 | ISBN 9781501727108 (cloth ; alk. paper) | ISBN 9781501727115 (pbk. ; alk. paper)
Subjects: LCSH: German drama—Early modern, 1500–1700—History and criticism. | German drama—18th century—History and criticism. | Fools and jesters in literature. | German drama (Comedy)—History and criticism.
Classification: LCC PT638 (ebook) | LCC PT638 .L36 2018 (print) | DDC 832/.009—dc23
LC record available at https://lccn.loc.gov/2018021945

Geschäftige Torheit ist der Charakter unserer Gattung.
Busied folly is the character of our kind.

—IMMANUEL KANT,
CONTEST OF THE FACULTIES

Contents

ACKNOWLEDGMENTS

This book has accompanied me far longer than I might have once hoped or expected. Along the way, I have experienced unusually generous support from people and institutions across the academic world. It may take a village to raise a child, but some of us need even more than that to emerge from intellectual adolescence. Since any attempt to list everyone deserving of mention would prove an ultimately doomed act of self-indulgence, I wish to express my appreciation, in a blanket fashion, to the many people in Chicago, Konstanz, Basel, Berlin, and Princeton whose passion and intelligence have contributed to my life in immeasurable positive ways. There are a few individuals whom I must mention by name, as I cannot imagine I would have written this book without them. I feel very grateful to Allison Fleming, whose generous help and quick hands made it possible for me to work while living as a nomad. I also owe thanks to Kelly

Rafey, who read and commented on an earlier draft of this book. Juliane Vogel first sparked my interest in drama; her singular insight into literary form has inspired me in decisive ways. For more than a decade now, David Wellbery's unflagging encouragement and incisive mind have guided me in my attempt to become a student of literature. Among the many people who showed me such humanity when it mattered most, I owe special thanks to Yanoula Athanassakis, Andrew Dechet, Linda Grenis, Inka Mülder-Bach, Jonny Thakkar, Joseph Vogl, and Nikolaus Wegmann. Friendships with Seth Kimmel, Bodo Hoffmeister, Nathan Rothschild, and Joshua Schapiro have propelled me forward in the best of times and propped me up in the worst of times. Over the years, I learned in unique ways from the conversations and experiences I shared with Saskia Haag. Finally, my heartfelt thanks go out to my two sisters, their families, and my parents. I dedicate this book to Anna Philomena, who is never far from my mind.

PERSISTENCE OF FOLLY

INTRODUCTION

The overarching theme of this book is the historicity of theatrical and dramatic form. It aims to show that an underappreciated figure, the stage fool, played a decisive role in the birth of German literary drama. Admittedly, the fool provides an improbable focus for a book-length study. For long stretches of the story told over the following chapters, there were no instances of literary greatness to vaunt; and the German tradition is not known for the clowns and fools celebrated in, for instance, Shakespeare's oeuvre. That being said, this book does include analyses of some of the most acclaimed voices in the history of German letters, as well as two of the greatest comic works from the years around 1800, Johann Wolfgang von Goethe's *Faust* and Heinrich von Kleist's *Der zerbrochne Krug (The Broken Jug)*. But to understand the continuity between these literary masterpieces and the tradition of the stage fool, it is necessary to broaden the scope of our historical view and to expand it to include a corpus of works far beyond what

has typically earned a place in studies of classical German literature. Doing so will bring into perspective the broad range of cultural factors that conspired, over the course of the seventeenth and
eighteenth centuries, to make the fool into a fixture of stage performances and debates over their proper configuration. The following chapters seek to understand what gave the fool such staying
power *and* what changes this form experienced in the course of
its long career. Answering these questions will mean considering
the many reworkings and redeployments—some unacknowledged,
some willfully artistic—that made a figure seemingly incompatible
with serious literature pivotal to the effort, during the latter half
of the eighteenth century, to create a German literature of world-
historical rank.

To analyze the fool as a historically variable dramatic and theatrical form is to revise a prominent mode of inquiry that has organized literary-historical investigation since its very beginnings. This
approach can be found in the first and perhaps greatest literary
critic in the European tradition, Aristotle, whose fourth-century
BCE treatise known as the *Poetics* has shaped the terms of debate
more than any other text. It is essentially impossible for us to imagine what literature would be if Aristotle had not passed down this
text to posterity, particularly because he utilizes a classificatory
practice, derived from his logical and natural scientific texts, to
divide up genres of poetry and separate them from other kinds of
writing. Aristotle's argument that poetry can be organized in terms
of comedy, tragedy, and epic is, ultimately, akin to his conviction
that cognate divisions are possible among kinds of living beings.
When we forfeit the notion that poetic kinds are natural and given,
however, it becomes necessary to explain the cultural mechanisms
that allow for and encourage their perpetuation in time. The preeminent approach to this question—What encourages the reproduction
of literary forms?—is to consider the efforts of individual artists
to preserve established forms through intentional acts of creative
appropriation. But the artistic accomplishments of monumental
individuals can provide only a partial explanation for the persistence of dramatic forms. An adequate explanation of *broad-based*

conventional practices must look beyond the achievements of exceptional individuals to consider a range of cultural-historical and discursive factors. Because the fool was just such a conventional form, the task of this study is to grasp the reasons underlying both its unspectacular persistence across vast stretches of time *and* its innovative appropriation in the hands of artists such as Goethe and Kleist.

The fool is a form whose significance can be discerned, as Friedrich Nietzsche's genealogical method suggests, only in terms of "its actual use and integration into a system of ends" (*thatsächliche Verwendung und Einordnung in ein System von Zwecken*).[1] Expanding the discussion of this dramatic and theatrical form to a larger network of goals means looking beyond the field of the literary proper, beyond plays and aesthetic treatises, to other contexts that address the place of comic theater in the weave of life. Unexpected deviations in the conception of the fool resulted as much from poetological disagreements over the proper way to write a play as from arguments over the broader civic potential of comic theater. Treating the fool as a form that persisted across the seventeenth and eighteenth centuries within an encompassing "system of goals" means examining its place in a broad swath of discussions on the relationship between text and performance, tradition and innovation, the individual nation and the broader European context, and more. These are the competing forces that allowed for the fool's perpetuation and modification over time.

The vicissitudes of the form of the fool are evidence of the deep cultural need to regulate laughter. In other words, controversies surrounding the fool's status as a figure worthy of celebration or scorn were rooted in concern with the individual and collective effects of different varieties of comic speech. Although it can easily escape attention, one of the most basic distinctions organizing cultural activity and its analysis is the difference between humorous

---

1. Friedrich Nietzsche, *Zur Genealogie der Moral*, in *Sämtliche Werke: Kritische Studienausgabe in 15 Bänden*, ed. Giorgio Colli and Mazzino Montinari (Berlin: De Gruyter, 1999), 5:313.

and serious modalities of human behavior.[2] Discourses on the significance of joking and techniques of soliciting laughter, extending from classical antiquity to the present day, often brush up against but fail to directly address the fundamental importance of this distinction. Just as laughing and crying stand opposed as distinct manifestations of human expression, so the serious and the humorous issue from two distinct and opposed attitudes, two distinct and opposed ways of experiencing life and finding meaning in it.[3] A version of this distinction can already be found in ancient Greek and Roman rhetoric, and the construction of this distinction there can help sharpen our own methodological stance. The rhetorical tradition stresses the need for public speakers to intuit the line between seriousness and jest, and develop the ability to solicit each mood separately, under the appropriate circumstances, and to the proper degree. A directive attributed to the fifth-century BCE sophist Gorgias, later enthusiastically endorsed by Aristotle in his own treatise on rhetoric, suggests that a public speaker should "destroy their opponents' seriousness with laughter and their laughter with seriousness" (τὴν μὲν σπουδὴν διαφθείρειν τῶν ἐναντίων γέλωντι, τὸν δὲ γέλωτα σπουδῇ).[4] However, just because the two species of speech are opposed does not mean that they should be used indiscriminately. Quintilian, the first-century CE Roman rhetorician, accordingly disparaged Cicero as overly humorous and Demosthenes as overly serious. Much like Greek and Roman orators before him, Quintilian asserts that the proper apportionment of light- and heavyheartedness is necessary to establish and maintain internal coherence. The premise of this historical typology, as well as Gorgias's prescript, is the belief that seriousness and joking form an opposition and, even more, that

---

2. There is a brief but insightful discussion of the "dialectic of play and seriousness" in Stephen Halliwell, *Greek Laughter: A Study of Cultural Psychology from Homer to Early Christianity* (Cambridge: Cambridge University Press, 2008), 19–38. I strongly recommend the methodological observations in Mary Beard, *Laughter in Ancient Rome: On Joking, Tickling, and Cracking Up* (Berkeley: University of California Press, 2014), 23–69.

3. Helmuth Plessner, *Laughing and Crying: A Study of the Limits of Human Behavior*, trans. James Spencer Churchill and Marjorie Grene (Evanston, IL: Northwestern University Press, 1970).

4. Aristotle, *Rhetoric* 1419b3–5.

they can counteract one another. In a crucial formulation, Quintilian writes, "We understand as a joke that which is the opposite of serious" (*iocum vero id accipimus quod est contrarium serio*).[5]

Despite the appearance of a watertight division, the traditional distinction is weighted disproportionally toward the side of seriousness: humor enters into rhetorical typologies only insofar as it serves an ulterior purpose of promoting serious contents. The risible worth attending to is essentially a more gripping, pleasurable, and efficacious avenue for arriving at a destination that is no less available along a more earnest route. In rhetoric, laughter-provoking speech is only a peer to serious speech insofar as it can contribute to the final purpose of rhetoric in general—whether that goal be civic or philosophical.[6]

The basic structure evident in the rhetorical distinction is, in fact, common to a group of seemingly discrepant theories, including several modern ones, which are far removed and seemingly more radical. While the ancients expressed exclusive interest in those jocular modes of speech that communicated subjects of import, the modern tendency has been to insist on the subterranean seriousness of even the most trivial forms of speech or sign-making. Two distinctive permutations of the opposition between seriousness and levity have made a huge impact over the last century. First, modern anthropologists and semioticians have endeavored to expose the "human seriousness of play," to show that human society is held together by shared meanings that are evident in even the most mundane and mindless rites, rituals, signs, or statements.[7] Within this scheme, the analytic task is to show that all human activity, no matter the context, is meaning-making, and that this meaning is the glue that holds together a society. There is a second, equally prevalent strand, which seems irreconcilably different, but in truth possesses a deep structural affinity. It has become a near-theoretical commonplace to claim, in line with highly celebrated thinkers from Henri Bergson and Sigmund Freud to Mikhail Bakhtin and Mary Douglas, that joking and laughter are

---

5. Quintilian, *The Orator's Education*, trans. Donald A. Russell (Cambridge, MA: Harvard University Press, 2001), 2:72.

6. See the historical account in Quintilian, *The Orator's Education*, 1:257–417.

7. See Victor Turner, *From Ritual to Theater: The Human Seriousness of Play* (New York: Performing Arts Journal Publications, 1982).

defined in terms of their "subversive effect on the dominant structure of ideas."[8] These authors developed trenchant theories, each
deserving of meticulous attention, that are united in the assertion
that joking speech possesses the capacity to challenge and subvert
conscious thought, rationality, bodily control, or hegemonic social
structures. In this respect, they are also unified in the assertion that
joking copes with matters of ultimate importance to the individual
human being and for society.

Missing from these theories is a type of laughter that does not serve
a higher purpose, which is sometimes called, in thoroughly uncom-
ical jargon, autotelic laughter. What of this sort of humor? What
of the varieties of speech and gesture that cause a good chuckle and
nothing more—which do not solicit deeper reflection, but instead
provide a distraction from heavy-duty thoughts and concerns?
These, too, are subject to policing and controlling, and can thus
be shaped and changed. What is more, these, too, can serve a purpose. One does not have to look hard to find historical examples
of entertainment—from public spectacles in Rome to American
romcoms—that would be unfairly assimilated into the category
of the serious. I wish to claim that something similar is at work
in the first appearance of the stage fool in the German-speaking
lands. Here, a variety of comic theater was born that aimed to
pass the time, to supply ephemeral amusement, and to strive for
nothing more than to bring the audience pleasure. His first appearance on the stage could be described in terms of the typical
American-English locution "It's just entertainment."

A more supple and encompassing distinction between the risible and the serious can help account for the historical alterations to which the stage fool was subject. The hallmark of the
fool may have always been humor, but he also went from being
a figure featured in contexts without any aspiration to coun-
termand authority or challenge norms to serving as the comic

---

8. The phrase is from Mary Douglas, "Jokes," in *Collected Works* (New York:
Routledge, 2010), 5:146–164, here 150.

engine of some of the most profound plays in the German literary tradition. The heuristic potency of a distinction between the risible and the serious depends on its capacity to account for such historical changes, to describe modifications in the purpose and execution of theatrical communication. For this reason, we might think of the serious and the risible as occupying different spaces on a continuous line, with some regions of overlap where they seem one and the same, and other disparate zones of complete antithesis. This view can be understood as the radicalization of a stunning observation from Jean Paul's *Preschool of Aesthetics* (*Vorschule der Aesthetik*, 1804/1812), one of the most technically insightful aesthetic treatises in the German tradition. Jean Paul postulates that "one could make on every planet a different kind of literature out of the serious and the jocular" (*aus Scherz und Ernst in jedem Planeten eine andere Dichtkunst setzen könnte*), and continues by saying that literature is *per se* a mode of human expression "connected to time and place."[9] The different historical embodiments of the fool, therefore, are essentially different ways of negotiating this fundamental distinction. Literature is not based on an exclusive either/ or, but on space- and time-specific combinations of these two kinds of speech. We find a related idea in Goethe's references to his own works, during his later years, as "very serious jokes."[10] Goethe here identifies his literary productivity as inhabiting a place toward the center of the continuum of the joking and the serious. To modify perhaps the most famous formula for the aesthetic around 1800,

---

9. Both quotations from Jean Paul, *Werke* (Munich: Carl Hanser Verlag, 1973), 5:92. The programmatic importance of the distinction between "serious" and "comic" literature for Jean Paul's classifications cannot be overestimated. Literature can, in his view, have either an objective (serious) or a subjective (comic) thematic focus (5:67). Jean Paul's analysis of humor provides a good test case for the claim I am making, namely, that we are not dealing with irreconcilable opposites, but rather poles along a continuous line, with antithesis as well as overlap. For a probing explication, see Paul Fleming, *The Pleasures of Abandonment: Jean Paul and the Life of Humor* (Würzburg: Königshausen und Neumann, 2006), esp. 44–57.

10. Letter, 3/17/1832, FA II 11:555.

from Kant's *Critique of the Power of Judgment* (*Kritik der Urteils-kraft*, 1790), we might say that the joking character of Goethe's literary works means they lack an instrumental purpose, while their serious engagement with issues of fundamental importance in life lends them their purposive shape.

It is thus reasonable to conjecture that literature, as a time- and place-specific mode of creative expression, depends on an alchemy of the serious and the joking, not their irreconcilable opposition. The great benefit of this claim for the history of the stage fool is that it forces us to expand the field of inquiry beyond linguistic or properly literary phenomena and to remain sensitive to variation over time. By looking at more than plays and aesthetic treatises, it will also become possible to approach the fool as a historically variable form, rather than as a static character or type. Whereas the notion of character typically provides a qualitative description of a human being with a unique biography, and a type invokes a static mold, the notion of form is significantly more elastic. It has the virtue of not picking out any biographical qualities as essential or terminological tendencies as definitive. Instead, it locates the fool as a dramatic and theatrical phenomenon that survived through its incessant regeneration. By that, I mean that as the fool was taken up repeatedly as a theme in discourse and a presence on the stage, the encompassing "system of ends" within which the fool was situated also underwent major changes. The form of the fool was, on the one hand, portable: it could migrate from the stage into poetological discourse, into discussions of the well-ordered polity, and so on. But the form was also mutable: the transposition into new argumentative settings wrought significant changes in the potential assigned to the fool's comic practice. Looking back at the seventeenth and eighteenth centuries, it seems that the fool was, for some, the main attraction of an entertainment-driven show, and for others, a vulgar distraction from the edifying potential of drama; for some, a community-building comic force, and for still others, an underappreciated tradition that could revitalize the stage culture.

In the domain of dramatic and theatrical forms, the cardinal rule is to adapt or perish. And so if the fool persisted in time through adaptation, it is worth searching for an underlying logic to these changes. The guiding claim of this study is that throughout the seventeenth and eighteenth centuries, the fool consistently provides a medium through which the most basic elements of drama and theater could be distilled, debated, and tested. I claim that the emergence of German literary drama, viewed in retrospect, cannot be severed from the ongoing controversies that surrounded the fool. Paradoxical as it may sound, a profoundly unliterary and emphatically theatrical figure contributed in essential ways to the creation of German literary drama.[11]

At the same time, identifying the fool as a form is not without risk. Broadly speaking, within twentieth-century scholarship, the analysis of form has often entailed a sequestering of literary objects from broader social-historical issues, with an emphasis instead on the internal organization of individual works and the complexities of their linguistic patterns. My intention is to use the concept of form for the exact opposite purpose. I wish to understand what forces, beyond the imagination of the solitary author, secured the centuries-long persistence of the fool as a dramatic and theatrical form. Accordingly, I approach the vicissitudes of form in connection with the broader cultural context, not in isolation from it. And as a further consequence, the individual and unique work does serve as the sole crucible of analysis. Since the fool was a widespread, general role, not an individual character, so too the following discussion draws on a rich body of evidence.

With this methodological framework in place, it is worth saying a word about the notion of origins in the title of this book. As a point

---

11. My aspiration to provide a succinct and coherent account of certain origins of German literary drama has led me to exclude another context, within which the theatrical fool traced a singular trajectory. The Viennese folk theater, which has been the subject of a large body of exceptionally meticulous research, does not figure in this book. Its origins, development, and outgrowths ultimately unfold in very different ways than elsewhere in the German-speaking world, and for this reason I have elected not to examine it in close detail. To do the unique and fascinating Viennese tradition justice would have, unfortunately, exploded the frame of this study.

of contrast, let us return to the first account of the origin of a dramatic form. Aristotle's *Poetics* gives us a narrative of the steady emergence of an ennobled genre from archaic—we might say, pre-poetic—prototypes. In book 4, he claims that tragedy began as improvisatory choral songs and only progressively emerged into what we would recognize as a *bona fide* genre. The ennoblement and consolidation of the genre comes about through two simultaneous procedures. On the one hand, there is a shedding of impropriety, through a "step-by-step" (κατὰ μικρὸν) process that "brought about many changes" (πολλὰς μεταβολὰς μεταβαλοῦσα) until it reached "its own nature" (τὴν αὑτῆς φύσιν).[12] This civilizing process is accompanied by the addition of more dialogic complexity into the plays. First there was only the chorus singing and dancing in unison, then there was the chorus and one additional role, then two, then three. Genuine tragedy comes about in the twin passage from the simple to the complex and the raw to the cultivated. Aristotle provides us with a fairly simple story of things getting better; he accounts for the existence of the most venerated literary genre by showing how a certain set of elements undergoes a process of self-improvement. Tragedy emerges from the division and recombination of a basic set of properties until "its own nature" comes to full flower.

Today, we might well have a knee-jerk aversion to the teleological direction of Aristotle's narrative of origin. It is easy to feel some discomfort with the idea that, from the very beginning, inchoate choral songs and dances were aiming toward the perfection or entelechy of fourth-century BCE tragic poems. And yet there is little controvertible about the claim that, viewed in retrospect, the constitutive elements of tragedy came about through a process of progressive accrual and transformation; the intermediate steps within this process then culminated in the birth of a full-fledged form. Even if we deny that there can be a complete and enduring form of tragedy, according to "its own nature," by pursuing an origin story, we still leave open the possibility of anticipatory stages of incompleteness.

---

12. Aristotle, *Poetics* 1449a12–15.

At the same time, it is worth emphasizing that Aristotle's account radically limits the sorts of causes deemed relevant to the making of genuine tragedy. He makes no mention of different domains of society, nor of influences from other cultures, or the mandate of religious, civic, or scholarly authorities. Instead, tragedy emerges through the persistent labor of solitary poets, whose searching efforts eventually draw out the genre's intrinsic possibilities and bring about its fully developed state.

It is a near truism today, meanwhile, that the course of history is unpredictable and its significance prone to multiple, retrospective interpretations. The contrast to Aristotle's teleological arrangement is crucial not because it illustrates the wrongheadedness of each and every origin story, but rather because it helps us recover, in the absence of natural necessity or intentional design, the improbability of the pivotal presence of the fool in drama and theater for two centuries. The task, therefore, is to discover underlying developmental patterns without subscribing to a predetermined narrative that imagines the modernization process as a forward march of cultural refinement. That is to say, the persistence of folly throughout the eighteenth century runs athwart well-worn narratives about the eighteenth century as the moment of an enlightened assertion of rational control. Just as the eighteenth century cannot be understood as the moment that reason overcame religious superstition, so too should it not be treated as the moment when literary earnestness replaced preliterary folly.

For the period between roughly 1730 and 1810, the fool provides a prism through which two rudimentary but utterly pressing matters came into view, both related to the relationship between the two seemingly self-evident terms *drama* and *theater*. The first matter pertains to the question, What is the theater for? And the second, What is a dramatic text? In the final analysis, these are not two questions but rather interdependent ways of thinking through a single historical state of affairs. For a core controversy running through the eighteenth century was the relationship between the fixed and controllable dramatic text, on the one hand, and the singular and therefore always unforeseeable actuality of performance, on the other. The fool was uniquely ambidextrous, playing a pivotal role on each side of the distinction and imposing, by the end of the eighteenth century, a higher unity on them both. These two questions are, properly speaking, historical questions, and therefore the narrative I build in this study proceeds chronologically. That is not to say that it proceeds through a paratactically arranged sequence of events. Instead, the four parts of the study, each subdivided into four succinct chapters, argue that the fool is one of the chief pillars in the internally dynamic and contentious process that gave rise to German drama and theater.

The starting point of this book, it bears emphasizing, lies outside the gamut of what is ordinarily treated as modern German literature. Laying the foundation for the chapters to come, part 1 investigates the process of cultural transfer that brought the fool to the German stage at the turn of the seventeenth century and that provided for his immense popularity. My objective in this part of the book is to understand how scrappy traveling players from England, who came to the German-speaking lands in search of gainful employment but lacked facility in the local tongue, created a veritable star. Part 1 shows that the distinctive practice of stage interaction associated with the fool was deeply connected to the contexts in which the itinerant acting troupes performed. Examining a rich body of scripts as well as the extant testimonial evidence, I distill the fool's patterns of dialogue participation. While much of his art was improvisatory, the fool's comic interventions come at specific junctures and possess a consistent significance. My overarching claim is that the fool provided the centerpiece of a commercially driven performance culture that placed greater emphasis on sustained entertainment than on coherence of plot. His characteristic joking techniques were responsible for arresting the audience's attention and comically deflating the concerns of quotidian life. Part 1 demonstrates the interdependence of the concrete circumstances of performances and the telltale conventions of the fool's stage role.

Expanding the historical trajectory into this largely uncharted territory allows me, in part 2, to account for the complexities of an intensely dynamic and oft-neglected epoch, the years between 1730 and 1750. During this period, conventionally referred to as the early Enlightenment, the fool became a crucial object of dispute among reform-minded scholars and playwrights. The aspiration to endow the theater with a moral and aesthetic purpose, reformers claimed, required limiting the fool's comic prerogative. The reform project returned again and again to the story of a spectacular auto-da-fé in which the fool was supposedly banished, once and for all, from the stage. My argument concentrates on two components of the early Enlightenment endeavor to overhaul the theatrical culture. The first was a strict conception of the comedic genre. Although ostensibly modeled on ancient Greek and Roman sources, the design of early Enlightenment comedy was equally inflected by contemporary concerns, in particular by the desire to craft a moral message and to block the fool's comic interventions. In addition, the early Enlightenment sought to use the print medium as a tool for altering performance standards. Translations, new compositions, and anthologies became the key mechanisms for improving the stature of the German stage. Contrary to scholarly consensus, I claim that the fool did not simply disappear from the stage to make space for compositionally conventional, classicizing dramas. Instead, the early Enlightenment evinced a nuanced and internally conflicted attitude toward the capacity of laughter-provoking folly to make theater flourish.

In part 3, I turn to the latter half of the eighteenth century, during which questions concerning the relationship between the theater and the broader nexus of social life come into sharper focus. I begin by discussing a widely influential discourse on the role of the government in assuring the well-being of its citizens, the so-called *policey*. The fool was conceived of as a mechanism for ensuring that members of society had the entertainment necessary to recover from the day-to-day life of labor. I then move to the debates over the potentially salubrious effects of laughter on both the individual and the larger social community. In the final two chapters of part 3, I advance the claim that the fool plays a pivotal role in perhaps the most important project of the late eighteenth century, the attempt to create a nationally distinctive mode of dramatic composition and theatrical performance. A broad spectrum of authors and critics turned to the fool as a resource for the propagation of performance conventions specific to German culture. I show that the use of folly as a nation-building instrument hinges on the belief that the comic, rather than the tragic, depends on and fosters local custom. In the latter half of the eighteenth century, the fool returns to the stage as a socially binding force.

In part 4, my approach switches in a significant way. Rather than considering large-scale phenomena by synthesizing large quantities of evidence, I focus my attention on the role of the fool as he appears in two works by the two greatest German playwrights around 1800, Goethe and Kleist. I claim that the fool functions in their plays as a model of theatrical presence, as the guarantor of intimacy between the figures on stage and the audience. Across his long and storied career, Goethe asserts that the early Enlightenment banishment of the fool was based on a mistaken assessment of both the elementary function of theatrical entertainment and the artistic potential of this once-beloved figure. I show that the scenic construction and overarching patterns of significance in Goethe's 1808 *Faust* tragedy cannot be properly understood without acknowledging their debt to the fool. In the final chapter of the study, I draw out the brilliant recasting of the fool in Kleist's 1811 comedy, *The Broken Jug*. Kleist's play amounts to a subtle but penetrating reflection on the possibility of a literary rendering of the fool in the early decades of the nineteenth century. His comedy profoundly thematizes the tension in eighteenth-century Germany between, on the one hand, the broader European literary tradition since classical antiquity and, on the other, the immensely popular tradition of the stage fool. These phenomenal literary achievements, I claim, stand in productive dialogue with a tradition that subsequent scholars have typically dismissed as a trivial forerunner to serious works of literary art.

Part I

The Fool at Play

Comic Practice and the Strolling Players

Stultorum plena sunt omnia.

The world is full of fools.

—The fool in an adaptation of
Andreas Gryphius's *Papinianus*, and Cicero

1

Birth of a Comic Form

German theater—and, in particular, its early modern ancestor—is not especially well known for its sense of humor. But the lack of acclaim is not for lack of evidence: beginning around 1600, comic elements reigned supreme on the stage. In fact, during the period before German-speaking towns could espouse a local theater building, no single factor ensured a leavened atmosphere with the same effectiveness and frequency as did the stage fool. A verbal and gestural wild-card figure, the fool dazzled audiences with song and dance, and used rude jokes to provoke their laughter. He was more protean and less rooted in a specific social context than the court fools that still today in the twenty-first century occupy a vivid place in our cultural imagination. At the same time, the stage fool shared with his royal cousin a strong penchant for the irreverent and salacious. While the court fool belonged, in general, to a structured social-political environment, the German stage fool flourished on the makeshift stages lacking for luster that first began to sprout up,

through an improbable turn of events, across the German countryside around 1600. His unlikely appearance raises the question, Whence did he come? His long-lasting presence, meanwhile,
presses the related query, What provided for his success? In order
to trace the beginnings of the German stage fool and account for
his centrality to the flourishing dramatic and theatrical culture that
arose in the seventeenth and eighteenth centuries, we must look at
a little-known process of transfer that brought English players and
their plays to the German-speaking lands. However some caution
is necessary in approaching these plays—their language, their integrity, their form—for they testify to a process of transmission
quite different from what ordinarily falls under the category of "literary tradition."

It may seem strange to imagine traveling English players as the
decisive point of departure for a genealogy of German drama. After
all, the beginning marked out by the sudden appearance of
English-speaking players around 1600 was anything but a glorious one. The traveling groups of players numbered fewer than
ten and scarcely more than twenty, and they spent long stretches
of time on the road in search of a paying audience. Despite their
tireless efforts, they seem to have rarely emerged from a pitifully
impecunious existence. The itinerant and often penurious lifestyle of troupes means that material evidence of their concrete situation is rather scant. Moreover, the fool's lifeblood was the live
unfolding of a stage performance, especially spontaneous gesture
and improvised expression. A historical reconstruction thus cannot rely on the highly educated authors of the seventeenth century,
among whose writings very few traces of the fool can be detected.
And the English traveling players traced a different path than
the *commedia dell'arte* troupes, whose improvisatory scenarios
were enjoyed by the political elite and within courtly contexts as
early as 1568.[1] The fool of English extraction, by contrast, first

---

1. Although the scholarship once conflated the fool of English extraction and
the tradition of the *commedia dell'arte*, the two lineages can, at least for the seventeenth century, be kept largely separate. See, most recently, Ralf Böckmann, *Die
Commedia dell'arte und das deutsche Drama des 17. Jahrhunderts* (Nordhausen:
Verlag Traugott Baut, 2010). See also Peter Sprengel, "Herr Pantalon und sein

gained a foothold, around 1600, in a milieu without lofty artistic ambitions, which made liberal use of translations or loose adaptations from preexisting playtexts. Wherever he appeared, the fool delighted with a unique blend of immediate recognizability and humorous surprise. From his first appearance, the fool was, in a word, a hit.

Although the historical record leaves no doubt as to the overwhelming success of this impertinent jokester, the cause of that success is less easy to identify. In contrast to a genre such as tragedy, we cannot chalk up his long and widespread career to the imprimatur of aesthetic experts or the rigors of humanistic training. Reverence for traditional poetic forms was nowhere to be found in those settings where the fool beguiled audiences. Moreover, dictates such as (good) taste and novelty did not provide direction for the popular stage of the seventeenth century, and traveling players did not feel the sway of rhetorical and aesthetic dictates. In general, early modern German playtexts seldom circulated in authoritative editions (the sort a modern reader might expect), and they almost never commanded fidelity from actors.[2] While the early seventeenth century did see a movement aspiring to establish German as a language for the making of poetry, such efforts took place in elite scholarly venues far removed from the traveling troupes that first brought the fool into existence.[3] Indeed, the fool gained traction in a world far less concerned with poetic authors or texts than with just giving audiences a gripping show.

Knecht Zanni: Zur frühen Commedia dell'arte in Deutschland," in *Wanderbühne: Theaterkunst als fahrendes Gewerbe*, ed. Bärbel Rudin, Kleine Schriften der Gesellschaft für Theatergeschichte 34/35 (Berlin: Gesellschaft für Theatergeschichte), 5–18.

2. On the emergence of dramatic authorship in the broader European context, see Julie Stone Peters, *Theatre of the Book, 1480–1880: Print, Text, and Performance in Europe* (Oxford/New York: Oxford University Press, 2000).

3. The project of putting German-language poetry on the international map has been the subject of a major body of research, most often focused on Martin Opitz (1597–1639). For a sound introduction to the topic, see Wilhelm Kühlmann, *Martin Opitz: Deutsche Literatur und deutsche Nation* (Heidelberg: Manutius, 2001).

So what led theatrical troupes to put the fool front and center? At first glance, it is hard to understand what could make even the most malleable figure appealing enough that his presence in play after play would be a source of enthusiasm and amusement rather than a bore. Here we stumble on a second, equally puzzling question: What gives license to speak of *a* fool or *the* fool, of a single conventionalized figure? It seems obvious that it would not make much sense to treat every stage appearance as unique and different. But by virtue of what? To return to the previous grammatical contrast: What makes any individual fool an instance of *the* fool? These are all questions clustered around what one might call the reproduction of a theatrical form. The biological ring of the term *reproduction* need not be cause for concern; at issue here is a distinctive way of interacting on the stage, from the words chosen to how the fool speaks them, from his position within the cast of characters to the attitude he assumes toward them.

Instead of proceeding on the basis of historical generalization, it is worth considering a text first published during the latter half of the eighteenth century, but that properly belongs among the materials at the center of part 1 of this study. The play, an adaptation of Shakespeare's *Hamlet*, discloses decisive features of the fool's stage activity, and its analysis can provide methodological orientation for the following chapters. The example is particularly revealing because of its high degree of conventionality, something that a modern reader can easily skip over in sheer excitement of discovering a version, albeit radically altered, of perhaps the best-known play in the English language.

The surviving German adaptation of *Hamlet*, it bears emphasizing, is an acting script, not a dramatic text in the ordinary sense of the word. While the German-language play overlaps on a schematic level, a few times even up to the level of a whole scene, with the Shakespearean play, it would be a mistake to treat the adaptation as a translation. But the difference between the Hamlet adaptation and a dramatic text extends beyond the difference visible today on the printed page. Rather, the acting script is of a different categorical order than that of a dramatic text; it is even tempting to say, in more traditional philosophical jargon, that the two are different kinds of material substance. But the terminology is not as important as the recognition that the division between these two types or classes (acting script/dramatic text) does not just depend on surface characteristics like formal or verbal organization, but also on how the acting script or dramatic text ordinarily gets used. For the purpose of marking out extreme poles, we might think of a dramatic text as a kind of poetic composition defined by its fixity: it has been uniquely written and edited and, by and large, can be attributed to an author. An acting script, meanwhile, carries on its existence in the more open-ended, presentist world of theatrical performance. It can be expanded and contracted, modified and recast. Furthermore, its relationship to authorship is more nebulous and prone to variation from performance to performance and context to context. This chapter and the three that follow focus attention primarily on acting scripts; dramatic texts come into view in part 2.

The distinction, even if rough-and-ready, helps make sense of the mechanisms that allowed the German *Hamlet* to endure, such that copies can now be found in university libraries and on the Internet.[4] It also helps to make sense of the fact that the survival of the adaptation is due to unplanned and uncontrolled circumstances of appropriation and transformation, not the willful bequeathing of a work by a great author to an unversed audience. The version that survives today is based on a printed edition from 1778, itself based on a manuscript from around 1710.[5] The acting script bears the sort of two-part title typical of seventeenth-century German plays: *Tragedy of Fratricide Punished, or Prince Hamlet of Denmark*. The modified title testifies to a long period of circulation among traveling players who certainly did not treat any particular script they came across as authoritative or as commanding fidelity. In fact, something like the surviving adaptation had probably been used by actors in Germany since the early decades of the seventeenth century, even though no version seems to have found

---

4. At present the German *Hamlet* adaptation, as well as an English translation, is available for download at https://archive.org/details/shakespeareinger00cohnrich.

5. For the historical record, see Wilhelm Michael Anton Creizenach, *Die Schauspiele der englischen Komödianten* (Berlin/Stuttgart: W. Spemann, 1889), 144.

its way between bound covers until much later. It is crucial to keep in mind that when *Hamlet* first appeared in the German-speaking world, the theatrical culture where it found a home did not even identify plays with authors, nor did it feel the need to search for or treat one version as original and final. The proper name of the Bard, in other words, only became an identifying marker for the *Hamlet* adaptation long after the play first began its career on the German stage. While in the first half of the seventeenth century authorship was becoming increasingly important to English publishing practices, in no small part due to the popularity of Shakespeare himself, the very same period the German-speaking theatrical world showed little concern for original authorship and, in general, allowed for free tinkering with every part of the play, from plot construction to title, to fit the needs and desires of actors.[6]

The liberties taken with the Shakespearean play shine through most forcefully in the latitude afforded a figure utterly alien to the original: a court jester by the name of Phantasmo.[7] Of course, English theater in Shakespeare's own time had a sparkling tradition of fools and clowns, and no one exploited the available conventions

6. The importance of Shakespeare's First Folio to the emergence of dramatic authorship has been studied in Douglas A. Brooks, *From Playhouse to Printing House: Drama and Authorship in Early Modern England* (Cambridge: Cambridge University Press, 2000), 66–103. In Germany, there is a lineage of dramatic authorship within educated circles beginning around 1650. Andreas Gryphius (1616–1664) and David Caspar von Lohenstein (1635–1683), among other lesser-known playwrights, composed tragedies, many of which were intended for stage performance. However, the inclusion of copious scholarly annotations in their published plays indicates that these authors were interested in textual circulation in a fashion utterly alien to the traveling players. For instance, when one of Gryphius's tragedies was adapted by traveling players, the author's name is nowhere to be found, and the manipulation of the acting script is rampant. I discuss this matter in greater detail in chapter 4.

7. The play has been reprinted, along with an English translation, in Albert Cohn, *Shakespeare in Germany in the Sixteenth and Seventeenth Centuries: An Account of English Actors in Germany and the Netherlands and of the Plays Performed by Them during the Same Period* (London: Asher & Co, 1865), 237–304.

with the same acuity as did Shakespeare.[8] Without question, a figure like Phantasmo would have been unthinkable without the influence English actors had in the first half of the seventeenth century in the German lands. That being said, this figure is far removed from what one might expect from the fools and clowns that inhabited the Elizabethan comic imagination. This difference, the following discussion will show, supports the claim that the German stage fool was a distinct theatrical form.

The divergence between adaptation and original asserts itself from the start and remains consistent throughout. In the version performed by German traveling players an introductory prologue mixes Christian and pagan themes, as four chthonic spirits of classical Greece set up a moralizing frame for the modern tragedy of Danish aristocracy. And then, in its main body, the play includes the court jester Phantasmo who, with relentless barbs, solidifies the initial impression that the German adaptation is far from Shakespeare's universe. By any estimation, the play possesses highly unusual internal heterogeneity: while the prologue announces a story of providential justice, the ensuing tragedy puts a figure front and center who, in his trivializations of the ongoing action, constantly threatens to spill the play over into farce.

For a sample of the sort of material an analysis of the German stage fool must account for, consider the following pivotal moment in the play. When Hamlet's desire for vengeance for his father's death has reached its peak intensity, and Ophelia is crestfallen but has not yet gone mad, the fool arrives on an empty stage and remarks, "Everything has now become fantastical here at court. Prince Hamlet is crazy, Ophelia is crazy. In sum, it has become so crazy here that I almost want to leave, myself."[9] This comment seems inconsequential enough, especially to a modern reader expecting Shakespearean nuance. There is, indeed, little

---

8. The Shakespearean fool has been the subject of much scholarly discussion. I recommend in particular Richard Preiss, *Clowning and Authorship in Early Modern Theatre* (Cambridge: Cambridge University Press, 2014).

9. Cohn, *Shakespeare in Germany*, 277.

artistry to be unearthed here, no hidden aesthetic dimension to vindicate. Nonetheless, much can be learned from this simple passage, particularly concerning the German stage fool's integration into the plays performed by traveling players across the early modern period.

Consider the way this scene positions the fool within the sequence of events. He appears here in the guise of commentator, and offers his viewpoint as the opening to a scene. In so doing, he addresses the audience directly with words that serve to belittle elements of the plot that others in the play treat with utmost gravity. All of these are noteworthy dimensions of Phantasmo's utterance because—this can only be asserted at this juncture, but should emerge as fact in due course—they are utterly commonplace. Even though the play may have survived oblivion merely because of the exalted status of the English original, a fortuitous fact that can easily make Phantasmo seem exceptional, he assumes exactly the role one would expect from a stage fool among the traveling troupes in Germany during the early modern period.

Before drawing any general inferences, a second example deserves attention: this time, the fool Phantasmo in dialogue with Ophelia. The scene begins with Phantasmo alone on the stage, Ophelia to join him soon. Before she makes her entrance, he sets up the ensuing dialogue:

> Wherever I go or linger, the simple girl Ophelia comes after me out of every corner. I can find no peace from her; she's always saying I am her beloved; but that's just not true. If only I could hide so she wouldn't find me. Now the devil's at it again: here she comes again.[10]

And with that Ophelia storms onto the stage, proclaiming that she has just visited a priest who has consented to marry her and Phantasmo the very same day. Surprised by the announcement, the fool consents, but goes on to make certain she is aware of his desperate need to consummate as soon as possible. Before the scene

---

10. Ibid., 283.

comes to a close, Ophelia thrashes him for his vulgar remarks and flees the stage in a fit. The scene thus blends salacious joking with slapstick—two elements of licit impropriety facilitated by the unique position of the fool in the dialogue. On a thematic level, we see the fool here recasting love as a mere obsession and connubial romance as corporeal satisfaction. The fool's coarse humor, here as elsewhere, possesses a hypertrophic masculine dimension; it reduces the love between a heterosexual pair to the man's pleasure. At the same time, the scene subjects the fool to violence, pointing to the transgressive character of his speech act that, at the same time, remains essentially inconsequential. In this way, the fool's expression of a masculine desire, at once drastically reduced to a single element and playfully exaggerated, is marked as a harmless pecadillo, a tolerated impropriety.

As the scene underscores this masculine dimension to the fool's role, it maintains a number of striking similarities with the previous example. Of particular importance is the fool's assumption of the role of commentator. He appears on the scene before Ophelia, installing a frame for the ensuing action. In the final moment of slapstick, his commentary is revealed for what it was all along: a laughter-provoking infringement on the sense of propriety that governs the rest of the play. Even if the other figures in the play lack the linguistic nuance and poetic beauty we identify with Shakespeare, they nonetheless display a strong penchant for pathos and grandiloquence. Phantasmo's role, meanwhile, makes it difficult to know just how seriously the tragic dimension of the play should be taken.

In both foregoing instances, it is important to keep in mind that the play is not intended as parody; the adaptation does not presuppose knowledge of a real *Hamlet*. Actually, Shakespeare's *Hamlet* remained basically unknown and unperformed in the seventeenth and early eighteenth centuries, aside from versions like this one with Phantasmo. Until an epoch-making explosion of enthusiasm beginning in the late 1760s, Shakespeare was a nonentity in the German-speaking world. His plays largely made their way through the German-speaking lands as stock in an inventory of translated adaptations for itinerant players.[11] Despite the temptation to treat this play and the fool in it as specimens of the broader European "Shakespeare reception," there is good cause to resist the idea that any author, especially one bearing the laurels of literary greatness, was coming to the awareness of a new public here. At least from the perspective of seventeenth- and early eighteenth-century German theater, there is little special about this play. Rather, the adaptation is noteworthy because, especially in its deployment of the fool, the play is so humdrum.

I have emphasized the fool's strategy for framing scenes in order to make clear that he introduces a parallel, comic avenue running alongside Hamlet's tragedy. Such scenes accompany others more directly cognate with Shakespeare's original. And yet the adaptation does not show an obvious concern with the convergence, or even bare compatibility, of these two avenues. The acting script lacks any moment that might support the belief that Phantasmo's role amounts to a full-fledged subplot that, in its reflection of the main action, contributes to a complexly integrated play. Although the play assigns Phantasmo the role of debasing the main action, the values espoused in his remarks do not form a contrast with the values outside of them that spectators or interpreters could synthesize into a coherent stance.[12] Perhaps most importantly, Phantasmo's machinations are of a different ilk than the riddles, witty wordplay, and semantic inversions that characterize the fools populating Shakespeare's universe. Instead, the roughly hewn nature of the two aforementioned passages

---

11. Johann Elias Schlegel's comparison of Shakespeare and the seventeenth-century German playwright Andreas Gryphius is a true historical anomaly. Writing in 1741 on the occasion of a translation of Shakespeare's *Julius Caesar*, Schlegel endorses the enterprise but remains highly critical of this particular execution. His commentary is particularly unique since Schlegel read English and offers a measured defense of Gryphius, whose style had fallen into disrepute during the first half of the eighteenth century. See Johann Elias Schlegel, "Vergleichung Shakespears und Andreas Gryphs bey Gelegenheit einer Uebersetzung von Shakespears Julius Cäsar," in *Werke*, ed. Johann Heinrich Schlegel (Frankfurt am Main: Athenäum, 1971), 3:27–64. I return to the eighteenth-century fascination with Shakespeare in chapter 11.

12. In this respect, I believe his role is fundamentally different from the sort of subplot construction we find in Elizabethan drama. See Jonas A. Barish, "The Double Plot in 'Volpone,'" *Modern Philology* 51, no. 2 (1953): 83–92; Richard Levin, "Elizabethan Clown Subplots," *Essays in Criticism* 16, no. 1 (1966): 84–91.

disappoints the modern reader's hope that Phantasmo might offer the sort of dramaturgically integrated derision that we find in figures like Dogberry of *Much Ado About Nothing* or even Rosencrantz and Guildenstern in *Hamlet*.[13] The contrast between the English clown and the German fool is, of course, very important, but must await a fuller treatment in chapter 2.

For the time being, it is worth drawing out some of the structural features of the fool's role revealed in these two episodes from the *Hamlet* adaptation.

Dialogic Integration In the foregoing scenes from the *Hamlet* adaptation, the content of Phantasmo's speech cannot be dissociated from its position in the encompassing nexus of dialogue. The *what* of his statements and the *from where* are inextricably connected. The commentary he provides on the other members of the fictional universe—here Hamlet and Ophelia—functions by jutting out of the environing dialogue. He frames the events onstage before they transpire and casts them in a tone that differs strongly from the one struck by others in the play. It is helpful to imagine the fool as a kind of switch operator, flipping from an austere vantage point to one of playful disparagement.

The discrepancy between the fool and the other dramatis personae issues from his distinctive way of relating to the most basic element of theater: dialogue. The interweaving of verbal and gestural action on the stage—the integration of words and movements—constitutes the signature mechanism by means of which theater creates a fictional world. Dialogue in theater is modeled, to varying degrees and standards of fidelity or artfulness, on the manifold and historically variable ways human beings interact face-to-face.[14] In order

---

13. The surviving adaptation has a scene that is perhaps a far-fetched mutation of the gravediggers. Two robbers (ruffians in Cohn's translation) encounter Hamlet, whom they threaten to kill. After Hamlet has accepted his fate, the two robbers fumble the execution and, rather preposterously, end up shooting themselves. See Cohn, *Shakespeare in Germany*, 285–288.

14. The relationship between theater and face-to-face interaction is the subject of the underappreciated essay by Dietrich Schwanitz, "Zeit und Geschichte im Roman—Interaktion im Drama: Zur wechselseitigen Erhellung von Systemtheorie und Literatur," in *Theorie als Passion*, ed. Jürgen Markowitz, Rudolf Stichweh, and Dieter Baecker (Frankfurt am Main: Suhrkamp, 1987), 181–213. It may seem

to analyze the theatrical situation in this adaptation, therefore, it is helpful to consider the contrast between fictional dialogue and the conditions under which ordinary conversation gets off the ground. In particular, it is worth recalling that interlocution demands a minimum common ground among statements, including both linguistic formulation and meaning. Communication, that is, depends on the articulation of differences on the basis of, to use a well-worn metaphor, a shared space of intelligibility. Dialogue is not made up of atom-like utterances; the words evince a dynamic of back-and-forth, of understanding and misunderstanding, of agreement and disagreement.[15] Too much difference, and a statement seems peculiar; too much similarity, and dialogue comes to a standstill. One of the key interpretive dimensions of watching or reading a play is, then, understanding the balance of continuity and difference in sequences of dialogue. And this includes registering the anomalous moments, when dialogue does not interlock at all or deviates from its usual proportion of continuity and difference. Humor, it deserves emphasizing, often depends on just such abrupt deviations in the flow of speech.

A fool like Phantasmo, meanwhile, furnishes the play with an exceptional degree of discontinuity, when compared to the other utterances making up the fabric of the fiction. To put it figurally, the fool's utterances and gestures are fringes in the weave of dialogue. In his role as commentator, Phantasmo introduces a view of the events that seems to stand both inside and outside the patterns of face-to-face interaction. He phrases things in ways others cannot and recasts the tragic events in the most trivial terms.

---

that I am unduly leaving aside the possibility of a purely monological theater. I believe that is only partially true, insofar as monologue only becomes theater by virtue of its placement within a dialogic setting, before an audience. For this reason, I distinguish in chapter 3 between fiction-internal and fiction-external axes of communication. The potential existence of experimental forms of modern or contemporary theater that conform to neither axis of communication is not germane to the present, historically rooted analysis.

15. On dialogue structure, I recommend in particular Jan Mukařovský, *The Word and Verbal Art: Selected Essays* trans. John Burbank and Peter Steiner (New Haven: Yale University Press, 1977), 81–115.

He breaches the flow of dialogue and upbraids protagonists with abandon. He jumps out onto the stage and informs the audience of things in words that are sometimes mirthful and sometimes more caustic. All the while, though, his statements rely for their relevance on their thematic connection to the rest of the dialogue. The fool is, importantly, not talking about something completely foreign or unfamiliar, but instead channeling a distinct perspective on the fiction. Hence the switch operator—only he can participate in the ongoing dialogue and then, at will, alternate the frame.

In both of the two brief scenes from the Hamlet adaptation, the fool's position in the dialogue is further defined by its incidental or opportunistic quality. That is to say, his foremost skill lies in his ability to seize on a statement or a scene as the occasion for a comic intervention. On the basis of his loose dialogic integration, the fool offers a sort of hermeneutic fork in the road—shall we take things seriously or not?—and the play on the whole pursues both paths with insouciant disregard for their overall compatibility.

Form as Practice   Thinking of Phantasmo in terms of his locus in the dialogic interplay provides the basis for the recognition that one and the same figure—the fool—assumes dozens of guises and in myriad contexts. Patterns in the configuration of dialogue are, in essence, the units that hold together the diversity of the fool's stage appearances. Concentrating attention on such repeated structures entails leaving out certain other modes of investigation to account for his unforeseeable genesis and resulting permanence. For instance, it does not involve chronicling stage appearance after stage appearance, beginning with debut and continuing for decades, in pursuit of lines of influence. And for good reason: the fool is not a human being with a biography, and the parameters of his narrative are not birth, life, and death. The fool is, instead, a conventionalized figure, a theatrical form, brought to life under multiple sobriquets, clad in varying costumes, and embedded in different plots. Throwing light on such a form requires making its constitutive parts clear and showing how they fit together. And this because the form in question—the characteristic kinds of activity executed by the fool—constitutes what we ordinarily think of as a *practice*. The formal unity characteristic of the fool must be elaborated in terms of a constitutive practice.

Treating figures like Phantasmo as manifestations of a theatrical form also steers the discussion away from two ready-made terminological schemata. The first is captured by the locution "stock character," used commonly in both colloquial and academic discourse. This schema is used to indicate a sort of cookie-cutter persona, distinguished by signature personality traits that remain recognizable in play after play.[16] According to this line of thought, the fool is something like a skeletal type, a rube or buffoon. Accounts of the comedy genre, particularly of its flowering in classical antiquity and the Renaissance, have often involved the identification of a set repertoire of such character types that participate in rigid plot patterns. And continuities between ancient and modern comedy are often explained in terms of the repetition of such standard and set elements. But such an approach ignores the sort of cultural-historical vicissitudes that stand at the center of this study.

A common procedure in discussions of the fool is to turn to the early modern distinction between a person deprived of adequate mental wherewithal (the *Naturnarr*) and a witty and rollicking jokester (the *Kunstnarr* or *Schalksnarr*).[17] This model of analysis, however, draws on a preexisting category the stage fool ostensibly falls under, without explaining what makes this category hang together in the first place, needless to say endure over time. So unless we suppose there is some sort of primordial human need fulfilled by jokester figures—a difficult claim to defend—the assertion of a ready-made category does not assist in uncovering the fool's genesis or explaining his reproductive mechanism. A more fruitful avenue

---

16. This mode of analysis reached its theoretical acme in the still deeply impressive study by Northrop Frye, *Anatomy of Criticism: Four Essays* (Princeton: Princeton University Press, 2000).

17. Edgar Barwig and Ralf Schmitz, "Narren, Geisteskranke und Hofleute," in *Randgruppen der spätmittelalterlichen Gesellschaft*, ed. Bernd-Ulrich Hergemöller (Warendorf: Fahlbusch Verlag, 2001), 239–269.

of inquiry is, so the basic claim of this study, to gain a firm grip on both the overarching theatrical context and the patterns of stage interaction that integrate the fool into dialogue. The goal, in other words, is to uncover the organizational principles of dialogue, the distinctive ways of going on, that allowed for the fool's spectacular diversity of embodiments while still maintaining enough consistency that he could be understood as a distinct role.

Context-Sensitivity of Form An analysis of the fool involves the consideration of structures of dialogue as well as of the larger environment—to put it simply, of form and context. Understanding how fool figures could be freely inserted into plays such as Shakespeare's *Hamlet* demands an appreciation of the highly unusual theatrical culture within which the fool gained a foothold. This means exploring how the happenstance arrival of English strolling players around 1600 and even more unexpected success of itinerant theatrical troupes over the ensuing decades gave rise to a new variety of theater, utterly different from more familiar modern counterparts. The traveling troupes inhabited a theatrical sphere lacking venerated tradition and strict ceremony, without the aspiration to everlasting fame or artistic greatness. Their plays were lavish in liberal adaptation and playful improvisation, focused on crowd pleasing and commercial success. And the centerpiece of it all was none other than the stage fool.

My insistence on the context-sensitivity of form is motivated by the chasm separating the seventeenth-century fool from the category we typically call literature. In the classicizing movements that run through the modern age, plot structures and generic categories made their way from antiquity into the modern period via translation and adaptation in the Latinate world of the social and political elite. The reproduction of classical forms was, in essence, a disciplined procedure; it emerged out of a philological tradition invested in ensuring the preservation of ancient knowledge. It further depended on a broad array of ancillary forces, including educational venues, religious and political authorities, and poetic handbooks. Procedures of imitation or emulation labored to accomplish the conformity of new poetic productions to established standards. The entire enterprise had as its foundation a reverence for the ancients that has occasionally come under fire but has nonetheless remained a major force up to the present day. The reproduction of classical forms, however interesting in its own right, cannot supply a model for understanding how the *Hamlet* adaptation survived for so long, and how the figure of the fool found a place in this play and so many like it. In lieu of supporting institutions—church, university, or others—to celebrate the preeminence of ancient forms and command their imitation, the subsistence of the fool for expanses of time largely depended on factors internal to the conventionalized role itself. The stage presentation he embodied, in other words, contained many of the means by which the role endured across time. Indeed, the appearance of the fool in play after play depended on the exercise of a recognizable stage practice—which, if popularity is any indication, provided audiences with abundant pleasure.

Template as Reproductive Mechanism   The origins of this stage figure are located in a deracinated and informal theatrical world. This means, firstly, that the conventions of the stage were not dictated by an authoritative mandate of any sort and, secondly, that the traveling troupes made their living by constantly moving about and looking for sufficient payment to survive. What is more, the fool belonged to a culture of playmaking that seems, in light of more modern expectations, highly unorthodox, particularly given the malleability of acting scripts and the reliance on commercial conditions defined by relentless travel. For all these reasons, it makes good sense to think of the plays put on by the strolling players of the seventeenth century as much closer to familiar oral traditions like the folktale or epic song than modern written literary genres like the novel or even the modern dramatic text.[18]

---

18. The scholarship on oral literature is insurmountably vast. In my thought on this subject I have been particularly inspired by the pioneering research conducted on the Homeric epics and on folktales. In place of a litany of scholarly references, I shall therefore mention only two I particularly recommend: Gregory Nagy, *The Best of the Achaeans: Concepts of the Hero in Ancient Greek Poetry*

The printed edition of the *Hamlet* adaptation, for instance, ultimately amounts to a template that could be tailored to fit the immediate needs of actors, instead of a rigid blueprint for uniform stagings. As templates, scripts were used as supple instruments that could sponsor a multiplicity of different theatrical realizations. Much as forms like the folktale and epic song depend on unsystematic channels of proximate communication—passing from generation to generation through the act of face-to-face retelling, relishing in improvisation on the basis of rudimentary structures, and imbuing no single version with exalted status—the printed version of our *Hamlet* adaptation does not possess the authoritative and authentic character of a set literary text. Although only a single version of the adaptation has survived, it must be treated like a palimpsest of decades of informal transmission. The play withstood the test of time almost exclusively through live performances in town squares and royal courts. Accordingly, to read or study a scene repeatedly, submitting it to close scrutiny, is to engage in an interpretive act that would have been unthinkable during the era of traveling theatrical troupes. What appears today as a fixed play, with every word and scene in its proper place, is, in truth, the post hoc calcification of a more fluid phenomenon.

The media-historical status of the *Hamlet* adaptation—its template-like nature—deserves particular emphasis. Like many surviving plays, it derives from makeshift scripts that had been used primarily by the acting troupes themselves. Text and textuality entered the picture only in a very loose and impermanent sense, and certainly not as the material anchor for the singularity of a literary work. It seems that a typical troupe would have been in possession of only a single copy of each acting script in the repertoire, and it belonged to the manager of the troupe. It was used, not as a fixed substrate to which fidelity was required, but as an outline that could be filled in, even substantively altered, by an acting troupe as needed. Good evidence for approaching the

(Baltimore: Johns Hopkins University Press, 1999); Vladimir Propp, *Morphology of the Folktale*, trans. Laurence Scott (Austin: University of Texas Press, 1968).

Hamlet adaptation as based on a template structure can be found already in the first major collection of plays featuring the fool, which appeared in 1620. The title page announces the wish that print circulation will allow actors to recreate "the manner of performance" and thereby ensure the "amusement and satisfaction of the spirit (*Gemüt*)."[19] In other words, the collection—which consists of translations of English plays, a few original German compositions, and a stockpile of interludes—was intended to equip acting troupes with the material required to continue functioning as a performance outfit and to spur on the popularity of acting and theatergoing.

Within this realm of informal circulation and unconstrained adaptation, the fool inhabited a particularly open-ended role. Although Phantasmo's commentaries and interjections may appear in the printed edition as fully articulated utterances, they are in fact markers of a more freely manipulable discourse. The most instructive trace of the liberty afforded the fool is the presence in many surviving acting scripts of stage directions indicating that he should continue on extemporaneously. These could be as simple as "action here,"[20] "jumps around and is funny,"[21] or "strange antics."[22] Other plays left entire scenes for improvised song or dance to be filled out according to the prerogative of the actor.[23] One adaptation of the English play *Old Fortunatus*, originally written by Thomas Dekker (ca. 1572–1632), includes five moments in the play when the text simply says, "Now Pickelhering plays," indicating the insertion of a fully improvised song and dance.[24] Another stage direction

---

19. Manfred Brauneck and Alfred Noe, *Spieltexte der Wanderbühne* (Berlin: De Gruyter, 1970), vol. 1, unnumbered cover page.

20. Johann Georg Schoch, *Joh. G. Schochs Comoedia Vom Studenten-Leben* (Leipzig: Johann Wittigauen, 1658), 42.

21. Ibid., 67.

22. Brauneck and Noe, *Spieltexte der Wanderbühne*, 1:544.

23. Reinhart Meyer, "Hanswurst und Harlekin, oder: Der Narr als Gattungsschöpfer: Versuch einer Analyse des komischen Spiels in den Staatsaktionen des Musik- und Sprechtheaters im 17. und 18. Jahrhundert," in *Schriften zur Theater- und Kulturgeschichte des 18. Jahrhunderts* (Vienna: Hollitzer, 2012), 295.

24. For the German adaptation, see Brauneck and Noe, *Spieltexte der Wanderbühne*, 1:128–209.

instructs the fool to perform "fantastic antics" with props like a dagger, perhaps indicating the insertion of a brief juggling show.[25] Yet another has him do something very similar with a glass that eventually falls and shatters.[26] In all of these instances, it seems to have been the actor's prerogative to contract or expand such bouts of comic play to fit the circumstances of a given venue or event. One can, perhaps should, imagine that each of the scenes with Phantasmo was accompanied by a dashing gambol or an unexpected verbal jest.

Phatic Structure of Play   The word *play* describes precisely what the fool does. *Play* points to a quality of the fool's conduct, of how he interacts on the stage.[27] The fool's verbal and gestic interventions are exceptional moments in the rhythm of a performance, defined by the very absence of plot-driving information. The activity of the fool on the stage is play in the sense that it offers a hiatus, a circumscribed break, from the main action. The place of the fool within the performances of itinerant troupes is much like the place of play in ordinary life: it is an ulterior activity, taking place beside and along with ordinary life.[28] As play, the fool's remarks are not superfluous or meaningless; his words and deeds are invested with their own expressive potential and significance. The fool's play is something that "interpolates itself as a temporary activity satisfying in itself and ending there."[29] His antics have no need for the participation of other dramatis personae; they subsist on their own, often adding nothing informative and instead just seeking to gratify the audience. Because of this self-enclosed status, the fool's interventions can be as audacious as a lampoon of the main action or as whimsical as a surge of leaping and spinning.

---

25. Brauneck and Noe, *Spieltexte der Wanderbühne*, 2:509.

26. Ibid., 2:180.

27. My thoughts and terminology here are deeply indebted to the pioneering study of Johan Huizinga, *Homo Ludens: A Study of the Play-Element in Culture* (London: Routledge, 1949).

28. For insightful remarks on this structure, see Roger Caillois, *Man, Play, and Games* (Urbana: University of Illinois Press, 2001), esp. 43.

29. Huizinga, *Homo Ludens*, 9.

Such mirthful capsules of dialogue also remind the audience that the show is a show and just pretend.[30] For this reason, the fool operates as a champion of *the* play—that is, of the fictional simulation contained in time and space. In this broader sense, too, the fool functions as an exponent of the play as "a temporary activity satisfying in itself and ending there."[31] The fool can ostentatiously direct attention to the fictive character of the play without undermining its ability to captivate audiences. However strange it may initially seem, the fool's exposure of the play as a play is a strategy of heightening the experience of illusion. It is a technique of phatic communication, of ensuring the sustained attentive contact between audience and theatrical fiction.[32] As an example of such phatic immediacy, consider Phantasmo's remark that the events involving Hamlet and Ophelia are so ridiculous that he himself might abandon the court. Of course, he does no such thing, and the audience's anticipation grows only more intense.

The structure of play associated with the fool ensured his abiding success. In every instance, he was a figure of transgressive masculinity who afforded spectators the pleasure of hearing about themes barred from ordinary discourse. That is, the fool's distinctive form of play provided a moment when social values held in high esteem could be openly mocked simply for the enjoyment of throwing treasured forms of significance, even if only momentarily, into the wind.[33] The pleasure associated with the fool was that

---

30. See Huizinga, *Homo Ludens*, 8. For this reason Roger Caillois, in the above-mentioned study, treats the fictional status of games as the sixth and final of the essential qualities of play.

31. As above, Huizinga, *Homo Ludens*, 9.

32. For this terminology, see Bronislaw Malinowski, "The Problem of Meaning in Primitive Languages," in *The Meaning of Meaning: A Study in the Influence of Language upon Thought and of the Science of Symbolism*, ed. Charles Kay Ogden and Ivor Armstrong Richards (New York: Harcourt Brace, 1945), 296–336.

33. It is reasonable to speculate that there is something idic about the fool's playful transgression of behavioral norms. In many instances, he does profess an infantile indulgence in instinctual pleasures and libidinal release. I have ultimately avoided the Freudian vocabulary for fear that it would provide an overly rigid framework for understanding the interplay of institutional, media-historical, and discursive forces that altered the fool's role, especially over the course of the

of momentary abandon, often through vulgar speech and gesture. The privilege of such transgression was afforded only to the fool, with his exaggerated caricature of male desire. As a consequence, we can say that the sequestering of the meanings conveyed in his interventions provided the precondition for their presence. The fool negates the meanings conveyed by other figures in the play from within an insular sphere, and such separation licenses the audience's enjoyment of what would otherwise be illicit.[34]

To understand how the fool goes about this, it is important to avoid ranking his role, or even the plays in which he participated, as either trivial or profound, as high or low. At issue is not whether the *Hamlet* adaptation possesses the linguistic beauty and nuanced construction of the original Shakespeare play. After all, this was a theatrical environment that was unbothered by, perhaps even unacquainted with, the desire to make great art. From the arrival of English players around 1600, it took over a hundred years for reform-minded poets and scholars to make the fool into the centerpiece of a discussion concerning the superior potential of a more sophisticated theater. But before we investigate the complexities of these later developments, including the pivotal role the fool played in them, we have to comprehend the conditions under which he first flourished.

---

eighteenth century. The idic thesis was famously advanced in Sigmund Freud's *Der Witz und seine Beziehung zum Unbewussten* (1905).

34. In thinking through the relationship between the fool's insularity and the overarching semantic structure of plays, I have found Hans-Ulrich Gumbrecht's reformulation of the concept of carnival highly instructive. See Hans-Ulrich Gumbrecht, "Literarische Gegenwelten, Karnevalskultur und die Epochenschwelle vom Spätmittelalter zur Renaissance," in *Literatur in der Gesellschaft des Spätmittelalters* (Heidelberg: Winter Verlag, 1980), 95–144.

2

Strolling Players and the Advent of the Fool

The years around 1600 mark a watershed moment in the history of German theater. Importantly, though, the process that established the fool in the German-speaking lands was not an articulated project with proponents and detractors; nothing about it was planned or inevitable. It was an unforeseeable explosion of enthusiasm, followed by an equally improbable run of success. When in the 1590s a small ragged band of English actors made its way across the Channel, through the Low Countries, and into the western part of what is now Germany, they could very well have come and gone without leaving a lasting footprint. Instead, they precipitated a major shift in the conventions of theatrical performance. The coming century was witness to the abiding presence of professional troupes passing under the name Engelländische Komödianten, which led to the establishment of theatrical conventions that remained vital long after the earliest traces of this history—especially the use of the English tongue—had passed into oblivion. Given that no one orchestrated, planned, or even served as theoretical advocate for the fool's rise to popularity, his beginnings possess a haphazard quality; indeed they were not just contingent, but also recognizable as such only after the fact. One consequence of the fool's unplanned rise to popularity is that it traced a path through historical epochs that the dominant narratives of history treat as fundamentally separate. Equally importantly, the process of transfer that breathed life into the stage fool does not fit neatly within the divisions among modern nation-states and their putatively unique cultures. The history of the stage fool is, rather, a history of interference across temporal as well as linguistic-cultural boundaries.

It bears mentioning at the outset that the decision to begin this story of the German stage fool with the English troupes dislodges a story of origin that has long seemed unassailable. This account, that is, does not begin with the form of improvisatory, comic theater known as *commedia dell'arte*, which spread beyond the Italian border over the latter half of the sixteenth century and, among other places, into the German-speaking territories. The Italian term originally meant roughly "professional acting show," but came to refer to a cohort of regionally specific theatrical personalities, with distinct costumes and character traits. Over the course of time, manuals codified scenarios that could be played out in varying ways and inventoried types of improvisatory sequences that could be added on. Quite early in their career, in 1568, such *commedia dell'arte* troupes made their way into the German-speaking lands and, indeed, drummed up interest in some social circles.[1] In particular, Italian acting made its impact in princely courts that hosted the players and among the social elite as they made their educational peregrinations across Europe.

Although scholars of German literature have often lent *commedia dell'arte* pride of place in the historiography of German comic theater, there are compelling considerations that speak against such an approach. For one, Italian troupes relied heavily on gesture and

---

1. See Ralf Böckmann, *Die Commedia dell'arte und das deutsche Drama des 17. Jahrhunderts* (Nordhausen: Verlag Traugott Baut, 2010), 46ff.

mimicry that was immediately intelligible (and humorous) to spectators in the German-speaking lands, but never put down linguistic or geographic roots there. What is more, their performances took place in the rarified environment of the court, and, at least in the seventeenth century, textual traces of their mode of performance are surprisingly rare. Despite the early arrival of Italian *commedia dell'arte* troupes, in fact, it took another one hundred years before the comic servant figure with the sobriquet Harlequin made regular appearances in German-language plays—and, even then, via the French *comédie-italienne*, and not via Italian channels of transmission. Although eighteenth-century writers sometimes conflated and sometimes held apart the English fool and the French-Italian Harlequin, the crucial transformations that took place in the early decades of the seventeenth century pertained exclusively to the former.

Although part 1 of this study focuses primarily on the tradition of the Engelländische Komödianten, with comparatively little attention spent on the French-Italian lineage, it does not thereby engage in the search for a point of absolute beginning along a timeline or reconstruct theatrical event after event.[2] The attempt to trace out the movements of individual troupes across the German countryside can too easily lose itself in a microhistory that fails to illuminate the larger-scale

---

2. The task of tracking single troupes, writing history of the theater in a single town, and drawing out of lines of influence has been nobly undertaken a number of times over the last century, often in fastidious detail. In addition to the large corpus of literature on the topic from the late nineteenth and early twentieth centuries, impressive microhistorical reconstructions of the itineraries of individual troupes have been undertaken over the last four decades by Bärbel Rudin. I have made reference to many of her essays, where relevant, below, but recommend them generally to the reader interested in a more granulated picture of individual troupes. The recently revised and published study by Peter Brand is, to be sure, the most exhaustive discussion of the very earliest stage of this history. See Peter Brand and Bärbel Rudin, "Der englische Komödiant Robert Browne," *Daphnis* 39 (2010): 1–134. A comprehensive account of the English troupes and their aftermath can be found in Ralf Haekel, *Die englischen Komödianten in Deutschland: Eine Einführung in die Ursprünge des deutschen Berufsschauspiels* (Heidelberg: Winter Universitätsverlag, 2004). For the discussion of a single town, see Markus Paul, *Reichsstadt und Schauspiel: Theatrale Kunst in Nürnberg des 17. Jahrhunderts* (Tübingen: Max Niemeyer Verlag, 2002).

historical processes that are ultimately of interest here. The following pages work toward resolving a basic question: How did context shape the emergence of and abiding popularity of the fool? How did the life of traveling theatrical troupes in the seventeenth century give rise to a comic force that deserves reference in the singular, that is, as *the* fool? Which circumstances assisted in the consolidation into a unique theatrical form? Since a decisive goal of part 1 is to understand what allowed the fool to appear in a multitude of stage events, repeating the same sorts of words and engaging in the same sorts of actions, our analysis must look beyond a one-by-one recounting of those very same events. It must look for commonalities in the composition of theatrical troupes, their repertoires and lifestyles, and the relationship they entertained with audiences. These are the contextual factors that contributed to the genesis of the practice of stage interaction that will come into focus in chapter 3.

Gaining a clear-eyed perspective on German-speaking theater throughout the seventeenth century, but especially at its start, demands that we strip away the familiar trappings of modern theater: buildings, regularly scheduled performances, publicity outlets, authors, and regular theatergoers. Indeed, to speak of the theater in the singular projects a consolidation that emerged only more than a century later. When the first acting troupes arrived around 1600, theater took place irregularly and in disconnected institutional settings, in the absence of any professional training or the potential for a career as a paid actor. Its three main venues were communal fairs, royal courts, and schools. None of these bore a strong resemblance to the playhouses that would gain a foothold in urban centers during the closing decades of the eighteenth century and become increasingly dominant in the course of the nineteenth century. Two of these three institutions provided the fertile ground for the growth of a novel and, as it turned out, enduringly popular mode of theatrical presentation.

The inclusive town fairs and the exclusive princely courts, in particular, became the institutional platforms upon which the fool first captivated audiences with his intoxicating verve and impishness. Despite the dissimilar social-economic composition of these two settings, both responded with enthusiasm to the first forays of English actors in the German-speaking territories. The mere fact that both of these environments proved hospitable to the fool thwarts the temptation to apply the grab-bag term that has enjoyed currency in academic discourse over recent decades for such phenomena, namely, Mikhail Bakhtin's concept of the carnivalesque.[3] For Bakhtin, the fool amounts to a fundamentally transgressive or emancipatory force, opposed to the quotidian life of social hierarchy and inhibition. But it would be a mistake to begin with a celebratory image of the fool and his role, one that attributes to him both an overarching purpose and a predetermined set of semantic possibilities. While the fool often antagonized the values propounded by other members of the fictional world represented on the stage, his stage activity is not worthy of unqualified glorification. What is more, the different phases of the fool's long history—from widespread success in the seventeenth century to vituperative attacks and then enthusiastic revival in the eighteenth century—each embedded the fool within a different conception of the internal coherence demanded of a play as well as the purpose the theater, taken as a whole, should serve. Working too closely with the concept of the carnivalesque risks obscuring the fine-grained differences in the composition and function of comic theater between the first arrival of the fool around 1600 and the explosion of literary interest over two hundred years later.

Playmaking was a central part of German carnival. The calendrical cycle of Christian holidays, especially Shrovetide, gave rise to a rich heritage of theatrical performance, particularly during the fifteenth and sixteenth centuries.[4] Its single exponent still widely recognized today—in no small part due to Richard Wagner's mid-

---

3. This line of thought is ubiquitous in the scholarship, largely because of the immense influence of Mikhail Bakhtin's study of Rabelais and the medieval carnival. However appealing it may seem to understand the tradition of the stage fool as evidence of a subversive force against "official" culture, the evidence speaks against such a monolithic approach. For the pioneering study, which has produced an abundance of epigonal discourse, see M. M. Bakhtin, *Rabelais and His World* (Bloomington: Indiana University Press, 1984).

4. A succinct presentation of the carnival environment in Nuremberg is provided in Samuel Kinser, "Presentation and Representation: Carnival at Nuremberg, 1450–1550," *Representations* 13 (1986): 1–41. See also the very useful typology of different carnival plays in Anette Köhler, "Das neuzeitliche Fastnachtspiel

nineteenth-century opera—the Meistersinger and cobbler named Hans Sachs (1494–1576), lived at the tail end of this line. Even though the guild of performers known as the Meistersinger lived on into the seventeenth century, their popularity steadily diminished beginning with the arrival of traveling English players in the 1590s.[5] The sort of plays Sachs and his colleagues put on generally consisted of a small handful of roles distinguished by social position or profession (doctor, servant, farmer, etc.). The plays were performed impromptu by amateur actors in public houses without a stage. Among the many reasons that Hans Sachs (unlike many of his predecessors and successors) secured a place in literary history, two in particular stand out. First, he did not exploit themes related to the confessional battles that wrought havoc on the German territories during the sixteenth century. The second reason is a consequence of the first: his brief sketches of cuckolds, rubes, and foolhardy masters, in the end, resonated well with the comic imagination of later generations. Evidence of this is the fact that when the aspiration to write histories of German drama gained traction around 1800, Hans Sachs earned a place as revered forefather. Over the same years, a massive corpus of playwrights who focused on biblical narratives, colored by interconfessional strife, fell essentially into oblivion.[6]

Even though Shrovetide and carnival plays have found a prominent place in the broader literary-historical consciousness, they were by no means the most influential public festivals for the history of German theater. By the end of the sixteenth century, Shrovetide playmaking forfeited pride of place to biannual commercial fairs

---

(1600–1800)," in *Fastnachtspiel—Commedia dell'arte: Gemeinsamkeiten—Gegensätze* (Innsbruck: Universitätsverlag Wagner, 1992), 103–117.

5. Paul, *Reichsstadt und Schauspiel*, 30–36.

6. An example of this historiographical shift is the relatively minor role Sachs plays in Carl Friedrich Flögel's *Geschichte der komischen Litteratur*, which appeared in four volumes between 1784 and 1787. See the remarks in Carl Friedrich Flögel, *Geschichte der komischen Litteratur* (Liegnitz/Leipzig: David Stegert, 1787), 4:291–294. By contrast, August Wilhelm Schlegel—following a number of his contemporaries from Goethe to Tieck—isolates only Sachs for detailed attention while ignoring nearly all the other sixteenth- and seventeenth-century playwrights. August Wilhelm Schlegel, *Vorlesungen über dramatische Kunst und Litteratur* (Leipzig: Weidmann, 1846), 2:401–403.

around such holidays as Easter, Michaelmas Day, and Pentecost. Towns from Leipzig to Frankfurt, from Basel to Graz, hosted fairs that became as much platforms for economic activity as magnets for traveling performers, confidence men, and quacks. Since the Middle Ages, groups of minstrels and mountebanks had been known under the rubric Farhendes Volk, the traveling or itinerant people. Whereas this group suffered stigmatization, essentially regarded as swindling vagabonds, the English theatrical players that arrived in the decades around 1600 were accorded a more privileged status.[7] Upon their arrival, towns consistently granted the English comedians the license required to set up their boards and sell their wares, which included as much music and dance as playmaking. The home of the acting troupes became the town square, especially in the bustling weeks when the major towns hosted their fairs. For the duration of the seventeenth century, acting troupes did well at securing the necessary municipal permissions, even though their itinerant lifestyle and impecunious existence meant that they were lastingly associated with unseemly social groups.

Just as the diversity of town fairs offered ample opportunity to supply a paying audience with a novel performance, the sheer quantity of German-speaking principalities meant that courtly entertainments were also in high demand. Although the houses of German-speaking princes never reached anything near the level of opulence and profligacy that, for instance, seventeenth-century French royalty could espouse, theatrical performances were regular installments in dozens of German-speaking courts, including Braunschweig-Wolfenbüttel and Wolgast, Dresden and Heidelberg, Munich and Vienna, just to name a few. Although courts maintained a strong preference for French drama and Italian opera, traveling theatrical troupes with translations of English plays and original German compositions also made inroads into the courtly milieu.[8]

---

7. See Ernst Schubert, *Arme Leute, Bettler und Gauner im Franken des 18. Jahrhunderts* (Neustadt an der Aisch: Gegner & Co., 1983); Schubert, *Fahrendes Volk im Mittelalter* (Bielefeld: Verlag für Regionalgeschichte, 1995).

8. The presence of traveling players in courtly contexts has been discussed in detail in Harald Zielske, "Die deutschen Höfe und das Wandertruppenwesen im 17. und frühen 18. Jahrhundert—Fragen ihres Verhältnisses," in *Europäische*

There can be little doubt that the English traveling acting troupes that first visited the fairs and courts around 1600 encountered (and quickly electrified) an otherwise lackluster theatrical landscape. But how are we to think of the existence of these small bands?

The English players made their way to Germany from London, an urban center supporting multiple stages and acting companies, during periods when the theater was closed because of contagion or political mandate.[9] In general, English companies spent some time in the provinces, in rare instances venturing onto the Continent, but London was undeniably the epicenter of their activity.[10] It is crucial to emphasize that the English players arrived on the Continent at a moment when clowning had become intensely controversial in England.[11] On the one hand, some currents in England opposed roles, as Sir Philip Sidney put it, "with neither decency nor discretion."[12] It had become current, to quote Hamlet's famous instructions to his visiting players, that they should "let those that play your clownes speak no more than is set down for them."[13] At the same time, complex verbal and gestural clowning remained a fixture at many of the London playhouses. Within the German context, meanwhile, linguistic barriers demanded simplicity, gave free rein to improvisation, and amplified the musical and gestural dimensions of theatrical expression. The characteristics of play and wit, which were most strongly associated with the English clown, were reinvented in the German context as an exceedingly coarse brand of extemporized humor.

Hofkultur im 16. und 17. Jahrhundert: Vorträge und Referate, ed. August Buck (Hamburg: Hauswedell, 1981), 521–541.

9. Among studies of traveling English acting troupes and the London scene, I have found Andrew Gurr's work particularly informative. Andrew Gurr, *Playgoing in Shakespeare's London* (Cambridge: Cambridge University Press, 1987); Gurr, *The Shakespearian Playing Companies* (Oxford: Clarendon Press; New York: Oxford University Press, 1996).

10. Alan Somerset, " 'How Chances It They Travel?' Provincial Touring, Playing Places, and the King's Men," *Shakespeare Survey* 47 (1994): 45–60.

11. Richard Preiss, *Clowning and Authorship in Early Modern Theatre* (Cambridge: Cambridge University Press, 2014).

12. Sir Philip Sidney, *The Prose Works of Sir Philip Sidney*, ed. Albert Feuillerat (Cambridge: Cambridge University Press, 1968), 3:39.

13. *Hamlet* 3.2.40–47.

Even before the ravaging of the Thirty Years' War began, the German territories found themselves in a fragmented political order and without a central metropolis that might serve as a hub of cultural activity. Visiting acting troupes were hence relegated to a punishing regiment of travel across astonishingly vast stretches of land, from Berlin to Basel and Strasburg to Prague. In small caravans of horse-drawn carriages, which were as much a means of locomotion as makeshift abodes, the actors spent time in all corners of the German-speaking world. Although they often performed in municipal buildings, they also often brought along primitive wooden stages to set up in the town square or wherever else the local municipal authorities would allow them. Although they were at first dominated by only male actors, we know that, by the second half of the seventeenth century, troupes in the German-speaking lands included both sexes. As one might expect from their itinerant lifestyles, husband-and-wife couples became regular installments. To give the two most famous examples, Catharina Elisabeth Velten (1646–1712) and Johannes Velten (1640–1693) were preeminent on the theatrical scene during the closing decades of the seventeenth century, while Friedericke Carolina Neuber (1697–1760) and Johann Neuber (1697–1759) became key players in the early decades of the eighteenth. Both instances were also second-generation acting families. Professional acting was, in short, a family affair.

The influx of Englishmen was strongest in the decades around 1600, but their influence—both in terms of personnel and repertoire—would have remained nonexistent if some among them had not quickly mastered the local language and begun to adapt their plays to make them appeal to audiences. A few Englishmen seem to have had a particular knack for the entrepreneurial and managerial role. For instance, from 1608 on, John Green led a troupe, which was taken over in 1628 by a longtime member, Robert Reynolds.[14] Another major English manager was George Jolly (fl. 1640–1673), who led a troupe of German actors for over a

---

14. For the generational connections among these actors, see Brand and Rudin, "Der englische Komödiant Robert Browne," 92 and 97–98.

decade around midcentury.[15] All of these men led troupes of German-speaking and almost exclusively German-born actors; their own heritage and role in charge, however, meant that English plays secured a place at the center of repertoires.

The impact of English actors was sudden and profound as they crisscrossed the German-speaking territories with a repertoire of enough plays to remain in a single place for at least one to two weeks and, in some rare occasions, even longer.[16] One can expect that they had about two dozen plays in their repertoire, about as many as any English acting company of the same period.[17] At first, acting scripts consisted entirely of materials freely adapted from plays that had already proved themselves on the English stage. Almost immediately, new German compositions and adaptations joined in the fray.

The earliest extant play list, submitted in 1604 to the town council of Nördlingen as part of the troupe's request for permission to perform, indicates how quickly the actors adapted to their new environment.[18] Although modern historians first took notice of the list because it attests to the first staging of *Romeo and Juliet* on the Continent, the name Shakespeare, importantly, appears nowhere on it. The tragedy of ill-fated lovers appears rather inconspicuously as the seventh in a list of ten plays distinguished only by title. By contrast, the most extensive surviving early play list is an inventory of

---

15. Robert J. Alexander, "George Jolly [Joris Joliphus], Der wandernde Player und Manager," *Kleine Schriften der Gesellschaft für Theatergeschichte 29/30* (1978): 31–48.

16. The permissions have been particularly well documented for the early decades of the seventeenth century, in no small part due to the interest in the activities of English players on the Continent. The most impressive case study of a single troupe, with rich documentary evidence, is Brand and Rudin, "Der englische Komödiant Robert Browne." A diverse array of further municipal permissions has been discussed in Bärbel Rudin, "Pickelhering, rechte Frauenzimmer, berühmte Autoren: Zur Ankündigungspraxis der Wanderbühne im 17. Jahrhundert," *Kleine Schriften der Gesellschaft für Theatergeschichte 34/35* (1988): 29–60.

17. Preiss, *Clowning and Authorship in Early Modern Theatre*, 18.

18. Haekel, *Die englischen Komödianten in Deutschland*, 105. Haekel also provides a number of other early lists, all of which attest to the same shift in the early 1600s to the German language.

forty-two performances by John Green's troupe at the Dresden court in June 1626; plays by Marlowe, Shakespeare, Thomas Dekker, and Thomas Kyd are listed anonymously together with many others.[19] Green was traveling with a repertoire large enough that a different play could be performed each night for more than one month—much longer than a typical sojourn—and the play list tells us that spectacular titles and tantalizing plot synopses were his pivotal advertising devices. Using acting scripts as loose templates for their performances, troupes like Green's showed no interest in authorial attribution, and audiences seem to have been equally uncurious.[20]

Although diversity of repertoire allowed for longevity and flexibility, an additional factor proved important to success. Take the example of Carl Andreas Paulsen (1620–1679), who led his troupe around the German-speaking world beginning in the 1650s. During a particularly long residence in Nuremberg in the summer of 1667, Paulsen and his group received permission to perform as "English Comedians," a term that was used in the seventeenth century more as a strategy to attract audiences than as a statement of national provenance.[21] In the course of at least thirty performances, Paulsen's group put on plays ranging from a derivative of Shakespeare's *Titus Andronicus* to an adaptation of Daniel Casper von Lohenstein's *Ibrahim Bassa*, in addition to a smattering of other German, French, and Italian pieces. In the following year, however, municipal authorities rejected Paulsen's application with the statement that the stagings tended to "mix in irritating things and farce" (*ärgerliche sachen und possenspiel miteinzumischen*).[22]

---

19. For the complete list, see Haekel, *Die englischen Komödianten in Deutschland*, 111–114.

20. We might understand the German disregard for authorship as a more radical version of the contemporary English situation. By and large, authorship was of dwindling importance in the London theater industry. However, names like Shakespeare were becoming increasingly known, and print editions of plays did become available in select instances, even though the circulation remained rather small. For a critical discussion of this issue, with a focus on Shakespeare and references to the vast body of literature, see Douglas A. Brooks, *From Playhouse to Printing House: Drama and Authorship in Early Modern England* (Cambridge: Cambridge University Press, 2000), 14–64.

21. Paul, *Reichsstadt und Schauspiel*, 173.

22. Ibid., 174.

The condemnation of disjointed plays interspersed with comic, and evidently galling, skits alludes to a problem of theatrical form. A loose conception of internal continuity and the amplification of comic effects were the bedrock of the fool's success.

With a full repertoire and a vigorous travel schedule, the actors took part in a motley spectacle that looked quite different from modern plot-driven theater. Among the contextual factors that helped shape the fool's unique practice of producing comic effects, one deserving of attention is the competition for attention within the broader spectacle. A play in the town square was not a stand-alone entertainment to which audiences devoted exclusive attention for the duration of a narrative. Plays were, instead, intermingled with a heterogeneous array of routines of song, dance, and acrobatics. The greatest German picaro novel, Grimmelshausen's *Simplicissimus Teutsch* (1668–1669), includes an informative description of the place of the fool at the town fairs. The novel's concluding section begins with a comparison between the eponymous protagonist and the sort of farceurs and funnymen that had populated the town square:

> Carnival-barkers and quacksalvers . . . enter the open marketplace with their Hans Wurst or Hans Supp. With the first cry and fantastical crooked leaps of the fool they attract a greater throng and more listeners than the most zealous pastor.

> Marckscheyer oder Quacksalber . . . wann er am offnen Marckt mit seinem Hanß Wurst oder Hanß Supp auftritt/ und auf den ersten Schray und phantastischen krummen Sprung seines Narren mehr Zulauffs und Anhörer bekombt/ als der eyfrigste Seelen-Hirt.[23]

This passage provides a good sense of the general atmosphere where the fool had his home. For one, it testifies to the enthusiasm

---

23. Hans Jakob Christoffel von Grimmelshausen, *Continuatio des Abentheurlichen Simplicissimi oder der Schluß Desselben* (Mompelgart: Johann Fillion, 1669), n.p. For the modern reprinting, see *Hans Jacob Christoffel von Grimmelshausen, Simplicissimus Teutsch* (Frankfurt am Main: Deutscher Klassiker Verlag, 2005), 564.

of audiences for the fool, here under the interchangeable monikers Hans Wurst and Hans Supp. But it also gives an impression of acoustic and visual pageantry that accompanied the traveling players. Plays earned a place in a hodgepodge of attractions that, as Grimmelshausen notes, offered a profane diversion of greater fascination than a pastor's promise of spiritual redemption. At the annual fair and in the town square, all sorts of entertainers were ruthlessly competing for attention and money.

We find the very same sort of insistence on the sensational at the first stationary playhouse in Germany, Nuremberg's Fechthaus or Fencing House, built in 1627–1628. The roofless square building, with three floors of galleries, hosted circus entertainments like tightrope walking, choreographed bear and ox hunts, and acrobatics in addition to playmaking.[24] Performances took place during daylight hours on a wooden stage that could be assembled and disassembled as needed. Although the excitement surrounding the English actors undoubtedly contributed to the municipality's decision to build the Fencing House, playmaking alone was not enough to keep the doors open—especially as the financial impact of the Thirty Years' War made itself felt. The copperplate engraving (fig. 1) of the Fencing House from around 1720 gives us some idea of the scripted hunts. Within the broader German-speaking context, Nuremberg actually appears quite exceptional; other towns made due with makeshift setups, often in public spaces, well into the latter half of the eighteenth century.

But how did traveling troupes first establish themselves and achieve enough popularity that, within a few decades, the first experiments in public playhouses, like the one at Nuremberg, made even remote economic sense? Let us return to the years around 1600. The unwitting pioneer of these developments was an actor named Robert Browne (1563–ca. 1621), who had spent decades in English companies in and outside of London. With a group of about ten players, many of whom had been associated with an English company called the Admiral's Men, Browne headed out in

---

24. See Paul, *Reichsstadt und Schauspiel*, 40–55.

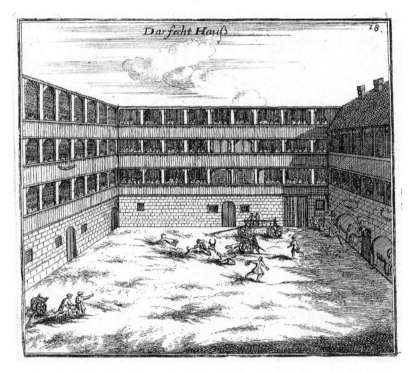

Figure 1. Das Fechthaus in Nuremberg. Copperplate by Samuel
Mikovíny from *Nurembergische Prospekte* ca. 1720.

search of employment around 1590, a time when the plague was
ravaging the city and the London theaters were closed.[25] While a
lack of steady income and an impoverished lifestyle were hallmarks
of an actor's day-to-day life in England, the troupe enjoyed unexpected economic success on the Continent. So even though the itinerary of relentless travel just barely elevated members of the troupe
above the level of subsistence, this was a marked improvement over

---

25. The convincing evidence in favor of this reading was first outlined by
Brand. To be brief, the passport the men carried, written by the benefactor of the
Admiral's Men and Charles Howard (1536–1624), refers to the troupe as *mes
jouers et serviteurs.* The letter is reprinted in full in Brand and Rudin, "Der englische Komödiant Robert Browne," 120–121.

sure poverty and possible death from the London plague. Despite significant obstacles to success, including language itself, the English players secured enough pay to warrant multiple visits over the coming years and even to spawn offspring troupes.

The conditions under which Browne's troupe first performed shaped the strategies they used to flourish. Indeed, their lasting resonance can be attributed to two instances of resourceful stagecraft. The very linguistic barrier that made a warm welcome so unlikely also propelled gestural effects, song, and dance to the forefront of the stage.[26] In addition, although the English troupes, unlike Italian ones, quickly showed a willingness to learn German and to adapt their plays to local preferences, firsthand accounts of spectators give the impression that when it seemed impossible to capture the audience's attention with dialogue, the comic register, and especially nonlinguistic elements, became the primary means of theatrical address. A 1597 poem about the Frankfurt fair, for instance, identifies as the English troupe's key attributes "bawdy jest and comic strokes . . . antics and salacious jokes."[27] An English traveler from the same period, Fynes Moryson (1566–1630), was baffled by the popularity of "stragling broken Companyes."[28] The "wandring Comedyians," he observed "hauing nether a Complete

26. In addition to Brand's exhaustive study, I have also found helpful the concise discussion in Willem Schrickx, "English Actors at the Courts of Wolfenbüttel, Brussels, and Graz during the Lifetime of Shakespeare," *Shakespeare Survey 33* (2007): 153–168. There is a vast body of older research dating back to the nineteenth century, much of which is gathered and reviewed in J. G. Riewald, "The English Actors in the Low Countries, 1585–c. 1650: An Annotated Bibliography," in *Studies in Seventeenth-Century English Literature, History, and Bibliography,* ed. G. A. M. Janssens and G. A. M. Aarts (Amsterdam: Rodopi, 1984), 157–178. On the broader European context, I recommend in particular Jerzy Limon, *Gentlemen of a Company: English Players in Central and Eastern Europe, 1590–1660* (Cambridge: Cambridge University Press, 1985).

27. This translation is from Ernest Brennecke, *Shakespeare in Germany, 1590–1700, with Translations of Five Early Plays* (Chicago: University of Chicago Press, 1964), 8.

28. Fynes Moryson and Charles Hughes, *Shakespeare's Europe; Unpublished Chapters of Fynes Moryson's Itinerary, Being a Survey of the Condition of Europe at the End of the 16th Century* (London: Sherratt & Hughes, 1903), 476.

number of Actours, nor any good Apparell, nor any ornament of the Stage" are "more descruing pitty then prayse, for the serious parts are dully penned, and worse acted, and the mirth they make is rediculous, and nothing less then witty."[29] Having thoroughly denounced the quality of the acting by the traveling players, Moryson goes on to paint a picture that reveals quite a bit about the form of their performances:

> The Germans, not vnderstanding a worde they sayde, both men and wemen, flocked wonderfully to see theire gesture and Action, rather than heare them, speaking English which they vnderstood not, and pronowncing peeces and Patches of English playes, which my selfe and some English men there present could not heare without great wearysomeness.[30]

This passage speaks to the rapport between stage and audience. Moryson recognizes that the very strategies that made the actors successful with German audiences also made them appear vapid to an English spectator. In particular, the focus on corporeal devices, even in the absence of linguistic intelligibility, ensured the rapt attention of men and women who did not understand English. As a consequence, the actors felt little need to sustain a continuous plot, instead using abbreviated slices of plays to keep audiences fully engaged. As Moryson's remarks make clear, the transfer to a new context compelled the small bands of English actors to change their strategies for soliciting and sustaining the audience's attention. Even if the English theater of the late sixteenth century did not possess the strict standards of compositional unity that one finds in, say, French classicism, it seems that the relocation to the German territories shifted the accent even further in the direction of an internally heterogeneous and discontinuous construction—a *pieces-and-patches construction.*

The derisive observations of the English traveler Moryson hint at, but do not yet make explicit, the ludic presence that achieved fame over the seventeenth century. Meanwhile, a 1601 chronicle of the town Münster attests that the performances by visiting English

---

29. Ibid., 304.
30. Ibid.

troupes were largely unintelligible but for "plenty of tricks and gags" interspersed by the fool.[31] A poem about the Frankfurt fair from a few years earlier similarly locates comic gesture at the center of its remarks. It paints a picture of a highly informal environment in which the players on the stage do "such crooked things / that they often must laugh themselves." If their motivation is "taking money from the people," the poem tells us, the means by which they do it is fairly straightforward: "The fool causes the laughter."[32]

There is good reason to believe that a single member of Robert Browne's group played an exceptional role in sparking the love affair with the fool. At the turn of the seventeenth century, a socially diverse array of German-speaking audiences at both public fairs and royal courts fell under the spell of an actor named Thomas Sackville (d. 1628). He seems to have possessed superlative gifts as a dancer, musician, and improvisator. Even though it is quite clear that Sackville, in particular, pioneered the new role of the fool—in no small part to circumnavigate the linguistic barrier that initially separated him from the audience—the sobriquet he used, Jan Bouschet, was never substantively attached to a single actor. Instead, the role was immediately recognized as an iterable form, a way of acting and interacting that could be reproduced. While Sackville achieved a good deal of notoriety, it was not he, but his role, that made a lasting impact. Both on the stage and in writing, the role of the fool, under a single and soon familiar sobriquet, quickly entered into wider circulation. Consider the following two textual examples, one related to the court context, and the other to the fair. These examples lend support to a perhaps initially bewildering claim: what happened with the arrival of Browne's troupe

---

31. Helmut G. Asper, *Hanswurst: Studien zum Lustigmacher auf der Berufsschauspielerbühne in Deutschland im 17. und 18. Jahrhundert* (Emsdetten: Lechte, 1980), 26.

32. The original lines from which I have quoted are the following: "Vnd Agieren doch so schlecht sachen / Das sie der poszn oft selbst lachen, / Das siesz Gelt von den Leuten bringen / Zu sich, vor so närrische Dingen, / Der Narr macht lachen, doch ich weht / Da ist keiner so gutt wie Jan begehtt." Ernst Kelchner, "Sechs Gedichte über die Frankfurter Messe," *Mittheilungen des Vereins für Geschichte und Althertumskunde in Frankfurt am Main* 6 (1881): 373.

was not imposition of a set type to which subsequent instantiations of the fool were beholden; it was the emergence of a much more elastic and variable theatrical form.

Perhaps the largest body of plays from around 1600 that feature the fool were written by Jakob Ayrer (1544–1605), who spent the last decade of his life as a civil administrator in Nuremberg. Ayrer probably came into contact with the English strolling players in 1593,[33] and began integrating a figure who, by his own account, "dresses like the English fool,"[34] into many of the approximately six dozen plays he wrote in his leisure. In fact, Ayrer's posthumously published five-volume corpus of plays is replete with instances of the English fool, including multiple roles that are variations on Sackville's sobriquet, Jan Bouschet. Ayrer composed highly moralizing plays—some closer to the Hans Sachs Shrovetide tradition, some closer to English song-and-dance numbers, some rewritings of episodes from Roman history and the Bible—in which a figure called Jahnn (with some variation in spelling) assumed the role of a comic servant, often characterized by idleness and gluttony, and repeatedly suffering the abuse of his superiors. In a good number of instances, Ayrer also has the fool speak an epilogue, ensuring that the play ends with an unequivocal moral message. Even without looking at the individual plays in minute detail, a striking structural feature of Ayrer's writing immediately sticks out: he composed his plays without any hope that Sackville himself, or for that matter any other English actor, would ever play the role of the fool.

Something very similar can be seen at work in the plays of another author from the early 1690s, Duke Heinrich Julius of Brunswick (1564–1613). As he was a member of the educated elite and the ruler of one of the most important northern German territories, the duke's plays testify to the power of the fool to electrify people from all socioeconomic groups. In 1693–1694, after he had

---

33. Brand and Rudin, "Der englische Komödiant Robert Browne," 33.

34. The relevant stage direction indicates that a figure is meant to enter the stage *kleidt wie der Engellendisch Narr*. Jakob Ayrer and Adelbert von Keller, *Ayrers Dramen* (Stuttgart: Litterarischer verein, 1865), 1:22.

hosted the group of strolling players led by Browne and featuring Sackville, the duke published a collection of plays that testifies to his fascination with the English acting troupe. As a pious Protestant, Duke Heinrich Julius possessed a fondness for biblical themes, and he drew upon his humanistic education in crafting a play after the Roman comedian Plautus.[35] But he also installs a fool, whom he identifies sometimes as a *morio*, the Latin equivalent of the German *Narr* and English *fool*. While the duke had been deeply impressed by Sackville, he was also concerned enough about the textual circulation of his plays that he revised and republished them a second time approximately a decade after they first appeared in print and after Sackville himself could no longer have possibly played the role.[36]

Beyond Ayrer and Duke Heinrich Julius, there were still more writers who populated their plays with a fool named Johann.[37] But none of the other texts or their authors ever achieved much fame. On the contrary, notions of originality, as well as the identification of the play with the voice and experience of a unique individual, had little relevance to the success of the plays featuring the fool. It would be more accurate to say that these writers understood their activity as part of an ongoing chain of production that allowed for the unrestricted appropriation and redeployment of preexisting narratives, with the expectation that their own rewritings would become the subject of further appropriations and redeployments. A similar fluidity underlies the use of the fool in plays by Ayrer and Duke Heinrich Julius; they treat the fool as a theatrical convention detached from any single actor or script that could be deployed in new plays in accord with a standard purpose.

---

35. On potential Italian influences on von Braunschweig, see Böckmann, *Die Commedia dell'arte und das deutsche Drama*, 62–68.

36. Helga Meise, "Narrheit in den Dramen Heinrich Julius' von Braunschweig-Wolfenbüttel und Lüneberg," in *Der Narr in der deutschen Literatur im Mittelalter und in der frühen Neuzeit*, ed. Jean Schillinger (Bern: Peter Lang, 2008), 171–180.

37. See, for instance, Johann Neudorf, *Asotvs Das ist COMOEDIA vom verlohrnen Sohn, auß dem 15. Capitel S. Lucae* (1608; Goslar: Geschichts- und Heimatschutzverein Goslar e.V, 1958); Hektor Conradus, *Necrobaptista: Die Historia von Johanne dem Teufer / Wie er von Herode Gefangen / vnd wie er jm endlich das Heubt abschlagen Lassen* (Uelzen: Michael Kröner, 1600).

Another set of examples, this time with a significantly longer historical trajectory, clusters around the sobriquet Pickelhering.[38] It appears to have come into more widespread use during the first two decades of the seventeenth century as the sobriquet for an English actor named George Vincent (d. 1647). A formerly prominent actor from the company Queen Anne's Men, Vincent began touring the Low Countries and German-speaking territories around 1616 with a troupe led by John Green.[39] Vincent lived until about 1650, but by that point the name Pickelhering was no longer associated with him alone, having by then become a conventional calque for the fool.[40] Much like the name Jan Bouschet, the role of Pickelhering quickly became unmoored from a single actor and remained so for almost two centuries. When a massive collection of English plays appeared in print in 1620, the name was well-enough known to be used as an advertisement on the title page.[41] In fact, for the duration of the seventeenth century, the fool possessed such central importance that the name Pickelhering by itself worked as a magnet to attract audiences. The earliest playbills from the 1650s tout the presence of a "very funny Pickelhering,"[42] or prominently list the name Pickelhering at the very center of a broad swath of plays to be performed. The earliest surviving playbill from a performance of the immensely popular Faust story, from 1688 in Bremen, announces that the play will feature not just "the life and death of the great Arch-Magician D. Johannes Faustus," but also

---

38. The text name first appears in Christopher Marlowe's *Doctor Faustus*, when the allegorical embodiment of gluttony refers to his godfather as Peter Pickelherring. For an attempt to uncover the etymological origin of the sobriquet, see John Alexander, "Will Kemp, Thomas Sacheville, and Pickelhering: A Consanguinity and Confluence of Three Early Modern Clown Personas," *Daphnis* 3, no. 4 (2007): 463–486.

39. Willem Schrickx, " 'Pickelherring' and English Actors in Germany," *Shakespeare Survey* 36 (1983): 135–147.

40. When the English name Pickelherring became a German calque, its spelling became highly irregular. For the sake of simplicity, I refer to Pickelhering, which seems to me most commonly used.

41. Manfred Brauneck and Alfred Noe, *Spieltexte der Wanderbühne* (Berlin: De Gruyter, 1970), vol. 1.

42. Wilhelm Michael Anton Creizenach, *Die Schauspiele der englischen Komödianten* (Berlin/Stuttgart: W. Spemann, 1889), xxv.

"Pickelhäring's entertainments from beginning to end."[43] Much like the sobriquet Jan Bouschet, Pickelhäring also cut across social and political strata, as his role in a 1686 play performed on the occasion of the meeting in Regensburg of the Imperial Diet of the Holy Roman Empire makes clear.[44] This remained true at least until 1794, almost 170 years after the stage fool first appeared in the German-speaking world.[45]

Make no mistake, in the early decades of the seventeenth century, Jan Bouschet and Pickelhering were by no means the only sobriquets under which the fool circulated. There were many others either implicitly or explicitly identified as variations on the fool. Some names—like Traraeus, Grobianus, Schrämgen, and Morohn—appear to have been used just once.[46] Others like Kilian Brustfleck had their heyday, but then died off before long.[47] Names like Harlequin and Hanswurst, meanwhile, find only sporadic mention in the seventeenth century, before really catching fire in the eighteenth.[48] The latter two names, in fact, achieved such notoriety that they became synonymous with the role of the fool.

---

43. Willi Flemming, *Deutsche Literatur: Sammlung literarischer Kunst- und Kulturdenkmäler in Entwicklungsreihen* (Weimar: Böhlau, 1931), 3:203.

44. Anonymous, *Comoedia, Bitittult Der Flüchtige Virenus, Oder Die Getreue Olympia* (Regensburg: Johann Georg Hofmann, 1686).

45. Anonymous, *Pickelhärings Hochzeit Oder Der Lustig-singende Harlequin* (Fröhlichshaussen, 1794). This text provides a particularly apposite example, since it is actually based on a play about the marriage of Harlequin, a popular theme in the latter half of the eighteenth century, but it uses the name Pickelhäring in the title. The 1794 publication is a reprint of a play that first became available around midcentury.

46. Traraeus appears in *Tragoedia genandt Der Großmüthige Rechts Gelehrte Aemilius Paulus Papinianus* in Flemming, *Deutsche Literatur*, 3:138–201. Grobianus plays the fool in *Tragaedia von Julio und Hyppolita* in Brauneck and Noe, *Spieltexte der Wanderbühne*, 1:427–459. For Schambitasche, see *Comoedia von König Mantalors unrechtmäßessigen Liebe und derselben Straff*, ibid., 2:311–401. And Morohn figures centrally in *Tragi Comedia*, ibid., 2:451–551. This counts, of course, as only a small sampling of the abundant names for the fool.

47. Christian Neuhuber, "Der Vormund des Hanswurst: Der Eggenbergische Hofkomödiant Johann Valentin Petzold und sein Killian Brustfleck," *Daphnis 35* (2006): 263–299.

48. See Asper's monumental study, *Hanswurst*. On the use of Harlequin and Scaramouche, see Walter Hinck, *Das deutsche Lustspiel des 17. und 18. Jahrhunderts und die italienische Komödie: Commedia dell'arte und Théâtre italien* (Stuttgart: Metzler, 1965).

Part 2 will explore in greater detail the unique trajectory that these two sobriquets traced across the German-speaking world and, in the case of Harlequin, across Europe.

At least as far the theatrical role of the fool in the seventeenth century goes, nothing really hangs on the moniker itself. So much can be gleaned from the career of the most famous German play of all. The 1688 rendering of the Faust story in Bremen featured a fool named Pickelhäring, while one from Frankfurt approximately fifty years later nominates Hans Wurst for the role. Different troupes seem to have preferred one name over the other, and each performance certainly allowed for a good amount of liberty in what was said and done, but underlying the onomastic variations is but one comic form. The formation of a conventionalized fool role was, as one can tell from the Faust comparsion, a way of affording audiences a familiar point of orientation. Plays changed from day to day as troupes passed through town and worked through their repertoire. But audiences always knew the pieces-and-patches construction of plays would provide ample doses of the fool, sometimes between scenes, sometimes within them, and sometimes after the show. In order to see what made the fool's comic practice hang together, across his various instantiations and sobriquets, it is necessary to have a closer look at his integration into the dialogue and scenic action. This is the task to which we now turn.

3

PRACTICE OF STAGE INTERACTION

If the fool appeared under so many guises and as part of so many different plays, what supports the commonsense view of these as just so many realizations of one and the same theatrical form? In the first chapter, I introduced the provisional claim that a figure like Phantasmo from the *Hamlet* adaptation is best identified in terms of characteristic ways of interacting onstage. Now the task is to marshal broad-based evidence for the assertion that the fool should be investigated in terms of his place in the larger fabric of the play. Untangling the threads that hold the fool together with the rest of the fictional world requires responding to two straightforward questions. Are there recognizable patterns to the fool's participation in plays, especially to the sequences of dialogue in which he is involved? And, if so, do these patterns produce similar sorts of (local and global) effects within the respective encompassing play? These are questions of a general scope bearing on crucial methodological issues. At the same time, they avoid a biography-like account of stage appearance after stage appearance and move beyond self-evident descriptions of the fool as funny or off-color, irreverent or lewd, which may be true but are also uninformative. The above questions, by contrast, isolate the structure of dialogue as the key to grasping the formal element that lends unity to the fool.

The most rudimentary dimensions of the fool's abiding stage presence can be described in terms of a simple paradox. To wit, the fool is uniquely able to participate in the fictional world as a full-fledged member, yet he is also able to step outside it and address the audience directly. Discerning the implications of this rudimentary doubleness—his status as an agent both inside and outside the fiction—will require an up-close look at the fool *in actu*, as he conducts his comic work. The following observations on the fool's comic strategies avoid the search for some buried profundity, instead tracking, as value-neutrally as possible, his effects on environing words and actions. Within the overarching mission of part 1—to understand how and why the fool was featured with such frequency and longevity—this chapter explores the core possibilities that his involvement provided the dialogue. In other words, the present task is to describe the game rules that the fool plays by.

Before laying out the parameters of dialogue within which the fool moves, it is important to register that, in nearly every instance, he stands on a particular rung in the social hierarchy: namely, the position of the male servant. This point is so obvious that its importance can be easily overlooked. The unique possibilities for play available to the fool are based on the fact that, as a servant, he is installed in what the anthropologist A. R. Radcliffe-Browne referred to as a "joking relationship."[1] That is, the fool interacts with others by means of "a peculiar combination of friendliness and antagonism" and of "permitted disrespect."[2] The fool's place within

---

1. The term was not originally Radcliffe-Browne's, but he wrote the foundational studies in anthropology on the subject. See A. R. Radcliffe-Browne, "On Joking Relationships," in *Structure and Function in Primitive Society* (New York: The Free Press, 1965), 90–104.

2. Radcliffe-Browne, "On Joking Relationships," 91.

the play is defined by such an exceptional privilege to mock and make fun of the other characters.

Of course, the use of a servant role for configuring a joking relationship was not new to German plays. The comic servant had a long tradition in European theater, extending back to the Greeks and Romans.[3] In a radicalization of tendencies that can be found across European theatrical history, the seventeenth-century German tradition sequestered comic play to a single figure, allowing only the fool to strike certain thematic chords: only the wily servant employed scatological humor, referred unsolicitedly to sex, professed his willingness to perform any act for pecuniary reward, and made light of death and suffering. The main elements in his thematic repertoire are all drawn from the corporeal dimension of human activity, including coitus, defecation, inebriation, satiation, and expiration. In addition, the fool is almost always associated with the bald acquisition of money. Furthermore, all of the fool's utterances take place within a stratified social situation, organized around a cleft separating servant from master. A prominent linguistic index of the social distinction underlying the joking relationship, meanwhile, is the fool's use of crude dialect. One of the hallmarks of an entrance into the fool's space of play, however brief or extended, is the abrupt switch in linguistic code. In aberrant pockets of speech, the fool temporarily transports the dialogue to less formalized and more vulgar regions, profoundly altering the verbal register and semantic tenor of the dialogue. Evidence of this verbal discrepancy can be found from the 1590s well into the eighteenth century.

The permission to introduce what would have otherwise counted as improper and therefore illicit contents, particularly against the conventions of social hierarchy, cannot be detached from the fool's masculine identity. The fool's rampant impropriety, including the

---

3. Most famously, of course, Plautus, who will figure in our discussion in part 2. For the foundational discussion of the servant in Plautus, see Eduard Fraenkel, *Plautine Elements in Plautus*, trans. Tomas Drevikovksy and Frances Muecke (Cambridge: Cambridge University Press, 2007), 159–172.

sexual debasement and celebration of debauchery, depended on his double role as male and servant. While the social-economic position of underling affords him a vantage point from which he can freely poke fun, the particularly salacious content of his joking is a gendered privilege. The fool invariably treats sex as a form of corporeal satisfaction, with the sole purpose of providing the man with gratification.

Consider how the following two scenes choreograph the relationship between the fool and the other dramatis personae. The expositions of the two dramas published in a 1630 collection of plays for traveling acting troupes, *Comedy of the Small Lad Cupid* (*Comoedia und Macht des kleinen Knaben Cupidinis*) and *Comedy of Aminta and Silvia* (*Comoedia von den Aminta und Silvia*), introduce fools with differing names but imbued with an identical ambiguity.[4] In the first play we have a fool named Hans Wurst; in the second, one called Schrämgen. Both plays begin when a member of the nobility happens upon an unknown person, who, in exchange for financial reward, is willing to spend some time as his lackey. In one play, he is called a "funny man" and "fool," in the other the "servant of all servants."[5] In both, the fool enters the fictional world as a figure without family or friends, without a background or personal history. When asked, "Who are you then?" the fool replies with such uninformative formulations as "I am a man" or the Latin equivalent "ego sum homo."[6] In yet another play, we see the fool describe himself as "nothing," sometimes as "totally nothing at all," and at the very most as "something."[7] Such formulations are strategic assurances of the fool's distinct status among the dramatis personae. The fool is neither fully somebody nor merely nobody. He belongs to a general category that lacks for individuating

---

4. The two scenes I discuss can be found in Manfred Brauneck and Alfred Noe, *Spieltexte der Wanderbühne* (Berlin: De Gruyter, 1970), 2:18–25 and 103–107.

5. See Brauneck and Noe, *Spieltexte der Wanderbühne*, 2:20, 22, 106.

6. Ibid., 2:36.

7. See the two servants in *Niemand und Jemand*, reprinted in Willi Flemming, *Deutsche Literatur: Sammlung literarischer Kunst- und Kulturdenkmäler in Entwicklungsreihen* (Weimar: Böhlau, 1931), 3:73–131.

properties; as an everyman, he is poised to curry the favor of every audience member, while also remaining open to continuity with innumerable future embodiments.

In a state of hierarchical diminution and figural indeterminacy, the fool enjoys special license to speak. The key mode in which he exploits his joking relationship is spontaneous and unsolicited interjection. Duke Heinrich Julius exploited this attribute in his *Von der Susanna* (*Tragedy of Susanna*, 1593), which lends the fool a prominent place among the thirty-four total parts. The fool goes under the sobriquet Johan Clant, whose role is listed as the *morio*. In the course of a discussion between the husband and wife concerning the moral instruction of their daughter in "fear of God, honor and virtue, according to the law of Moses," the fool unexpectedly intrudes on the stage and repeatedly interrupts the conversation.[8] He inserts his lowly voice into the father's intricate perorations, tossing in sarcastic remarks about "what a good teaching" the father is offering.[9] The contrast between the pious discourse of husband and wife, on the one hand, and the fool's playful interjections, on the other, bifurcates the dialogue, installing a comic view at odds with the father's moral message.

The fool's joking relationship with his master, as the next scene in Duke Julius's play makes clear, detaches the fool's comic effects from the overarching dramatic plot. Immediately after the dialogue between husband and wife, the fool appears onstage with a lock covering his mouth, which does little to inhibit his ability to cajole father and daughter about the validity of the biblical commandments. He responds, for instance, to the father's extensive remarks on the observance of the Sabbath by saying, "Well, that is good, because I do not like to work. I wish that it were Sunday every day, because then I would be able to do nothing."[10] It is

---

8. Julius Heinrich and Wilhelm Ludwig Holland, *Die Schauspiele des Herzogs Heinrich Julius von Braunschweig, nach alten Drucken und Handschriften* (Stuttgart: Litterarischer Verein, 1855), 6.

9. Ibid., 10.

10. Ibid., 11.

remarkable that this commentary is made despite the lock, thereby exposing the weak demands for verisimilitude that govern these plays. Particularly important for understanding the structural role of the fool, meanwhile, is what happens immediately after his interjection. That is, upon his demeaning of the holy day of rest, father and daughter continue their dialogue as though nothing unusual had been said. Their piety, in other words, remains immune to the fool's impiety. Like a switch operator, to return to a metaphor from chapter 1, here again the fool flips to a separate and alternative comic voice, while on a parallel line the play goes on as before.

The specificity of the joking relationship means that allowances for such verbal play and code switching are restricted to the fool. Accordingly, there is no instance in the seventeenth-century tradition sparked by the English players, at least that I know of, where the fool's ribaldry and baseness spread to other members of the dramatis personae, creating a sort of comic contagion that threatens the seriousness of the main plot. Large-scale devolutions of this sort do happen—but in plays of different artistic ambition and rank than those put on by the traveling players. In this context, the fool's role was, rather, to punctuate the ongoing action with his humor, with interjections that, again in the words of the anthropologist Radcliffe-Browne, "within any other context would express and arouse hostility."[11] And yet such hostility remains absent, precisely because the fool's interventions remain encapsulated in the dialogue.

The fool's permission to switch the linguistic and semantic codes that govern the dialogue, to insert a brief interval of play, maintains a loose and associative connection with the main action. His encapsulated moments of play amount to semantic distortions, small-scale interruptions that deflate, even if only temporarily, the significance of the play's events. The sort of momentary deviation that we have just seen in the passage from Duke Heinrich Julius's *Susanna* was, I would claim, the widespread and long-lasting signature of the fool.

---

11. Radcliffe-Browne, "On Joking Relationships," 91.

Let us focus in on a characteristic scene from the *Tragedy of Julio and Hypollita* (*Tragaedia von Julio und Hypollita*), a play loosely based on Shakespeare's *Two Gentlemen of Verona* that was published in the first collection of plays associated with the English actors. The play features a fool named Grobianus, who plays a supporting role in the central romantic intrigue. The plot is simple: a prince betroths his daughter to a Roman named Romulus (not the mythical one), who, upon departing to inform his family of his engagement, is betrayed by his friend Julius. When Romulus returns to find his friend Julius and fiancée Hyppolita married, a bloody conflict ensues. The betrayal at the center of the play depends on the fool's cooperation: he is responsible for delivering a fabricated letter to the fiancée Hyppolita, which is meant to convince her to abandon her original lover. When asked to deliver the letter, the fool responds, "Good sir, what wouldn't I do for money? If I could get money for it, I would call my mother a whore and my father a rogue. I will loyally execute your order."[12] And with that, the fool's intervention is complete, and the dialogue returns to its usual level of formality. Again, pointing to the vulgar content of the fool's response cannot fully capture the conventional quality of the episode; it is equally, if not more, important to notice that the ensuing dialogue continues on undeterred, taking no note of a deviation in the stream of dialogue.

Before moving on, there is one further facet to the scene worth noting. Although the fool's remark does not fit with the register of the surrounding dialogue, it does conform to a familiar pattern of communication, namely, request and affirmative response. Keeping this structure in mind, it becomes clear that the scene is internally disjointed: on the one hand, there is the fool's exact verbal formulation, including its semantic content, and, on the other, the skeletal pattern of dialogue it signals for the other members of the dramatic fiction. The distinction between Grobianus's words and their purpose in the flow of dialogue is instructive. It demonstrates that in many instances his utterances are, in a crucial sense, for the audience, and not for the other members of the theatrical fiction, even if he does not

---

12. Brauneck and Noe, *Spieltexte der Wanderbühne*, 1:435.

address the audience directly. The fool's participation in the dialogue, rather, evinces a doubleness—at once part of the dialogue and radically deviating from it. The fool offers a moment of play that aims at soliciting laughter from the audience, while also sustaining the question-response pattern and thereby advancing the forward march of the plot. This passage makes clear that, although encapsulated as miniature episodes of jest, the fool's utterances maintain a minimal level of structural integration with the surrounding dialogue.

Another example from later in the century will help make this unusual economy of continuity and discontinuity clearer. The drama *Der Jude von Venetien* (*The Jew of Venice*, uncertain dating), which loosely draws on Shakespeare's *Merchant of Venice*, is based on a manuscript that was probably written down around midcentury by an actor named Christoph Blümel, a member of the traveling company led by the last English-born manager, George Jolly.[13] However, the attachment of a name to the manuscript should not distract from the fact that we are dealing with an acting script, which is to say, with a textual artifact resulting from decades of informal circulation. Strolling players put on a German version of Shakespeare's play as early as 1626, and the surviving version is probably the result of approximately forty years of liberal adaptation.[14] Although the play bears traces of the Italian tradition of the *commedia dell'arte*, it employs the fool in a manner closer to the German fool than the comic servant Launcelot Gobbo in Shakespeare's original.[15] Consider the opening of the first act, a conversation between a king and a prince

---

13. See the discussion of the origin of the German adaptation and its English (re-)translation in Ernest Brennecke, *Shakespeare in Germany, 1590–1700, with Translations of Five Early Plays* (Chicago: University of Chicago Press, 1964), 105–110.

14. Ralf Haekel, *Die englischen Komödianten in Deutschland: Eine Einführung in die Ursprünge des deutschen Berufsschauspiels* (Heidelberg: Winter Universitätsverlag, 2004), 111–114. On Blümle's participation in the Jolly troupe, see Robert J. Alexander, "George Jolly [Joris Joliphus], Der wandernde Player und Manager," *Kleine Schriften der Gesellschaft für Theatergeschichte 29/30* (1978): 32. See chapter 2, above, for a brief discussion of Jolly.

15. For an attempt to treat the play as a blend of English and Italian conventions, see Ralf Böckmann, *Die Commedia dell'arte und das deutsche Drama des 17. Jahrhunderts* (Nordhausen: Verlag Traugott Baut, 2010), 100–105

of Cyprus. In a sequence alien to the English original, the prince asks for his father's leave to warn the Venetian Republic about the recently banished Jews. After the king assents, the fool, under the moniker Pickelhäring, requests permission to accompany the prince on his journey. The ensuing dialogue employs a degree of internal discontinuity that strongly resembles the other examples I have already introduced:

> PICKELHÄRING: Oh, yes, Majesty, let me go along. Even if I am a rogue, I cannot remain at home.
> KING: If you cannot, then we must permit it. But take good care of our son, and remain with him at all times, in order to make sure he doesn't fall into bad company.
> PICKELHÄRING: I will take care. If he wants to go to church, I'll show him the way to the whorehouse.
> KING: Because it is decided, beloved son, you shall not postpone this trip any longer.[16]

It is striking that the fool's promise to take the prince to the brothel rather than the church does not rend the fabric of the dialogue. The king understands the fool's outrageous remark, it seems, as an ordinary expression of assent, even though it does not cohere with the register or content of the conversation otherwise. As in the previous example, only the question-response structure of the dialogue remains in place; the exact meaning of his words goes unnoticed.

However easy it is in printed versions of these plays to skip over moments like these, their prevalence can only lead us to believe that we are dealing with an elementary pattern in the fool's comic practice, one of his signature forms of play. In both passages cited above, the integration of the fool into the dialogue preserves the continuity of question and answer, while also allowing for the articulation of linguistically aberrant, comic meanings. The utterances provide evidence of a recognizable structure that seems to have been the cornerstone of the fool's abiding success in engaging the audience's attention.

---

16. Flemming, *Deutsche Literatur*, 3:211.

The fool's participation in the stage action takes place along two axes. In fact, all communication on the stage—whether gestural or verbal, explicit or tacit, spoken or silent—means engaging in a face-to-face communicative setting in two distinctive ways at the same time. In general, theater takes place via a fiction-internal dimension of dialogue—the back-and-forth among fictional personae—and, at the same time, presents this fiction to an audience via a fiction-external dimension that remains, most of the time, unmarked and inconspicuous. Within the theatrical setting, the whole fiction is *for the audience*—fiction-internal communication is directed, in general, toward the audience, even if this fact is never acknowledged as such. For most of history and within most plays, the fiction-internal axis functions as the primary and uncontroversial means for conjuring theatrical illusion, while the fiction-external dimension of theatrical communication is kept in a state of latency or only utilized at structurally specific moments, such as in a prologue. Denis Diderot's famous "fourth wall" from the mid-eighteenth century, a version of which we will encounter in part 2, can thus be understood as a particularly restrictive approach to the fiction-external line of communication.

One heuristic benefit of drawing the distinction between fiction-internal and fiction-external axes of communication is that it allows historical differences to emerge into view. A wide-lens look at theater history reveals some situations in which its direct employment is thoroughly uncontroversial; others where only certain figures can freely manipulate it; others where its use is restricted to particular junctures like the prologue and epilogue; and still others where its direct use is proscribed. A second heuristic benefit of the distinction is that it helps us recognize that the fool's distinctive form of play depended upon the regulated use of the boundary between the inside and outside of the fictional world. For he is uniquely able to tarry on both sides, contributing to the ongoing stream of dialogue and also providing it with an external frame for the audience. In virtue of this capacity to step outside the fiction, the fool fostered a unique rapport with the audience, often serving as the onstage advocate for the audience's amusement.

With the distinction between these two communicative axes in hand, it is worth returning to the examples provided above. We have already seen that the fool's utterances leave the concatenation of fiction-internal utterances intact, despite their deviation from the semantic flow of content, as though the fool's remarks provided plot-driving information. This preservation of the continuous structure of fiction-internal dialogue, irrespective of what the fool actually does, means that the fool's play is encapsulated, and thus separated off from the rest of the action. This bifurcation between fiction-internal and fiction-external axes is illustrated in figure 2.

The division between internal and external communicative axes in a single utterance echoes another of the fool's fundamental comic strategies: the aside. This more familiar form of theatrical speech provides a straightforward mode of communicating with the audience and is the fool's most pervasive device for manipulating the boundary between fiction-internal and fiction-external communicative axes. In fact, the surviving acting scripts record myriad times when the fool turns to speak directly with the audience about a state of affairs currently transpiring or having just transpired.[17] This pervasiveness is attributable

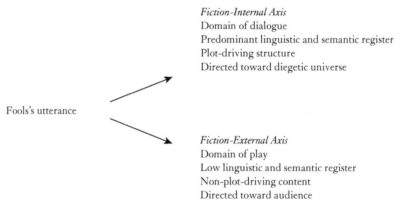

Figure 2. Fiction-internal and fiction-external bifurcation

---

17. The phenomenon of framing events onstage by means of an aside is extremely common. To just give examples from the first two collections of plays of the English players: Brauneck and Noe, *Spieltexte der Wanderbühne*, 1:11, 28, 29, 292, 344, 525, 526, 529; 2:35, 36, 38, 39, 48, 51, 54–55, 85, 88, 219, 239, 246, 248, 251, 261, 328, 361–362, 376–377.

to the effectiveness of the aside for reflecting on and reframing events taking place onstage. By contrast to the sort of bifurcated utterances schematized above, here there is no question-and-response skeleton, no simulation of a fiction-internal, plot-driving dimension.

This point is illustrated in a very successful play by Johann Georg Schoch (1627–1690), *Comoedia vom Studenten-Leben (Comedy of Student Life)*, which first appeared in 1657 and was reprinted in 1658, 1660, and 1668.[18] Schoch's deployment of the fool seems particularly noteworthy because it creates a strong dissonance with the play's overall moralizing mission. Ultimately, the play does not need to resolve the relationship between its edifying purpose and the fool's comic interjections. The use of the aside keeps his play within enclosed boundaries.

The opening scenes introduce, as was usual, the hierarchically structured joking relationship. The fool is given by a merchant and a nobleman as a servant to their two university-bound sons.[19] The play makes clear that the father intends for the servant to keep the young men in line, a charge that is radically at odds with his comic personality. For example, immediately before their departure for the university town, the fool accompanies one of the adolescent noblemen, Floretto, as he pays a visit to his beloved. When the young woman invites the nobleman to say his farewell, the fool speaks an aside concerning the young woman's ardent desire to embrace her beloved one last time: "Go on, you are on the right path, you poor simple pet."[20] These words, shared only with the audience, provide a fiction-external frame for what had come before and what will ensue. In the course of his remarks to the audience, the fool goes on to deride the girl's affection and boast about his master's sexual prowess: "My master arranges things, so that he can spoon out his

---

18. I refer to the 1658 edition, a digital copy of which is available through the Deutsches Textarchiv (http://www.deutschestextarchiv.de).

19. Johann Georg Schoch, *Comoedia vom Studenten-Leben* (Leipzig: Johann Wittigauen, 1658), 26.

20. Ibid., 47. For a similar episode, see p. 83.

desire and pleasure."[21] The fool uses the aside to encode his master's acts as emotional (and, it is implied, sexual) manipulation. In so doing, the fool also draws attention away from questions of moral culpability, offering the audience a moment to relish the moral transgression as it transpires on stage. In Schoch's drama, then, the fool propounds the very sort of moral dereliction that the drama otherwise works to contain. However, because this advocacy is restricted to the fool and, in this instance, to the aside, the fool is not unmasked as deserving of the audience's disapprobation. His role in Schoch's comedy is far too central and his portrayal far too endearing to support such a view. It makes more sense to think of these asides as momentary allowances for self-contained play that do not make the fool into an object of general derision. In other words, the fool exploits his liminal status in the dialogue to introduce a moral transgression that the course of the drama means to exclude. The term *liminality* accurately describes the sense in which Pickelhering's words or actions fall outside the scope of transgression that the play seeks to expose as morally depraved. When sequestered within the confines of the joking relationship, the fool's remarks and gestures create moments of licit (because restricted) enjoyment of the ordinarily illicit.

Comments by the fool, directed toward the audience and bearing on events within the drama itself, introduce what one might call a thin layer of self-reflexivity. I say *thin* because the act of framing does not undermine the simulation of a fictional world on stage, but rather intensifies it. The fool can restate for the audience what is going on, and such fiction-external reflection on fiction-internal communication remains unproblematic. For this reason, when the fool draws attention to events transpiring elsewhere onstage, this act of self-reference sidesteps paradoxes of drama-within-the-drama. Instead, it uses direct communication with the audience to encourage the spectator's sustained engagement with the performance.

---

21. Schoch, *Comoedia vom Studenten-Leben*, 47.

The privilege of liminality is clearly evident in the frame for the entire play that Pickelhering later provides. Although the concluding scenes had sought to show that the sons will have their moral integrity restored once they return home, the final words by the fool are an announcement of his own unflagging commitment to pleasure:

> So I will go along inside and rejoice too that I also made it back. I want to get so drunk that it will be a disgrace and sin. (*ad spectatores*) My good sirs! the fun is now done. If you didn't like it, I can't do anything about it. Nonetheless, I'm going to go have a fresh drink poured inside. Surely, we'll see each other again. And excuse my politeness, even though you haven't exactly seen much of it.

> So werde ich auch mit hinein gehen / und mich auch freuen / daß ich selber bin wieder kommen / ich wil mir zu sauffen daß es eine Schande und Sünde seyn wird / (*ad Spect.*) Jhr Herrn / die Lust wehre nun aus / hats euch nicht gefallen / ich kann nicht dafür / ich wil mir indessen drinnen ein frisches einschenken lassen. Wir wollen noch wohl wieder zusammen kommen / und verzeihet meiner Höffligkeit / ihr habt ihr aber nicht gar viel gesehen.[22]

Unlike the debauchery of the students, the fool's play is sanctioned. In being afforded the final word, he is nominated as a representative of the play. The fool's vow to return on another occasion, meanwhile, points to the serial or iterable quality of the fool. Because there will be subsequent plays, so too will there be subsequent fools in them.

Such jest was, it bears emphasizing, by no means limited to the verbal aside. It also included playful displays of bodily movement, from the isolated gesture to the more protracted comic dance. The interpolation of dance within scenes, much like the aside, stopped the fiction-internal flow of dialogue, allowing for the opportunity to frolic briefly before—and for—the audience. It is unfortunately difficult in most cases to say with certainty when these moments were inserted. Many plays from the seventeenth century, particularly those used by traveling players, lack stage directions entirely, which seems to indicate that the duration and exact placement of such dance numbers were the actors', or at least the troupe

---

22. Ibid., 192.

manager's, prerogative. That being said, the surviving playscripts have some trace indications of their presence. Textual markers exist, for example, in the play *Fortunatus*, an adaptation of Thomas Dekker's *Old Fortunatus* from 1599. In the German version, included in the 1620 collection of plays by the English traveling players, the text indicates three times that the fool, who is not included in Dekker's original, should interrupt the ongoing stage dialogue and provide some sort of visual amusement. The surviving text simply indicates: "At this point Pickelhering acts (*agieret*)."[23] While we cannot know exactly what these dances looked like, all three occur at key transitional moments, when there is a certain gap or the possibility of momentary relief. Such dance numbers, then, probably functioned as miniature intermezzi, when the audience could reduce its attentive effort and just enjoy the show.

To gain a slightly richer sense of the implications of interpolated dance episodes, let us return to the play about student life, with its fool called Pickelhering. Remember that this play was written in 1657, almost forty years after the English plays were first collected, and comes at a historical juncture when the conventionalized antics associated with the fool had already achieved widespread acclaim. Before the fool departs with the two sons for university, the merchant's wife provides the fool with two large sacks of money and beseeches him to use the funds wisely. She tells him to "take good care of the two / and let [her] know / if they are not pious." At this point her interlocutor responds with verbal affirmation. However, the sparse stage instructions indicate that mother's mention of potential improprieties rouses the fool's interest. In addition to seemingly harmless affirmation, he responds with a brief frolic. Of course, the contrast between verbal and gestural levels of expression is the key to the scene's comic effect. What is more, the division between fiction-internal and fiction-external axes of communication becomes visible here. That is, the mother does not notice or take umbrage at the fool's

---

23. For the *Fortunatus* adaptation, see Brauneck and Noe, *Spieltexte der Wanderbühne*, 1:128–209. The three points in the play where Pickelhering dances can be found at 150, 154, and 159.

bodily movements. If she had, she would not go on to entrust the fool with her son's well-being. The dancing moves exclusively along the fiction-external axis of communication, whereas his verbal affirmation utilizes the fiction-internal dimension of communication.

The aforementioned varieties of discontinuous verbal and gestural communication disclose a comic view on the drama's events that is shared only with the audience. One must keep in mind, though, that these are not instances of coloring outside the lines; such forms of direct address are uncontroversial. On the whole, that is, the interruption of dialogue by the fool's utterances fits comfortably within the stage fiction; the theatrical world to which the fool belonged was not equipped with an impregnable communicative-ontological boundary between plot events and the audience. The boundary separating the fiction and the real—stage and audience—is selectively permeable, allowing for the fool to switch back and forth across it without endangering the viability of the whole fiction. Indeed, this boundary became salient in the seventeenth century *as* the site for the fool's play. The fool utilized the fiction-external axis of communication to introduce a thin layer of self-reflexivity, which often served to enhance the audience's awareness of or to shape its attitude toward something happening onstage. And he also used short dance numbers to provide momentary respite.

In the pieces-and-patches construction that made up the performances by traveling players in the seventeenth century, the fool's interventions used the element of surprise as a key comic ingredient. In no small part because of this constant possibility of interruption, theatrical performance in this context tolerated a high degree of discontinuity in its simulation of a fictional world. The fool's antics could be as brief as an aside or short dance and could also extend into larger-scale comic improvisations and short dramatic sketches. His star role in interludes and postludes—referred to as *Zwischenspiele, Unterhandlungen, Aufzüge,* and *Nachspiele*—made them an essential ingredient in theatrical performance.

While the presence of such playlets surely reaches back to the predominately gestural performances of the earliest English acting

troupes, the practice of embedding short song and dance or dramatic numbers in performances remained nearly ubiquitous over
the ensuing decades. The historical record suggests that the interspersed mimic relied predominately on an originally Scottish song
and dance known in London as the jig.[24] Etymological features of
the term have led scholars to speculate that it first referred to "a type
of dance in which whirling and turning on the toe was a conspicuous feature."[25] The popularization of this dance in London during
the second half of the sixteenth century led to the application of the
name to a broad swath of ballads that were performed with a dance.
The jigs usually consisted of one to three persons singing rhymed
couplets, but the number of participates peaked at five. In England,
jigs were usually inserted into the middle of plays, especially between acts. When they were imported to the German context, such
numbers gained even more prominence, initially as a way of dealing with the linguistic barrier and eventually as a response to widespread enthusiasm.[26] Essentially every playbill from the seventeenth
century advertises the fool's capering "start to finish"[27] as well as in
a *lustiges Nachspiel,* or amusing postlude. Long after their origin
had been forgotten, the improvisational song-and-dance numbers
appended to and inserted in plays remained popular in the German-
speaking world.

In the interludes and postludes, the fool's play was allowed free
rein in a way that would have been impossible in the main body
of the drama. Sequestered from the main body of the play, the fool
became the ill-fated or triumphant hero of his own story, often in

---

24. On the tradition of the English jig, see the foundational study of Charles
Read Baskervill, *The Elizabethan Jig and Related Song Drama* (Chicago: University of Chicago Press, 1929). This volume also contains materials relevant to
the German tradition, beginning on p. 491. Baskervill drew many of his sources
from the earlier study of Johannes Bolte, *Die Singspiele der englischen Komödianten und ihrer Nachfolger in Deutschland, Holland und Skandinavien* (Hamburg/
Leipzig: Voss, 1893).

25. Baskervill, *The Elizabethan Jig,* 15.

26. A number of interludes and postludes related to the tradition of the English
jig have been gathered in Baskervill, *The Elizabethan Jig,* 491–589.

27. See the Faust playbill in Flemming, *Deutsche Literatur,* 3:203.

a tale of love or romantic intrigue. At the same time, the hierarchical social construction of the joking relationship persevered in veiled form. Rather than the lowly servant-fool coupled with a noble master, here the fool often appeared in a rustic milieu, set off from the urban population that typically frequented the performances by traveling players. The scenes seek to reconstruct a skeletal, typological picture of rural life, as evident in the appearance of the fool alongside a figure simply referred to as "the neighbor."[28] In a small-scale and intimate town context, the fool gets caught up in the sort of romantic intrigue and financial wrangling that seems to have possessed nearly universal appeal. For instance, a characteristic interlude explores the domestic life of the fool, casting him opposite an imperious and upbraiding wife. Others explore his sexual prowess.[29]

One instance of the interlude that enjoyed an unusually long career was known in English as *Singing Simpkin*, until it became popular in German under the title *Pickelhering in der Kiste*.[30] The example is informative in a few key respects. First, it provides an indication of how popular these playlets featuring the fool were. For instance, a Dutch version of the same interlude, penned by Isaak Vos, appeared in 1705 on the basis of performances at the Amsterdam city theater, the Shouwburg. This means that the Dutch were still performing the piece one hundred years after the German version first appeared in print. Aside from a few variations, the surviving English and German texts are alike. Both tell the story of a woman with an insatiable sexual appetite who hides her two lovers from each other and disguises both from her husband. In the English version, the clown, named Simpkin, plays one of the duped lovers. But the example is also revealing because of a major change that takes place in the switch from English to German. In

---

28. See, for instance, the dramatic interlude in *Schoch, Comoedia vom Studenten-Leben*. See also Brauneck and Noe, *Spieltexte der Wanderbühne*, 1:581–639. A very similar social scheme is also at work in the song interludes reprinted in Brauneck and Noe, 2:402–449.

29. Brauneck and Noe, 1:559–580.

30. For a facing-page bilingual edition, see Bolte, *Die Singspiele der englischen Komödianten*, 50–62.

the adapted version, the fool is no longer beaten off the stage by the woman's husband. Instead, the fool triumphs over the other lover and the husband, and the piece ends with him headed to bed with the woman. Perhaps unlike any other example, this one shows just what the different dimensions of the fool's comic practice collectively aimed for: the licensed, because contained, pleasure in the illicit. Whether hinted at in the form of an aside or acted out in a supplementary play, the fool provided a temporally and narratively circumscribed indulgence of the audience's desire to experience otherwise forbidden pleasures. Because everything he said and did was in jest, his transgressions against social norms could be written off as the source of harmless pleasure.

4

THE FOOL'S SPACE AND TIME

The fool does not stand alone. Although the foregoing three chapters have not addressed issues concerning overarching plot organization and devoted little attention to the other figures on the stage, it would be a mistake to think of the fool either as a wholly autonomous agent or as a mere add-on. The fool only existed through his participation in a larger theatrical affair. That is to say, the structural import of his various strategies for soliciting laughter always arose in tandem with the pieces and patches they accompanied. This encompassing, composite whole is paramount to understanding the fool's part.

Speaking of wholes can summon to mind images of tightly reticulated and causally interconnected unities, of plotlines without adventitious additions or dissevered joints. But this conception is too limited. A more historically sensitive approach has to account for theatrical wholes that are more tightly or more loosely held together, with gradations of unity, instead of presupposing the existence of a gold standard. What one theatrical culture may regard as integrated can seem tattered to another, and vice versa. Take the example of the unity of place: that a play might switch locations between scenes did not seem controversial to, among others, Elizabethan English playwrights and theatergoers, but contemporary critics inspired by (and, in this respect, taking liberties with the text of) Aristotle regarded such changes as a threat to the internal coherence of a play. Classicizing critics thus advanced principled claims about the requisites of theatrical unity, and in doing so sought to undermine the experience of audiences that clearly felt such plays hung together more than well enough. From today's vantage point, it seems best to avoid the assumption that there is a single yardstick for unity, handed down by classicizing critics, and to forgo use of a crude binary opposition (e.g., open/closed). Rather than supposing there are dramatic or theatrical forms that are, per se, unified or disparate, it is preferable to see theatrical unity itself as a variable and context-specific measure, vulnerable to historical and cultural change.[1] One and the same theatrical performance can appear in one context as disturbingly disjointed and chaotic; in another as gripping *by virtue of* its internal diversity. As has by now become clear, the fool's rupturing of the dialogue, in fact, contributed essentially to the success of theatrical performance.

In the absence of a fixed paradigm for dramatic or theatrical unity, it becomes clear that the tertium, the unit for measuring an open form against a closed form, is the moving target in need of a description. A more fine-grained vocabulary would suggest that different theatrical cultures possess varying criteria of openness and closure, as well as varying dramaturgical strategies for satisfying such criteria. By recognizing that the openness or closure of a form cannot be determined independent of historical context, it is possible to avoid simply repeating the critical gestures of a particular theatrical culture. We can then turn our attention to the different standards of unity—of a theatrical performance and, eventually,

---

1. For an influential formulation of a more restricted notion of unity, see Victor Klotz, *Geschlossene und offene Form im Drama* (Munich: Hanser Verlag, 1960).

a dramatic text—that prevailed under different historical circumstances. The claim that the fool belonged to a whole, with which this chapter began, is meant to suggest only that the fool came into being in connection with environing utterances, roles, scenes, plot trajectories, and even stage spectacles. The pressing question is, now, how this interlacement was configured. Or, to remain within the same metaphorical register, how taught or slack were the crisscrossing strands?

A key indication of the way in which the fool related to the encompassing whole can be found in the term used to describe him from the turn of the seventeenth century into the eighteenth: *kurzweilig*.[2] The composite adjective is built out of two lexical components: *kurz*, referring to a short length, and *weilig*, referring to a period of time. To get at the heart of its meaning, it is helpful to think of its opposite, *langweilig*, a word more easily translated into English: "boring." *Kurzweilig* is not a sophisticated philosophical term, nor is it in any way obscure. But its meaning is nonetheless complex, ranging from *"amusing"* to *"entertaining,"* and entailing a diversity or variation in experience. Something that is *kurzweilig* unfolds as a varied succession of appearances in such a way that time itself passes imperceptibly. In the phenomenon of *Kurzweil*, rapid augmentation engenders rapt attention. The word enjoys a privileged place in the description of the fool, because it brings into close proximity two features definitive of his role: deviation from the established course of dialogue and absorption in the present moment. In spite of the potentially cumbersome effect on English diction, I use the German word *kurzweilig* over the following pages. I do so to emphasize the central role of the combination of alternation and presence that describes the fool's place in the encompassing theatrical event.

Kurzweilig is used as an attribute of the fool in three distinct but related situations. First, other members of the dramatic fiction address him as if he possessed this special quality. When he is

---

2. For the sake of clarity, I have modernized the spelling of *kurzweilig*. The seventeenth-century spelling is *kurtzweilig*. The importance of the term was observed already in Jean Paul, *Werke* (Munich: Carl Hanser Verlag, 1973), 5:161.

first beckoned onto the stage in Duke Heinrich Julius's 1593 play, *Vincentius Ladislaus,* for instance, Duke Siluester refers to the fool as his "*kurzweiligen* counsel."[3] We see the same sort of description in plays like the 1630 *Aminita and Silvia,* published in the second major collection of English plays, and the 1686 *Virenus,* performed on the emperor's name day in Regensburg.[4] Each of these scenes is orchestrated in the same way: one character expresses ignorance regarding the identity of a new character entering the stage. The matter is quickly cleared up when the unknown person is referred to as *kurzweilig,* and therewith revealed as the fool. A second context in which *kurzeilig* is an attribute of the fool is the list of *dramatis personae* typically included at the beginning of a printed play. To give an early example, Johan Bannser is listed as the *kurtzweilig* counsel in Elias Herlicius's 1601 rewriting of Duke Heinrich Julius's *Vincentius Ladislaus.* In much the same way, Johannes Riemer (1648–1714) refers to Chambre as the *kurzweilig* Frenchman in his 1681 tragedy about Maria Stuart.[5] The third context is the fool advertised as *kurzweilig* in the playbills that were distributed in advance of performances. An adaptation of the great Dutch tragedian Joost van den Vondel's (1587–1679) *Gebroeders* announces that the "*kurtzweiligen* Pickel-Häring" will make an appearance.[6] A 1671 playbill from the town of Rothenburg ob der Tauber in Franconia promises more of the same.[7] This list could be expanded to include a legion of additional

3. Julius Heinrich and Wilhelm Ludwig Holland, *Die Schauspiele des Herzogs Heinrich Julius von Braunschweig, nach alten Drucken und Handschriften* (Stuttgart: Litterarischer Verein, 1855), 526.

4. Manfred Brauneck and Alfred Noe, *Spieltexte der Wanderbühne* (Berlin: De Gruyter, 1970), 2:103. Anonymous, *Comoedia, Bitittult Der Flüchtige Virenus, Oder Die Getreue Olympia* (Regensburg: Johann Georg Hofmann, 1686), n.p. The latter instance occurs at the end of the second act.

5. Johannes Riemer, *Der Regenten bester Hoff-Meister oder lustiger Hoff-Parnassus* (Leipzig: Weißenfels, 1681), 284.

6. Rudin, "Pickelhering, rechte Frauenzimmer, berühmte Autoren: Zur Ankündigungspraxis der Wanderbühne im 17. Jahrhundert," *Kleine Schriften der Gesellschaft für Theatergeschichte* 34/35 (1988): 30.

7. The playbill is reprinted in Rudin, "Pickelhering, rechte Frauenzimmer, berühmte Autoren," 42, and transcribed on 45.

announcements.[8] Thus, the denomination *kurzweilig* did more than identify an ordinary character trait; it persisted for the entire seventeenth century as a way of distinguishing the fool's import in the entire theatrical event. For this very reason, advertisements and lists of *dramatis personae* found the term an effective way of identifying the presence and purpose of the fool within the larger tapestry.

Kurzweilig gathers under a single heading the two formal processes that are distinctive of the fool: departure from the main dialogue and investment in the immediately present instant. As chapter 3 showed in detail, the fool relates to the encompassing whole primarily through disjointed, encapsulated interventions. Whether through a single utterance, a short dance, or a brief interlude, the purpose of the fool's involvement was always to introduce a momentary comic effect that, as a delimited sphere of play, runs alongside large-scale plot designs. As a rupture in the tone and meaning of dialogue, the fool transports it, for a brief moment, to a world defined by creaturely desires and pecuniary acquisitiveness. He is woven into the theatrical spectacle as a moment of indulgence and thereby a reprieve from ordinary dealings and concerns. His is a domain of play freed from concerns of past and future, utterly ignorant of moral duty and divine retribution.

This can all sound rather exalted, but the signature of this figure was, of course, the utterly mundane. And as deeply rooted in the fleeting pleasures of the here and now, the fool bore the potential for cynical and vacuous denial of meaning. While, in most instances, the encapsulation of his interventions restricted their impact, there are still others where this sequestering is incomplete. Such circumstances allow the meaning of the fool's utterances to emerge more clearly. The most popular and often-performed play of the traveling stage troupes, an adaptation of the German Baroque tragedy

---

8. See the rich inventory of playbills collected in Bärbel Rudin, "Von Alexanders Mord-Banquet bis zur Kindheit Mosis: Eine unbekannte Kollektion von Theaterzetteln der Wanderbühne," *Daphnis* 35 (2006): 193–261, especially 194, 201, and 209. See also Johann-Richard Hänsel, *Die Geschichte des Theaterzettels und seine Wirkung in der Öffentlichkeit* (Berlin: E. Reuter, 1962), 107 and 277.

by Andreas Gryphius (1616–1664) entitled *Großmüthiger Rechts-gelehrter oder Sterbender Aemilius Paulus Papinianus* (*The Mag-nanimous Jurist Aemilius Paulus Papinianus*, 1659), possesses a fool figure dislodged from the ordinary joking relationship and im-bued with exceptional potency. Importantly, the fool is not in his usual servant role in the adaptation of Gryphius's tragedy. He assumes a position that mirrors, albeit distortedly, that of Gryphius's hero, the chief Roman jurist Papinian. Traraeus, as the fool is called, is referred to as a "spoiled jurist," capable of redoubling and disfigur-ing the hero's every move.[9] The transposition from servant role to parallel jurist allows for a more pronounced view of the relation-ship between the fool's strategies of play and the encompassing whole to which he belongs.

The adaptation was first staged in 1677 and maintained its place until 1745—all told, a nearly seventy-year career in front of audiences. Gryphius's tragedy of the ill-fated and unwaveringly virtuous Roman lawyer makes an odd choice for an adaptation. The author was a jurist himself, with a sound humanistic educa-tion and strong Lutheran convictions, and as a result his play is laden with political and religious significance, along with ornate language and copious erudite references.[10] Once the strolling play-ers got their hands on it, however, they disposed of much of this. The adaptation evinces a radical reduction in semantic complexity,

---

9. Willi Flemming, *Deutsche Literatur: Sammlung Literarischer Kunst- und Kulturdenkmäler in Entwicklungsreihen* (Weimar: Böhlau, 1931), 3:138.

10. For a general overview of the author's career, see the now-classic essay by Conrad Wiedemann, "Andreas Gryphius," in *Andreas Gryphius*, ed. *Harald Stein-hagen and Benno von Wiese* (Berlin: Erich Schmidt Verlag, 1984), 435–472. The Papinian tragedy has been the subject of a number of incisive analyses over re-cent years. I have found three discussions particularly insightful: Wilfried Barner, "Der Jurist als Märtyrer: Andreas Gryphius' Papinianus," in *Literatur und Recht: Literarische Rechtsfälle von der Antike bis in die Gegenwart*, ed. Ulrich Mölk (Göttingen: Wallstein Verlag, 1996), 229–242; Rüdiger Campe, "Theater der In-stitution," in *Konfigurationen der Macht in der frühen Neuzeit*, ed. Rudolf Behrens and Roland Galle (Heidelberg: Universitätsverlag, 2000), 258–287; Karl-Heinz Habersetzer, *Politische Typologie und dramatisches Exemplum: Studien zum his-torisch-ästhetischen Horizont des barocken Trauerspiels am Beispiel von Andreas Gryphius' Carolus Stuardus und Papinianus* (Stuttgart: Metzler, 1985).

particularly in the amount of background knowledge required to make sense of the play. Clearly, the traveling players did not demand an elite education of their audiences. Many of the characteristic features of Baroque tragedy—from the elevated status of the hero to the eschatological backdrop and the political message—are suddenly transformed. And, almost as a matter of course, the introduction of a fool establishes an additional strand of significance completely incompatible with the original.

Although a protracted comparison between original and adaptation would lead far afield, I would like to draw out some of the salient features of the adapted play, with particular focus on the status of the fool as *kurzweilig*. Of interest is the way in which the adaptation distorts Gryphius's celebratory portrayal of the tragic hero, especially of his culminating deed of tragic gravitas: death. The trivialization of death is not unique to this play; no one, no matter how virtuous or innocent, is immune to his ridicule. Perhaps more importantly, no event, no matter how high it is ordinarily honored, is fortified against the fool's attack on its significance. His belittlement of death is, in particular, a siege on deeply cherished values. To give one noteworthy example, in a gesture that would solicit disdain from the modern Shakespeare enthusiast, we see the fool mocking Juliet's suicide in the surviving acting script of *Romeo and Juliet*.[11]

The Gryphius adaptation opens with two parallel monologues. In the first, the noble jurist Papinian enters the stage lamenting his unwarranted vulnerability for having scaled "the paramount peak of honor." In the other, the fool steps out onto the stage announcing, with a proverbially puffed-up chest, the sight of "justice riding into the horizon of my erudition." The self-inflating and celebratory proclamation of one jurist reverses the desperate cry of the other.[12] By counterposing these two figures—one suffering at

---

11. Albert Cohn, *Shakespeare in Germany in the Sixteenth and Seventeenth Centuries: An Account of English Actors in Germany and the Netherlands and of the Plays Performed by Them during the Same Period* (London: Asher & Co, 1865), 391–394.

12. Compare Flemming, *Deutsche Literatur*, 3:140–141 and 144–145.

the hands of injustice, the other diminishing the import assigned to justice—the adaptation is able to transform even the most austere moments in Gryphius's tragedy into risible spectacle. A good example of this is a scene featuring a soothsayer named Thrasullus. In the original, the royal prophet paints a picture of the potential doom for the Roman Empire born by the internecine conflict between the two coemperors. In the adaptation, meanwhile, the fool interrupts the soothsayer's rumination, pestering the diviner to let him in on his future chances for marriage and wealth.[13] As one would expect, the soothsayer is unperturbed, even offering genuine prognostications in response to the fool's petty questioning.

These sorts of moments run throughout the play. None is more striking than the fool's remarks when he intrudes on one of the coemperors of Rome lying dead on the floor. The fool storms onto the stage in response to a desperate cry for help, but he has little assistance or consolation to offer. Standing over the emperor's corpse, he pronounces with stinging mockery, "So who strangled the poor devil? He is lying there and is bleeding like swine. He's got four or five wounds; there is no pulse. He's given up the ghost."[14] In keeping with the fool's signature encapsulated play-structure, the dialogue then moves forward as though the fool had not uttered a word. The other figures on the stage continue their cries of lament—"Murder, murder! We are betrayed!"—while the fool makes light of the horror they feel. The scene relies on a clean-cut opposition between the fool's play, on the one hand, and the acute sense of political and personal catastrophe, on the other. This internal duplicity is completely consistent with the earlier discussion with the soothsayer. In this case, though, the death of the emperor—an event of chief political and religious significance in Gryphius's play—is not simply made light of; it is recast in the most brutal terms. When the emperor's murder is described as the expiration of the lowliest creature, it is robbed of all its imperial gravity and reduced to a banal corporeal occurrence. By the same token, the repercussions of the emperor's death for the future of

---

13. Ibid., 3:154–156.
14. Ibid., 3:160.

Rome are inconsequential to the fool. He introduces a comic frame incongruous with the somber scene, one that expresses indifference to what has already transpired and what is yet to come. It amounts to a radical deflation of the value of life itself.

The subsequent section of the scene is equally noteworthy. In an especially grotesque description, the fool remarks that the emperor Bassian fleeing the stage, having just killed his coemperor, looks "as if he had gorged himself on ten peasants [*sic*]."[15] Immediately thereafter, the dead emperor's mother falls unconscious on the stage, stunned by her son's death. The fool, meanwhile, is unaffected by the violence and the distraught mother. Staring at her unmoving body on the ground, he again introduces commentary that robs the scene of all gravity: he observes, "Even more foolish antics (*Narrenpossen*)."[16] As he then takes stock of the tragic turn of events, his appraisal shows no sensitivity to the potential impact of the death of the co-emperor or the unconscious queen. "What should we do now?" he asks. "This thing is going to be crazy."[17] The fool's running commentary, laced with the usual derision, unfolds according to a telling structure. He recasts the protagonists as fools and the events as folly. Within the circumscribed domain of his commentary, he inverts the relationship between earnest and frivolous, the pathetic and the comic. Since the fool acts as a doppleganger of the protagonist Papinian—one might say, crisscrossing the comic track with the tragic plot—he interferes more than is usual. To be more exact, he redoubles the patterns of significance that run through the tragedy, offering the spectator the occasion to see things in a tragic as well as in a comic light. This sort of redoubling, which produces interferences between comic and tragic registers, will become essential in part 4 of this study, when we turn to literary dramas by Goethe and Kleist.

At present, it is worth taking a look at an additional scene that explodes tragic conventions. In the final scene of the play, the fool provides commentary on the death of the tragic hero, Papinian.

---

15. Ibid.
16. Ibid., 3:161.
17. Ibid.

It must be kept in mind that in Gryphius's tragedy, Papinian is distinguished by his steadfast virtue, resistance to courtly intrigue, and fidelity to the letter of the law. The original play is organized around the ambition to demonstrate Papinian's time-transcendent exemplarity. In the version featuring the fool, however, the hero's death is reduced to base everydayness. This debasement comes out in the fool's take on tragic death:

> The case between the emperor and Papinian has come to a bloody close. Whether it occurred *per fas* or *nefas* I'll leave to the jurists to decide. Not the great *capitolium*, not the councilors of Rome, not the garrison cut off his neck but rather the emperor. But I know he regrets it: he was a bit of furious. I feel bad for the good Papinian. But what's it matter? My laments can't bring him back to life.

> Dieser Proceß zwischen dem keyser und Papiniano hat ein blutiges end genommen / ob es *per fas* oder *nefas* geschehen, laß ich die Herren Juristen urteilen / nicht das große *Capitolium*, nicht die Rathsherren zu Rom, nicht das Lager hat ihm den halß abgesprochen, sondern der keyser / aber ich weiß das es ihm gereuet: er ist etwas furiös gewesen / der gute Papinianus trauert mich, aber was hülffts, ich kan ihm mit meinen klagen nicht wieder lebentig machen.[18]

In this passage, the fool employs forensic vocabulary—Latin legal terms meaning "by right or wrong"—in the interest of undoing the identification of Papinian with the principle of justice. The question of whether the emperor's execution of Papinian conformed to justice is introduced only to be dismissed as a vain inquiry. His remarks do not locate culpability beyond the scope of the knowable so much as they treat questions of responsibility as unworthy of serious consideration. He sees no need for eternal lessons in justice or for reflection on the past. The fool's commentary reduces the transpired events to theater in the purest sense—to a fleeting spectacle, after which life simply goes on.

This final passage of the *Papinian* adaptation showcases the temporal order furnished by the fool, what I earlier called immersion in the present moment. For him, there are no enduring

---

18. Ibid., 3:199.

questions, no timeless moral lessons, no death lament, no tragic gravitas—just the indulgence in the now and the pleasure of switching, however briefly, to a viewpoint of unalloyed frivolity. In his intrusions and commentaries, his dances and gesticulations, he tears asunder the stream of dialogue, the accretion of meaning, the heightening of tragic pathos. The solace offered in his play is the pleasure of the here and now. The fool inhabits the onrushing present, the vanishing interstice into which he can cast his comic light all about.

In another one of his plays, Gryphius includes the advice that the fool should "adorn the play like sauerkraut does the bratwurst."[19] The image is a brilliant comic reversal. In order to understand it, one must recall that, contrary to modern-day baseball-game gastronomy, the bratwurst traditionally sat atop a bed of sauerkraut. Gryphius here seems to indicate that the fool can be thought of only as a supplement, insofar as he, qua foundational element, undoes the very logic of supplementation. His comic interventions may be parasitic upon the main body of the play, deviating from and often radically altering its significance, but these supplementary interventions are also the foundation upon which the play as a whole is built. In the seventeenth century, the fool's presence defined an entire theatrical culture, one that depended upon his machinations to secure the interest of audiences night after night, in town after town, year after year. Under conditions of relentless travel, with the ever-present need to attract a paying audience, theatrical players had to make sure that the experience of theatergoing would provide delight for the duration of a performance. The fool's name was disseminated in advance, and he played an important role within scenes, between scenes, and at the end of the show. He was the sideshow that essentially ensured the success of the play, as he ushered the burdens of quotidian life into the background and enchanted audiences with the evanescent rapture of the profane.

---

19. "Er muß das Spiel zieren / wie die Bratwurst das Sauerkraut." Andreas Gryphius, *Dramen, ed. Eberhard Mannack* (Frankfurt am Main: Deutscher Klassiker Verlag, 1991), 587.

Part II

Fabricating Comedy and the Fate of the Fool in the Age of Reform

Diese Zeiten sind größtenteils Zeiten der Kindheit unseres guten Geschmacks gewesen. Kindern gehöret Milch und nicht starke Speise.

These times have been largely the childhood of our good taste. Children need milk and not heavy fare.

—Gotthold Ephraim Lessing,
Beyträge zur Historie und Aufnahme des Theaters

Ein Thier heranzuzüchten, das versprechen darf—ist das nicht gerade jene paradoxe Aufgabe selbst, welche sich die Natur in Hinsicht auf die Menschen gestellt hat?

To breed an animal with the prerogative to promise—is that not precisely the paradoxical task which nature has set herself with regard to humankind?

—Friedrich Nietzsche,
On the Genealogy of Morality

5

MAKING COMEDY WHOLE

Eighteenth-century German literary drama possesses a notorious origin myth. Like most stories of this variety, it did not appear immediately conspicuous as fantastical or foundational. With enough time and repeated retelling, though, a single story appeared to most writers as the mark of a radical break with the past and the start of something new. The myth in question concerns the moment in which the fool passed from a crowd favorite to the object of derision, indeed the pariah, among an ambitious group of scholars, playwrights, translators, and theater directors. The protagonists in the story are the two central figures in early eighteenth-century German theater, the director and actress Friedericke Caroline Neuber and the professor from Leipzig, Johann Christoph Gottsched (1700–1766).[1] Together, they spearheaded a reform movement that

---

1. For much of history, the consensus has been that Caroline Neuber was a devotee of Gottsched. She came under his influence in many decisive respects, as

would send shock waves through the decades to follow. They allegedly collaborated in an act that would have been highly improbable just a decade or two earlier, but which epitomized the spirit of the 1730s: they tried to make the most beloved single stage persona in the German-speaking world into an outcast. Neuber was not the first German-speaking actress to take up arms against what she regarded as crass varieties of commercial theater.[2] But her rumored act of, to put it emphatically, ritual exorcism had particular appeal among her contemporaries. Even more important than the occurrence of the event itself was, to be sure, the way it became a touchstone for historical self-positioning and self-diagnosis over the following years. The myth became a mechanism for reflecting on the order of meaning appropriate to the stage, for assessing its social purpose, its relationship to textual fixity, to the tradition of ancient Greek and Roman comedy, and more. As it was recounted

---

should become clear over the following chapters. But two key historical details speak against such a view of Neuber's relationship to Professor Gottsched as overly servile. First, she and her husband possessed artistic ambitions that set their traveling troupe apart from others long before they made Gottsched's acquaintance. In fact, in the forty-forth installment of his journalistic project *Die Vernünftigen Tadlerinnen* from October 1725, Gottsched has nothing but words of praise for the serious quality of their troupe years before he entertains closer involvement with German theatrical culture. See Johann Christoph Gottsched, *Die Vernünfftigen Tadlerinnen: Erster Jahr-Theil* (Frankfurt/Leipzig: Brandmüller, 1725), 348–351. In addition, it seems that Caroline Neuber's affiliation with Gottsched and her opposition to the stage fool were both shaped by commercial considerations. Her troupe, which was formed after the dissolution of a prominent acting troupe, the "Hoffmansche Schauspielergesellschaft," did not have an actor well suited to play the role of the fool. The actor responsible for the role, Joseph Ferdinand Müller, joined a rival troupe, and Neuber's decision to perform without a fool figure seems to have been motivated, at least in part, by her desire to give her own troupe a distinctive identity. A good review of the facts and the literature on the subject, albeit with a speculative conclusion, can be found in Daniela Schlet-terer, "Die Verbannung des Harlekin—programmatischer Akt oder komödiantische Invektive?," *Frühneuzeit Info* 8, no. 2 (1997): 161–169.

2. The other notable case of an actress-director who defended a culturally ennobled concept of the theater was Catharina Elisabeth Velten, who lived from approximately 1650 to 1715. For her defense of the theater, which at the time of its publication enjoyed some acclaim but went without a long-lasting impact, see Carl Niessen, ed., *Frau Magister Velten verteidigt die Schaubühne: Schriften aus der Kampfzeit des deutschen Nationaltheaters* (Emsdetten: H. & J. Lechte Verlag, 1940).

and passed down, the story allowed various authors to reflect on successes and failures of German theater.

So what was the origin story? Around 1737 the actress and director Neuber put on either a prelude or postlude that culminated in the ritual-like ostracism of the fool. Of course, thrashing and chasing the fool off the stage were standard-fare slapstick; but in this case, the episode appeared, or at least was taken as, literal. The exact title or content of the play did not make its way into the historical record, for all that really mattered to contemporary accounts were the skeletal details. Here is the Swiss critic Johann Jakob Bodmer's unspectacular but typical telling of the story from 1743: "In a play, Mrs. Neuber, banished the Harlequin . . . from the stage. From this point on, the Harlequin was never again seen, even in the comedies performed by her troupe."[3] Criticism of the fool's role had, in the early 1730s, become commonplace in the pages of critical handbooks and journals, particularly those written by Gottsched himself. With Neuber's intervention, censure of the fool became the subject of a live display and, eventually, lore. Her act of violent exclusion was understood as the founding gesture in a reform project capable of having a lasting impact. The fool's absence ostensibly paved the way for the emergence of a culturally ennobled stage, comparable to its European counterparts and in line with ancient precedent. At first, the story of the fool's banishment was recounted in a triumphant tone; already by midcentury, however, detracting voices made themselves heard. Either way, the story had staying power. In fact, it maintained a formative but largely unexamined role in narratives of the development of German theater throughout the eighteenth century to Goethe's death in 1832, and even today.[4] In his widely influential study of the carnivalesque in Rabelais, no one less than Mikhail Bakhtin identified the controversy over the fool instigated by Gottsched as "an essential change" for the history of "literature, as well

3. Johann Jakob Bodmer, *Critische Betrachtungen und freye Untersuchungen zum Aufnehmen und zur Verbesserung der deutschen Schau-bühne* (Bern, 1743), 11.

4. For Goethe's remarks in the course of his autobiography *Dichtung und Wahrheit*, see FA I 14:616–617. Perhaps the most influential historical account is Eduard Devrient, *Geschichte der deutschen Schauspielkunst* (Leipzig: J. J. Weber Verlag, 1848), 2:35–37.

as in the field of aesthetic thought."[5] For nearly two hundred years, the supposed banishment of the fool has epitomized the zeal of theatrical reform that prospered in the eighteenth century.

The foregoing description of German drama's founding myth involved a terminological slippage that requires explanation. Versions of the story that circulated in the first half of the eighteenth century often spoke of the Harlequin, rather than employing more general terminology. It might be thus reasonable to suppose, as many critics have, that a comic presence derived from the Italian *commedia dell'arte* and the French *comédie-italienne* provided the flashpoint for early Enlightenment critics. But this viewpoint fails to make sense out of the (admittedly murky) theatrical situation in the early decades of the eighteenth century. To be sure, a three-volume prose translation of Molière, which appeared in 1694, exerted a marked influence on educated writers such as Christian Reuters (1665–1712), and beginning around 1710 the names Harlequin and Arlequino began to appear on the German stage.[6] While adaptations from the French and Italian encouraged the popularity of the name, there is no evidence that the role was played any differently than other instantiations of the fool figure had been. Indeed, where plays and advertisements from the seventeenth century had announced the presence of a Pickelhering, it now became increasingly common in the early decades of the eighteenth century to perform the same scripts with the name of the fool switched to Harlequin.[7] There is also evidence of some casts where one and the

5. Mikhael Bakhtin, *Rabelais and His World* (Bloomington: Indiana University Press, 1984), 35.

6. For Reuters, see the introduction to Christian Reuters, *Werke in einem Band*, ed. Günter Jäckel (Berlin: Aufbau Verlag, 1965), 5–31. On the transformations around 1710, see Bärbel Rudin, "Der Prinzipal Heinrich Wilhelm Benecke und seine 'Wienerische' und 'Hochfürstlich Bayreuthische' Schauspielergesellschaft: Zur Geschichte des deutschen, insbesondere des Nürnberger Theaterwesens im ersten Viertel des 18. Jahrhunderts," *Mitteilungen des Vereins für Geschichte der Stadt Nürnberg* 62 (1975): 179–233, esp. 191–193.

7. See Ingo Breuer, "Wi(e)der die falschen Possen? Zur Rezeption von Luigi Riccobonis theatertheoretischen Schriften bei Gottsched und Lessing," in *Deutsche Aufklärung und Italien*, ed. Italo Michele Battafarano (Bern: Peter Lang Verlag, 1992), 67–86, esp. 68–74.

same play was sometimes performed with a fool named Harlequin, sometimes with a fool named Hanswurst. Furthermore, the seminal speeches and treatises by Gottsched, which began to appear around 1730, use the term Harlequin as a general category and not as a proper name.[8] As a consequence, the claim that Caroline Neuber banished the Harlequin from the stage, in the parlance of the 1730s and 1740s, did not mean a specifically French or Italian manifestation of the fool. At stake, rather, was the elimination of the standardized role also known at the time as the comic persona or *lustige Person*.

The early Enlightenment effort to transform the stage, putatively founded in the banishment of the fool, relied on two categories that thus far have been essentially absent from this study: comedy and drama. These are unusual omissions. After all, this study has thus far concentrated on obviously related matters, such as the fool's laughter-provoking effects and multiple dimensions of his integration into the design of a play. I have avoided use of the terms *comedy* and *drama* because they will now describe, in a precise fashion, two strategic dimensions of the early Enlightenment reform project. Comedy and drama, that is, point to decisive formal and media-historical mechanisms that permeated the attempts to alter the theatrical landscape between 1730 and 1750. They were two key mechanisms in the project of "literarizing" the German theater.[9] This chapter will address the circumstances that assigned the comedic genre a central role. Chapter 7 will then head into the territory of drama. Part 2, on the whole, addresses the integral steps in the large-scale endeavor to make performed theater into a literary enterprise, founded on dramatic texts composed according to strict generic standards. In this respect, the early eighteenth century offered a distinct version of the seismic shift in the relationship

---

8. Although Gottsched initially entertained drawing a distinction between the German "Hans Wurste" and a more civilized "Harlekin" of French extraction, he abandoned this position by the time he wrote his most influential texts on the theater. For the initial position, see Johann Christoph Gottsched, *Der Biedermann*, ed. Wolfgang Martens (Stuttgart: Metzler, 1975), pt. 2, 136.

9. For a valuable discussion of "literarization" processes in general, see Alexander Beecroft, *An Ecology of World Literature: From Antiquity to the Present Day* (London: Verso, 2015), esp. 11ff.

between text and performance that took place across Europe in the seventeenth and eighteenth centuries and that gave rise to such prominent playwrights as Molière and Marivaux in France and Goldoni and Gozzi in Italy.[10]

Whereas these few canonical Italian and French writers, each in his own way, integrated and transformed the tradition of the *commedia dell'arte*, including the beloved Arlequino/Harlequin, the German theatrical reform movement began with an act of radical exclusion. The drastic nature of this founding gesture was not lost on contemporaries, who, over the course of time, inscribed the story of the fool's banishment with ambivalences. Take the following account. Johann Friedrich Löwen, director of the pioneering but short-lived National Theater in Hamburg, remarks in his *Geschichte des deutschen Theaters* (*History of German Theater*, 1766):

> Neuber and the Harlequin: *Gottsched* was heavily opposed to this innocent. He demonstrated to *Neuber* that, by virtue of all the rules of good taste, no Harlequin was to be tolerated on a well-constructed and moral stage (*auf einer wohleingerichteten und gesitteten Bühne*). He advised her to exile this wrongdoer from the theater ceremoniously. *Neuber* conceded, and promised *Mr. Gottsched* not just to banish the fool, but even to bury him. What joy for taste, and for *Mr. Gottsched*.[11]

Everything in this passage hangs on the sarcasm and scorn of the final sentence. To be sure, here Löwen identifies Neuber's harsh treatment of the fool as the founding gesture for the formation of a theater that aspired to meet the standards of good taste. Deriding the fool's banishment as a Pyrrhic victory, Löwen's history of the German stage—probably the first such history in the German language—ultimately acquits the fool of any culpability. A bit later the author goes on to refer to Neuber and Gottsched's act as an "auto-da-fé," providing a hyperbolically religious framework for

---

10. For an older discussion of this transformation from which I have repeatedly drawn inspiration, despite some disagreement over details, see Richard Alewyn, "Schauspieler und Stegreifbühne des Barock," in *Mimus und Logos: Eine Festgabe für Carl Niessen* (Esdetten: Verlag echte, 1952), 1–18.

11. Johann Friedrich Löwen, *Geschichte des deutschen Theaters*, ed. Heinrich Stümcke (Berlin: Ernst Frensdorff, 1905), 30.

the understanding of the fool as intrinsically deleterious.[12] Whereas in the 1730s the fool had appeared a threat to taste, a mere three decades later Löwen describes his banishment as an act of misguided persecution.

In the above passage, Löwen establishes a sense of ambivalent continuity with the fervor that had gripped the protagonists of his story. The flagrancy of his description reveals that he already recognizes the mythic role of the episode. In truth, a single stage event did not irreversibly change the conventions governing an entire stage culture, nor could it have. It was clear already to Löwen that he was dealing with an event that had symbolic value far outweighing the facts of the matter. In its retellings, the story allowed for the articulation of a number of crucial questions. Was the fool an innocent scapegoat or genuine villain?[13] And, either way, did his banishment encourage the coalescence of a new theater? If a new form of theater was coming into existence, could this happen in a punctual act, just by supplanting old predilections with new ones? Or did theatrical reform necessarily entail a more temporally protracted and gradual process? On a more global level, was the notion of reform advanced by Gottsched and embodied by Neuber and her troupe an innovative advance or a mistaken detour? In order to explore answers to these questions, it is first necessary to lay out the initial design of the reform project.

Neuber's banishment of the fool, under the aegis of Gottsched, is not just of historiographic import; it also brings into relief key methodological issues. The myth, that is, demonstrates the following truism: continuity cannot be taken for granted—not in general, and certainly not when it comes to theatrical conventions.[14] The point is worth making because the fool, as part 1 has shown, was

---

12. Ibid., 31.

13. The scapegoat structure has been most influentially theorized in Rene Girard, *Violence and the Sacred*, trans. Patrick Gregory (Baltimore: Johns Hopkins University Press, 1979).

14. For particularly insightful remarks on the problem of continuity in literary history, see Jürgen Link, "Was heißt: 'Es hat sich nichts geändert'? Ein Reproduktionsmodell literarischer Evolution mit Blick auf Geibel," in *Epochenschwellen und Epochenstrukturen im Diskurs der Literatur- und Sprachhistorie,*

the champion of discontinuity on all levels. No level of dialogue or scenic atmosphere was fully fortified against his intrusions. His unique capacity to storm onto the stage, suspending the flow of dialogue and interrupting its course, might lead one to suppose that everything would proceed cohesively if not for his presence. Without this agent of discontinuity, one might suppose, continuity should just emerge on its own. Neuber's myth gains purchase by concretizing the view that exclusion of the fool and institution of a new theatrical culture are two faces of the same coin. But continuity, much like its opposite, has to be produced, and this by means of intermediate steps of various techniques and procedures.

Perhaps the most distinctive hallmark of the intellectual currents conventionally referred to as the early Enlightenment, at least within the theatrical arena, was the institution of continuity on multiple levels.[15] Figures like Gottsched and Neuber, as well as a number of other writers and scholars in their orbit, made it their project to alter the internal cohesion of stage performances. This involved an intricate conception of what a play should be and what the theater was for. According to the traditional philosophical language prevalent among reformers, it was necessary to articulate the "essence of plays" (*das Wesen der Schauspiele*) in light of their "final purpose" (*Endzweck*).[16] Such analytic terms make sense only in light of the view that the theater could be submitted to "a test or examination" at the hands of "the scholar who has philosophical

---

ed. Hans Ulrich Gumbrecht and Ursula Link-Heer (Frankfurt am Main: Suhrkamp, 1985), 234–250.

15. The reference to the period between 1730 and 1750 as the early Enlightenment is not entirely unproblematic. In using this term, I have no desire to make an ambitious historiographical claim or to take a stance in ongoing debates about the varied uses of Enlightenment as a periodization term. I use the concept rather thinly, as a tag for a group of advocates for theatrical reform who possess a shared, albeit nonuniform, field of concerns. On the problems plaguing the concept of Enlightenment in contemporary historiography, see Simon Grote, "Review-Essay: Religion and Enlightenment," *Journal of the History of Ideas* 75, no. 1 (2014): 137–160.

16. Both pieces of terminology are from Christlob Mylius, "Eine Abhandlung, worinnen erwiesen wird: Daß die Wahrscheinlichkeit er Vorstellung, bey den Schauspielen eben so nötig ist, als die innere Wahrscheinlichkeit derselben," *Beyträge zur critischen Historie der deutschen Sprache, Poesie und Beredsamkeit* 29 (1742): 297–322, here 297 and 302.

insight into the rules of the arts."[17] Those possessed of the reform spirit believed themselves able to uncover the theater's genuine reason for existing, even if its concrete manifestations had thus far fallen short and even if all its constitutive elements required overhaul.

Although harangues of the fool's "jokes and farces that grieve the Holy Spirit, vex the youth, and plant many harmful things in the eyes and hearts of idle (*müßigen*) spectators" had been voiced before, the interweaving of theoretical and practical endeavor made the early Enlightenment reforms uniquely effective.[18] Their impact was shaped by a broad-based program for the encouragement of scholarly critique, a practice of philosophically and philologically attuned deliberation over successes and failures in poetry.[19] The early Enlightenment practice of critique rested on the assertion that venerated relics of antiquity and untested contemporary works equally rewarded analysis in terms of a canon of poetic principles and regulations. A steady flow of long-form treatises and journal articles, often engaged in a pugilistic back-and-forth, became one of the key mechanisms for the improvement of German poetry. Although minor differences in the conceptual architecture and philosophical genealogy were visible among participants, there was a widespread sense that poetic critique was both the product of and an instrument to "judge the perfections or imperfections of things" (*Vollkommenheiten oder Unvollkommenheiten der Dinge zu urtheilen*).[20] Such judgment

---

17. Johann Christoph Gottsched, *Versuch einer critischen Dichtkunst vor die Deutschen* (Leipzig: Bernhard Christoph Breitkopf, 1730), 2 (of preface without page numbers). Unless otherwise noted, all references to Gottsched's epoch-making poetic treatise are to its first edition.

18. Paul Jacob Marperger, *Beschreibung der Messen und Jahr-Märkte* (Leipzig: Johann Friedrich Gleditsch and Son, 1710), 2:209.

19. Concentrated analysis of this phenomenon, with heavy emphasis on media-historical dimensions, may be found in Steffen Martus, "Negativität im literarischen Diskurs um 1700," in *Kulturelle Orientierung um 1700*, ed. Sylvia Heudecker, Dirk Niefanger, and Jörg Weschke (Tübingen: Max Niemeyer Verlag, 2004), 47–66. More expansively and with a longer historical trajectory: Steffen Martus, *Werkpolitik: Zur Literaturgeschichte kritischer Kommunikation vom 17. bis ins 20. Jahrhundert* (Berlin: De Gruyter, 2007), esp. 113–201.

20. This phrasing, which is indebted to Alexander Gottlieb Baumgarten's aesthetics, is used on multiple occasions in Georg Friedrich Meier, *Abbildung eines Kunstrichters* (Halle: Carl Hermann Hemmerde, 1745). Although it is convention

proceeded on the basis of ostensibly timeless, universal guidelines for the construction of poetic utterances. The insistence on rudimentary but crudely employed rationalist principles for the practice of critique—above all, the principles of noncontradiction and sufficient reason—was more than a game of philosophical analysis. In fact, it fit within a larger media enterprise, aiming at putting German theater on a par with that of other European nations. The project of improving the quality of German theater required the establishment of feedback loops between critical commentary and the composition of new plays. Reformers asserted that such circuitry would be "beneficial for the Germans" by fostering "beauty in speech and thought."[21] In order to be successful, the reform movement had to do more than supply abstract theoretical accounts and critical evaluations of individual plays. Progress in "theatrical poetry" demanded that a "lack of printed pieces" (*Mangel gedrückter Stücke*) be dealt with.[22] In other words, concepts would not do; a broader practice of composition and publication was required.

The reform project relied on two factors: an increase in the number of plays published according to specific compositional standards and a tighter integration of text and performance. Acting troupes had to put on "pieces that have been learned by heart word for word,"[23] and writers had to attend not just to "the quantity of pieces, but to the kind and good construction of them (*Art und gute Einrichtung derselben*)."[24] These ends were pursued within

in literary histories to emphasize the agonistic relationship between figures like Meier and Gottsched, these differences emerged within the shared domain of rationalist critique. I return to some of the philosophical differences between early Enlightenment camps in chapter 9.

21. Meier, *Abbildung eines Kunstrichters*, 1–2.

22. Johann Christoph Gottsched, *Die deutsche Schaubühne nach den Regeln der Griechen und Römer* (Leipzig: Bernhard Christoph Breitkopf, 1741), 2:3–42, here 18. The lack of published German-language plays became a trope repeated countless times across the eighteenth century, but not entirely in line with publication and performance history. See Thorston Unger, "Das Klischee vom Mangel an deutschen Stücken: Ein Diskussionsbeitrag zur Internationalität des Hof- und Nationaltheaters," in *Theaterinstitution und Kulturtransfer*, ed. Anke Deten, Thorston Unger, Brigitte Schultze, and Horst Turk (Tübingen: Gunter Narr Verlag, 1998), 1:233–247.

23. Gottsched, *Die deutsche Schaubühne*, 2:25.

24. Ibid., 2:29.

the bounds of a learned society, in speeches and pet journalistic projects, but also by acting troupes like the Neubers'. Although some attention was paid to the practices and training of actors, the reform project had at its foundation a conviction in the transformative power of texts.[25] We can see as much in the diagnosis of a particularly prevalent ailment, namely, the fact that the "poets are guilty" of making the audience "laugh, when one cries, and cry, when one laughs."[26] And so a canon of rules had to be drawn up—rules that would ensure that plays treated two opposing varieties of human expression, laughter and tears, more felicitously. Indeed, for much of the eighteenth century, whenever there was a desire to demonstrate the "essence and specific character" (*Wesen und eigentümlichen Charakter*) of comedy and tragedy respectively, this generic difference was supported by a sanitary effort to "establish the ground (*Grund*) from which on the one side the necessity of laughter, and from the other the necessary permissibility of tears could flow."[27] Following the "rules and examples of theatrical poetry"[28] could control the flow of laughter and tears, thereby ensuring consistency in the meanings produced in a play and the emotional responses afforded the spectator. Within this model, rigid generic boundaries should serve to distinguish different varieties of affect and to contain them within separate domains. And with the institution of a purified comedy and tragedy, there would then be no room for the "Harlequin and Hans Wurst, who, with their ridiculous farces and undignified banter have spoiled everything that could have been in accord with the rules."[29]

---

25. Acting reforms played a more significant role in the latter half of the eighteenth century. See Alexander Kosenina, *Anthropologie und Schauspielkunst* (Tübingen: Max Niemeyer Verlag, 1995).

26. Heinrich Samuel von Brück, "Gedanken von der Dichtkunst überhaupt," in *Der deutschen Gesellschaft in Leipzig eigene Schriften und Uebersetzungen* (Leipzig: Bernhard Christoph Breitkopff, 1735), 1:2–31, here 20.

27. Christian Ernst Schenk, *Komisches Theater* (Breslau: Carl Gottfried Meyer, 1759), 7–8.

28. Anonymous, "Nachricht von der uefnter der Presse befindlichen deutschen Schaubühne," *Beyträge zur critischen Historie der deutschen Sprache, Poesie und Beredsamkeit* 23 (1740): 521–526, here 525.

29. This quotation is from a review of a widely circulated translation of a French speech and newly written treatise on the value of a rehabilitated stage. See

One of the chief mechanisms for the transformation of the stage was comedy itself. But comedy was more than just a conventional form. Consider what Neuber and her husband wrote in a 1737 application for a license to perform in the city of Hamburg: "Comedy seeks to make evident the difference between virtue and vice, and to reveal the necessary consequences of both."[30] The content of the definition is not as important as the context in which it is provided. The Neubers introduce poetological principles—in particular, those concerning the general usefulness of comedy—in the hope of recruiting the support of the city council. The deployment of a morally inflected conception of the comedic genre meant to assure the municipal authorities that the troupe's performances would further the effort "to purify the German stage of all its mess (*von all dem Wuste zu reinigen*)."[31] To be sure, the Neubers' general sense of purpose as well as their specific attunement to genre owed quite a bit to the theoretical head of the reform movement, Gottsched. The first version of his expansive poetic treatise *Versuch einer critischen Dichtkunst für die Deutschen* (*Attempt at a Critical Art of Poetry for the Germans*, 1730) contains a kindred characterization of comedy as the "imitation of a vicious action, which, by virtue of its risible essence, can amuse the spectator at the same time that it edifies him" (*Nachahmung einer lasterhafften Handlung, die durch ihr lächerliches Wesen den Zuschauer belustigen, aber auch zugleich erbauen kan*).[32] In alignment with his broader approach to generic divisions, Gottsched defines comedy in terms of a representational content (human vice) and spectatorial response (laughter).

But relying from the start on a statement bearing on content and response risks obscuring the reasons why genre became an

---

Anonymous, "Des berühmten französischen Paters Poree Rede von den Schauspielen: Ob sie eine Schule guter Sitten sind, oder seyn Können? übersetzt. Nebst einer Abhandlung von der Schaubühne, heraus gegeben von Joh. Friedrich Meyer," in *Beyträge zur Critischen Historie* 9 (1734): 3–29, here 22.

30. Letter reprinted in Friedrich Johann Freiherrn von Reden-Esbeck, *Caroline Neuber und ihre Zeitgenossen: Ein Beitrag zur deutschen Kultur- und Theatergeschichte* (Leipzig: J. A. Barth, 1881), 204–207, here 205.

31. Ibid., 204.

32. Gottsched, *Versuch einer critischen Dichtkunst*, 594.

attractive way of conducting the business of theater.[33] It is important to shift from the standard question, What is a comedy? to the more practice-oriented question, What does calling something a comedy accomplish? Orienting the discussion in this way allows us to investigate what the concept of genres, including comedy, does. And it also focuses attention on the concrete circumstances that made the comedic genre into an organizing concept for the theatrical reform movement. Included among these circumstances is the contrast between the use of genre as a means for the "purification" or *Reinigung* of the stage in the early eighteenth century and the altogether different, more chaotic approach to genre in the seventeenth.[34]

Considered abstractly, genre distinctions function as a classificatory mechanism for achieving the semblance of coherence on two levels: both in the composition of individual plays and in the (prospective as well as retrospective) classification of multiple plays into a group. The concatenation of elements in a play and the formation of a classificatory standard are ultimately both procedures for creating, among other things, consistent patterns in plot organization, character deployment, and verbal register. The difference between these two levels is ultimately one of scale: the one bears on the individual; the other, the class.

Genre distinctions play a decisive role in two distinct communicative settings. They appear as self-ascriptions—for instance, as paratextual markers—and, in addition, as second-order distinctions in the discourse about poetry. In both instances, genre works to establish similarities or equivalences. Obvious though it may sound, classification depends on naming, which provides for the formation, iteration, and recognition of distinct groups. It may be natural to suppose that comedy and tragedy constitute standard

---

33. The pioneering discussion for my own approach to questions of genre is Wilhelm Voßkamp, "Gattungen als literarisch-soziale Institutionen," in *Textsortenlehre—Gattungsgeschichte*, ed. Walter Hinck (Heidelberg: Quelle & Meyer, 1977), 27–43.

34. The use of cognate forms of the verb *reinigen* (purify) by and with reference to the reform movement is so widespread that any reference to a single instance would be misleading.

rubrics that, even if not always uniform in content, consistently provide the parameters for dividing up the field of plays and playmaking. This intuition is supported by the widespread use of the two lexemes *die Komödie* and *das Lustspiel* in German, not unlike the use of *comedy* in English. While the lexical connections and connotative linkages to the Roman and ancient Greek nomenclature and *comedy/die Komödie* may not always be evident to modern speakers, their origin is less than mysterious. In both languages, words are coordinated with themes, objects, and affects, thereby orienting the expectations of writers, readers, listeners, and spectators of plays and standing in a latent opposition to *tragedy/die Tragödie/das Trauerspiel*. But from a historical perspective the categorizing function of such terminology is surprisingly unstable. Indeed, the imposition of onomastic consistency—particularly on the level of first-order paratexts—is a major innovation of the early Enlightenment.

To bring this historical point into relief, consider the situation in the seventeenth century. Among the traveling players of the seventeenth century, genre distinctions figured prominently in advertisements or *Theaterzettel*.[35] Itinerant companies possessed an overwhelming penchant for identifying their plays as *tragedies*, even though the use of this term was by no means systematic. In other words, the term *tragedy* did not form part of a larger generic order. Within this context, there was no consistent differentiation of the social rank of the characters appropriate for the various genres, nor a distinction among different modalities of speech, nor a distribution of thematic foci. Traveling players may have called their plays tragedies, but the utility of the term lay in its vague associations and allure rather than in any classificatory stringency.

Plays published by learned playwrights attest to an even more unsystematic approach to genre distinctions. The proliferation of paratextual markers gives an impression of a hodgepodge of genre names lacking for rhyme or reason. In the plays written by Andreas

---

35. See the discussion in Johann Richard Hänsel, "Die Geschichte des Theaterzettels und seine Wirkung in der Öffentlichkeit" (PhD diss., Freie Universität Berlin, 1962), esp. 103–155. See also George W. Brandt, ed., *German and Dutch Theater 1600–1848* (Cambridge: Cambridge University Press, 1993), 71–73.

Gryphius and Christian Weise (1642–1708), for instance, we find such unfamiliar terms as *Schimpff-Spiel, Schertz-Spiel,* and *Ein lächerliches Schau-Spiel.*[36] Other unfamiliar names that enjoyed currency include *Misch-Spiel,*[37] *Freudenspiel,*[38] and *Lust oder Freudenspiel.*[39] Despite appearances, this list does not attest to a byzantine system of nomenclature; it rather indicates an unexacting approach to genre distinctions as well as a comfort with unorthodox terms.

The contrast between the seventeenth-century onomastic conventions and those of the early Enlightenment could not be starker. Beginning around 1730, a single terminological equivalence—between *die Komödie* and *das Lustspiel,* between Greek and German nomenclature—became a crucial mechanism in the overhaul of compositional and performance practice. Reformers believed that the development of a homogeneous terminology and a restricted notion of genre could prove vital in the effort to fuse text and performance. A unified notion of comedy—one entailing the "imitation of vices worthy of laughter" (*Abbildung auslachenswürdiger Laster*)—could help make sure that theater fulfills its final purpose of providing for the "edification of spectators."[40]

Reformers like Neuber and Gottsched aimed to replace the comic practices sponsored by the fool by publishing generically uniform texts. They argued that printed comedies could form the

---

36. On Gryphius's use of the term *Schimpff-Spiel* in the title to *Absurda Comica. Oder Herr Peter Squentz,* and its possible connection to Hans Sachs, see the commentator's notes in Andreas Gryphius, *Dramen,* ed. Eberhard Mannack (Frankfurt am Main: Deutscher Klassiker Verlag, 1991), 1138ff. Gryphius gives the title *Schertz-Spiel* to *Die geliebte Dornrose* (1661) and *Horribilicribrifax* (1663) contained in the same volume. The name *Ein Lächerliches Schau-Spiel* is used by Christian Weise for a very lengthy interlude first performed in 1685 and then published in 1700. See Christian Weise, *Sämtliche Werke,* ed. Hans-Gert Rolloff (Berlin: De Gruyter, 1991), 2:249.

37. Kaspar von Stieler, *Ernelinde oder Die Viermahl Braut* (Rudolstadt: Caspar Freyschmidt, 1665).

38. Justus Georgius Schottelius, *Neu Erfundenes Freuden Spiel Genandt Friedens Sieg* (Wolfenbüttel: Conrad Buno, 1648).

39. Johannes Rist, *Depositio Cornuti Typographici, D.i. Lust-Oder Freuden-Spiel* (Lüneberg: Stern, 1654.

40. Mylius, "Eine Abhandlung, worinnen erwiesen wird," 302.

foundation for a theater that could "amuse" in a "rational and purified manner" (*vernünftige und geläuterte Art*).[41] *Comedy* was deployed to combat a figure so "devoid of good gags . . . that he could not say anything funny without injuring the rules of respectability."[42] Generic purity required the elimination of "jokes and grimaces," which had no place in the pen of "a true author of comedies" (*eines wahren Comödien-Schreibers*),[43] who instead should adhere to the "rules of the . . . masters" and make the stage "moral."[44] Comedy thus became an instrument for insuring continuity on the level of text as well as performance—indeed of using textual continuity as the basis for performative continuity. The *comic play* of the fool had to be harnessed by means of the *comedic genre*. Or, put differently, the large-scale continuity of the comedic genre—the unity of the individual play with a governing class—should ensure the small-scale continuity in the individual performance. Importantly, using a unified comedic genre for the "improvement of the German stage" amounted to the imposition of what would, in the course of the eighteenth century, become the kind of play audiences cherished most.[45] In the latter half of the century, comedies amounted to by far the majority of the repertoire of essentially every major acting troupe. In some troupes, comedies were performed five times as often as tragedies and up to three times as often as the increasingly popular opera.[46] As popularity increased, the designation remained consistent from troupe to troupe and year to year.

The fusion of text and performance under the aegis of comedy depended on a close connection between first- and second-order use of genre distinctions. Printed plays, that is, had to accord with

---

41. Gottsched, *Die deutsche Schaubühne*, 1:21.

42. Gottsched, *Der Biedermann*, pt. 2, 136.

43. Ibid., pt. 2, 178.

44. Ibid.

45. Gottsched, *Die deutsche Schaubühne*, 2:9.

46. See the statistics in Reinhart Meyer and Rainer Gruenter, "Der Anteil des Singspiels und der Oper am Repertoire der deutschen Bühnen in der zweiten Hälfte des 18. Jahrhunderts," in *Das deutsche Singspiel im 18. Jahrhundert* (Heidelberg: Winter Universitätsverlag, 1981), 27–76.

formal and terminological distinctions used in theoretical discourse. The importance of generic distinctions can be gleaned from the basic structure of Gottsched's *Versuch einer critischen Dichtkunst*: it consists of two parts, the first devoted to a philosophically oriented account of the nature of poetry and the poet, the second to the elaboration of the poetic genres. Meanwhile, the title of the eleventh chapter of the second part, "Von Comödien oder Lustspielen," points to the decisive terminological equivalence between ancient and modern paradigms, and its place within a systematic framework is evident in the fact that it follows immediately after the chapter "Von Tragödien oder Trauerspielen." Underlying this division is the recursive structure of critique. Gottsched's elaboration of the fundamental concepts of poetic activity and its constitutive forms serves the express purpose of guiding contemporary and future poets, whose works could, in turn, become the subject of subsequent critical discourse. In order to fulfill this charge, he subdivides his discussion of the comedic genre (and all others respectively) into "historical-critical" and "dogmatic" portions.[47] Whereas the first section assesses the shortcomings and accomplishments of various instantiations of comedy beginning with its putative origin in archaic times up to the present day, the latter part provides a more abstract discussion of formal characteristics, peppered with a small number of examples.

The implications of this subdivision will come into sharper focus over the next three chapters. For now, it is important to note its connection to the epoch-making interlacement of text and performance. The purpose of the historical-critical section of Gottsched's text is, as the name indicates, to assess concrete manifestations of comedy—and yet this appraisal is founded on formal principles elaborated in the dogmatic section. The author well realized that as contemporary poets engaged with his treatise, he would have to revisit the historical-critical discussion. In other words, he designed his treatise taking into account potential

---

47. Although introduced earlier in the treatise, the distinction organizes the chapter devoted to comedy. See Gottsched, *Versuch diner critischen Dichtkunst*, 548.

feedback loops between his critical discussion and future poetic production—and, accordingly, he continued to revise and expand his treatise through its fourth edition in 1751. In this final version, for instance, he pivots from critical to dogmatic observations with a word of praise for the role of "a small theatrical library of printed plays" (*eine kleine theatralische Bibliothek gedruckter Schauspiele*) in the steady improvement of the German stage.[48] The placement of this remark at the turning point in the chapter underscores the sense in which the critical reflection continuously tracks and adapts to the treatise's reception by playwrights. But the publication of plays alone was not enough to satisfy his reform aspirations. Generic purity can be accomplished, in Gottsched's view, only once a supply of strictly constructed plays has entered into print circulation and is "being dutifully performed" (*fleißig aufgeführret*).[49]

Gottsched's theoretical articulation of the comedic genre might seem nothing more than another instance of the sort of handbook for poetic composition that had enjoyed strong currency since the Renaissance. In truth, though, it subtly breaks with this lineage. Beginning with Martin Opitz's *Buch von der deutschen Poeterey* (*Book on German Poetry*, 1624) and continuing until Magnus Daniel Omeis's *Gründliche Anleitung zur teutschen accuraten Reim- und Dichtkunst* (*Fundamental Instruction in the Art of Accurate German Rhyme and Poetry*, 1704), scholars drew on structures from the art of rhetoric in order to account for poetic forms. Remarks on how to make a play commenced with a concern for proper method for finding its objects and themes (*inventio*), arranging them (*dispositio*), and then putting them into verbal formulation (*elocutio*). Within this tradition, discussions of genre constituted the transitional point between the first two elements in this list and the third—that is, between finding the proper words (*verba*) for the referential objects (*res*) of a play.[50] We see this alignment clearly in Opitz, when he uses the term *comoedia* as a heading for

---

48. Johann Christoph Gottsched, *Versuch einer critischen Dichtkunst vor die Deutschen* (Leipzig: Bernhard Christoph Breitkopf, 1751), 643.

49. Ibid.

50. On the importance of the *res-verba* distinction, see Ludwig Fischer, *Gebundene Rede: Dichtung und Rhetorik in der literarischen Theorie des Barock in Deutschland* (Tübingen: M. Niemeyer, 1968), 101ff.

a genre defined by the persons and events that appear in the poem; comedy is the genre of the lowly and quotidian. Because it deals with topics like betrothal and marriage, servant intrigue, and the shortsightedness of youth, the gravest error among those "writing comedies" is that they have "introduced emperors and rulers," who have no place in poems dealing with such base matters.[51] For Opitz, genre amounts to equivalence between the social rank of the persons depicted on the stage and the style of writing employed, a long-standing approach founded on the rhetorical principle of *decorum*.[52] Preoccupied with the question of how to compose a "poetic play" or *ein poetisches Schauspiel*, to use a phrase of Georg Philipp Harsdörffer's, seventeenth-century handbooks actually showed little interest in performance practices.[53] Comedy, in their hands, was not a device for the transformation of stage practices, but instead a time-transcendent, immutable form. For this reason, very little attention was paid to contemporary stage practice in the elaboration of the compositional rules organizing *comoedia*.[54] Second-order discourse on comedy in the seventeenth century, to borrow Gottsched's terminology, was entirely dogmatic.

---

51. Martin Opitz, *Buch von der deutschen Poeterey*, ed. Wilhelm Braune and Richard Alewyn (Tübingen: M. Niemeyer, 1963), 20.

52. Ursula Milden and Ian Rutherford, "Decorum," in *Historisches Wörterbuch der Rhetorik*, ed. Gert Ueding (Tübingen: Max Niemeyer Verlag, 1994), 2:423–452.

53. Georg Philipp Harsdörffer, *Poetischer Trichter: Die Teutsche Dicht- und Reimkunst, ohne Behuf der lateinischen Sprache, in VI. Stunden Einzugiessen* (Hildesheim/New York: G. Olms, 1971), 2:78.

54. To outline the standards of a *poetic play* was to engage in an enterprise entirely separate from the "people who make their profession with wanton and vexing plays, and make money by feeding vice into the hearts of people through their eyes." The original text reads: "die Leute / so von solchen liederlich- und ärgerlichen Schauspielen Beruf machen / und um das Geld den Leuten die Laster durch die Augen in das Herz spielen." Magnus Daniel Omeis, *Gründliche Anleitung zur teutschen accuraten Reim- und Dichtkunst* (Nuremberg: Wolfgang Michahelles und Johann Adolf, 1704), 248–249. This harangue by Magnus Daniel Omeis (1646–1708) is not a further installment in the long line of Christian-inspired attacks on all forms of theatrical spectatorship; it is a dismissal of the particular "nasty jokes and antics which often transform a theatrical play into swine's play." In talking about the presence of the fool in comic interludes, he writes, "Ich sage Scherz-Reden; und vertheidige nicht die garstige Zotten und Possen / welche öfters die Schau-spiele in Sau-spiele verwandeln" (236).

But its dogma is without the early Enlightenment philosophical un-
derpinnings and imputation of a final cause.

As the collaboration between Neuber and Gottsched makes
clear, the unity of first- and second-order conceptions of comedy
in the early Enlightenment was programmatic. Its telos was the
extension of the empire of texts onto the stage. In order for the reform enterprise to succeed, intractable theatrical forces—above all,
the fool—had to be contained. The utility of the myth with which
this chapter began consisted in showing that the elimination of the
fool, which in the mid-1730s was just a theoretical possibility, could
also lead to the transformation of stage performance and textual
composition. Johann Christoph Gottsched launched the reform
movement at that time in a cascade of speeches and published texts
championing the need for terminological rigor, a new discipline for the
production of comic effects, and a new practice of textual composition and performance. His ideas spread, playwrights composed
according to professed standards, and Neuber provided the endeavor with theatrical legitimacy. Even though over time, the early
Enlightenment conception of theatrical reform became subject to
scrutiny and revision, one thing remained true over the decades to
come: the name of the game was comedy.

6

BIASES IN PRECEDENT

Nowhere was the call for German comedy made with the same stridency and eventual resonance as in the poetological writing of the professor from Leipzig Johann Christoph Gottsched. The treatise he reworked again and again throughout his life is organized around the division between, on the one hand, the elaboration of universally binding standards of composition and, on the other, the description of the vicissitudes of poetic forms across epochs and through different linguistic traditions. He deduces the former from an order intrinsic to nature, while he assesses the latter on the basis of concrete historical developments. In Gottsched's hands, critique became a technical term for the examination of individual works and entire linguistic traditions, measured against putatively time- and place-independent standards. That being said, a closer look reveals a deeper—if unacknowledged, even unconscious—interdependency of historical variations and supposedly

transcendent poetic tenets. A battery of historical examples provides the basis for the presentation of formal and thematic principles, as historical phenomena are evaluated in light of the privileged
place assigned to the ancient Greeks and, even more so, to the Romans, whose achievements are identified as the purest embodiment
of the laws of nature. In this way, dogma and history equally participate in the articulation of comedy—not through a strict division of
labor, but through a process of mutual contamination.

That a genre like comedy could be explained in a dogmatic fashion at all—merely in terms of accord with time- and place-indifferent
principles of nature—itself counted as a dogma of Gottsched's
critical enterprise. As the reform project picked up steam, however, historical self-reference became ever more important, informing both definitions of genres and assertions of their applicability.
Considered abstractly, the early Enlightenment was responsible for
what we might call a temporalization of comedy and especially its
relationship to the fool.[1] The principled account of generic categories and their concrete historical manifestations became, over the
course of the first half of the eighteenth century, ever more closely
connected, especially as means to think through the appropriate
mechanisms for improving the German stage.

The temporal ensconcement of critique was most patent in the
mediating role of examples. Without reference to the past, it was
impossible to explain the formation of comedy and of genre, in
general, as a classificatory device. Reliance on the authority of ancient Greece and Rome was, of course, anything but new at the turn
of the eighteenth century, and even the chosen terminology—the
reference to *Muster* or *Exempel*, models or examples—had a longer history. For most of the early modern period, poetic manuals
drew on the rhetorical structure of the exemplum, itself a concept inherited from the ancient Greek παράδειγμα. An eminently
practical device, the exemplum is a work (or part thereof) that
authoritatively illustrates a class of phenomena. Poetic manuals

---

1. This temporalization is undoubtedly connected to the temporal specification
of knowledge Michel Foucault identified as characteristic of the period around
1800. See Michel Foucault, *The Order of Things*, trans. Alan Sheridan (New York:
Pantheon, 1970).

used exempla as instruments for teaching how to reproduce certain salient features; critical judgment (*iudicium*) was called for, as the eminent humanist Julius Caesar Scaliger writes, in order to "select in each instance the best for imitation" (*optima quaeque seligamus ad imitandum*).[2] Up to the early Enlightenment, the critic had to supply the poet with exempla conforming to canonical, formal criteria and thus worth using as scaffolding for new compositions. The exemplum was not scrutinized for shortcomings or used as the basis for innovation; its utility for the practice of composition lay in its self-evidence and immediate applicability.

The practice of critique provided, in the early eighteenth century, the framework within which exempla could be used for judging contemporary and past poetic works. Critique was a practice of pointing out shortcomings, of improving by way of negating, even "negating tradition" itself.[3] Gottsched's discussion of modern poetry, for instance, has just as many words of praise for the unparalleled achievements of the French as of biting censure for the unruly shortcomings of the Italians.[4] He proceeds in this schoolmasterly fashion because all linguistic and cultural traditions belong to a single taxonomy, organized in terms of a universally applicable set of value-laden criteria. Even though each culture possesses its own distinct taste, each can be evaluated for its conformity to a

---

2. Scaliger, *Poetices libri septem* VI, 44; quoted in Steffen Martus, *Werkpolitik: Zur Literaturgeschichte kritischer Kommunikation vom 17. bis ins 20. Jahrhundert* (Berlin: De Gruyter, 2007), 68. For a deconstructionist analysis of exemplarity, see John D. Lyons, *Exemplum: The Rhetoric of Example in Early Modern France and Italy* (Princeton: Princeton University Press, 1989).

3. See the discussion in Wilfried Barner, "Über das Negieren von Tradition: Zur Typologie literaturprogrammatischer Epochenwenden in Deutschland," in *Epochenschwelle und Epochenbewußtsein*, ed. Reinhart Herzog and Reinhart Koselleck (Munich: Wilhelm Fink Verlag, 1987), 3–52. Unlike the *exempla* used in moral-didactic contexts, poetic handbooks had up to this point little use for illustration by way of failure. On the latter tradition, see Reinhart Koselleck, "Historia Magistra Vitae: Über die Auflösung des Topos im Horizont neuzeitlich bewegter Geschichte," in *Vergangene Zukunft: Zur Semantik geschichtlicher Zeiten* (Frankfurt am Main: Suhrkamp Taschenbuch Wissenschaft, 1989), 38–66.

4. See Johann Christoph Gottsched, *Versuch einer critischen Dichtkunst vor die Deutschen* (Leipzig: Bernhard Christoph Breitkopf, 1730), 590–592.

universal and unchanging metric. As a classificatory system with its source in the "unchanging nature of things themselves" (*der unveränderten Natur der Dinge selbst*), genre applies to different traditions while at the same time remaining indifferent to spatiotemporal or cultural coloring.[5]

The complications of this taxonomic scenario are manifest in the anthologies of plays published under the title *Die deutsche Schaubühne*, which contained plays written in the German language "according to the rules and examples of the ancients."[6] The inscription of the collection with the marquee of the ancients simultaneously demarcates and effaces the temporal signature of poetic rules. They are said to emanate from a distinct historical and cultural point of origin at the same time that this point of origin is denied a sponsoring role in the validity of the rules they exemplify. Gottsched's paradoxical move is characteristic of his transitional place in the history of European poetics. On the one hand, he still belongs to a tradition of erudition, which uses exempla as a mechanism for the inculcation of poetic rules worth adhering to; on the other, he advances a philosophical program with claims to spatiotemporal transcendence. Because the identification of shortcomings became, in the early eighteenth century, an indispensable and productive component of critique, however, the ancient Greeks and Romans could serve as the privileged donors of exempla while still being subject to (at least some) negative evaluation. The coup of Gottsched's use of genre to encourage the improvement of the German stage lay in his tendency to exploit both the cachet enjoyed by antiquity and the unimpeachable claim to a time- and space- (and thus culture-) independent notion of reason.

To put it colloquially, Gottsched is trying to have his cake and eat it too. How can genres like comedy—and their constitutive formal features—stand both inside and outside of time? Despite initial appearances, it is important to ask how the comedies published under

---

5. Gottsched, *Versuch einer critischen Dichtkunst*, 103.

6. Johann Christoph Gottsched, *Die deutsche Schaubühne nach den Regeln der Griechen und Römer* (Leipzig: Bernhard Christoph Breitkopf, 1742), vol. 1, title page.

Gottsched's aegis can, at once, accord with concrete ancient Greek and Roman paradigms and, at the same time, enjoy a legitimacy guaranteed by "the unchanging nature of things themselves"? The answer, of course, is that comedy cannot be both necessary and contingent, both culturally specific and transcendent. Although Gottsched claims to be elaborating on the ageless conditions of comedy and be publishing exempla to encourage the promulgation of the genre, his project is, in fact, suspended between the past and the future, and he uses the reference to ahistorical dictates of reason as the justification for his modeling of the present upon the past. The underlying motivation for the duplicity is clear enough: his poetological reflections, speeches, journalistic projects, and publishing endeavors were intended as practical instruments for improving the supposedly deplorable state of theatrical performance. Because Gottsched viewed the publication of poetic rules and of new plays as essentially practical in purpose, it ultimately makes good sense that his elaboration of comedy is suffused with explicit and implicit references to the concrete historical world, both of the past and of the present.

For the larger developments in the course of the eighteenth century, in Gottsched's wake, it is important to notice the two basic functions assigned to the formation of the comedic genre, both of which lend a veneer of seriousness to the theater and thereby alter its cultural standing. First, the articulation of the unity of comedy through an exploration of its history amounted, at bottom, to a narrative of (potential) continuity between the past and the present. And, as a consequence, this history also provided a way to censure illegitimate models and celebrate worthy ones, pointing out the desired direction for the future.

Unsurprisingly, the line between illicit and licit comedy says more about the contemporary preoccupation with the stage fool than the objects it purports to be about. Within this division, the stage fool leads a veiled existence in the critical discussion of the two great comedic forerunners from ancient Rome, Plautus (ca. 254–184 BCE) and Terence (ca. 195–159 BCE). Gottsched's conception of ancient precedent—of a canon against which contemporary creations could be measured—gave strong preference to Terence as the antecedent more worthy of imitation. Not much later, in Gottsched's wake, the young Gotthold Ephraim Lessing (1729–1781) prompted a reassessment of Plautus, tipping the scales the other way. The differing assessment of these two Roman authors is not a matter of literary historical trivia. Instead, it inhabits the center of early Enlightenment definitions of the legitimate boundaries of the comedic genre, including the place of the fool within it. In the early eighteenth century, comedy's terminus a quo was also its terminus ad quem.

So how does the Leipzig professor portray the first of the great Roman comedians, Plautus? Gottsched's approach is highly polemical. He takes a single ambivalent and controversial statement from Horace's *Ars poetica* (*Art of Poetry*, 19 BCE) and uses it to license a wholesale dismissal of the Roman comedian. Drawing on Horace's poem, Gottsched claims that Plautus is deserving of censure for having accommodated the "taste of the riffraff" (*Geschmacke des Pöbels*).[7] The Roman comedian had interspersed his plays with "many nasty jokes and base grimaces" (*viele garstige Zoten und niederträchtige Fratzen*).[8] The crucial point here is that Gottsched justifies his rebuke of Plautus with terminology lifted from his own discussions of the stage fool.[9] Not only had Gottsched used the language of contamination in a speech from 1729 to describe the interventions of the fool, but he also uses the same terms later in his chapter on comedy from the *Critische Dichtkunst* to epitomize the contemporary taste of "the common people" (*das gemeine Volck*). The less dignified theatergoers of his own time "always have a greater taste for the antics of the fool (*Narren-Possen*)" than for "serious matters."[10] These quotations disclose a number of the core features of the reform movement as Gottched conceived it: (1) the division between the frivolous and the serious; (2) the degradation of the existing theater as a public entertainment forum; (3) the dismissal of the fool because of his use of frivolity. The presence of the fool, in other words, is an appeasement of the corrupt taste

---

7. Gottsched, *Versuch einer critischen Dichtkunst*, 588.

8. Ibid.

9. See, for instance, nearly the exact same language in Johann Christoph Gottsched, *Der Biedermann*, ed. Wolfgang Martens (Stuttgart: Metzler, 1975), pt. 2, 136.

10. Gottsched, *Versuch einer critischen Dichtkunst*, 586.

of the riffraff and a failure to cultivate a stage culture for "great men" who must "develop their taste for German plays."[11] In other words, Gottsched characterizes Plautus's appeal in the very same terms as that of the stage fool: both are attractive to the common people by means of a low brand of humor. In his later revisions of the commentary on Horace, Gottsched makes this connection increasingly explicit, claiming that Plautus's missteps should be a lesson to contemporary actors to cease mixing improvisational jokes into a dramatic text with clear authorship.[12] Although he does not make reference to any particular contemporary stage figure, there can be little doubt he means the stage fool's improvisation.

Strangely, Gottsched fails to say which particular feature of Plautus's plays he regards as analogous to the antics of the fool and therefore worthy of censure. A plausible answer can be be gleaned from the contrast to his remarks on the other Roman comedian, Terence. Whereas Plautus sought the approval of the plebeians of his day, Terence was known for his "commerce with the most noble Romans." Along the same lines, Gottsched attributes to Terence a number of other qualities that clearly distinguish him as the privileged forebear of German comedy. His plays are "rule-governed (*regelmäßig*), and include the most mannerly comic speeches (*die artigsten Scherzreden*) full of salt and spice."[13] Terence also develops figures with "character"—not fleeting jokes or grimaces. He imitates "nature" so precisely that "one does not believe one is seeing a picture of nature, but instead nature herself."[14] As with his description of Plautus, Gottsched is here drawing on a humanist commonplace, this time from the Roman compendium *Attic Nights* by Aulus Gellius (125–180).[15] The nature captured by Terence is not nature as it is now, but as it should be according to the principle of reason. He put "a very honorable expression even into the mouth of the lowliest

---

11. Ibid., 602.

12. Gottsched, *Versuch einer critischen Dichtkunst* (1751), 42.

13. Gottsched, *Versuch einer critischen Dichtkunst* (1730), 589.

14. Ibid.

15. Aulus Gellius, *Attic Nights* 3.3. There the claim is attributed to the earlier grammarian Marcus Terentius Varro (116–27 BCE).

slaves and maidservants," a strong contrast to the lowly joking
associated with the servants in Plautus. In a final brushstroke,
Gottsched claims that "Terence knew how to make his comedies
sufficiently funny without a comic persona."[16] The comparison
between the two Roman comedians reaches its conclusion, then,
with the claim that Terence's greatness issues from his exclusion
of the stage fool.

Terence, in short, possesses attributes that are the opposite of
those of his Roman counterpart. He appeals to the upper social
echelon, uses a refined speech register, and forgoes the use of
the fool. This asymmetry is not a matter of historical fact, but
rather Gottsched's own biased viewpoint. The opposition between the two playwrights allows him to delineate a boundary
between a pristine and a defective model of comedy, on the basis
of which future comedies can be composed. The retrospective
glance is simultaneously a directive for the future; diagnosis is
prognosis. The presentist coloring of history is particularly clear
in Gottsched's discussion of the "taste of a poet," in the course
of which he argues that the poet should never accommodate
himself to "the taste of the world, of the great mass, or the
ignorant riffraff" (*Geschmacke der Welt, des großen Haufens,
oder des unverständigen Pöbels*). The task of the proper poet is
rather "to purify (*läutern*) the taste of his fatherland, his city,
his court."[17] In addition, the social implications of the difference
between Plautus and Terence are clear in a remark that Gottsched makes concerning a play written by his wife, Luise Adelgunde Gottsched (1713–1762), whose *Die ungleiche Heirath*
(*The Uneven Marriage*, 1743) appeared in the fourth volume
of his *Die deutsche Schaubühne*. Gottsched says of his wife's
play that "the moral teaching that governs there will be just
as irreproachable as the style, which tastes more of the beautiful nature of Terence than the more lowly and farcical (*nied-
riger und possenhafter*) nature of Plautus."[18] Thus, Gottsched's
own aspiration to write and publish rule-bound dramas, which

16. Gottsched, *Versuch einer critischen Dichtkunst*, 601.
17. Both quotations from Gottsched, *Versuch einer critischen Dichtkunst*, 113.
18. Gottsched, *Die deutsche Schaubühne*, 4:10.

guided both his poetological activities and his work as the editor of *Die deutsche Schaubühne*, has as its champion Terence and as its pariah Plautus.

The question which of the two Roman comedians is definitive of the comedic genre quickly became the subject of some controversy. And this was because Gottsched's effort to institute generic unity did not (and could not) decide once and for all the nature of comedy; it initiated a temporally extended project, oriented around the desire for generic unity, to which others also contributed. The open-ended character of the reform movement is clear in the alternative history of the comedic genre proffered by the young Gotthold Ephraim Lessing. When the twenty-year-old Lessing devoted his energies to a revision of Plautus's standing in literary history, he did so in the attempt to alter the direction of Gottsched's generic project. Lessing, too, believed that the path toward theatrical reform in Germany would only stand on solid ground only once generic boundaries—boundaries fortified by reference to venerable authors and texts—had been established. Like the professor from Leipzig, Lessing asserted that the imitation of exemplary sources (*Muster*) offered the best means of improving the contemporary theatrical landscape. He too devotes his energies to "collecting the rules" from the "ancients and moderns," and then employing them in the "judgment of the most recent theatrical plays."[19] In his own practice of critique, Lessing develops a more supple understanding of the implications of spatiotemporal and cultural difference for a principled account of genre. Whereas Gottsched cherished French authors above all others, Lessing believed from a young age that the reform project would profit more from cultivating a close relationship with the English theatrical tradition.[20] And while Gottsched expressed disdain for the preferences of the "riffraff" and celebrated plays putatively directed to the social elite, Lessing believed the preexisting conditions on the German stage possessed resources that, with some reworking, could alter the sorts of plays that all kinds of spectators take pleasure in.[21]

19. Gotthold Ephraim Lessing, *Werke und Briefe*, ed. Jürgen Stenzel (Frankfurt am Main: Deutscher Klassiker Verlag, 1989), 1:727.
20. See Lessing, *Werke und Briefe*, 1:729.
21. See the closing remarks in Lessing, *Werke und Briefe*, 1:732–733.

Much of Lessing's early writing can be described as the attempt to shift, often quite delicately, Gottsched's theatrical reform project so that it conformed to what Lessing sees as the immanent and imminent needs of the German stage. Lessing, in fact, argues that Plautus stood at a historical and cultural juncture very much akin to his own. And so he uses his reflections on Plautus as the opportunity to articulate his own take on the theatrical reform project. Lessing not only composed a breathtakingly erudite text entitled *Abhandlung von dem Leben, und den Werken des Marcus Accius Plautus* (*Treatise on the Life and Works of Plautus*, 1750), but he also translated, introduced, and engaged in published debate on Plautus's *Captivi* (*Prisoners*). In addition, Lessing produced a fragmentary translation of the *Stichus* and wrote a short play bearing the title *Justin*, based on Plautus's *Pseudolus*.

As a talented young scholar, Lessing realized that Gottsched's condemnation of Plautus rested on a single line from Horace, rather than an even-handed consideration of his plays. And so Lessing sought to show up his senior colleague. His apology for the Roman poet takes the form of a treatise, full of references to ancient as well as modern authorities, and as such constitutes a work of erudition much akin to the sort that the Leipzig professor wrote. Lessing even goes so far as to counterpose Horace's critical remarks—in Gottsched's translation, it warrants mentioning—with the most venerable humanist scholars, including Joseph Justus Scaliger (1540–1609) and his student Daniel Heinsius (1580–1655), both of whom defend the Roman comedian. The core of Lessing's own appraisal of Plautus is lifted from the preface to Anne Le Fècre Dacier's (1645–1720) French translation of Plautus. There is good reason to believe that Lessing's use of a French text is the attempt to marshal evidence from a source that might appeal to the predilections of the always-francophilic Gottsched. And yet the young Lessing is engaging in more than just philological swordplay; he is trying to make a substantive argument for Plautus's contemporary relevance. Among the reasons Lessing enumerates, two deserve emphasis. First, what seem at first irredeemably indecent passages in Plautus's plays are, in truth, nothing more than evidence of his transitional role in the steady improvement of Roman literature. In addition, since comedy consists of more than a single verse or passing joke, a critic must consider the compositional whole of the play before passing judgment.

The translation of Plautus's *The Prisoners*, a play that Lessing refers to as "one of the most beautiful to ever make it to the stage," aims to show the soundness of this reasoning.[22] The translation, in fact, amounts to a strategic response to the reform movement according to Gottsched's design. At the close of his prefatory remarks, Lessing asks, "Is there anything better one could do [than publish the Plautus play] to impede to some extent the present onset of backwards taste in comedies?"[23] Lessing derides Gottsched's own attempt to shape the comedic genre, while positioning his own translation as an antidote. Once Plautus is granted a fitting place in literary history, Lessing asserts, the reform of the contemporary stage will be set on the right track.

Lessing turns to Plautus in order to recraft the dynamic relationship between cultural context and dramatic innovation, especially as it pertains to the use of historical precedents or *exempla*. He believes that the critics and playwrights must draw on the past in ways that respond to the concrete deficiencies and possibilities of the present. Ultimately, Lessing envisions his own role in German theater as akin to Plautus's role in Roman history. Plautus began, Lessing writes, "to fabricate (*verfertigen*) his plays when the Roman people were still used to the satire plays that had hitherto dominated the stage."[24] The satire play that Lessing has in mind is characterized by coarse humor and design—dramatic features that Plautus could not entirely disavow if he wished to earn the

---

22. Lessing, *Werke und Briefe*, 1:766.

23. "Könnte man was bessers tun, den itzt einreißenden verkehrten Geschmack in den Lustspielen einigermaßen zu hemmen?" Lessing, *Werke und Briefe*, 1:767.

24. "Als Plautus anfing seine Stücke zu verfertigen, das römische Volk noch an die Satyren, welche vorher den Schauplatz besessen hatten, gewöhnt war." Lessing, *Werke und Briefe*, 1:752. Based on a widespread etymological practice, Lessing conflates the satyr and satire. Here he seems to mean the genre of satire, though it is likely that he associated Roman satire with the Greek satyr play. See also Lessing, *Werke und Briefe*, 1:1085.

applause and adoration of his audience. Lessing claims that Plautus brilliantly accommodated himself to the taste of the public, rather than imposing foreign standards onto it. He uses Plautus as the key paradigm for his own efforts to create a comedic genre, because this Roman encouraged the improvement of his own stage through measured continuity with the immediate past, and not an abrupt break with it. In Lessing's view, Gottsched's project is irredeemably doomed because it invests everything in fashioning an entirely new theater based upon an abrupt return to an imagined antiquity. His own vision of improvement seeks to fit with the gradualness of historical change itself.

Lessing's celebration of Plautus responds to Gottsched's dismissal of the stage fool in surprising ways. In fact, Lessing's apology for the Roman comedian is indebted in large part to the latter's use of a figure known as the "parasite."[25] First emerging in the so-called Middle Comedy of ancient Greece, the parasite was an popular stock role when Plautus had his career in the third century BCE. In the Greek and Roman traditions, the parasite was an itinerant and impoverished figure, who supplicated the wealthy to sustain himself and performed brief comic speeches, mockery, or tricks in return.[26] Gottsched and Lessing's divergent assessment of Roman comedy is attributable to the presence of the parasite as a central figure in eight of Plautus's plays, while the comic figure makes only two appearances in Terence's extant corpus of works. Furthermore, when the parasite does appear in Terence's plays, he does so in a subdued role, without many of his hallmarks—for example, his rapacious appetite and incessant begging.[27] On the basis of this signal difference, it becomes clear that we should take the parasite as a means for differentiating the positions in the debate

---

25. The general importance of the parasite in modern literature has been researched admirably. See Glenn Yaffee, "The Figure of the Parasite in Renaissance Comedy" (PhD diss., University of Toronto, 1983); E. P. Vandiver Jr., "The Elizabethan Dramatic Parasite," *Studies in Philology* 32, no. 3 (1935): 411–427.

26. On the history of the parasite, with particular attention to the processes of transmission between ancient Greece and Rome, see Andrea Antonsen-Resch, *Von Gnathon zu Saturio: Die Parasitenfigur und das Verhältnis der römischen Komödie zur griechischen* (Berlin/New York: De Gruyter, 2004).

27. Antonsen-Resch, *Von Gnathon zu Saturio*, 221–226.

between Gottsched and Lessing over the composition of the comedic genre. What else could the professor from Leipzig have meant when he championed Terence's avoidance of the "comic persona" (*lustige Person*) and derided Plautus's affinity with the bawdy humor of the lower classes?[28]

Lessing's reversal of the privilege accorded to Terence cuts to the core of his grievance with Gottsched's vision of theatrical reform. An anonymous letter sent to Lessing, the argumentative tenor of which echoes Gottsched's own statements, indicates the umbrage some took at the attempt to rehabilitate Plautus. This letter, which Lessing himself published in his *Beyträge zur Historie und Aufnahme des Theaters* (*Contributions to the History and Implementation of the Theater*, 1750), asserts that Plautus's plays are "completely and totally not rule-governed."[29] Among the supposed flaws in Plautus, the anonymous author condemns his use of the parasite as the most egregious. The condemnation is justified on the basis of the equivalence with the modern fool. "One sees clearly," the author claims, "Plautus used the parasite for the same final purpose as the moderns have enlisted the Harlequin."[30] The author proceeds, then, to champion the impeccable imitation of nature in Terence, especially its contrast to the fatuous fool in Plautus. Echoing the very same source that Gottsched employed in his discussion of comedy in the *Critische Dichtkunst* (Aulus Gellius's *Attic Nights*), the anonymous author claims of Terence that "of all the comic poets he knew how to express character so completely that if nature had wanted to speak herself, she would have had to make use of his [Terence's] words."[31]

---

28. Gottsched, *Der Biedermann*, pt. 2, 139.

29. Lessing, *Werke und Briefe*, 1:848. I take up the reasons for my unconventional translation of the noun *Aufnahme* at the start of chapter 9.

30. "Man sieht wohl, Plautus hat den Parasiten zu dem Endzwecke gebraucht, wozu die Neuern den Arlequin aufgeführet haben." Lessing, *Werke und Briefe*, 1:837.

31. "Doch hat Terenz vielleicht auch hier den Plautus übertroffen, weil Varro schon gesagt, daß er unter allen komischen Dichtern die Charactere so vollkommen auszudrücken gewußt, daß wenn die Natur selbst hätte sprechen wollen, so würde sie sich seiner Worte haben bedienen müssen." Lessing, *Werke und Briefe*, 1:858.

In his response, Lessing defends Plautus as an author who advanced a program of theatrical reform similar to Lessing's. His argument is rooted in the conviction that an appraisal of poetry—whether past or present—cannot succeed without a deep understanding of the history and culture to which it belongs. "It is the greatest injustice," Lessing asserts, "that one can commit against an ancient writer if one judges him according to the finer ethical standards of today."[32] But his defense of Plautus extends beyond an appraisal of the differences between the Romans and the Germans. Lessing seeks to undermine the alleged formal shortcomings in Plautus. Regarding the parasite, he concedes, "If one takes away the slaves and parasites from Plautus's comedies, there will indeed be few or no bad jokes left over."[33] But this would be a mistake because, he goes on, "it was his [Plautus's] intention to make this jokester (*Lustigmacher*) despised."[34]

When Lessing refers to the parasite as a jokester (*Lustigmacher*), he positions his remarks in the terminology introduced by Gottsched and thus within the early Enlightenment discourse on the unity of the comedic genre. Identifying the parasite with the fool was a position Lessing held for the duration of his career. In the eighteenth installment of his *Hamburgische Dramaturgie* (*Hamburg Dramaturgy,* 1667–1669)—written a full seventeen years after the translation of Plautus—Lessing posed, yet again, the question about the relationship between ancient and modern jokesters: "Was their parasite something other than the Harlequin?"[35] The parallel between the modern stage fool and the Roman parasite thus remained salient for Lessing long after Gottsched's death and after the early Enlightenment reform project had been surpassed by new endeavors. But Lessing's technique for defending the parasite and, in turn, the fool relies upon a surreptitious argumentative

---

32. "Es ist die größte Ungerechtigkeit, die man gegen einen alten Schriftsteller ausüben kann, wenn man ihn nach den itzigen feinern Sitten beurteilen will." Lessing, *Werke und Briefe,* 1:860.

33. "Wenn man aus den Lustspielen des Plautus die Knechte und Parasiten wegnimmt, so werden in der Tat wenig oder gar keine schlechten Schwerze übrig bleiben." Lessing, *Werke und Briefe,* 1:869.

34. Lessing, *Werke und Briefe,* 1:869.

35. Ibid., 6:271.

move, namely, the recoding of the parasite as a figure who exposes moral failures. Importantly, Lessing makes allowances for the fool, not as the champion of play, as in part 1, but instead as the figure whose risible shortcomings provide instruction. The laughter he provokes is directed at persons (in the theatrical fiction) who cannot properly distinguish right from wrong. In Lessing's hands, the stage fool does not, per se, warrant inclusion or exclusion; the decisive factor is, rather, how he is used.

One can safely presume that Lessing knew his incarnation of the fool did not align with the fool common in German theater up until this point. His early texts introduce subtle but profound recoding of the fool's identity and purpose. According to the theory of poetic innovation that Lessing advocates, such reworking of preexisting materials is the precondition for genuine theatrical reform. Whereas Gottsched thinks of comedy as a codified set of criteria, identical in every time and place, that should be realized, Lessing articulates a more dynamic and historically malleable conception of the genre. His openness to the transitional position inhabited by Plautus not only indicates his own ambition to serve as a similar bridge, but also develops a normative conception of genre that is responsive to context. He further accuses Gottsched of sealing the formal boundaries of the comedic genre too tight and dogmatically disapproving of the parasite—missteps that make him blind to Plautus's real virtues and thwart his attempt to improve German theatrical culture. Lessing still advocates rule-governed playmaking in concert with standards of generic unity. But his project is to show that the true master of a genre is he who can alter the rules within the preexisting confines, thereby developing a generic form that will appeal to audiences.

7

Sanitation and Unity

The debate over the history of the comedic genre that took place between approximately 1730 and 1750 amounted to more than a protracted deliberation over which of the two Roman comedians was worth imitating. The controversy over the parasite figure was an essential element in the project of constructing a unified comedic genre. Indeed, what may initially appear as an antiquarian quibble was, in truth, a disagreement over the legitimate form of comedy. For instance, when Gottsched dismissed Plautus for his "nasty jokes and base grimaces" while celebrating the portrayal of "character" in Terence, he simultaneously expressed his favor for a particular configuration of events in a play and, by consequence, his preference for a particular articulation of theatrical performance. And Lessing's approach took the opposite perspective, favoring a type of theater that is more accommodating of the fool. In their attempts to justify their respective positions, these two humanistically educated writers buttressed their assessments with an array of references—sometimes implicit, sometimes explicit—stretching from Horace and Aulus Gellius to Scaliger and Dacier. But we should not miss the wood for the trees; there is more at stake here than humanistic jousting. These are all authors who would have been bewildered at the use German critics were making of their arguments.

In order to place the generic pedigrees established by Gottsched and Lessing in the appropriate framework, it is important to recognize that these two writers inhabit differing positions within a shared paradigm, which we might call, in terminological shorthand, drama. In assigning drama significant analytic weight, this chapter employs the concept in a thicker sense than is usual. Drama here seeks to capture something more specific than just a single branch in the traditional triad of poetic genres alongside epic and lyric. In the early Enlightenment, drama was more than just a strategy for arranging words, personae, or events; it was, equally, a strategic use of the print medium.[1] Drama, in this instance, marks out a historically specific unity of design and matter, of the configuration of fictional elements within a material format. To be sure, the strategic importance and persuasive power of a textually framed notion of drama proceeded from the controversial status of—indeed, the desire to rein in, either by wholesale elimination or acts of rehabilitation—the paradigmatic figure of improvisation and theatricality, the fool.

By paying close attention to the interlacement of form and matter in drama, it is possible to sharpen the rough-and-ready distinction, familiar from chapter 1, between the mutable acting script and the fixed text. In the early Enlightenment context, two forces shaped the notion of drama: the avowed belief in the power of the textual medium to seize hold of theatrical performance and a novel conception of the internal makeup of comedy.[2] These two forces

---

1. For a focused study of the triadic division during the modern period, see Stefan Trappen, *Gattungspoetik: Studien zur Poetik des 16. bis 19. Jahrhunderts und zur Geschichte der triadischen Gattungslehre* (Heidelberg: C. Winter, 2001).

2. My argument is intended to lend more precise analytic shape to issues first raised in Georg Lukács, "Zur Soziologie des modernen Dramas," *Archiv für Sozialwissenschaft und Sozialpolitik* 38 (1914): 303–345 and 662–706. Lukács's essay

conspired to make the following statement become not just possible, but commonplace:

> Whoever wishes to be in charge of the stage must keep a sharp watch that no word is spoken by an actor on the stage that is not contained in a play that has been completely written down and handed in for him to censor.

> Wer also immer der Schaubühne vorzustehen haben möchte, muß scharf darauf sehen, daß kein Wort von einem Schauspieler auf der Bühne gesprochen werde, daß nicht in dem vorher gänzlich schriftlich abgefaßten und ihm zur Censur eingereichten Stücke befindlich sey.[3]

In this passage, the compositional fixity of the playtext assumes a programmatic significance fundamentally different from that found in the theory of poetry up to this point. In the first half of the eighteenth century, drama became a mechanism for rethinking and, moreover, remaking the entire enterprise of theater, from its performance culture to its sense of purpose and the social esteem it enjoyed.

In what follows, I refer to the drama-theater dyad in order to describe the textual medium's assertion of control over the theatrical performance. The imposition of a classical form—the imposition of comedy—can be understood as the attempt to use textual fixity and compositional unity to control the irruptive and interruptive presence of the fool. Comedic drama became, in short, a tool for renovating the prevailing stage culture, including its most popular avatar.

The emphasis on textuality in the early Enlightenment reform project was connected to the social and institutional vantage point of its participants. By the end of the 1720s, when Gottsched first developed an interest in the theater, he was already head of Leipzig's most prominent literary society, the Deutsche Gesellschaft (German Society).

---

also forms the foundation of another study I have found profoundly instructive: Kurt Wölfel, "Moralische Anstalt: Zur Dramaturgie von Gottsched bis Lessing," in *Deutsche Dramentheorien: Beiträge zu einer historischen Poetik des Dramas in Deutschland*, ed. Reinhold Grimm (Frankfurt am Main: Athenäum Verlag, 1980), 56–122.

3. Joseph Heinrich Engelschall, "Zufällige Gedanken über die deutsche Schaubühne zu Wien, von einem Verehrer des guten Geschmacks und guter Sitten," in Philipp Hafner, *Burlesken und Prosa*, ed. Johann Sonnleitner (Vienna: Lehner Verlag, 2007), 252–271, here 267

This collective was modeled on the literary societies (*Sprachge-sellschaften*) that had, since the early seventeenth century, devoted their energies to the improvement of the German language and vernacular poetry. Sprouting up in university towns across the German-speaking world, the learned societies before Gottsched spent their time delivering scholarly lectures and reciting original poetry, but had not yet shown much interest in commercial theater.[4] Perhaps more than any other society, the Deutsche Gesellschaft had a passion for texts, particularly ones that fit with its cultural chauvinism. For instance, a huge portion of the funds available to the Deutsche Gesellschaft was spent collecting German vernacular texts of all varieties for its ever-growing library. Already by the early 1720s, the group possessed around a thousand volumes of German vernacular poetry.[5] While this may initially sound like a small number, especially in comparison to the private scholarly libraries of the time, which sometimes reached 35,000 volumes, such collections tended to consist of Latin, French, and Italian texts.[6] The Deutsche Gesellschaft, meanwhile, collected German-language texts with an obsessive zeal. The interweaving of cultural-linguistic and national identity is evident in a poem Gottsched wrote in 1722, where he declares his goal to shine on the "German language greater rays of light" and thereby ensure that "the fatherland may rest in golden peace."[7]

---

4. Detlef Döring, "Die Anfänge der literatur- und sprachwissenschaftlichen Studien an der Leipziger Universität bis zur Mitte des 18. Jahrhunderts," *Jahrbuch für Internationale Germanistik* 44 (2012): 103–138, 111.

5. An earlier iteration of the German Society, called the German-Practicing Society (Teutsch-übende Gesellschaft) possessed more than one thousand volumes in 1723, and was steadily adding new ones as they became available. The details of the split between the German Society and the German-Practicing Society have been recounted in Detlef Döring, *Die Geschichte der Deutschen Gesellschaft in Leipzig: Von der Gründung bis in die ersten Jahre des Seniorats Johann Christoph Gottscheds* (Tübingen: Max Niemeyer Verlag, 2002), 205–227.

6. For a good overview of the library culture at the time, with particular emphasis on the private libraries of scholars, see Paul Raabe, "Gelehrtenbibliotheken im Zeitalter der Aufklärung," in *Bibliotheken und Aufklärung*, ed. Werner Arnold and Peter Vodosek (Wiesbaden: Otto Harrassowitz, 1988), 103–122.

7. Johann Christoph Gottsched, *Der deutschen Gesellschaft in Leipzig gesammlete Reden und Gedichte* (Leipzig: Breitkopf, 1732), 2.

For Gottsched and those working in his wake, the improvement of the German language and print culture went hand in hand. We can get an impression of the connection from an encomium he wrote on the fifteenth-century inventor Johannes Gutenberg (1400–1468). Gottsched takes up the theme in 1740, a good decade into his involvement with the overhaul of the theater.[8] In a speech peppered with erudition and patriotism, Gottsched claims that the fame of Germany in 1740 far exceeds that of any other nation in the history of mankind because of the invention of movable type. The core of Gottsched's argument is that the invention of Gutenberg's press was not simply an advancement in the forward march of knowledge or technology; it effected a tectonic shift in the entire "shape" or "Gestalt" of knowledge.[9] By "reproducing (*vervielfältiget*) to an astonishing extent" texts that would have otherwise remained rare, Gutenberg's invention increased the sheer number of books available and radically expanded the number of people able to access them.[10] A similar sort of *Gestalt* change was at stake in his own effort to use print dramas as instruments to alter the broader cultural reception of the theater.

The creation of drama consisted of two steps: first, the inscription of a text with edifying content; and, second, the yoking of performance to textual compositions. Taken together, these steps aimed at ensuring that comic theater would no longer address "amusements of the body" but instead gain access to "amusements of the understanding."[11] This distinction between pleasure of the mind and of the body comes from a 1690 speech by the theologian

---

8. Gottsched understands Gutenberg as the inventor of "the art of printing books" or *Buchdruckerkunst*. See Johann Christoph Gottsched, *Gesammlete Reden* (Leipzig: Bernhard Christoph Breitkopf, 1749), 125–172.

9. Gottsched, *Gesammlete Reden*, 133.

10. See the animated remarks on the triumph of print in Gottsched, *Gesamlete Reden*, 150.

11. Martin Stern and Thomas Wilhelmi, "Samuel Werenfels (1657–1740): Rede von den Schauspielen," *Daphnis* 22 (1993): 73–171, here 131. The denunciation of sensory experience in the Enlightenment reform movement has been the subject of a large body of research. I recommend, in particular, the discussion under the heading of antitheatricality in Christopher J. Wild, *Theater der Keuschheit— Keuschheit des Theaters: Zu einer Geschichte der (Anti-)Theatralität von Gryphius bis Kleist* (Freiburg im Breisgau: Rombach, 2003), esp. 167–262.

Samuel Werenfels (1657–1740). Although little known today, the Latin text of Werenfels's speech was translated into German on two separate occasions as part of the post-1730 theatrical reform movement, finding supportive readers in Gottsched and Lessing.[12] The alignment between Werenfels and the reform movement can be ascribed to his stalwart belief that once the rational faculty took the helm, "the craft of the Pickelhering" would give way to a "school of virtue."[13] The potential success of the endeavor rested on the assumption that, as the lexicographer Zedler put it, just because "plays should be of use . . . need not diminish amusement, even if this enjoyment is not due to some so-called Harlequin."[14] Figures like Werenfels and Zedler argued that a theater of genuine moral utility depended on the eradication of the purposeless and intrinsically anarchic sensory pleasure provided by the stage fool. Insofar as pleasure counted as one of the—in some instances even the primary—purposes for the existence of drama, it had to issue from the perception of "order and perfection" (*Ordnung und Vollkommenheit*).[15] Spectators would then take pleasure in plays about "the most serious philosophical truths, yes, even religious quarrels."[16] The major gamble of the early Enlightenment movement was that a rational form of pleasure could be had in rigorously constructed dramas, and that this pleasure could attract and retain a paying audience.

The impassioned sanitization of the German stage had its roots in the conviction that the theater, if properly orchestrated, could inculcate reason in spectators with unique efficaciousness. Among poetic

---

12. Martin Stern, "*Über die Schauspiele*: Eine vergessene Abhandlung zum Schultheater des Basler Theologen Samuel Werenfels (1657–1740) und ihre Spuren bei Gottsched, Lessing, Gellert, Hamann, und Nicolai" in *Théâtre, nation & société*, ed. Ronald Krebs and Jean-Marie Valentin (Nancy: Presses Universitaires de Nancy, 1990), 167–192.

13. Stern and Wilhelmi, "Samuel Werenfels (1657–1740)," 105.

14. Johann Heinrich Zedler, *Grosses vollständiges Universal-Lexicon aller Wissenschaften und Künste*; cited from the online version (http://www.zedler-lexikon.de).

15. See Johann Elias Schlegel, "Von der Nachahmung," in *Werke*, ed. Johann Heinrich Schlegel (Frankfurt am Main: Athenäum, 1971), 3:95–176, here 134.

16. Gotthold Ephraim Lessing, *Werke und Briefe*, ed. Wilfried Barner (Frankfurt am Main: Deutscher Klassiker Verlag, 1989), 1:883.

forms, Gottsched claimed, only theater relates its contents "with vivid colors (*lebendigen Farben*) before one's eyes."[17] If a properly constructed drama underwrites theatrical performance, he continues, it would surpass all other poetic forms because it provides "so to speak, not an image, not a portrait, not an imitation any longer, but the truth, nature herself, that one can see and hear."[18] He champions the theater as a passive sensuous experience that can contribute to the slow process of advancing human reason:

> The improvement of the human heart is, to be sure, not a task that can be accomplished in a single hour. A thousand preparations, circumstances, much thought, conviction, experience, examples and encouragement are required before a vicious man lets go of his ways. Enough that one throws one seed after another into his heart. In due course, the seed will blossom and bear fruit.

> Die Besserung des menschlichen Herzens ist fürwahr kein Werk, welches in einer Stunde geschehen kann. Es gehören tausend Vorbereitungen, tausend Umstände, viel Erkenntniß, Ueberzeugung, Erfahrungen, Beyspiele und Aufmunterungen dazu, ehe ein Lasterhafter seine Art fahren läßt.[19]

Gottsched believes that a properly constructed theater could attract an audience as well as a theater featuring the fool, but with the added benefit of offering moral improvement.

Before taking a closer look at the compositional standards of drama, it is worth pointing out that belief in the viability of an intellectual, text-based theater had potential pitfalls. Even Gottsched's adamant supporter, Caroline Neuber, thematized the tension between her own theoretical commitments and the practical need for commercial survival. In a prelude entitled *Die Verehrung der Vollkommenheit durch die gebesserten deutschen Schauspiele* (*Reverence of*

---

17. Johann Christoph Gottsched, *Versuch einer critischen Dichtkunst vor die Deutschen* (Leipzig: Bernhard Christoph Breitkopf, 1730), 569.

18. "Es ist, so zu reden, kein Bild, keine Abschilderung, keine Nachahmung mehr: es ist die Wahrheit, es ist die Natur selbst, was man sieht und höret." Gottsched, *Versuch einer critischen Dichtkunst*, 569.

19. Gottsched, *Versuch einer critischen Dichtkunst*, 572.

Perfection through the Improved German Plays, 1737), Neuber identifies her bind as a director:

> It should please the wise world and the riffraff too,
> And both are cut from different cloth,
> Whoever comes between the two, has no safeguard.
> The one ridicules him, if he deviates from the rules,
> The other scolds him, if he demonstrates the rules.
> The artist is left bare and driven to despair,
> When he is cursed and derided for his art and industry.
> Otherwise, I would have the desire for it.

> Sie soll der klugen Welt, dem Pöbel auch gefallen,
> Und beyde Theile sind von unterschiedener Arth,
> Wer zwischen beyde kömmt, ist schlecht genug verwahrt.
> Der eine lacht ihn aus, wenn er von Regeln weichet,
> Der andre schählt auf ihn, wenn er die Regeln zeiget,
> Da steht der Künstler blos und wird verzagt gemacht,
> Wenn man ihm Kunst und Fleiß verflucht und verlacht;
> Sonst hätt ich Lust dazu.[20]

This excerpt from Neuber describes a potential discrepancy between the ambitions of the reformers and the predilections of theatergoers. The source of the audience's displeasure, as related here, is the insistence on rule-bound playmaking—the very same rules that, according to the reform program, should ensure the compositional integrity of a drama. But the reform project aimed at nothing less than eliminating, in Gottsched's characteristically supercilious phrasing, "the nasty taste of the great mass" (*der üble Geschmack des großen Haufens*).[21] Neuber too aspired to alter what she referred to as the predilections of "the riffraff which had been nourished by earlier bands of comedians" and their "rude antics" (*grobe Possen*).[22]

---

20. Friederike Carolina Neuber, *Poetische Urkunden*, ed. Bärbel Rudin and Marion Schulz (Reichenbach: Neuberin Museum, 1997), 1:136.

21. Gottsched, *Versuch einer critischen Dichtkunst*, 116.

22. See the early letter from Johann Neuber to Gottsched in Friedrich Johann Reden-Esbeck, *Caroline Neuber und ihre Zeitgenossen: Ein Beitrag zur deutschen Kultur-und Theatergeschichte* (Leipzig: J. A. Barth, 1881), 96.

The reform movement sought to accomplish a revolution in taste through the publication of dramas. The essential first task was to translate and craft original texts that could form the substrate of ennobled theatrical performances. What reformers called a "purified" and "rational" stage culture would only come about by means of the transposition onto the stage of "purified" and "rational" dramas, which would in time alter the preferences of audiences.[23] Perhaps the most revealing testament to the irreducibly textual nature of early Enlightenment drama was Gottsched's groundbreaking publication project, *Die deutsche Schaubühne* (*The German Stage*, 1741–1745). Comprised of six volumes of translations and original compositions, Gottsched's collection aimed at much more than just finding a sympathetic readership. The anthology put into print circulation plays to reach "the clever minds, which are showing themselves here and there among young poets," inspiring them to "send [Gottsched their own] pieces." The professor promised to "make [the plays] known, insofar as they are rule-governed," as part of his campaign to "save the honor of German wit and reputation" (*zu Rettung der Ehre des deutschen Witzes und Namens*).[24] He hoped his collection of published dramas would become part of a larger circuitry, in which dramas would find readers and encourage imitation. Because the cycle gives rise to feedback loops—more dramas reaching more readers and encouraging more imitation—growth in the circulation of properly constructed dramas could be logarithmic. An indication of the publication project's overarching goal can be found in the title *Die deutsche Schaubühne*, which points beyond the printed page to the performance venue. Along the same lines, the professor celebrates his texts as vehicles for "progress" in the field of "theatrical poetry" (*theatralischen Poesie*), a hybrid denomination that absorbs the act of theatrical realization into the craft of poetic

---

23. Gottsched, *Die deutsche Schaubühne nach den Regeln der Griechen und Römer* (Leipzig: Bernhard Christoph Breitkopf, 1742, 1:21.
24. Ibid., 2:42.

composition.[25] Accordingly, the entire cycle of production and consumption demands that "different troupes of German actors" make use of the volumes "to amuse spectators in such a reasonable and purified manner" (*ihre Zuschauer auf eine so vernünftige und geläuterte Art zu belustigen*).[26] And to ensure harmony between the activity of actors and the "rules of theatrical poetry," Gottsched collected in each volume of *Die deutsche Schaubühne* six plays, "in alternation a comedy and a tragedy, always three of each genre."[27]

In light of Gottsched's identification of the bond between drama and theater as the crux of reform, it is worth taking a closer look at the internal construction of drama itself. As a point of departure, let us briefly return to the generic histories from chapter 6. Recall that Gottsched distills two different avenues for the production of comic effects, one that he considers conducive to comedic reform, and another that he sees as destructive. His diagnosis of the two Roman poets sets into opposition two methods for producing comic effects: Plautus's spontaneous jokes and laughable interludes and Terence's internally coherent, dramatically unfolding characters. The uneven appraisal of these two comic forms depends, as we have seen, on the role of the parasite—present in Plautus's comedies and absent from Terence's. In much the same vein, Lessing defends the parasite by highlighting the figure's integration within a larger tapestry. Indeed, when accused of celebrating the parasite's "shallow jokes," Lessing responds that he has only done so "with respect to the whole and in view of the relevant nature" (*in Betrachtung auf das Ganze und in Ansehung der getroffnen Natur*).[28] Both elements of Lessing's defense are important. He adverts to a superior level of integration, an encompassing plot structure, from which the parasite has been illegitimately excised. And he also insists that the parasite can only be assessed in light of the set of traits, duties, and activities he

---

25. Ibid., 2:17.
26. Ibid., 1:21.
27. Ibid., 2:31.
28. Lessing, *Werke und Briefe*, 1:870.

embodies—in light, that is, of the character he represents.[29] Lessing resists dismissals of the parasite because he believes the role must be appraised according to higher-order synthetic principles—that is, principles of dramatic unity.

How does Lessing intend the reference to the whole or *das Ganze*? What constitutes the synthetic unity that one must take into account when judging a figure like the parasite? A basic framework for answering these questions, exhibiting the patina of venerated authority, was provided by the Horatian injunction that a poem must be both "simple and uniform" (*simplex . . . et unum*).[30] The first of these adjectives, simple or *simplex*, does not refer to a dearth of meaning or sophistication, but instead to the poem's possessing a single fold, a well-defined center of gravity organizing the whole. Thus a simplex poem will also be one without narrative splintering or unintegrated subplots. Horace defines what it means to be a single poem (*unum*) rather than multiple poems smashed together in terms of the exhibition of internal continuity (*simplex*).[31] A poem counts as one by virtue of its interlocking parts—in a more technical jargon, by virtue of its concinnity. Gottsched, meanwhile, rewrites the uniform cobelonging required for a poem to be *simplex* and *unum* in terms of stylistic criteria. He translates the formula as *schlecht* [*sic*] *und einfach*, which we might render as "plain and simple."[32] Unity, for him, can be achieved by heeding principles of stylistic coherence manifest on the level of dialogic-linguistic expression. For a poem to be *schlecht und einfach*, Gottsched remarks, it must avoid intermingling registers of speech, especially through

---

29. For Lessing's suggestion that the parasite represents a character type that has become alien by virtue of changes to the social institution of hospitality, see Lessing, *Werke und Briefe*, 1:776.

30. For the relevant passage, see Horace, *Satires, Epistles, and Ars Poetica, with an English Translation*, ed. H. Rushton Fairclough (Cambridge, MA: Harvard University Press, 1932), 452–453.

31. See the discussion in C. O. Brink, *Horace on Poetry: The "Ars Poetica"* (Cambridge: Cambridge University Press, 2011).

32. Gottsched, *Versuch einer critischen Dichtkunst*, 12.

the addition of lowly patois (his word is *kauderwelsch*).[33] It should not "mix up" different elements "as if one wanted to make all the different parts of one's clothing from a different color."[34] The comparison to textiles carries significant weight for Gottsched's understanding of the sort of homogeneity demanded of comedy. He remarks that a poem "must be cut from whole cloth like a good frock, not stitched together from different sorts of colorful rags like a Harlequin's smock."[35] A drama that is *simplex* and *unum* is one that possesses internal concinnity, and thus also one without the encapsulated comic effects of the fool. The heterogeneity of meanings and registers engendered by the fool has no place in Gottsched's conception of a comedy worthy of being referred to in the singular.[36]

The checkered garb worn by the Harlequin—and by consequence the fool himself—became the symbol of the violation of formal purity. To be *simplex* and *unum*, that is, entailed stylistic homogeneity and adherence to genre constraints. In Caroline Neuber's *Die Verehrung der Vollkommenheit*, the opposition between a garment cut of a single cloth and the composite garb of the fool becomes an allegory of unreformed and hence corrupt tragedy:

It is so motley, at one point sad, at another laughable,
Eventually I have to do both in a single play,
Now my art is like the colorful frock
Of a Harlequin.

Es ist so vielerlei, bald traurig, bald zu lachen,
Bald muss ich beydes wohl in einem Stücke machen,

---

33. Gottsched's telling description, "nicht gar zu bunt und kauderwelsch durch einander gemsicht"; Gottsched, *Versuch einer critischen Dichtkunst*, 12.

34. Gottsched, *Versuch einer critischen Dichtkunst*, 12.

35. "Ein gutes Gedicht muß aus dem vollen geschnitten werden, wie ein gut Kleid; nicht aus mancherley bunten Lappen zusammen geflickt seyn, wie ein Harlekins-Rock." Gottsched, *Versuch einer critischen Dichtkunst*, 12.

36. Lessing reflects on the meaning of *simplex* as part of his protracted discussion of the philologically controversial question of whether Terence's Latin texts imitate a single or multiple Greek originals. See Lessing, *Werke und Briefe*, 6:615–618.

Itzund ist meine Kunst als wie ein buntes Kleid
Von einem Harlekin.[37]

The opposed responses of laughter and sadness here represent the division between comedy and tragedy; the fool, their unwarranted intermingling. To remove the multicolored frock and to unify the fabric of genre are two sides of the same coin—the unified coin of a stylistically homogeneous drama.

The identification of the fool as a contaminating force, disturbing the installation of rigid generic categories, entailed the introduction of a new distinction between the necessary constituents of a play and its contingent inclusions. What may look like a recrudescent classicism, especially if early Enlightenment reformers are taken at their word, in fact required a novel delineation of the boundary separating essence and accident—or, better yet, between indispensable core and accidental superadded elements. This hygienic logic first emerged as part of Gottsched's 1729 defense of the tragic genre in front of fellow members of the Deutsche Gesellschaft. In his speech "Die Schauspiele und besonders die Tragödien sind aus einer wohlbestellten Republik nicht zu verbannen" ("Plays and Especially Tragedies Should Not Be Banned from a Well-Ordered Republic"), he concedes that "deeply rooted prejudices" have made plays "such a widely despised thing."[38] Gottsched charts a path to redeem theater in the eyes of the educated elites based on the division between "rule-governed and well-ordered" plays and the "monstrosities" of the traveling players.[39] The characteristic feature that separates orderly dramas and contaminated ones repellent to the learned is "the intermixed revelries (*untermischten Lustbarkeiten*) of the Harlequin."[40] The language Gottsched uses here is informative. He introduces the contrast between a rule-governed play—an unalloyed imitation of nature as it should be—and the presence of the fool. The latter amounts to an extrinsic element, a contaminating supplement, that inserts

---

37. Neuber, *Poetische Urkunden*, 1:138.
38. Gottsched, *Gesamlete Reden*, 564.
39. Ibid., 567.
40. Ibid.

itself illegitimately. A direct consequence of the division between the rule-governed core and the polluting addition is Gottsched's insistence on the difference between the plays performed on a purified stage (*geläutert*) and the mongrels or deformities (*Mißgeburten*) of the traveling stage. His goal is to excise what he identifies as the abject intruder and thereby encourage the development of a more perfect birth. This is the logic of exchange that lent plausibility to eighteenth-century theater's founding myth, with which part 2 began.

In adducing the concept of rule-governed to describe drama that adheres to standards of generic unity, Gottsched develops a concept that will accompany him for the duration of his career and shape his legacy. The term I have translated as "rule-governed" is in Gottsched's speech *regelmäßig*, which in this context also carries the connotations of regular, orderly, and even well composed. In articulating this foundational principle for his conception of drama, Gottsched draws on the notion of a "théâtre régulier," which was common currency in the French works he was studying.[41] In his hands, the concept comes to refer to the compositional standards that ensure the highest degree of accord with reason and therefore the most proximate imitation of nature.

Drama that is rule-governed and pure fits within clearly generic categories that ensure the felicitous imitation of nature. But what does this reference to nature entail and how does it impact the formation of a synthetic unity? Consider Gottsched's definition, which can be found in various permutations across the first half of the eighteenth century: "Comedy," he writes, "is nothing other than the imitation of a vicious action (*Nachahmung einer lasterhafften Handlung*), which by means of its comical essence can both amuse and edify the spectator."[42] As so

---

41. I do not think it is possible to trace Gottsched's use of this term back to a single source. Already in 1730 (a year after the speech to the Deutsche Gesellschaft) Gottsched lists around a dozen authors who have had a strong influence on his thoughts about poetry and to whom the term could be attributed. See Gottsched, *Versuch einer critischen Dichtkunst*, 11. Interestingly, he does not list François Hédelin d'Aubignac in this passage. The omission is curious, since the influence of d'Aubignac's treatise *La pratique du théâtre* (*The Practice of Theater*, 1657) is undeniable.

42. Gottsched, *Versuch einer critischen Dichtkunst*, 594.

often, the terminology is not wholly his own. It is lifted from the humanist toolbox and repurposed. In the background is, of course, the famous passage from book 6 of Aristotle's *Poetics*, in which the Greek philosopher describes tragedy as the "imitation of an action" (μίμησις πράξεως).[43] He argues that the action that forms the basis of a tragedy (Aristotle's immediate subject in the *Poetics*) is the purposive activity of a human being through which he or she pursues an end with ethical content. Aristotle's calls such an activity *mythos,* and Gottsched, following his French sources, calls it the *Fabel.* Because an action takes time to unfold, comedy requires that its constitutive narrative elements stand in causal relation with one another, each contributing to the formation of a coherent story. But, much more than his classical ancestors, Gottsched is concerned that the syntactic array of elements making up the plot (*mythos, Fabel*) exhibit stylistic homogeneity. He insists that the contrasts among the figures—their registers of speech as well as the meanings they convey—resolve into a single moral picture. Needless to say, exactly this sort of integration was violated by the comic practice of the fool.

The concinnity of drama was founded upon the logically antecedent claim that "all the rules of the art of poetry can be derived" from the lawful "imitation of nature."[44] The suggestion that imitation formed the foundation of poetry had a pedigree reaching back to Plato and Aristotle. But the philosopheme was as much a founding gesture of the early Enlightenment conception of genre as it was a fuzzily defined term that allowed for differing positions to be staked out. At first, the foundational principle Gottsched appropriates from his teacher Christian Wolff and introduces to his contemporaries is that every form of poetry admits of greater or lesser accuracy in the portrayal of an extrinsic reality.[45] The rules

---

43. Aristotle, *Poetics* 6 (1449b24).

44. See the description of Gottsched's own educational path in Johann Christoph Gottsched, *Erste Gründe der gesamten Weltweisheit, Praktischer Teil* (Leipzig: Bernhard Christoph Breitkopf, 1762), 35 (of the unpaginated preface).

45. The dependency of Gottsched's writings on Wolff has been developed in Ruedi Graf, *Theater im Literaturstaat* (Tübingen: Max Niemeyer Verlag, 1992). On the distinction between the rhetorical tradition and Gottsched's philosophically inflected notion of rules, see Klaus Berghahn, "Von der klassizistischen zur klassischen Literaturkritik 1730–1806," in *Geschichte der deutschen Literaturkritik*, ed. Peter Uwe Hohendahl (Stuttgart: J. B. Metzlersche Verlagsbuchhandlung,

for poetic composition are meant as the best avenue for imitating nature to the most perfect degree, for creating a maximally verisimilar work within conventional parameters of decorum. A characteristic formulation from the early Enlightenment would have it that "verisimilitude in poetry and therefore also in plays overall" (*Wahrscheinlichkeit in der Dichtkunst, und also auch in den Schauspielen überhaupt*) consists in "a similarity between that which has been depicted and that which tends to happen."[46] Subordinated to a higher principle of reason, the task of the poet in imitating nature is fundamentally adjudicative and value-laden. To imitate nature means understanding the difference between "right and wrong use" of our mental facilities, to know "the nature and constitution of our thought."[47] And so the verisimilar imitation of details lifted from experience is not enough; the poet and actor must possess knowledge of how things should be both epistemically and morally, including the appropriate representation of social rank and political order, and transpose this knowledge, with the highest possible degree of fidelity, onto the poem. According to this notion of verisimilitude (*Wahrscheinlichkeit*), the fiction, including its linguistic formulation, is coordinated with a notion of genre itself beholden to an extrinsic order of nature.

The value-laden notion of imitation provided the precondition for making the theater into an intellectual enterprise, a school of virtue. More than just entertain, a poem had to unfold a "highly instructive moral principle" (*einen lehrreichen moralischen Satz*)

1985), 10–75. The longer philosophical tradition has been discussed in Hans Blumenberg, " 'Nachahmung der Natur': Zur Vorgeschichte des schöpferischen Menschen," in *Ästhetische und metaphorologische Schriften*, ed. Anselm Haverkamp (Frankfurt am Main: Suhrkamp, 2001), 9–46, esp. 41–45. The prevalent focus in literary histories on the miraculous or *das Wunderbare*, which provided for controversy between Gottsched and his contemporaries, such as J. J. Breitinger, whom Blumenberg discusses, risks overvaluing a metaphysical dimension to the early Enlightenment debates over poetry—what counts as possible?—at the expense of a shared moral foundation.

46. Christlob Mylius, "Eine Abhandlung, worinnen erwiesen wird: Daß die Wahrscheinlichkeit er Vorstellung, bey den Schauspielen eben so nötig ist, als die innere Wahrscheinlichkeit derselben," *Beyträge zur critischen Historie der deutschen Sprache, Poesie und Beredsamkeit* 29 (1742): 301.

47. Johann Christoph Gottsched, *Der Biedermann*, ed. Wolfgang Martens (Stuttgart: Metzler, 1975), pt. 2, 81st installment.

formulated in advance by the poet.[48] The principle of dramatic unity demanded a strict moral economy according to which all included elements of a play flow into the uniform communication of higher-order moral truths. The wager of the early Enlightenment reform movement—perhaps the wager that damned it to an ambivalent response over the following decades—was that such a conception of drama could also become a theater worth seeing. A decisive inheritance of the hard-edged and overcerebral articulation of early Enlightenment drama was the controversy it created over the need for poetry to be beholden to an external conception of nature. To a number of later critics, Gottsched's subordination of poetry to nature appeared so extreme in its initial formulation that it seemed implausible and in need of revision.

One heated quarrel among reformers pertained to the question of whether comedy could be written in verse or must, as the alignment of verbal register and social rank in the rhetorical tradition would have it, be composed in plain prose.[49] The controversy provided early Enlightenment critics a vehicle for negotiating the constraints or liberties of comedy as a poetic form. Ultimately, the debate over verbal structure (verse/prose) only made sense in the framework of a theatrical reform project with an insistence on unified dramatic form as its basis and principal tool. The most progressive stance was staked out by Johann Elias Schlegel, who asserted that a poet "determines in all imitations of nature how and how far he wants to imitate it."[50] He supports his view with the remark that verse (*gebundene Sprache*) and prose (*ungebundene Sprache*) are fundamentally different raw materials for the composition of poems that create different possibilities of form. Assessments of a poem must consider first and foremost the quality of its synthesis of these raw linguistic materials. Arguments like Schlegel's, while

---

48. Gottsched, *Versuch einer critischen Dichtkunst*, 133.

49. For Gottsched's remarks on the matter, see *Versuch einer critischen Dichtkunst*, 600. For a defense of Gottsched's position, see Anonymous, "Versuch eines Beweises, daß eine gereimte Comödie nicht gut seyn könne," in *Beyträge zur critischen Historie der deutschen Sprache, Poesie, und Beredsamkeit* 23 (1740): 466–485. The contrary view was advanced in Schlegel, *Werke*, 3:73–94.

50. Schlegel, *Werke*, 3:75.

still a far cry from conceptions of aesthetic autonomy from the end of the eighteenth century, show how assessment criteria for poetic works were slowly becoming attentive to the work as a unified whole. He argues that a poem's verisimilitude consists in rendering a poetic object in which its "parts have a proportion" equivalent to the "parts" of "the original."[51] This argument allows him to maintain that a felicitous comedy will also owe its success to an external nature, while insisting that any evaluative judgment must be guided by the synthetic unity of dramatic form.

What is true of a formal class also turns out to be true on a more encompassing cultural scale. Once again, the younger generation of early Enlightenment reformers utilized dramatic unity to articulate arguments that surely vexed Gottsched. Lessing challenges his senior colleague by insisting on the power of cultural difference. Against the professor's belief in universally applicable assessment criteria for the imitation of nature, Lessing argues that the developmental trajectory of each culture is distinct. He lays the foundation for his position when he argues:

> I would wish that a man, a skillful and clear-headed man knowledgeable in such matters, would judge the changes and vicissitudes of the German stage in the same way that foreigners have investigated their own, and then give rational rules for its improvement. Every people and every age has, in this respect, something special.

> Ich wünschte, daß ein der Sachen verständiger, geschickter und gesetzter Mann die Veränderungen und Abwechslungen der teutschen Schaubühne auf eben die Art wie die Ausländer die ihrige untersuchte, beurtheilte, und vernünftige Regeln zu deren Verbesserung gebe. Jedes Volk und jede Zeit hat hierinnen etwas besonderes.[52]

The task of the "composer of a comedic staging" is to adjust his poem to the "kind of risibility" in his particular culture.[53] The form of verisimilitude required by a felicitous poem depends, accordingly, "not on nature, about which we know so little; it [verisimilitude]

---

51. Ibid., 3:76–77.
52. Gotthold Ephraim Lessing, *Schreiben an das Publicum, die Schaubühne betreffend* (Frankfurt/Leipzig, 1753), 2.
53 Ibid., 15, 13.

must be derived from the stories, and namely the most common stories [of a given culture]."[54] Thus we can see the success criteria for a theatrical performance are still rooted to a notion of verisimilitude, achieved through the labor of poetic composition, but now adjusted to the peculiarities of cultural-historical context.

The modifications to the notion of verisimilitude proposed by Schlegel and Lessing amount to a reassessment of the implications of dramatic unity. Drama constitutes a (still limited) synthetic whole, not absolutely beholden to an external nature, but instead conditioned by the conventions internal to the form itself. These are claims to form-independence only possible in light of a shared conception of rule-governed dramatic composition as the key to theatrical reform.

---

54 Ibid., 16.

8

COMEDIC PLOT, COMIC TIME, DRAMATIC TIME

The previous three chapters have shown that the early Enlightenment campaigned for the imposition of a certain type of comedy and drama. On a superficial level, the early Enlightenment installation of a generically unified drama appears as a recovery of the Aristotelian standards of unity of time, place, and action, along with the Horatian belief that a poem should be morally instructive. This line of thought is entirely correct, but it is also unilluminating. It tells us little about the underlying reasons for and procedures supporting the creation of the ennobled dramatic poem. In order to illuminate the specific use of rule-governed, generically unified, and textually codified dramas as instruments for theatrical reform, it is helpful to frame the early Enlightenment reforms as a rearticulation of comic time, organized around the differing modalities of joke and character. This chapter shall demonstrate that the overhaul of comedy and drama attempted to control the temporality of playmaking.

The following pages can be understood as spelling out the implications of a formal problem articulated much later in the eighteenth century by Johann Joachim Eschenburg (1743–1820): "But in general the comic of comedy does not consist merely in individual statements and humorous gags (*einzelne Reden und witzigen Einfällen*), but rather must arise out of, and have sufficient ground in, the plot itself (*Handlung selbst*)."[1]

Let us recall that the discussion of the parasite in chapter 6 distinguished between two distinct strategies for arranging comic elements within a play, strategies that were formal and independent of the theme or content of individual utterances. Comic effects, one could say on the basis of that analysis, can be either punctual or syntactic; they can consist in momentary gestures or remarks, as in Plautus, or in narrative threads developed and sustained for the duration of the play, as in Terence. One might also think of this opposition in the more technical vocabulary developed by the linguist Roman Jakobson (1896–1982), who distinguished between paradigmatic and syntagmatic dimensions of poetic language.[2] According to this schema, the comic strategies of the fool elaborated in part 1—punctuality, detachment, encapsulation, extemporaneity—fall under the category of the paradigmatic. These strategies were also the ones that came under fire during the early Enlightenment, which sought stricter forms of syntagmatic or synthetic continuity.

In order to draw out the intimate connection between the institution of a morally univocal plot structure and the temporality of the comic, consider an example that is tellingly difficult to place in a specific epoch. Christian Friedrich Henrici (1700–1764), who published under the pseudonym Picander, wrote plays that resemble the ones composed during the early Enlightenment, but in several

---

1. Johann Joachim Eschenburg, *Entwurf einer Theorie und Literatur der schönen Wissenschaften* (Berlin: Friedrich Nicolai, 1789), 227.

2. The application of Jakobson's helpful distinction was first undertaken in a brilliant essay on comedy that has remained, in my estimation, underappreciated. See Rainer Warning, "Elemente einer Pragmasemiotik der Komödie," in *Das Komische*, ed. Wolfgang Preisendanz and Rainer Warning (Munich: Wilhelm Fink Verlag, 1976). For the original Jakobson publication, see the essays collected in Roman Jakobson, *On Language*, ed. Linda R. Wauh and Monique Monville-Burston (Cambridge, MA: Harvard University Press, 1995).

decisive ways stand just beyond the Enlightenment's ambit. More than any other author of his day, Henrici inhabits a gray zone in which Enlightenment ideas were beginning to take shape but had not yet coalesced.

Two examples will have to suffice: first, Henrici's plays do not assign great importance to genre distinctions or to their role in the improvement of the stage; and, second, he is indifferent to whether or not his published plays will ever be performed.[3] At the same time, the title page to his 1726 collection makes clear that Henrici conceives of his plays as instruments of moral improvement.[4] Their declared purpose is the "edification and amusement of the mind," a reference to Horace's dictum that poetry must amuse or delight (*aut prodesse . . . aut delectare*), a dictum that Gottsched happily endorsed. And Henrici also blames the traveling players for the current disrepute of the stage. But, by Hernici's own lights, the moral instruction his drama aims to achieve is not possible without the fool, the comic persona, albeit absent "saucy and scurrilous" speech.[5] In other words, Henrici proposes to include the fool, but in an unfamiliar and purified guise, thereby ensuring that the Horatian mandate is fulfilled. While Henrici seems to be offering a Lessing-like defense of the fool *avant la lettre,* superficial impressions are misleading, and the reasons why say quite a bit about what the unity of plot meant to Gottsched and his followers. In truth, Henrici is highly influenced by the current conventions of the Parisian stage, especially in his use of the Harlequin figure.[6]

Henrici's play *Der academische Schlendrian (The Academic Slacker)* evinces a formal design utterly foreign to the dramatic comedies written between 1730 and 1750. It is prolix, its scene changes coincide with location changes, its cast of characters is imperspicuously numerous, and its plot is disjointed. Moreover,

---

3. See the "Preface to the Reader," reprinted in Reinhart Meyer, *Das deutsche Drama des 18. Jahrhunderts in Einzeldrucken* (Munich: Kraus, 1983), 4:3–14.

4. See the title page in Meyer, *Das deutsche Drama*, 4:1.

5. Meyer, *Das deutsche Drama*, 4:6.

6. The connections between Henrici and the French *comédie-italienne* have been discussed in Walter Hinck, *Das deutsche Lustspiel des 17. und 18. Jahrhunderts und die italienische Komödie: Commedia dell'arte und Théâtre italien* (Stuttgart: Metzler, 1965), 156–163.

the fool, named Harlequin, appears in nearly every scene, typically serving as a mocking confidant and recalcitrant servant who points out the moral shortcomings of others. By and large, comic effects in this play are produced by the fool's many pithy commentaries on his master's poor financial decisions and misguided romantic inclinations. And in engaging in such commentary the fool contributes essentially to making Henrici's play into an instrument of moral instruction.

Der academische Schlendrian manipulates the servant-master asymmetry in interesting ways. In the opening lines, the master asks his servant for money, and the servant in turn does not miss the opportunity to reprimand his master. The importance of the fool in scenes like this one is not so much his role as a plot-driving agent, but instead his commentary on the actions and utterances of others. This commentary, though, is not the form of jest we saw in part 1, but instead is now part of the moralizing mission of the play. The fool is no longer transgressive, but is instead the mouthpiece of transgression's pitfalls.

A striking example of the fool's ancillary role comes at the end of act 3, when one of the central figures appears onstage with a violin, declaring his love in a fusillade of arias and *da capos*. The show culminates, however, in the fool's unsolicited commentary: "That is a twisted prank (*ein vertracter Streich*)!"[7] The scene's comic effect depends, in no small part, on the fool accusing his master of committing a prank, the very thing a fool is typically guilty of. Three elements in the scene deserve emphasis, because they push Henrici's play just beyond the cusp of the Enlightenment reform project. First, the scene contains a musical performance in an otherwise spoken play, an admixture that runs contrary to Gottsched's strict demands for stylistic homogeneity. Second, the fool makes a joke by pointing out the absurdity of the lover's song—the sort of punctual capsule of mockery that the Enlightened sought to avoid. And thirdly, the fool inhabits a liminal position with respect to the events on the stage, insofar as he acts as commentator.

---

7. Meyer, *Das deutsche Drama*, 4:90.

As in the seventeenth century, the fool is here able to occupy a position on both sides of the distinction between fiction-internal and fiction-external communication. All three of these structural features run against the strict demands for plot continuity central to in the early Enlightenment.

Some conceptual clarification will help sharpen our analysis. This chapter began with the distinction syntagmatic and paradigmatic as a way to capture the varying assessments of Plautus and Terence. These terms offer an abstract rubric for understanding a broad swath of comic effects in the theater. Writers on playmaking at least as far back as Aristotle's *Poetics* have asserted that comic effects have their home in a self-sustaining plot, as the unfolding of a story, perhaps even an archetypal pattern of stories. Others have focused on the presence of comic episodes (gestures, jokes, miniature stock scenes) that are only loosely connected to a plotline. The celebration of the *commedia dell'arte,* of *lazzi,* of English clowns like Richard Tarlton, falls into this camp. Discussions of comic theater—be they explicit attempts to think about the organization of a genre or to understand laughter-provoking techniques on their own—can thus be grouped together under the opposition between punctual and syntactic conceptions of the comic.

Ultimately, it is not important for present purposes to endorse one or the other of these species as the source of true comedy. The distinction's utility lies, rather, in its role in shaping the early Enlightenment reform process, in which Gottsched and Lessing celebrated the syntagmatic dimension and denigrated paradigmatic comic effects. The seamless concatenation of plot elements and the exclusion of sporadic punctual comic effects provided the cornerstone for a unified comedic genre. Beginning with Gottsched and continuing on to Lessing, comedy required duration, not spontaneity. During this period, punctual comic effects were treated as morally dubious, while telling a continuous story appeared as necessary for moral instruction. The reform paradigm argued that only a poem that was, in Horace's words, *simplex et unum* could count as a genuine drama.

The form of comedy thus emerged through the distinction between punctual and durative modes of the comic—which is to
say, on the basis of a conception of comic time. But why is it that
the proper temporal mode appropriate to comedy and conducive
to instruction is duration, not punctuality? The answer cannot
be uncovered by looking only at the form. It is also important
to consider the value assigned to it. The problem of how to ex-
tract an abiding moral effect from an ephemeral performance
seemed particularly acute to Gottsched and his followers, not
least because their project was a reaction to the performance
style of the traveling players, who, as part 1 demonstrated, used
encapsulated episodes of play to celebrate the ephemeral and
entertainment-driven experience of theatrical performance. And
as part 1 also showed, the various strategies of interruption that
were the trademark of the fool were not perceived as a threat to
the overarching unity of a performance, but instead a contribution to entertainment. Gottsched and his followers accomplished
a reorchestration of comic effects, which classified interruptions
as extrinsic elements, as ruptures in what should be a syntacti-
cally unified fabric.

It is helpful to recall Gottsched's typical condemnation of the
traveling players. The fool, he says, "mixes in antics"—in other
words, he constitutes an superadded element that contaminates
or disturbs the main body of the play. By recoding the fool as
an alien body, an incursion, Gottsched installs a barrier between
the plot and encapsulated moments of comic play. A proper play
demanded a higher degree of closure, of internal continuity. This
demand betokened not simply a new form, but a recalibration of
the distinction between form and formlessness, between openness
and closure.

An example will help illustrate the exclusion of punctual
comic effects. In a prelude to *Die mit den freyen Künsten ver-
schwisterte Schauspielkunst* (*The Art of Playmaking and Its Kindred Liberal Arts*, 1745), Johann Christian Krüger (1723–1750)
provides an allegorical representation of the traveling players.
The portrait he paints depends on the distinctions that drive the

Enlightenment separation of its concept of comedic form from the itinerant players' comic strategies. Krüger's prelude appears in the sixth volume of Gottsched's *Die deutsche Schaubühne* and depicts the traveling players in the allegorical form of a farce (*Possenspiel*), a preferred term among contemporary reformers for the plays featuring the fool. The following ridicule of the spectators' response illustrates the desire for a new temporal constitution of comedy:

> He who lacks a heroic spirit
> Grows tired in two minutes of watching heroes.
> He's gotten enough if he is fascinated by the hero's clothes;
> Won't the fool come soon, he asks, as soon as the hero speaks.
> The fool attracts him with a step, wordplay;
> He perks up, as soon as he sees a figure like this.

> Wer keinen Heldengeist in seinem Busen hat
> Wird Helden anzusehn in zwo Minuten satt.
> Genug, wenn ihn das Kleid des Helden eingenommen;
> Spricht der, so fragt er schon, wird nicht der Narr bald kommen?
> Der ihn durch einen Schritt, ein Wortspiel an sich zieht
> Man lebt sich gleich auf, sobald man seines gleichen sieht.[8]

The prelude introduces a blatantly derisive characterization of the spectator's desire for immediate amusement. Within two minutes, the unenlightened spectator already lusts after the satisfaction offered by the fool, who will delight with a brief gambol or prank. Krüger paints a scene where spectatorship is charged with an enlivening desire: the fool's appearance breathes life into a monotonous, even empty, experience. In this short episode, spectatorial engagement is not achieved through continuous immersion in a plot, but rather through the punctual intrusions of the fool. Krüger's own stance is made clear when he has Apollo, patron god of the arts, respond to Farce by saying, "Such riffraff only pleases

---

8. Johann Christian Krüger, *Werke: Kritische Gesamtausgabe*, ed. David G. John (Tübingen: Niemeyer, 1986), 82.

the riffraff; / He whose thoughts are noble can never be a friend to folly."[9]

The theatrical reform movement thus recasts the fool as a formal problem—a problem of plot contamination. The unity of a play is codified as an internally coherent story line, and the fool's interruptions are detached entirely from the theatrical whole to which they had previously belonged. The sort of supporting role assumed by a figure like the Harlequin in the Henrici play—pointing out the shortcomings of his master, poking fun at him—has now become illicit. All punctual comic effects are coded as inimical to a coherent dramatic syntax. For these thinkers, a properly constructed play is defined by plot design, while the fool's encapsulated commentaries and interruptions are understood as forces that corrupt it.

The construction of comedic form in terms of a tightly bound syntax—as plot or *Handlung*—aims to achieve a particular end. That is, the selection and causal arrangement of dramatic elements aim to depict vice in a morally instructive way. The concatenation of scenes, events, and utterances in the dramatic plot is directed toward the demonstration of *moral failure*. In the absence of the fool, the depiction of a moral shortcoming becomes the origin of comic effects. But because a depiction of vice must fulfill a clear function, must instruct, comic playwrights of the reform movement also developed a particular way of representing moral shortcoming. Human defects or failures are featured in plays for the purpose of pointing out an avenue toward their repair or avoidance. Thus the functional imperative dictates that the errors and vices, with which the comedic genre busies itself, must lie within the scope of potential human intervention and rectification. The human being at the center of Enlightenment comedy is, in short, *fundamentally corrigible*, for the depiction of an intractable failure would not satisfy the demand for moral serviceability. Human finitude appears during this period exclusively under the guise of avertable failure.

A scene from the end of Luise Adelgunde Gottsched's *Die ungleiche Heirat* (*The Uneven Marriage*, 1743) illustrates the stakes of this anthropological design. Known to her contemporaries and

---

9. "Ein solcher Pöbel nimmt allein den Pöbel ein; / Wer edel denkt, kann nie ein Freund der Thorheit seyn!" Krüger, *Werke*, 82.

subsequent generations of scholars as the Gottschedin, Luise Adelgunde contributed her own translations and original compositions to her husband's reform project, and wrote with a hand almost as heavy as his. Through and through, her plays are tools for moral instruction, characterized by a zeal lacking for ambiguity or ambivalence. *Die ungleiche Heirat* relates the attempt of a bourgeois bachelor to marry into an aristocratic family. Although the portrait of the aristocracy is undeniably critical, it becomes clear that the focus of the comedy is not the profligacy of the aptly named Ahnenstoz family, but the bachelor's misunderstanding of his station in life. Upon making a second marriage proposal to an aristocratic woman, he is admonished:

> And I tell you, you err. You err very gravely, my dear Mr. Wilibald. I belong to the aristocracy, and though I know that you possess much reason and merit and skill, all of this does not change my opinion that a young noble maiden cannot live happily with you. Consider only what I have already told you! If you were of the nobility, you would be my favorite among my suitors; yes, I would prefer you to the most genteel of them. Now, however, I will hold to my rule. Make someone happy who is of the same rank as you, and let your appetite for the noble maidens fade.[10]

At the close of the comedy, a member of the nobility reprimands Wilibald for the failure to recognize his social constraints. In the end, his good intentions are revealed as misguided, as blind to concrete social reality. Although some of the comedy is devoted to the wanton lifestyle of the aristocracy, its primary focus is Wilibald's inability to judge right from wrong. Conspicuously absent is a scene of final reconciliation; this comedy, as many others in the early Enlightenment, ends not with a scene of social inclusion or a

---

10. "Und ich sage ihnen, daß sie sich irren. Sie irren sich gar erschrecklich, mein lieber Herr Wilibald. Ich bin von Adel, und weis zwar, daß sie viel Verstand, Verdienste, und Geschicklichkeit besitzen: allein dieß ändert meine Meynung noch nicht, daß ein Fräulein mit ihnen nicht glücklich leben kann. Bedenken sie nur alles, was ich ihnen schon gesagt habe! Wären sie von Adel, so sollten sie mir der liebste unter allen Freyer seyn; ja, ich würde sie den vornehmsten vorziehen. Nun aber bleibe ich bey meiner Regel. Machen sie eine Person glücklich, die ihnen am Stande gleich ist, und lassen sie sich den Appetit zu den Fräuleins vergehen." Gottsched, *Die deutsche Schaubühne nach den Regeln der Griechen und Römer* (Leipzig: Bernhard Christoph Breitkopf, 1748), 4:183.

betrothal, but instead with the demonstration that all the events in the comedy are due to injudiciousness, to the failure to know and pursue the proper course of action.

A nearly constant theme in Enlightenment comedy, blindness to proper moral judgment, is portrayed with a metadramatic valence in Johann Elias Schlegel's *Der geschäftige Müßiggänger* (*The Diligent Good-for-Nothing*, 1743). This comedy depicts the repeated failures of an apprentice jurist, Fortunat, to execute his assigned tasks. He is incapable of arriving at the appropriate place at the appropriate time, and is always preoccupied with anything and everything except for what is truly urgent. The comedy depicts a constant back-and-forth between Fortunat and his family, between the voice of responsibility and the youth who refuses to listen. While they attempt to convince him to attend to his professional responsibilities, he pursues his inconsequential interests. In a conversation between Fortunat and his stepfather, Sylvester, the son's failure is addressed with the sententious blatancy characteristic of so many of the plays written in Gottsched's purview:

> SYLVESTER: You act the whole damn day like you are the busiest man in the world. But I have never seen you do what you should be doing; or finish what you should, when you should.
> FORTUNAT: Father, I never do anything mischievous.
> SYLVESTER: Oh my! Whatever's useless, that's mischievous.[11]

This dialogue between father and son presents *in nuce* the problem that the subsequent scenes laboriously unfurl. Unable to recognize the moral truth his stepfather advocates, Fortunat catches himself in a repetitive loop, from which even the most strident interventions of mother and father cannot rescue him. This failure is described by the stepfather as Fortunat's incapacity to direct his actions toward an end with social utility. His failure is one of judgment, a

---

11. "Sylvester: Ihr thut den ganzen geschlagenen Tag, als wenn ihr der geschäfftigste Mensch von der Welt wäret. Aber ich habe noch nicht geshen, daß ihr was gethan hättet, was ihr gesollt habt; oder daß ihr gethan hättet, wenn ihr gesollt habt. Fortunat: Herr Vater, ich thue nie was Unrechtes. Sylvester: Je! was unnütze ist, das ist unrecht." Gottsched, *Die deutsche Schaubühne*, 4:266.

failure to recognize things as they in fact are. His dilatory flitting about results from a cognitive shortcoming: time and again Fortunat undertakes a project he does not pursue to its completion, instead allowing himself to become absorbed in whatever else he encounters. Indeed, the very notion of a project, of a course of action directed toward a finite end, would be an inapt description of what Fortunat does in this comedy; his actions are not capable of maintaining the continuity in time constitutive of this concept. Fortunat's activity lacks the unity of a sustained action—the capacity to maintain the continuous direction toward an end over time.

The exposition of this comedy also provides an unusually complex reflection on the nature of Fortunat's moral defect and its metadramatic ramifications. In the opening scene, Fortunat expresses his desire to make a portrait of his stepfather. The conflict that plays out in the dialogue between father and son is the result of Fortunat's failure to meet his professional responsibilities that morning. Instead, Fortunat had spent his time painting Aesop's fable "The Fox and the Grapes." Aesop's story of the fox who curses the grapes he cannot reach mirrors Fortunat's own shortcomings. The irony of Fortunat's choice to create a visual representation of this fable is that, like the fox, Fortunat does not fully execute the actions he undertakes. He is blind to the meaning of the image and thus blind to his own failures. Fortunat's obsession with painting, moreover, elicits his father's criticism that such activities lack utility. Unable to grasp the moral lesson of Aesop's fable, Fortunat simultaneously fails to recognize the utility of art. His is a cognitive shortcoming: the inability to see things as they are, even in the act of rendering their likenesses.

Such a cognitive failure is encoded as a moral failure in this play, indeed as the very inability to conceive of the moral purpose of art. One can even go so far as to say that Fortunat's myriad stillborn attempts to bring his projects to fruition result from the inability to order actions and events into a meaningful sequence—or better yet into a continuous syntactic unity. In fact, one might say this comedy portrays the competition between syntactic and punctual dimensions of the comic. It is ultimately concerned with the necessity of strict continuity among individual actions and episodes for the construction of a whole. The trips to the cobbler, to the chief advocate, to his client—these are so many actions that do not achieve the necessary continuity. It is not a stretch to suggest that Fortunat is an embodiment of the punctual dimension of the comic. Schlegel's drama itself performs in its syntagmatic array the failure of the punctual dimension of the comic.

One could easily add still further examples showing that the foundation of many plots in the early Enlightenment is the assertion that cognitive weakness causes moral failure. A comedy is a comedy because it tells the story of a figure's failure to adjust his or her view to accord with things as they are. This conception of moral failure is not unique to early Enlightenment comedy, but rather depended on a concurrent idea in moral philosophy. The salient conceptual heading in moral discourse was nothing other than the fool (*der Narr*). The entry under the lemma "Narr" in Zedler's *Universal-Lexicon* evinces a number of analogues with the comedic discourse I have been discussing. Zedler refers to a fool as someone who suffers from "weakness" issuing from a lack of "judgment."[12] A lack of *judicium* or *Beurtheilungs-Kraft* translates, according to Zedler, into a "ruin of the human will," which robs the human subject of "mastery over himself." Such vices as excessive ambition, greed, and lust all result from the mind's failure to achieve proper control over the will. The parallel with Schlegel's comedy is unmistakable. Fortunat's incapacity to accomplish any of his assigned tasks results not from an alternate understanding of the good but rather from a weak mind. One might say, then, that the signal accomplishment of early Enlightenment comedy was to banish one fool, the stage fool, only to replace him with another, the moral fool. The fool, according to this design, became a figure of human finitude.

---

12. Johann Heinrich Zedler, *Grosses vollständiges Universal-Lexicon aller Wissenschaften und Künste*; cited from the online version (http://www.zedler-lexikon.de).

Here it is helpful to recall a remark Lessing makes in passing about the difference between Plautus's fool and the modern one. In his eighth annotation to the translation of Plautus's *The Prisoners*, Lessing says that the modern reader may be able to learn a lot from the parasite, but that the creation of a similar comic role under modern conditions must proceed differently.[13] He remarks that whereas the ancients could use a single figure whose actions embodied comic failure, without investing in their psychology, a fool in the modern period is defined by his *Hirngespinste*, by the illusions and machinations of the mental faculty. The fool is reconceived by Lessing in terms of his psychological faculties.

The punctual dimension of the comic thus leads a subterranean existence in the early Enlightenment; it persists as a form of failure or shortcoming. The comic antics of the fool are not simply disavowed for once and all, but instead transformed into the failures of human judgment. The effects of this covert metamorphosis are especially evident in Lessing's *Der junge Gelehrte* (*The Young Scholar*, 1754).[14] The play was first performed in 1747 and 1748, years before its publication, and in a context closely connected to the reform movement. Lessing demonstrates a keen awareness not only of the conventions governing the attempt to bring forth a unified comedic genre, but also of the need to broaden and enrich them. Consonant with his remarks on Plautus, Lessing is more interested in the logic of a gradual transformation than in instituting an abrupt break with the past.

---

13. Gotthold Ephraim Lessing, *Werke und Briefe*, ed. Wilfried Barner (Frankfurt am Main: Deutscher Klassiker Verlag, 1989), 1:776.

14. My discussion of Lessing's comedy deviates in significant respects from the sort of analyses that have been advanced in the existing secondary literature. The literature has been largely preoccupied with the question of whether the protagonist is a one-dimensional character type, as one finds in many comedies of this period, or whether Lessing articulates a fuller vision of character. This discussion dates back at least to Erich Schmidt, *Lessing: Geschichte seines Lebens und seiner Schriften* (Berlin: Weidmann, 1923). It was revived in Hinck, *Das deutsche Lustspiel*. In the same vein, see Rolf Christian Zimmerman, "Die Devise der wahren Gelehrsamkeit: Zur satirischen Absicht von Lessings Komödie *Der junge Gelehrte*," *Deutsche Vierteljahrsschrift für Literaturwissenschaft und Geistesgeschichte* 66 (1992): 283–299.

Lessing's choice of a young scholar as the focus of his comedy is not without precedent. For instance, it is highly likely that the young playwright was recrafting the stock figure known as *Il dottore* from the *commedia dell'arte*. But Lessing's protagonist Damis is not simply a copy of the misanthropic know-it-all from the Italian improvisational stage. Rather, Damis evinces a stronger similarity to the type of comedic character we discovered in Schlegel's *Fortunat*. Like his contemporary, Lessing's protagonist Damis is distinguished by an inflated self-conception, especially an unwavering conviction of his own brilliance, that blinds him to his own limitations. He claims he is the master of languages ancient and modern, ostentatiously displaying his knowledge of Latin throughout the comedy. Despite Damis's expectation of victory in an academic competition announced in the very first scene of the comedy, his book is not accorded the recognition of his scholarly peers, and he ends the play in dejection. Particularly important for the present argument, however, are not so much the plot details as their structural configuration. It is crucial for the play's formal arrangement that the protagonist's swollen self-image ultimately hinders his ability to execute his many ambitious intellectual projects. In the words of his servant Anton, "everything" for the protagonist "is a transition."[15] Nothing, in other words, is ever completed; nothing stays the focus of his attention long enough to come to fruition; the self-effacement of onrushing time is, one might say, inscribed into the structure of Damis's personality. Damis the fool lacks a capacity for judgment that would enable him to establish the continuity in time necessary to complete his projects.

One can glean the importance of this governing feature of the protagonist's personality from a series of utterances made by Damis's father, Chrysander, in scene 4 of act 3. In a heated exchange, Chrysander attacks his son's self-righteous claim to infallibility. When Damis attempts to instruct his father that Socrates's Xanthippe was not an insufferable woman—contravening a standard humanist trope—his father responds with excoriation. At the end of the rant, Chrysander remarks, "So be quiet with your

---

15. Lessing and Barner, *Werke und Briefe*, 1:159.

foolish antics (*Narrenspossen*); I do not want you to instruct me otherwise."[16] The reference to Damis's behavior as "foolish antics" is not coincidental. This was the term that everyone from Gottsched to Lessing used to pick out the fool's punctual comic techniques. This was, indeed, the very form of the comic that the reformers wished to banish from the stage. In identifying his son's academic pretensions with the machinations of the fool, the father points out the continuity between this play and the comic tradition allegedly disavowed by the reform movement. The father indicates that punctual comic effects are not a formal feature of the play—not an element in dialogue—but instead a dimension of the protagonist's character.

As the scene continues, the central importance of Lessing's use of the ostensibly discredited concept of the fool becomes clear. Chrysander (the father) goes on, "You are such a fool (*eingemachter Narr*), such a bore—don't take it personally, my son—such an abstruse Pickelhering (*ein überstudierter Pickelhering*)—but don't take it personally—."[17] The father thus calls his own son by one of the most common traditional monikers of the fool. Lessing's artful coup is to conceive of the derided figure of the fool as a dimension of Damis's person, as a cognitive shortcoming. Punctual comic elements are recoded as Damis's myopic moral vision that inhibits him from achieving a proper view of the world. The exclusion of this comic form, constitutive of the moral serviceability of comedy, thereby reappears in Lessing's comedy on the level of the syntactic unfolding of character.

The function of the comedic genre and its representation of moral failure depend on each other. Whereas this connection has most often been conceived of in terms of moral messages inscribed in dramatic texts, the comedies by Schlegel and Lessing open up an alternative perspective. They indicate that Enlightenment drama, with its close ties to the theater, became a vehicle for the *training of moral capacities*. For these comedies were not just to be read; they

---

16. Ibid., 1:209.
17. Ibid.

were to be staged, alongside other similar stagings, and through the experience of repetition, to inculcate moral truths.

It is worth emphasizing the forms of moral breakdown to which Fortunat and Damis fall prey. Both are obtuse to moral judgment because of their inability to recognize the temporal unity of moral action. Fortunat vainly attempts to sustain an intention for the duration of a project and becomes immediately absorbed in the next activity that crosses his path. Damis, meanwhile, is so misguided as to the character of his intellectual capacities that he inflates his projects to the point where he properly completes none. This chapter has argued that this particular mode of moral shortcoming itself figures as the embodiment of the paradigmatic, laughter-provoking elements, the proscription of which provided the foundation of the comedic genre in the early Enlightenment. The fool, that is, becomes a flaw internal to the protagonist: his inability to achieve the temporal unity required for a moral action. Enlightenment comedy focuses on this form of moral failure in order to articulate the negative models that will train moral capacities in the spectator and reader. What the protagonist cannot do, the spectator must learn to do. In this sense, comedy is a form of theatrical training.

The discrete events depicted onstage train the spectator to recognize increasingly complex orders of causal unity—to recognize the syntax of a unified plot in the cases where a comedic protagonist (Fortunat, Damis) cannot. This is the function of Enlightenment comedy; this is its moral charge. Whereas the comedic hero remains in the thrall of the present, unable to connect a single moment with those before or after, the task of the spectator is to link scene with scene, act with act, into ever-increasing levels of causal complexity. The spectator should see the play as *simplex* and *unum*, whereas the protagonist notices only a disconnected array. As the moral failures of the protagonists issue from a weakness of judgment that inhibits them from seeing the *unum* behind the plurality of temporally unfolding events, the spectator becomes aware of and learns to avoid the moral pitfalls by learning to string together the unity of action. The identification of moral failure as fundamentally corrigible—its codification as cognitive

weakness—translates, dramaturgically, into training for the spectator in increasingly complex orders of causal unity. The inability of
the protagonist to link event to event, action to action, and scene to
scene shows the spectator how to recognize the drama's syntactic
whole—that is, the causal unity that would allow for the potentially successful pursuit of moral ends. Damis and Fortunat are,
to borrow Nietzsche's wording, animals unable to keep a promise. Enlightenment comedy tries to make humans of these brutes,
drilling into them the capacity to sustain an intention. As moral
failure arises from an incapacity to see a thought through to its
completion, the task of comedy is to eradicate the will of such a
lapse. The Enlightenment sought to banish the fool from the spectator, just as from the stage.

Part III

Life, Theater, and the
Restoration of the Fool

Unser Theater, seit Hanswurst verbannt ist, hat sich aus dem
Gottschedinismus noch nicht losreissen können. Wir haben
Sittlichkeit und lange Weile.

Since the banishment of Hanswurst our theater has not yet
been able to wrest itself free of Gottschedianism. We have
morality and boredom.

— Johann Wolfgang von Goethe
to Johann Daniel Salzmann, March 3, 1773

So lange wir uns in unsern Originalen noch sklavisch an
die Regeln halten, und nicht daran denken, der Deutschen
Bühne einen eigentümlichen Charakter zu geben; —so lange
werden wir uns nicht rühmen können, daß wir eine Deutsche
Schaubühne hätten, die diesen Namen mit Recht verdiente.

As long as we slavishly stick to the rules in our original
compositions, and do not think to give the German stage a
unique character, we will not be able to stake the claim to
having a German stage justly worthy of this name.

— Friedrich Nicolai,
Briefe, die neuste Litteratur betreffend 11 (1761)

9

POLICEY AND THE LEGITIMACY
OF DELIGHT

As we turn to the latter half of the eighteenth century, the conceptual focus expands to include a larger nexus of issues. The following chapters are concerned, in the most rudimentary formulation, with the ligature connecting the theater with life. These chapters look at changing attitudes concerning the relationship of the theater and its surrounding environment—in other words, at the social ontology of the theater. By this, I mean the diverse interchanges between the theater and the social world around it—on individual and collective, municipal and state levels—that define the theater as an institution. The point of departure in chapter 9 is a pivotal challenge to moral instruction as the key function of theatergoing. That will directly lead, in chapter 10, to debates over the propitious social effects assigned to the experience of laughter, particularly of laughter solicited by the fool. The revaluation of the pleasurable experience of laughter in the decades around 1750 is deeply connected to the central theme of chapters 11 and 12, namely, the

establishment of a distinctively German comic theater. The identification of comic theater's salubrious effects, it shall become
clear, goes hand in hand with the claim that comic theater, much
more than its more heavy-handed theatrical sibling, speaks to the
idiosyncratic features of a cultural group. Part 3 argues that the putatively native tradition of the stage fool provides one of the foundational elements in the effort to develop a culturally specific German
theater, equal to its European counterparts.

Before shifting to the decades after 1750, it is worth taking note
that critics of the first half of the eighteenth century were also focused on the potential utility of the theater for social life more
broadly. While the most obvious evidence of this dimension is
surely the programmatic reliance on the traditional injunction to
instruct, a subterranean but equally impactful set of concerns can
be tracked in the use of the expression *Aufnahme des Theaters*.
This phrase, which became a ubiquitous and unproblematic component of the reform jargon, refers to both the *reception* of the
theater and to its concrete *implementation*.[1] Within the predominant theoretical model of the early Enlightenment, ennoblement
proceeded with a two-pronged approach. Critics asserted that if
only actors and dramatists would adhere to stricter standards of
taste, then the Germans would "soon be able henceforth to boast"
of a theatrical culture "that need not fear the harshest critique and
most unfair foreigners."[2] On the most obvious level, this remark
by the ambitious duo Lessing and Mylius is about creating collective self-identification and communal pride by improving the
conventions of stage performance. A reformed stage would, they
claimed, be fortified against critique from non-Germans, especially
groups like the French and English, who already enjoyed a proud

---

1. Two programmatic instances beyond Gottsched are Johann Elias Schlegel,
"Schreiben von Errichtung eines Theaters in Kopenhagen" and "Gedanken zur
Aufnahme des dänischen Theaters," in *Werke*, ed. Johann Elias Schlegel (Frankfurt
am Main: Athenäum, 1971), 3:251–258 and 261–298. With a greater historical
resonance: Gotthold Ephraim Lessing and Christlob Mylius, *Beyträge zur Historie
und Aufnahme des Theaters*, vols. 1–4 (Stuttgart: Johann Benedict Metzler, 1750).
   2. Lessing and Mylius, *Beyträge*, 1:2.

theatrical tradition.[3] At the historical juncture when Lessing and Mylius made these remarks, around 1750, the theater to be received and implemented was a theater built around strict standards of compositional unity and verisimilitude. In other words, it was a theater founded on principles supposedly with universal applicability.[4] Advocacy for rule-governed drama, in a time- and place-indifferent sense, went hand in hand with the desire to attract and address "learned, upright, and artistically adept men."[5] This would be possible if the theater were guided by the faculty of reason, rather than the errant and unreliable senses. Only in the years after 1750, as this universal faculty forfeited its role as the organizing principle for the drama-theater dyad, did it become possible to ask a broader set of questions about the integration of theater with a regionally and temporally bound form of life—which is to say, with a culture.

In general, the pursuit of theatrical reform was connected to the desire to establish and maintain social order. A major potential benefit of playmaking, reformers claimed, was the production of moral, and thus social, conformity. There were theological dimensions to the moral enterprise, as one would expect, but the particular power of the theater consisted in its ability to provide instruction to a collective audience. But because this model of theatrical reform wore its academic pedigree on its sleeve, it did not take long for the bond connecting the theater to the environing social world to appear unstable. It became necessary to take into

---

3. The remarks by Lessing and Mylius stand on the cusp of but do not fully belong to the emphatic notion of culture that will concern us in chapters 11 and 12. My interest in the foundational role of comparison was initially inspired by Niklas Luhmann, "Kultur als historischer Begriff," in *Gesellschaftstruktur und Semantik* (Frankfurt am Main: Suhrkamp, 1995), 4:31–54.

4. In order to illustrate this point at greater length, one might look at how concepts such as imitation of nature (*Nachahmung der Natur*), verisimilitude (*Wahrscheinlichkeit*), or genre (*Gattung*) remained central to the dramaturgical writings of, among others, J. E. Schlegel and G. E. Lessing, even after they had abandoned the Gottschedian belief in a reform program indifferent to cultural and historical differences. For a related discussion, see chapter 11.

5. Christian Fürchtegott Gellert, *Gesammelte Schriften: Kritische, Kommentierte Ausgabe*, ed. Bernd Witte (Berlin/New York: De Gruyter, 1988), 5:149.

more serious consideration, without the same dosage of scholarly pretense, such questions as the following: Who ordinarily goes to the theater? Who is the theater for? What bearing should the spectators' motivations have on its proper configuration? What community-building purpose might the theater possess?

Disavowals of the early Enlightenment dogma that "the stage is made for truth" or that plays should be a "school for ethical behavior" (*Schule der Sitten*) became increasingly salient in the second half of the eighteenth century.[6] By and large, these objections emerged out of a realistic attitude about the ineluctable fact that people want the theater "to please and to entertain" (*zu gefallen und zu unterhalten*), not just to inculcate virtue.[7] This chapter shows that a discourse far afield of properly aesthetic or poetic inquiry, namely, *policey* or the *science of policey* (*Polizeiwissenschaft*), provided essential energies and argumentative resources for altering the theater's assigned purpose. Despite its etymological links with the modern term *police*, the body of texts on *policey* was not solely (or even predominately) concerned with preventing criminality or enforcing laws, and for this reason I retain, as is conventional, the archaic spelling throughout the following pages. The primary concern of this discourse was the organization of government and its capillary institutions for supplying the population with order and welfare. And it was this concern with the purpose of government that gave shape to the epoch-making idea that the theater is a forum potentially vital to a society's well-being. The discourse on *policey* lent credibility to the suggestion that the fool could be a decisive instrument for more effectively interweaving theater and its environing social world.

The connection between the fool and social well-being is not as counterintuitive as it may initially seem. After all, the fool had

---

6. See para. 19 in the unpaginated section of fundamental principles appended to Johann Franz Philipp von Himberger, *Von dem Systeme der Polizeiwissenschaft und dem Erkenntniß grundsatze der Staatsklugheit und ihrer Zweige* (Freiburg: Johann Andreas Patron, 1779).

7. Himberger, *Von dem Systeme der Polizeiwissenschaft*, para. 19.

become the subject of such controversy in the early Enlightenment because he embodied the capacity of theatrical performance, by means of its visual and acoustic show, to place the audience in a state of pleasureful thralldom. The big shift in perspective was simply that such pleasure was, in the years after 1750, understood as potentially salubrious both for the individual and for society at large. The most famous testament to this reconsideration of the fool, to which I shall turn in the closing pages of this chapter, is Justus Möser's *Harlekin oder Vertheidigung des Groteske-Komischen* (Harlekin or Defense of the Grotesque-Comic, 1761/1777). This text, which was highly indebted to the discourse on *policey*, sparked huge interest among many of the most influential writers of the day. In this chapter, Möser's *Harlekin* will emerge as the condensation of a historically specific way of thinking through the fool's purpose. Although Möser himself asserted that his text was a defense of a very particular embodiment of the fool—the Italian-French Harlequin—I shall argue that he utilizes concepts from *policey* that, in general, were not rooted to a specific theatrical tradition, but instead asserted folly's contribution to creating a productive society.

In order to trace the bare outline of the historical process at issue here, it is first necessary to gain some clarity about *policey*. Interest in the succor that the theater could and should provide was part of a vigorous *policey* discussion that sought to delineate, roughly speaking, the purview of governmental administration. Seeking to maximally enhance the health and wealth of the population, *policey* encouraged the government to rigorously track and control citizens' lives.[8] The term *policey* had been in circulation for quite

---

8. Usage of the term *policey*, in fact, reaches back to the end of the fifteenth century. It referred to regulatory mechanisms on city and territorial levels throughout the early modern period. The formalization of *policey* into an academic discipline and its penetration of the political sphere, however, gained momentum in the seventeenth century and and then emerged in full flower in the eighteenth century. See Gerhard Oestreich, "Policey und Prudentia civilis in der barocken Gesellschaft von Stadt und Staat," in *Strukturprobleme der frühen Neuzeit* (Berlin: Dunker & Humblot, 1980), 367–379. See the concise and programmatic presentation in

some time and was in no way limited to German-speaking contexts, but in eighteenth-century Germany it became the subject of a systematic and influential lineage of texts. Its concrete ramifications were, in no small part, due to the fact that it proliferated at the universities that served as training grounds for a growing milieu of bureaucratic officials. From today's vantage point, this body of texts seems to consist of part political philosophy, part economic theory, part plan for development of a governmental apparatus, and part moral sermonizing, but a number of recurrent themes, particularly concerning the theater, can be made out.

First, some points of orientation. The basic concern of *policey* was, as one treatise from the early eighteenth century puts it, providing for the "internal and external constitution of the state in order that both remain unified in an agreeable and enduring alliance" (*die innerliche und äusserliche Verfassung eines Staats / damit beyde Stücke / in einer angenehmen und dauerhafften Alliance, vereinbaret bleiben*).[9] But reflection on and prescription for the constitution of the state was, in this case, not a matter of delineating powers and limits of the sovereign's prerogative, as had been the case in the most influential political treatises from Machiavelli to Bodin and Hobbes. Law and the lawgiver had a subordinate role to play here. Instead, *policey* focused on a different constituent of the state—its population—with the aim of developing techniques to extricate as much economic output as possible and to make society as orderly as possible. By the 1750s the elaborate tomes dealing with the science of *policey* had become breviaries containing protocols for the growth of a governmental bureaucracy, whose duties included the demand that they grant the population a "pleasurable

---

Michel Foucault, " 'Omnes et singulatim': Toward a Critique of Political Reason," in *Power*, ed. James D. Faubion (New York: The New Press, 2000), 298–325. The theme is developed more extensively in Michel Foucault, *Security, Territory, Population: Lectures at the Collège de France 1977–1978*, trans. Graham Burchell (New York: Picador, 2007), esp. 311–361. The standard-bearing study of *policey* is still Hans Meier, *Die ältere deutsche Staats- und Verwaltungslehre: Ein Beitrag zu der politischen Wissenschaft in Deutschland* (Neuwied am Rhein: Luchterhand, 1966).

    9. Theodor Ludwig Lau, *Entwurff einer wohl-eingerichteten Policey* (Frankfurt am Main: Friedrich Wilhelm Förster, 1717), 4.

life" (*ein vergnügtes Leben*). This meant developing strategies for the optimal apportionment of bodily "satisfaction" (*Erquickung*) and "amusement" (*Ergetzung*).[10] With the aim of strengthening the population and thereby also the state, *policey* works as the "active hand and eye of the lawgiver,"[11] as a set of mechanisms that subtend the law and work toward creating "virtuous and useful burghers."[12]

As a fixture in *policey* discourse, the theater assumed a distinct functional role, determined by its potential as a "means for advancement of the general welfare" (*Beförderungsmittel der allgemeinen Wohlfahrt*).[13] It is important to notice that welfare contains two sets of interlocking concerns, namely, the aspiration to maximize the wealth (*Reichtum*) of a population as well the felicity (*Glückseligkeit*) of its members.[14] According to this scheme, the theater was worth supporting because it could encourage individual and collective prosperity. While some prominent writers still made occasional reference to the theater as a "school in ethics and virtue" (*Sitten- und Tugendschule*), the overwhelming tendency was to downplay its didactic dimension and amplify its propitious effects for the spectator's body and mind.[15] The theater earned a place as an instrument for "forcing the burgher to be happy," a covert

---

10. Ibid., 4–5. Oestreich introduces the concept of *Sozialregulierung* to describe the work of the *policey*. See Oestreich, "Policey und Prudentia civilis," 371.

11. Johann Franz Philipp von Himberger, *System der Polizeywissenschaft und dem Erkenntnißgrundsatze der Staatsklugheit und ihrer Zweige* (Freiburg im Breisgau: Johann Andreas Satron, 1779), 89.

12. Ibid., 70.

13. Ibid., 79. See Joseph Vogl, "Staatsbegehren: Zur Epoche der Policey," *Deutsche Vierteljahrsschrift für Literaturwissenschaft und Geistesgeschichte* 74 (2000): 600–626. On the relationships between the *policey* and theater, see Wolfgang Martens, "Obrigkeitliche Sicht: Das Bühnenwesen in den Lehrbüchern der Policey und Cameralistik des 18. Jahrhunderts," *Internationales Archiv für Sozialgeschichte der deutschen Literatur* 6 (1981): 19–51.

14. Joachim Georg Darjes, *Erste Gründe der Cameral-Wissenschaften* (Leipzig: Bernhard Christoph Breitkopf, 1768), 363ff.; Lucas Friedrich Langemack, *Abbildung der volkommenen Policei* (Berlin: Johann Jacob Schütze, 1747), 3.

15. Johann Heinrich Gottlob von Justi, *Grundriß aller Oeconomischen und Cameral-Wissenschaften* (Frankfurt, 1759), 15.

coercion accomplished by simply watching a play.[16] Let there be no misunderstanding: the campaign for the good of entertainment for the population went hand in hand with the injunction that plays should align with standards of conduct. It remained true that the theater could and should inculcate commendable values and behavioral patterns. The important point, though, is that moral lessons no longer stood at the forefront of the spectatorial experience; they were no longer conceived of as the bridge connecting theater and the social good.

Thus the *policey* discourse effected a twofold displacement from the reform trajectory traced in part 2. The first is concerned with the integration of the theater into a program to strengthen the internal constitution of the state. The second bears on the question of *whom the theater is for*. By framing the potential worth of the theater in terms of its societal use, this brand of governmental knowledge offered an alternative approach to audience. The theater, that is, should not just aspire to reach an elite subset of the population—the early Enlightenment's "learned, upright, and artistically adept men"[17]—but should provide service to a broader swath of the population. The function and scale of the theatrical enterprise, in short, emerged here within an alternative frame.

Because the material from part 2 of this study, in general, advanced a severely intellectualist curriculum, with a near-constant emphasis on reason, it required some conceptual labor to recode spectatorial pleasure as a social good. Unsurprisingly, *policey* authors did not open the floodgates to indulgence in unalloyed folly "at the expense of some one of the virtues."[18] There remained an abiding sense that "the enjoyments (*Vergnügungen*) by means of which a people seeks to fill its empty hours"[19] disclose the ethical character of that very same people. Gratifications of all sorts, including the theater, earned a place in the literature on *policey* only because of their ability to contribute to the final purpose (the

---

16. Himberger, *System der Polizeywissenschaft*, 89.
17. Gellert, *Gesammelte Schriften*, 5:149.
18. Langemack, *Abbildung einer vollkommenen Policei*, 48.
19. Ibid.

oft-used Aristotelian term of art is *Endzweck*) toward which all government must aim. To put it plainly, *policey* argued that it was good for the state if its population had a laugh now and again, but of the right kind of show.

Even though the expansive body of *policey* texts did not show any interest in issues related to theatrical and dramatic forms, they do say a lot about what a play should do and how it should function. A play conducts its essential work as a preventive mechanism, as part of a general governmental program for combatting an array of ailments, including illness, profligacy, and sloth. The theater, that is, appears as a precautionary measure—or mechanism of *Vorsorge*—much like governmental programs such as the creation of public avenues and secure public spaces, the encouragement of certain dietary habits within the population, and the maintenance of an educational system.[20] Such preventive measures were deemed necessary to make up for a certain built-in deficiency that hindered communal flourishing. Humans stand apart from other animal creatures, who "do everything possible according to their kind and composition to preserve themselves."[21] The human, by contrast, "poisons and degrades what is his own best [interest], not wanting to content himself with mere necessity, and doing everything for his own ruin and demise through insatiable and always fickle desires and demands."[22] In addition to concern with innate moral corruption and physical vulnerability, writers on *policey* worried that human life does not possess the teleological direction and sense of moderation required to achieve a proper communal existence.

A decisive cluster of perils, for which the theater serves as a potential corrective, pertrained to an unpleasant but indispensable part of life: work. Given its overarching desire to articulate strategies for achieving the population's maximal productivity, it is only natural that the effects of daily labor on the individual figured centrally in *policey* discussion. *Policey* writers argued that the

---

20. Johann Heinrich Gottlob von Justi, *Deutsche Memoires, oder Sammlung verschiedener Anmerkungen*, pt. 2 (Vienna: Jean Paul Krauss, 1751), 65–67; Langemack, *Abbildung der vollkommenen Policei*, 35–36.

21. Justi, *Deutsche Memoires, pt. 2*, 65.

22. Ibid., pt. 2, 66.

necessity of individual and collective labor brings with it a threat to "the greatest treasure on earth," namely, health.[23] Therefore, active measures must be undertaken in order to secure the proper level of industriousness. *Policey* turns to the theater because it "knows that the human powers (*Kräfte*) cannot bear constant and ongoing exertion and that they [the powers] diminish when they are constantly directed toward one sort of task."[24] Too much work does not just cause misery, but also reduces the contribution to the collective well-being. It is crucial, then, to "grant the population rest and to try to cheer them up with all sorts of entertainments (*Ergötzungen*) so that it can begin again with renewed powers and complete its work more happily."[25] The theater counts as just such a "reward" (music and dance also earn occasional, though markedly less frequent, mention).[26] The rather simple idea advanced in *policey* texts was that only a measured cadence of work and play will ensure maximal output in the former domain. Writers on *policey* thus admonish rulers that they should not "begrudge the people a permissible pleasure" (*dem Volke eine erlaubte Lust misgönnen*).[27] Or in a related formulation, "This wearisome life is, in any case, so full of suffering and tribulations that there is no need for governmental efforts to make enjoyment (*das Vergnügen*) and a permissible pleasure a rare thing for political subjects."[28]

Ensuring intervals of play as the complement to work has the further benefit of "enlivening the health" of political subjects, by "unburden[ing] the heart from worries (*Sorgen*)."[29] The pleasures

---

23. Ibid., pt. 1, 160.

24. Langemack, *Abbildung einer vollkommenen Policei*, 30. See also Darjes, *Erste Gründe der Cameral-Wissenschaften*, 422–423.

25. Langemack, *Abbildung einer vollkommenen Policei*, 49. See also Lau, *Entwurff einer wohl-eingerichteten Policey*, 56; Darjes, *Erste Gründe der Cameral-Wissenschaften*, 429; and Justus Möser, *Patriotische Phantasien* (Berlin: Verlag der Nicolai'schen Buchhandlung, 1858) 4:34.

26. Darjes, *Erste Gründe der Camera-Wissenschaften*, 429.

27. Johann Heinrich Gottlob von Justi, *Grundfeste der Macht und Glückseligkeit der Staaten* (Königsberg/Leipzig: Verlag Woltersdorfs Wittwe, 1761), 2:131.

28. Ibid.

29. From Ludwig Lau, *Entwurff einer wohl-eingerichteten Policey* (1717), quoted in Martens, "Obrigkeitliche Sicht," 23.

of theatrical spectatorship are a concession to the inevitable suffering demanded by labor productivity, and, if properly doled out,
such pleasures can actually enhance the overall well-being of the
population. The theater thus enjoys a unique potential to enhance
the social well-being of its audience and thereby maximize the effectiveness of labor.

Mention of collective pursuits and greater welfare should, however, not obscure the power structure that supports the entire *policey* discourse. Even though models of government often became
remarkably elaborate in this body of texts, the social groupings
remained commonplace. The standard conceptual constellation can
be grasped in terms of the distinction between, on the one hand, the
riffraff (*der gemeine Haufen, der Pöbel, der gemeine Mann,* and,
with some qualification, *das Volk*) and, on the other, those imbued
with reason, education, and a sound sense of propriety.[30] The earliest *policey* texts from the mid-seventeenth century, for instance, are
built around the opposition between the sorts of entertainments
appropriate to the elite authorities and ones potentially beneficial
to the everyman.[31] In the eighteenth century, meanwhile, *policey*
texts have remarkably little to say about courtly entertainments,
aside from the occasional exhortation to avoid princely profligacy.
At the same time, the established nomenclature and disciplinary
attitude toward the less esteemed social classes remain in place.
The persistence of an asymmetrical social and political nomenclature brings with it the sense that specific allowances had to be
made for those political subjects who preferred bodily enjoyment
to the "enjoyments of the spirit" (*Vergnügungen des Geistes*).[32] As
a spectacle for the uneducated classes, who are especially suscepti-
ble to their desires and senses, the theater can pacify common men
"so that [they are] at other times more industrious and orderly."[33]
According to this model, the theater became a technology for

---

30. Heinrich August Fischer, *Von der Polizei und Sittengesetz* (Zittau/Görlitz:
Adam Jacob Spielermann, 1767), 46–47.

31. For an instructive early instance, see Veit Ludwig von Seckendorff, *Teutscher
Fürstenstaat* (Frankfurt am Main: Thomas Mathias Götzens, 1660), 105–106.

32. Justi, *Grundfeste der Macht,* 2:273.

33. Möser, *Patriotische Phantasien,* 4:33.

regulating a social antagonism. Theater was identified, that is, as an instrument for forestalling the unrest, disorder, or torpidity to which the laboring class is prone. As a compensatory mechanism rooted in the staccato rhythm of work and play, including its supporting power structure, the following question earned an affirmative response: "Do the senses not have as much of a right to enjoyment as reason?" (*Haben die Sinne nicht so viel Recht zum Vergnügen, als der Verstand?*)[34]

Against this backdrop, it is worth turning to the most influential discussion of the role of comic theater, and especially the fool, from the mid-eighteenth century. *Harlekin oder Vertheidigung des Groteske-Komischen* (*Harlekin or Defense of the Grotesque-Comic*, 1761/1777) may perhaps not count as a household text today, but it made an immediate splash among a number of eminent writers. Möser's *Harlekin* earned extensive commentary from, among others, Thomas Abbt (1738–1766), Johann Gottfried Herder (1744–1803), Johann Wolfgang von Goethe (1749–1832), and Gotthold Ephraim Lessing. Given the dizzying mix of erudition, stridency, and playfulness with which the jurist and *policey* expert from the Westphalian bishopric of Osnabrück, Justus Möser (1720–1794), imbues his text, it is perhaps unsurprising that it solicited an impressive chain of responses. But its import, I argue, consists largely in its repurposing of the commonplace notion that spectatorial pleasure counted as a key mechanism of civic engagement.

There are essentially two interwoven strategies that make Möser's *Harlekin* so unique. The first consists of the combination of rhetoric and *policey*, bodies of knowledge that ordinarily had little overlap. These traditional bodies of knowledge conspire in pursuit of the second crucial dimension of the text, namely, the transformation of the hierarchical-political valence that typically supported defenses of the theater. That is to say, as the arguments from *policey* are infused with ones drawn from rhetoric, and vice versa, the asymmetrical social nomenclature outlined above gives way to a more inclusive vision of the theatrical audience.

---

34. Justi, *Grundfeste der Macht*, 2:378.

Spoken in the voice of the Harlequin, Möser's monologue vehemently rejects the staid earnestness of his predecessors and carves out a role for the fool in the creation of a more industrious society. Of particular importance for delineating the alterations to the relationship between theater and life that took place in the latter half of the eighteenth century is Möser's claim that his text can propagate "true taste," while still calling into question one of the pillars of the reform project, namely, the idea that comic theater must educate.[35] Möser's *Harlekin* expresses doubt that spectators are actually even drawn to the theater by an "affinity for improvement" (*Neigung zu Besserung*).[36] He advances the counterclaim that a spectator goes to the theater with "the desire to cheer oneself up and amuse oneself" (*sich aufzumuntern und zu ergetzen*).[37] Indeed, if one wishes to attribute any use to the theatergoer's experience, it will not lie in any moral instruction, but in the respite it provides from the day's labor. "We are merely seeking," Harlekin says of the typical spectator, "to soothe, to calm, to cheer ourselves, and to ready the tired spirit for more serious duties."[38] The excitation of the senses instills them new "vitality" (*Lebendigkeit*),[39] which in and of itself provides "a necessary and useful motivation" for theatergoing.[40]

These are all familiar tropes. But Möser takes the defense one step further when he asserts that the early Enlightenment reformers had failed to grant the body the "open-hearted laughter" it craves and requires, thereby causing a "suppression of good nature" and charting an all-too-austere avenue for theatrical reform.[41] In Möser's apology for the fool, tenets of *policey* become the means to think through the political utility of folly and to reevaluate the fundamental distinction between the serious and the mirthful.

---

35. Justus Möser, *Harlekin: Texte und Materialien mit einem Nachwort*, ed. Henning Boetius (Bad Homburg: Max Gehlen, 1968), 9.
36. Ibid., 16.
37. Ibid.
38. Ibid.
39. Ibid., 17.
40. Ibid., 16.
41. Ibid., 19.

Möser thus offers a wholesale revision of what comic theater is for. According to this new line of thought, laughter, as a form of corporeal excitation, restores "the badly rusted spirit back into a communally useful motion."[42] Members of society are driven to the theater out of the desire to have their spirits lifted, to find themselves uplifted and renewed. The pleasurable experience of laughter, issuing in the experience of rejuvenation, is the very source of the theater's social utility. The difference between the utility founded on *policey* principles and the early Enlightenment program can be understood as the switch from service to reason and service to mental and corporeal health, itself based on the more general goal of enhancing the productivity of the population. The overpowering excitement of laughter provides an avenue to "shake the lamed and stiffened nerves of a body" back to life, a life of labor and productivity.[43]

Chapter 10 will return to the social value of laughter. For the moment, it is important to notice the rhetorical strategies Möser employs to justify the theater. Throughout the early modern period, the standard formula, repeated with almost mechanical frequency, dictated that the capacity to "delight and improve" makes poetry a noble pursuit. The word typically translated in English as "delight" is Latin *delectare*; "improve," *prodesse*.[44] "Delight" is almost invariably rendered in German as *ergetzen* or, in modern orthography, *ergötzen*.[45] We require this basic piece of etymological background because Möser repeatedly refers only to delight or *ergetzen* (on its own) as justification for the theater. That is, he places all the weight on one side of the venerated Horatian formula, brushing aside the need to instruct. And placing all the emphasis on *ergötzen/delectare* means that the sensory pleasures of theatergoing, the rapture of laughter, is not reserved for only a subset of the

---

42. Ibid., 18.
43. Ibid., 19.
44. The mandate stems from Horace and is originally an "either/or" and not a "both." In the poetic manuals of the early modern period, however, the two elements in Horace's phrase were regarded as inseparable.
45. See the afterword in Möser, *Harlekin*, 86.

population—those unable to take pleasure in *Geist*—but is understood as beneficial to all.

Möser's defense of the Harlequin with its focus on delight did more than tip the scales in favor of one side of a traditional binary. It reinterpreted the independent legitimacy of each term. For in the first half of the eighteenth century, delight had not just been coupled with its more austere partner, instruction; it had been subordinated to it. Consider the elaboration of the traditional Horatian formula in the definition of a *play* or *Schau-Spiel* in Zedler's *Universal-Lexicon*. Consonant with the mainstream of humanistic learning, Zedler defines a play as "a theatrical presentation . . . through living persons that aims at the instruction and delight of the spectators (*Erbauung und Ergötzung der Zuschauer*)."[46] The other paragraphs of the entry make clear that this definition is meant to fend off religious condemnations of the theater. He accomplishes this goal by allowing for pleasure in the experience of theatrical spectatorship only as a means to make instruction palatable. Enjoyment is permissible just to ensure the spectator will be "led to a school from which he can get the best lessons and make for himself the finest rules."[47] At the same time, delight is inscribed with a perilous limit beyond which its effects become intractable. When unhinged from the principle of instruction, Zedler claims, plays encourage moral dereliction. And so he makes clear that "this enjoyment (*Vergnügen*) may not be owed to a so-called Harlekin."[48]

Möser's *Harlekin*, by contrast, denies the imperative that instruction stand at the center of the theatrical enterprise, and instead insists on the independent value of the "noble intention to delight (*ergetzen*)."[49]

And what good is delight? Here again, a set of classical tropes are put to work, this time concerning the nature of laughter. Since the classical discussions of laughter by the Roman orator Cicero

---

46. Johann Heinrich Zedler, *Grosses vollständiges Universal-Lexicon aller Wissenschaften und Künste*; cited from the online version (http://www.zedler-lexikon.de).

47. Ibid., 1040.

48. Ibid., 1041.

49. Schlegel, *Werke*, 3:271.

(106–43 BCE) and rhetorician Quintilian (35–100 CE), physical restoration had been identified as the ameliorative outcome of laughter.[50] Quintilian, for instance, defines the effects of laughter in terms of the verbs *refacere* and *renovare*.[51] This humanistic trope is one of Möser's subtle strategies for installing himself within accepted tradition, while still pointing out an alternative (that is, not educational) service of comic theater. His accomplishment is the expansion of the renovative capacity traditionally reserved for laughter and its application to the complete experience of comic theater.

The assertion of the fool's renovative effects is, in essence, the assertion of the fundamental worth of a good laugh. In fact, Möser's contemporaries regarded his advocacy for the fool as the attempt to locate comic theater in a legitimate sphere of meaning equal to life's more austere undertakings. The man of letters and mathematician Thomas Abbt corresponded with Möser around the same time that he published a review in the Berlin weekly *Briefe, die neueste Litteratur betreffend* (*Letters Concerning the Recent Literature*, 1759–1765). In his letters to Möser and his published review, Abbt indicates that he sees the fool's monologue as a potential way out of dead-end moralizing, while still aiming to "purify taste."[52] Abbt does not want to count among the "sect of funeral singers" who want nothing more than that "everything around us, even including the Harlekin, should become serious."[53] Against the chorus of solemn reformers, he insists "the improvement of morals" does not provide the "primary intention" for playwriting or for theatergoing and so enjoins the fool to "be kind enough to consort with us more closely so that we might thereby better pass the time."[54]

---

50. On the Roman oratorical context, with attention to both Cicero and Quintilian, see Mary Beard, *Laughter in Ancient Rome: On Joking, Tickling, and Cracking Up* (Berkeley: University of California Press, 2014), 99–127.

51. Quintilian, *The Orator's Education*, trans. Donald A. Russell (Cambridge, MA: Harvard University Press, 2001), 3:64–65.

52. Möser, *Harlekin*, 72.

53. Ibid., 63.

54. Ibid.

The reintroduction of the fool, therefore, entails two distinctive features. It will, first, counter the tendency to rob the theater of all its cheer, ensuring, second, that the spectator will enjoy the show. These two steps are rooted in a revaluation of the role of the senses, no longer attached to the asymmetrical social structure characteristic of the *policey* discourse. Consider this decisive passage:

> Indeed, may not enjoyment equally count as an intention? Is there not a moral enjoyment? And if nature provides us with gratifications that we may relish, then does art alone have impure hands, so that we must be ashamed to accept enjoyment from it and instead always demand utility? Harlekin rejoices when he beholds the blessed effects of the enjoyment he doles out to his listeners.

> In der That darf denn das Vergnügen nicht ebenfalls als eine Absicht gelten? Gibt es denn nicht ein moralisches Vergnügen, und wenn die Natur uns Freuden darreicht, die wir geniessen dürfen, hat denn die Kunst allein unheilige Hände, daß wir uns schämen müssen, vor ihr Vergnügen anzunehmen, und von ihr immer nur Nutzen fordern dürfen? Harlekin jauchzet, wenn er die seligen Würkungen des Vergnügens betrachtet, dass er seinen Zuhörern austheilet.[55]

Morality and utility still have a role to play in this scheme, but they are now downstream from the pleasureful absorption the theater should afford. A flourishing theater, it is becoming clear in the 1760s, depends essentially on the communicative rapport between stage and audience—a rapport most readily and effectively secured through the stage fool's presence. Only once the fool's "blessed effects" are fully felt will the theater be able to discharge its genuine vocation: providing the audience with *Gemüthsbelustigung*, a spirited elevation of the temper, that encourages a flourishing society.[56] By attempting to replace the pleasureful exchanges between fool and audience with austere tales of moral virtue, the reform program had caused its

---

55. Ibid., 68.
56. Anonymous, "Harlekin, oder Vertheidigung des Groteskekomischen," *Bibliothek der schönen Wissenschaften und der freyen Künste* 7, no. 2 (1762): 334–351, here 339.

own demise. Assigning theatrical pleasure its due place should, ultimately, allow for society to function more cohesively.

Möser's *Harlekin* participates in—one might even argue that it instigates—a realignment of the relationship between comic theater and life. Its signature gesture is the advocacy of a more inclusive approach to the sorts of meaning that deserve a place in social and political life. Making the rational faculties the sole custodians of all good taste had ignored the good that comes from the sensory experience of delight. If only the older strategies of merrymaking associated with the fool could now find a place on the stage, then the theater could serve its "salubrious" purpose—it could "ready the spirit for more serious duties."[57] There may be no play without work, but work needs play too.

---

57. Möser, *Harlekin*, 69 and 16.

10

THE PLACE OF LAUGHTER IN LIFE

In addition to providing an essential ingredient in the recipe for a flourishing society, the syncopation of work and play also provided latitude to redescribe the activity of theatergoing. Chapter 9 uncovered the modulation of the spectator's experience in *policey* discourse and the consequent function assigned to comic theater. But the defense of the pleasure provided by public entertainment also drew inspiration from a teleological account of laughter that had found partisans already in antiquity. Advocated most influentially by Cicero and Quintilian—but with lines of filiation reaching back as far as Plato and up through the church father Augustine of Hippo (354–430) and the medieval philosopher Thomas Aquinas (1225–1274)—the gold-standard apology for laughter pointed to its restorative and rehabilitative potential.[1] Of course, recovery

---

1. See Anton Hügli, "Lachen, das Lächerliche," in *Historisches Wörterbuch der Rhetorik*, (Tübingen: Max Niemeyer Verlag, 2001).

counts as an individual and social good only by virtue of its participation in a high-order good, namely, the universally binding good
of making one's labor and indeed one's life useful to the creation
of a flourishing society. Assigning worth to laughter because of its
subordinate usefulness raises a number of questions. Is this usefulness an unconditional effect of the bodily experience of laughter?
Or is its fit for a well-ordered society dependent on the cause of
laughter, on the statements and/or gestures that solicit the spectator's response? And if the worth of laughter is determined by the relationship to its external source, what conditions must be satisfied
in order for laughter to count as societally beneficial?

Whenever the causal source of laughter comes under consideration, regulatory forces are not far behind. And for as long as
laughter has been an object of knowledge—even, as we shall see,
of medical knowledge—the distinction between its proper and improper varieties has seemed necessary. It is important to note that
the word *regulation* need not bear the burden of heavy pathos; it
need not evoke, that is, the image of pernicious and suppressive
forces. Wherever human social life exists or has existed, norms of
propriety, even in matters of play, have played a form-giving role.[2]
Chapter 8 divided up these patterns in terms of their temporal organization, their paradigmatic punctuality or syntactic duration.
But that is only part of the equation. The appropriateness or in-
appropriateness of laughter, its permissibility for certain contexts,
depends on the kind of meaning transmitted in the act of laughter.
The disciplining of laughter, including its communicative and semantic dimension, figured centrally in the decades around 1750 in
assigning the theater the appropriate seat in life.

The purpose of this chapter, then, is to trace the transformations of the conceptual understanding of laughter that emerged in
response to the theatrical reform movement. The dynamism had its
source in a ferment of discontent, as visible, for example, in a sequence of slapstick scenes from one of the most irreverent and icon-
oclastic writers of the 1770s. The scenes in question, from Jakob

---

2. Johan Huizinga, *Homo Ludens: A Study of the Play-Element in Culture*
(London: Routledge, 1949).

Michael Reinhold Lenz's (1751–1792) *Der neue Menoza oder Geschichte des Cumbanischen Prinzen Tandi* (*The New Menoza or Prince Tandi of Cumba*, 1774), are especially apposite because they portray, with brevity and clarity, the critical nodes in changing attitudes toward the purpose of laughter. As a member of what became known as the Storm and Stress movement, comprised of an engaged circle of young artists and intellectuals in Strasbourg, Lenz was acutely interested in overthrowing the existing conventions of stage propriety. Lenz deserves attention not least because Storm and Stress writers, as Goethe later pointed out in his autobiography, possessed a strong fondness for the "absurdities of the clowns" (*Absurditäten der Clowns*).[3] While this fascination is also evident in Lenz's translations of Plautus and Shakespeare, the most telling evidence is from his original compositions. There, Lenz shows a strong interest in the idea that theatrical spectatorship should work as an instrument of restoring health to the laboring body. The two scenes that will concern us here thwart the early Enlightenment demand for the internal unity of plot, and constitute a sort of scenic addendum addressing the conditions of playmaking and theatergoing at large.

Lenz's comedy is about a visitor from an unfamiliar Asian land, who has come to Germany to "get to know the mores of the most enlightened European nations."[4] It characterizes the reform movement as fundamentally geliophobic, particularly in its identification of good taste that adheres to formal rules. The final sequence pits a young academic named Zierau against his father, the mayor of the town Naumberg and a faithful habitué of the fool's performances. The governmental role of the father can easily be skipped over, given that in the preceding five acts his position as mayor is unimportant. Even so, the exchange between father and son makes a subtle political statement, particularly because the former holds an official governmental position. The son, meanwhile, plays the role of an austere academic who has "sacrificed more than three years to the muses and graces in Leipzig."[5] Mere mention of this town in Saxony

---

3. Goethe, FA I 14:540.

4. Jakob Michael Reinhold Lenz, *Werke und Briefe in drei Bänden*, ed. Sigrid Damm (Frankfurt am Main: Insel Verlag, 2005), 1:133.

5. Ibid.

closely associated with Gottsched and other reform-minded lumi-
naries indicates that the son, Zierau, functions here as a fictional
proxy for the norms and aspirations of the early Enlightenment
reform movement. And so it comes as no surprise when he bran-
dishes the three Aristotelian unities (time, space, and action), crucial pillars of rule-based dramatic composition, in his assault on his
father's theatrical predilections. The father-son exchange, which by
the second scene breaks out into literal slapstick, executes a verbal
and corporeal attack on the veneration of rule-based drama and
theater.

The first of the two concluding scenes can be straightfor-
wardly summarized. After a long day of bureaucratic work, the
father-mayor expresses the desire to go to the puppet show. His
son refers to this activity as the pursuit of an illicit desire; doing
so is like "prostituting himself" night after night in depraved pursuit of sensual satisfaction.[6] The son's metaphorical projection
onto the domain of sexual misconduct establishes a connection
between laughter and sex. In other words, laughter itself is cast as
a corrupt species of enjoyment, at least so long as it is not yoked
to external regulating instance. In response, the mayor advocates
going to the puppet show for reasons that reveal a novel notion
of theatrical spectatorship, conceived in direct opposition to the
reform movement. "Today," the mayor explains, "I have written
until I am lame and blind. I have need of a laugh."[7] Underlying
these words is the familiar distinction between the serious business of work and the salubrious pleasure of theatrical spectatorship. He even goes so far as to announce his need for *Rekreation*,
a lexical choice more unusual in German than English, and thus
bearing almost technical connotations. And he also makes clear
that this relief will be supplied by none other than the fool, his
beloved Hanswurst.[8]

The contrast to his son's position could not be more flagrant. Zierau
insists that the performances of the fool do not live up to the standards
of good taste and thus cannot be a source of genuine pleasure. In his

---

6. Ibid., 188.
7. Ibid., 187.
8. Ibid., 188.

own formulation, "Pleasure without taste is not pleasure" (*Vergnügen ohne Geschmack ist kein Vergnügen*).[9] He tries to convince his father that the key to spectatorial pleasure lies in the adherence to the rules of dramatic composition ostensibly derived from ancient poetic authorities. And with this, the mayor agrees to go to the theater in order to test whether knowledge of poetic rules enhances his experience of theatrical performance. When the father storms back onto the stage at the start of the next scene, stick in hand, he claims that attentiveness to the rules of dramatic composition, to the fulfillment of Gottsched's classicizing standards, undermined his absorption in the play. "I counted and calculated and looked at my watch," the father complains as he beats his son. "I'll teach you to prescribe rules for how I should amuse myself (*wie ich mich amüsieren soll*)."[10] The father lambastes his son for averting his attention to rules that detract from his pleasure in viewing and that disturb his ordinarily rapt attention to the performance.

The father's verbal and physical explosion, which contains a litany of insults and accusations, also points to a deeper issue. Whereas the father wanted nothing other than the restoration provided by "that chap, that Hanswurst,"[11] the son prevailed upon him to commit himself to the "improvement of all arts"[12] in the name of taste. The scene thus counterposes two kinds of evaluative criteria for the theatergoing experience: broadly speaking, entertainment and education. Spectatorship, the father insists, becomes stale and artificial when its apprehension is mediated by a rule-based awareness rather than absorption. According to the view espoused by the mayor and implicitly endorsed by the structure of the text, the early Enlightenment program blocks the potential of rehabilitation from the day's labor and means having one's "pleasure ruined."[13] In the words of another of Lenz's comedies, "Does one always have to learn something? Isn't it enough if we amuse ourselves?"[14] Entertainment, that is, is presented as a

---

9. Ibid.
10. Ibid., 190.
11. Ibid., 188.
12. Ibid., 134.
13. Ibid., 190.
14. Ibid., 199.

value that alone justifies the theater and its audience, regardless of a performance's educational utility.

Before abandoning this example, a final point must be made concerning the confrontation between father and son. The final scenes of Lenz's comedy can also be read as a reversal of the symbolic ritual that, according to the reform movement's founding myth, had inaugurated a new way of conducting the business of theater. Rather than driving the fool from the stage in the name of *prodesse*—of improving taste by means of an educational mandate—here the representative of the body politic, championing a principle of *delectare*, expels the agelastic advocate of reform. Thus Lenz's scene presents us with the dramatized installation of the new conception of the theater—not one oriented toward generic and compositional unity, but toward the solicitation of laughter, culminating in individual restoration and collective coalescence. This sequence of scenes provides a verbal and corporeal agon that dramatizes the desire for a rupture with the key aspects of the reform program. Of particular importance for the following discussion is the link between theatrical spectatorship and pleasure, especially the pleasure of the physical act of laughter. So what are the lines of filiation and transformation that made it possible for the final scenes from Lenz's comedy to assume the shape they did? How could rule-governed drama come to seem anathema to the rapt enjoyment of spectatorship? These questions demand historical excavation.

Even though Lenz depicts the early Enlightenment program as the enemy of laughter, it would be a misrepresentation to call early Enlightenment writers fundamentally agelastic or geliophobic. Reform-minded writers did not proscribe all forms of laughter. Instead, they sought to articulate its rationally controlled and teleologically directed modalities by restricting the pool of acceptable causes.

The extreme demand for composure and deep misgivings about the explosion of laughter are nowhere more evident than in the sudden appearance in the first half of the eighteenth century of the *rührendes Lustspiel* or *weinerliches Lustspiel*, both of which stood in close proximity to the French *comédie larmonyante*. All three terms lack ancient pedigree and run athwart the traditional alignment of tragedy with tears and comedy with laughter. Even the mere appearance of these genres counted as an attempt to imbue comedy with the seriousness characteristic of the tragic genre and thereby to appropriate some of its esteem as well.[15] The idea of a comedy more tearful than hilarious found its most prominent champion in Christian Fürchtegott Gellert (1715–1769), a widely revered professor and philosopher in Leipzig. In addition to publishing plays that are, at least from our historical vantage point, barely recognizable as comedies except for their title pages and betrothal narratives, Gellert also authored a tractate in Latin on the virtues of a mirthless species of comedy entitled *Pro Comoedia Commovente*, which Lessing translated into German.[16] While the text bears all the familiar trappings of self-legitimization via classical references, its most revealing argumentative maneuver is the distinction between two forms of risibility: "a laughter aloud" and a laughter that takes place in the "innermost of the heart."[17] The seemingly preposterous classification of an inaudible species of laughter, which may have been intended as an echo of the medieval Christian trope of a *risus cordis*, functions in Gellert's apology as an attempt to fold comedy and tragedy into a single genre.[18] He sought to enhance the status of comedy by incorporating tragedy's gravitas while still allowing genre-specific, thematic foci. Gellert

---

15. Lessing characterizes the emergence of bourgeois tragedy and sentimental comedy as twin enterprises, based on the reduction in rank of the first and promotion in the second. See the introductory remarks in Gotthold Ephraim Lessing, *Werke und Briefe*, ed. Jürgen Stenzel (Frankfurt am Main: Deutscher Klassiker Verlag, 1989), 3:264–267.

16. The entire text has been reprinted in Christian Fürchtegott Gellert, *Gesammelte Schriften: Kritische, Kommentierte Ausgabe*, ed. Bernd Witte (Berlin/ New York: De Gruyter, 1988), 5:46–173.

17. Gellert, *Gesammelte Schriften*, 5:149.

18. See Marc Föcking, "'Qui habitat in caelis irrideibit eos': Paradiesisches und irdisches Lachen in Dantes *Divina Commedia*," in *Paradies Topographien der Sehnsucht, ed.* Claudia Benthien and Manuela Gerlof (Cologne: Böhlau Verlag, 2010), 77–98.

believes that, absent solicitations of laughter, such a comedy could provide the spectator with "a more serious emotion" (*Gemüths-bewegung*) and a "more composed gratification" (*eine gesetztere Freude*).[19] Brushing aside the explosive moment of laughter, which sets the body into wild motion and transgresses its boundaries, Gellert here imagines a perfectly continent and internally efficacious variety of laughter. Such laughter is not externalized; instead, it proceeds along a purely internal communicative channel that, by avoiding potential interruptions through the occasional audience guffaw, can relate issues of enhanced moral significance. This conception of laughter fit together with the conception of an internally unified comedic form that stood at the center of part 2.[20]

The appeal to a silent form of laughter rested on a division between the upper section of the body, home to positively valorized intellectual and emotional capacities, and the lower domain, where fleeting and compulsive desire is born. Accordingly, Gellert imagines a comedy without appeal to those "who wish to shake their bellies with a heavy laughter."[21] At the same time, the elimination of an undesirable corporeal response is part of an exercise in cultural aggrandizement, of altering the status of the genre by attracting a select audience. The shift in status demanded that comedy no longer cater to the predilections of the lower social classes, which supposedly cannot discriminate among varieties of laughter in a way that accords with the pedagogical mission of the theater.[22] Among writers from the first half of the eighteenth century, there was a widespread view that the sort of laughter enjoyed by the "ignorant rabble" appeals only to "the amusements of the

19. Gellert, *Gesammelte Schriften*, 5:149. For an important reiteration of the same distinction, buttressed by physiological assertions, see Carl Friedrich Flögel, *Geschichte der komischen Literatur* (Liegnitz/Leipzig: David Sieger, 1784), 1:31–33.

20. In this context, Lessing's observations from the *Hamburgische Dramaturgie* are worthy of close consideration. See Lessing, *Werke und Briefe*, 6:479–536.

21. Lessing, *Werke und Briefe*, 5:149.

22. A representative statement linking the reform movement and the disparagement of the baser predilections of the group identified as the rabble: "Die Poesie ist eine Kunst so der Wahrheit und Tugend viel Dienste thun kann, wenn sie in den Händen eines verständigen und redlichen Bürgers ist, und mehr nach den Regeln der Weltweisheit, als nach dem verderbten Geschmacke des unverständigen Pöbels eingerichtet wird." See Johann Christoph Gottsched, *Der Biedermann*, ed. Wolfgang Martens (Stuttgart: Metzler, 1975), pt. 2, 123.

body," while paying little heed to the more noble "amusements of the understanding."[23] The power of this distinction rested on its crisscrossing of physiological and anthropological divisions with stereotypical gestures of social condescension. These dimensions coincide in their ahistorical character. Just as the dispositions of the upper and lower domains of the body are unchanging, so too is the riffraff forever driven by the need for base and fleeting amusement. Improvement of the meanings transmitted in comedy fit together with an improvement of the social groups addressed by the theater.

Although Gellert's fantasy of a "laughter of the heart" undoubtedly marks out an extreme position, it points to a general trend that can also be noticed in more moderate positions. The tactical gambit of the reform program rested on the belief that "a comic object" (*ein komischer Gegenstand*) should not be unconditionally identified with "that which has something risible about it" (*etwas Lächerliches an sich*).[24] In other words, the goal was to draw a qualitative distinction between the broad class of things capable of soliciting laughter and the genuinely comical. Lessing, for instance, repeatedly expresses a cautious aversion to the corporeal expression of laughter, including in the introduction to his 1760 translation of the French lumière Denis Diderot (1713–1784), where he remarks, "The truly risible (*das wahre Lächerliche*) is not that which makes one laugh the loudest; and imperfections (*Ungereimtheiten*) should not just set our lungs in motion."[25] Insofar as laughter has a role to play, it must, rather, be subservient to a training in the recognition of moral failures and thus a stepping stone along the avenue of moral improvement. In much the same vein, Lessing elsewhere says that the "true universal utility" (*wahrer allgemeiner Nutzen*) of comedy

---

23. Martin Stern and Thomas Wilhelmi, "Samuel Werenfels (1657–1740): Rede von den Schauspielen," *Daphnis* 22 (1993): 131. Gellert taught at the university in Leipzig beginning in 1745. Despite quibbles and minor differences, Gellert undoubtedly participated in the same general movement, characterized by common concerns and reform aspirations, with his colleague at the university, Gottsched.

24. Christian Ernst Schenk, *Komisches Theater* (Breslau: Carl Gottfried Meyer, 1759), 51. This rather unknown text by Schenk also contains the lengthiest programmatic elaboration of comedy in the terms set forth by Gellert. See pp. 51–88 in the same volume.

25. Gotthold Ephraim Lessing, *Werke und Briefe*, ed. Wilfried Barner (Frankfurt am Main: Deutscher Klassiker Verlag, 1989), 5/1:16.

"lies in laughter itself, in training this capacity to detect the risible (*das Lächerliche*)."[26] These remarks delineate a qualitative boundary between the expressive, corporeal dimension of laughter—its volume or intensity—and its long-lasting, ratiocinative repercussions. The distinction between these two temporalities was based on the hierarchical rank of the faculty of reason above the senses, passions, and affects. Lessing, for one, identifies the absence of a substantive connection to more epistemically and morally focused ratiocination as the source of the overwhelming mediocrity in mid-eighteenth-century German theater. As he observes in his *Hamburgische Dramaturgie*, whoever "wants more than to convulse with his belly, whoever also wants to laugh with the understanding (*mit dem Verstande lachen will*)," abandons the theater after a single visit.[27] We can legitimately take Lessing's diagnosis from 1768 as one of the culminating gestures in an epochal project of cultivating a species of laughter harnessed by reason and thus capable of improving aesthetic taste in general and the theater in particular. It does not take much imagination to hear an echo of Lessing's remark in Lenz's play, particularly in the association of laughter with prostitution.

But what does it mean to "laugh with the understanding," to imbue laughter with a rational content and purpose? To answer this question and round out the picture of the early Enlightenment, it is helpful to consider another text: the most protracted attempt to craft a regime of laughter compatible with the "purification of taste."[28] In the treatise *Gedancken von Schertzen* (*Reflections on Jokes*, 1744), by Georg Friedrich Meier (1718–1777), reason

---

26. "Ihr wahrer allgemeiner Nutzen liegt in dem Lachen selbst; in der Überung dieser Fähigkeit das Lächerliche zu bemerken." Lessing, *Werke und Briefe*, 6:323.
    27. Lessing, *Werke und Briefe*, 6:656.
    28. The phrase is used explicitly and programmatically in the treatise I am discussing. See Georg Friedrich Meier, *Gedancken von Schertzen* (Halle: Carl Hermann Hemmerde, 1744), 2. As a student of Baumgarten, Meier's conception of taste differs in certain respects from Gottsched's. Meier insists on an impermeable boundary separating the higher and lower mental faculties, and relegates taste to judgments concerning the perfection—that is, the beauty—of objects that humans become aware of via their lower faculties, in this case the senses.

serves as the tribunal over laughter. A student, translator, and biographer of the man often referred to as the pioneer of the science of aesthetics in Germany, Alexander Gottlieb Baumgarten (1714–1762), Meier was a close observer of the contemporary debates over the possibility of a philosophically grounded demonstration of the rules of artistic, especially poetic, production. Jokes belong to the domain of taste because their acceptable forms are all, in Meier's view, verbal formulations; yet words are spoken and understood with the lower mental faculties, the senses. Since he structures his text more like a rhetorical manual than a commentary on artworks, its task is to categorize, explain, and provide rules for the construction of laughter-provoking statements in much the same way that rhetoric had traditionally treated persuasion. At issue in the treatise is a conception of the joke that is much broader than an ossified verbal formula, incorporating, even if often dismissively, almost all spontaneous as well as rehearsed verbal and gestural acts that can call forth laughter.

The treatise's structuring opposition between jokes in accord with and those contrary to taste falls out along lines defined by the distinction between, roughly speaking, the deliberations of the mind and the disinhibitions of the body. Again, physiological-anthropological distinctions intersect with social ones. For the division between the upper and lower domains of the body is supported, in turn, by reference to the erratic antics of the fool. The following passage warrants being quoted in its entirety, since it cuts to the heart of the opposition between, on the negative side, the irrational and basely instrumental machinations of the body and, more affirmatively, the cool and controlled activity of reason:

> Whoever makes his body, by means of industry and practice, into an instrument for the amusement of others, deserves the unequivocal disdain of rational people. Jokes that are related with incongruous and extreme distortions of the face and inhuman twisting of its parts belong on the stage. And even there, they have already been chased away. A speech that is related with a grimaced face is a joke that belongs to a vulgar and raffish taste.

Wer seinen Körper durch Fleiß und Uebung zu einem Werckzeuge, andere Leute zu belustigen, macht, verdient ohnfehlbar die Verachtung vernünftiger Leute. Schertze, die mit ungereimten und ausserordentlichen Verzuckungen der Gesichtszüge, und unmenschlichen Verdrehungen der Teile desselben, vorgetragen werden, gehören auf die Schaubühne, und da hat man sie schon weg gepeischt. Eine Rede, die mit einem Fratzen-Gesichte vorgetragen wird, ist ein Schertz der für einen groben und pöbelhaften Geschmack gehört.[29]

The background to this passage—much like the scenes from Lenz's *Der neue Menoza*—is, of course, the notorious story of Caroline Neuber's banishment of the fool, the founding myth of the Enlightenment reform movement. Meier understands his own text as offering a conception of laughter that does not depend on gesticulations and wordplay, but that culminates in an act of ratiocination. The characteristic comic strategies of the fool treat laughter as an end in itself, as a self-fulfilling species of sensory pleasure, whereas a more rational mode of the comic treats laughter as subordinate to higher-order cognitive activities. The form of laughter deserving of approbation, meanwhile, is founded on and culminates in what the treatise calls "wit" or *Witz*. A joke in good taste depends on the speaker's ability to "to test and to judge" the sources and implications of a joke before they are being made; it requires deliberation and patience, not spontaneity and celerity.[30] If the rational power of wit is in command, a joke will depend on comparisons among mental representations, on the discovery and elaboration of the way things stand objectively.[31] A joke in good taste is, then, one that unearths unexpected relationships among mental representations (*Vorstellungen*) of objects; a joke is an instrument for fabricating new knowledge. According to this scheme, joking may come to the surface in speech and therefore count as a sensory experience, but its ultimate worth is dictated by subservience to higher-order forms of reasoning. Because wit allows for crafting combinations between seemingly disparate or disanalogous entities, laughter expresses the listener's discovery of a connection where one had hitherto been undisclosed.

---

29. Meier, *Gedancken von Schertzen*, 114.
30. Ibid., 6.
31. See Ibid., 19ff.

In a move that reveals the extreme limitations of the theory, Meier claims that any pleasure to be had in jokes is secondary to their intellectual accomplishment. Viewed from a distanced historical perspective, the claim that laughter should be caused by the discovery of knowledge may well be little more than the illusion of a stalwart rationalist. After all, the joke, according to this model, is not pleasureful play but a veridical mode of world observation. The basic premise of this intellectualist approach—which comes to expression in Gellert, Lessing, and Meier, but that, in truth, amounts to a broad-based historical trend—is that the body must be subjugated to the command of reason.[32]

Treating jokes as a form of knowledge making, and laughter as an internalized sentiment, can make the act of theatrical spectatorship seem like high-powered ratiocination. Perhaps unsurprisingly, though, subsequent years brought resistance to this perspective. Countervailing voices did not champion the irrational or the anarchic; instead, the reassessment of laughter's value remained, in an indispensable sense, internal to the project of creating social order through the exclusion of supposedly improper, deleterious, or useless forms of laughter. That being said, anachronic and retroleptic strategies provided decisive instruments in breaking with the reform program.

It is impossible to tell the story of the comic in the eighteenth century as a forward march of the civilizing process, nor can one speak of ever more expansive suppression. On the contrary, a general mood of dismissiveness toward Gottsched and company became audible in complaints that he had made the stage overserious and had mistakenly banished from the stage "the sole doctor for a large number of men" (*der einzige Arzt für eine grosse Anzahl Menschen*).[33]

---

32. In addition to the passages from Gellert and Lessing that I have already cited, see Johann Christoph Gottsched, *Versuch einer critischen Dichtkunst vor die Deutschen* (1730), 601; and, more expansively, Gottsched, *Critische Dichtkunst* (1751), 654.

33. Remark by Thomas Abbt, reprinted in Justus Möser, *Harlekin: Texte und Materialien mit einem Nachwort*, ed. Henning Boetius (Bad Homburg: Max Gehlen, 1968), 68.

The intrinsic potential of the theater, including the salubrious individual and collective function it might discharge in a well-ordered society, demanded the restoration of antecedent forms of the comic.

The reference to the fool as the "sole doctor for a large number of men" contains two features worthy of closer consideration: the reference to the fool's presence as therapeutic and the characterization of his palliative effects as essentially collective. In these two predications, we can track tectonic shifts in the conception of theatrical mirth. Perhaps most consequentially for the history of German dramatic literature, these shifts led to a categorical revaluation of the fool.

A good impression of the shifting conceptual landscape can be gathered from the theater by the doctor from Heidelberg Franz May (1742–1812), who published a text under the revealing title "On the Influence of Comedies on the Health of Working Citizens" ("Von dem Einfluß der Komödien auf die Gesundheit arbeitender Staatsbürger," 1786).[34] May, who maintained an active engagement with the theater in the neighboring town of Mannheim, declares that the early Enlightenment movement had, to their peril, failed to realize the beneficial effects that the "farcical Hanswurst" has to offer "for the well-being of the state and its citizens."[35] He goes on to say that "those improvers of the German stage" did not grasp that "laughter causes (*beibringen*) the spectators' nerves profitable convulsions."[36] By banishing the fool from the stage, the reform movement had disregarded the "health of the citizens" and their "lethargic bellies," which are vulnerable to "constipation in the lower region of the body."[37] But an ample dosage of explosive and uncontrollable laughter "sets the circulation of blood into a faster movement."[38]

Adverting to palliative physical effects in the act of laughter, as May does, simultaneously displaces the regulatory role of reason

---

34. Franz May, *Vermischte Schriften* (Mannheim: Neue Hof- und akademische Buchhandlung, 1786), 42–50.
    35. Ibid., 43.
    36. Ibid., 45.
    37. Ibid., 43.
    38. Ibid., 44.

characteristic of early Enlightenment writers. This rigorous emphasis on reason set aside, laughter was now afforded new functions and new possibilities. And yet there persisted a disciplinary impetus. Because of the ineluctably corporeal nature of laughter, discussions on the subject in the latter half of the eighteenth century faced a distinctive challenge: to understand laughter as a physical, bodily function while ensuring its difference from the affects and capacities of brutes. This entailed more than simply defending the Aristotelian argument, taken from book 3 of his treatise *De partibus animalium*, that laughter is a distinctively human capacity, also a theory commonplace in the eighteenth century. It further required an explicit distinction between "animalistic laughter" and the "external laughter" that was a dignified, healthful response to humor.[39]

Thus a two-pronged compensatory strategy emerges in response to the dogma of reason. On the one hand, laughter was characterized as the motor response to a "variety of pleasant sensations (*Empfindungen*)."[40] In particular, it was sensations of external objects that caused a "convulsing of the nerves."[41] The nerves constituted, according to the prevailing physiological model of the time, the mediating instance between the inner domain of subjective experience and the outer world.[42] This division between the cause of sensation and its subjective experience made it possible to at once provide a general defense of laughter's social utility *and* limit it according to standards of propriety. For the intersection of *policey* and medical knowledge suggested that "laughter is beneficial for health" and health is the cornerstone of good governance.[43] The mere excitation of laughter, with its attendant benefits, made up for an intrinsic deficiency of the human

39. Ibid., 49.

40. Johann Christoph Adelung, *Über den Deutschen Styl: Zweiter und Dritter Teil* (Berlin: Christian Friedrich Voß, 1785), 193.

41. Ibid., 199.

42. On the far-reaching consequences of this model, see Albrecht Koschorke, *Körperströme und Schriftverkehr* (Munich: Wilhelm Fink Verlag, 2003), esp. 112–129. For a representative discussion concentrated on the phenomenon of laughter, see Ernst Platner, *Neue Anthropologie für Aerzte und Weltweise* (Leipzig: Siegfried Lebrecht Crusius, 1790), 1:388–414.

43. Flögel, *Geschichte der komischen Litteratur*, 1:123.

body, namely, its proneness to exhaustion. By restoring the body, laughter allowed for the continuation and enhanced productivity of labor. The sheer enjoyment of laughter, causally related to the excitation of nerves by impingements of the external world, had to align with some basic standards of good taste, and then it could fulfill its service to society.

Although formal descriptions were not forthcoming, prospective calls for one figure in particular played a prominent role in the effort to jolt the German theater back to life. Advocates for the banished fool's return sought to counteract the "unnatural earnestness" that the reform movement had instituted.[44] Instead of opening the floodgates to all varieties of the comic, critics continued to insist on the categorical distinction between ridicule (*Verlachen*) and laughter (*Lachen*), which had been a mainstay in manuals on rhetoric since Roman antiquity.[45] What is more, they only made room for a fool who would not "spit nasty words at the ethically upstanding audience" (*Unflättereien auf das gesittete Publikum hin speien*).[46] The function of the fool was identified in his ability to "purify folly through folly" (*reinigt durch Narrheit von Narrheit*).[47] The task was then to come up with a model of the fool that could accomplish what, as Goethe writes in his first draft of the Wilhelm Meister novel, "the old philosopher promises of tragedy, namely that it purify the passions (*die Leidenschaften reinige*)."[48] Inoculation through laughter was the conceptual foundation for folly's place on the reformed stage.

Of course, much of this remains at best tentative, at worst woefully vague. But in order to understand how the fool's laughter-provoking presence should work, and why his presence became indispensable, we must fit together more pieces of the puzzle. In particular, we have to understand why the fool seemed a necessary instrument for laughter. Thus far in part 3, we have been concerned with the displacement

---

44. Quoted from Thomas Abbt's letter, reprinted in Möser, *Harlekin*, 63.
45. See, for instance, Lessing, *Werke und Briefe*, 6:322.
46. May, *Vermischte Schriften*, 44.
47. Flögel, *Geschichte der komischen Litteratur*, 1:28.
48. Goethe, FA I 9:132–133.

of the principle of reason as the source of laughter. Locating its cause in sensations and their purification, it bears particular emphasis, did away with a universal canon to which laughter must conform. Hence, it now became plausible to claim, incontrovertibly, that laughter can change "not just between different peoples (*Völkern*), but also in one and the same people at different points in time and among different social classes."[49] Our next task, then, is to grasp the sorts of regional and historical differences that impact the conduct of laughter.

---

49. Adelung, *Über den Deutschen Styl*, 204.

11

NATIONAL LITERATURE I

Improvement

Whose spirits should be rejuvenated, whose laboring bodies revitalized, by laughing at a play? The readily available response—that the theater is for the audience, with their exhausted bodies and depleted spirits—leads into a thicket of issues that, in fact, had a broad historical impact in Germany.[1] Part of the difficulty concerns the concept of *audience* itself, a noun that does not refer to a uniform group across time and space, but rather possesses a situation-specific meaning, shaped by multiple, varying factors. One approaches the concept of *audience* with caution because,

---

1. I leave aside lexicographical and conceptual-historical issues that would provide an additional line of inquiry. In the latter half of the eighteenth century, the meaning of the German noun *Publikum* was contested, not least because it had significantly more capacious definitions than English *audience*. On this issue, with further references, see Dorothea E. von Mücke, *The Practices of the Enlightenment: Aesthetics, Authorship, and the Public* (New York: Columbia University Press, 2015), esp. 181ff.

at this historical juncture, it is unthinkable without reference to signifiers such as nation and people, whose meanings are equally subject to ambiguity and controversy. Even though the latter half of the eighteenth century is associated, in aesthetic theory, most prominently with an emphatic notion of the artistic genius, spontaneously creative and untethered from the constraint of tradition, debates over comic theater and its German audience headed in the opposite direction: in that of traditional, calculated creativity that speaks to culturally inflected predilections.[2]

Taking on such charged signifiers as German nation, German people, German audience, head-on involves being flooded by the sheer quantity of potentially relevant evidence, so widespread is the interest in the meaning of these big concepts during the latter half of the eighteenth century.[3] For that reason, this chapter looks through a conceptual lens that I have employed repeatedly in this study and that functions as a key relay in the patterns of historical transformation during the latter half of the eighteenth century. It is striking that, beginning around 1730 and stretching to the turn of the nineteenth century, the envisaged transformation of the stage is chiefly described as a process of "improvement" (*Verbesserung*). Now it may seem a matter of definitional necessity that reform is a process of betterment, but merely acknowledging a teleology does not yet clarify the terminus ad quem, nor does it map out intermediary steps to get there. A major alteration in the vehicle and goal of improvement took place in the latter half of the eighteenth century once cultural difference—the difference, for instance, between the Germans, the French, and the English—became a decisive factor.

2. The locus classicus for the concept of genius is Jochen Schmidt, *Die Geschichte des Genie-Gedankens in der deutschen Literatur, Philosophie, und Politik*, 2 vols. (Darmstadt: Wissenschaftliche Buchgesellschaft, 1985). For a more concentrated and deeply insightful discussion, see David E. Wellbery, *The Specular Moment: Goethe's Early Lyric and the Beginnings of Romanticism* (Stanford: Stanford University Press, 1996), 121–183.

3. For a sociological analysis of this difficult concept, with attention to historical detail, see Bernhard Giesen and Kay Junge, "Vom Patriotismus zum Nationalismus," in *Nationale und kulturelle Identität: Studien zur Entwicklung des kollektiven Bewußtseins in der Neuzeit*, ed. Bernhard Giesen (Frankfurt am Main: Suhrkamp Taschenbuch Wissenschaft, 1991), 255–303.

As a matter of course, the meaning and the consequences of the concept of *culture* in this setting will require some interpretation. And so this chapter and chapter 12 unfold a single argument in two steps. The fool will temporarily fade into the background over the following pages, but he eventually reappears in the final stretches as an indispensable agent in the formation of German literature in an emphatic sense.

As a point of departure, it is worth taking note of the absence of the term *literature* in this study thus far, and of the privilege assigned to *poetry*, in spite of the reader who may associate the latter with the lyric. This terminological absence is not without reason. For one, the term *poetry* aligns more accurately with the terminology favored in the seventeenth and early eighteenth centuries. Particularly in second-order critical reflection, *Poesie* and *Dichtkunst* are the standard terms; over the latter half of the eighteenth century *Literatur* (for the fastidious, often *Litteratur*) becomes increasingly prevalent. The shift, broadly speaking, from poetry to literature was not a lexical trade-in, and a close lexicography would show that the French loan word never fully supplanted the other eighteenth-century terms. But I have hitherto avoided using the noun that we now feel most at home with—*literature*—for reasons as much analytical as historical. Literature carries connotations that map poorly onto the critical activity in the seventeenth century or in the age of Gottsched, but that do well at the historical crossroads around 1760.[4] The rise of a culturally inflected conception of literature has a lot to do, I wish to claim, with certain strategies of comparison that began to take hold starting around 1760.

The replacement of a poetic paradigm with a literary one was not instantaneous and intentional, but instead decentered and unplanned. It would be foolhardy, therefore, to try to summarize the entire debate over German literature from the second half of the eighteenth century; the following discussion focuses on a small number of representative samples from a close-knit discursive setting. The evidence comes

---

4. The most ambitious study of the shift from a rhetorically founded concept of poetry to the modern notion of literature is Rüdiger Campe, *Affekt und Ausdruck: Zur Umwandlung der literarischen Rede im 17. und 18. Jahrundert* (Tübingen: Max Niemeyer Verlag, 1990).

from a text entitled—in what is more than a happy coincidence—
Letters Concerning Most Recent Literature, a pseudo-epistolary
periodical centered in Berlin led by a small cadre of polymathic critics, scholars, and literary authors. Because of its focus on current
publications and the acuity of vision evident in many of the epistles,
this periodical can be seen as a nexus of the contemporary climate.
In this journal, German dramatic literature appears in still inchoate
terms, caught in a process of becoming.

To get an impression of the conceptual terrain, consider the concluding lines from the best-known and most revealing verbal
blast against Gottsched and his reform program:

> He [Gottsched] had the Harlequin ceremoniously banished from the
> theater, which was the greatest harliquinade that has ever been played.
> In short, he did not so much wish to improve our old theater as to be
> the creator of a totally new one. And of what sort? A Frenchifying one,
> without investigating whether or not this Frenchifying theater fit with
> the German way of thinking.

> Er ließ den Harlequin feierlich vom Theater vertreiben, welches selbst
> die größte Harlequinade war, die jemals gespielt worden; kurz, er wollte
> nicht sowohl unser altes Theater verbessern, als der Schöpfer eines ganz
> neuen sein. Und was für eines neuen? Eines Französierenden; ohne zu
> untersuchen, ob dieses französierende Theater der deutschen Denkung-
> sart angemessen sei, oder nicht.[5]

It is not difficult to read these rhapsodic sentences, published by
Lessing in 1759 as the seventeenth installment in the *Letters*, as a
death sentence for the reform program. Two surface features guide
this line of interpretation. First, Lessing mockingly cites the founding myth of the reform movement in order to decry its wrongheadedness and futility. And, second, he identifies Gottsched as

---

5. Gotthold Ephraim Lessing, *Werke und Briefe*, ed. Jürgen Stenzel (Frankfurt am Main: Deutscher Klassiker Verlag, 1989), 4:499–500. Although Lessing
is sometimes seen as a defender of the Italian-French Harlequin as separate from
other traditions of the stage fool, this demonstrates that the Harlequin, for him,
was a general term for the fool. Surely a writer of Lessing's sharp wit would have
grasped the absurdity of deriding Gottsched's francophilic reforms while, in the
same breath, practicing it himself!

champion of a derivative French neoclassicism. The scapegoat transaction that should ostensibly have brought an ennobled theater-drama coupling into existence is, Lessing claims, a charade, a foolish concoction. The argumentative logic of these dismissals provides a constructive heuristic for our analysis. The above passage identifies defects in the temporal and cultural design of the early Enlightenment reform program, and as we sketch out the lines of attack against the early Enlightenment reform project, as well as the alternative paths that stretched along beside it, this brief but profound passage from Lessing will serve as our guide.

Lessing identifies a temporal scission at the heart of the reform program, a complete division between the before and after. Within this paradigm, there is no remainder of preexisting stage conventions that traverses the boundary of reform. In other words, Gottsched's reform paradigm was ostensibly based in complete, instantaneous transformation: that was then, this is now. As such, the old reform program remained indifferent to the formal configurations or thematic contents that had hitherto enjoyed currency among theatergoers, writers, and actors. It follows that the exorcism of the fool was more than the symbolic realization of Gottsched's disavowal of the past; it was the attempt to install, by fiat and in an instant, an entirely extrinsic model of theater. And so we might say that in these few short lines Lessing identifies a logic of *imposed improvement*.

His own proposal, by contrast, advocates attending to "our [the Germans'] old dramatic plays," to see what "impacts us better" (*besser auf uns wirkt*).[6] These simple phrases allow us to ascertain the temporal protocol according to which the alternative path of improvement should proceed. Lessing suggests that fundamentally altering the stage requires continuity between established conventions and future design. As Lessing had written already a decade earlier, the imposition of "rapid change" (*schnelle Veränderung*) is as "dangerous for taste as it would be for a child which one wanted to accustom to strong wine just after milk."[7] Alimentary

---

6. Lessing, *Werke und Briefe*, 4:500.
7. Ibid., 1:726.

and aesthetic maturation best proceeds, as he says, "step-by-step" (*Stufenweise*).[8] The extended simile comparing theater to infantile development, together with the description of its pace in terms of the regularity of a gross-motor movement, provides a framework for conceiving of reform and improvement. But the framework is more than just a verbal cipher, an inconsequential switch from a literal to a figurative discourse. It points to a redrawing of the life-theater matrix, according to which the theater becomes a *vital extension* of its social environment.

This reorientation was not limited to a single writer. During the latter half of the eighteenth century, the patterning of improvement on the developmental rhythm of human life—and, in the same breath, decrying the mistaken derailment of such an organic trajectory—became the dominant way of identifying the wrongheadedness of Gottsched's reform program. Lessing's friend and former collaborator Friedrich Nicolai (1733–1811) remarked in 1761 and elsewhere among the *Letters* that "what one can say in a certain respect of good taste in Germany in general is valid specifically and in every respect of the German stage, namely that it is only still in its childhood."[9] Herder, in much the same vein, remarks in his commentary on the *Letters* that the German stage is akin to a "child that has become prematurely clever through imitation" (*ein Kind, das durch Nachahmen zu frühzeitig klug geworden*).[10] He offers the alternative recommendation that the theater should "work backwards" and only then proceed forward; he encourages the return to erstwhile conventions and then, from the vantage point of a recovered origin, paving contiguous steps for improvement.[11] In his first draft of the Wilhelm Meister novel, Goethe summons a corresponding image when he says that in the early Enlightenment reforms the "German stage threw away its

---

8. Ibid.

9. Friedrich Nicolai, "Von den Ursachen, warum die deutsche Schaubühne immer in der Kindheit geblieben," *Briefe, die neuste Litteratur betreffend* 11 (1761): 299–306, here 303.

10. Johann Gottfried Herder, *Werke*, ed. *Wolfgang Pross* (Munich: Hanser Verlag, 1984–2002), 1:339; see also 336.

11. Ibid.

children's shoes, before they were worn out, and had to walk barefoot in the meantime."[12] Such reiteration of a metaphorical scheme points to a shared sense that the path of improvement could not be charted in abstraction from the surrounding terrain. To be successful, innovation within the drama-theater dyad, rather, had to attend to the already existing ecosystem. Genuine innovation denies the possibility of a radical break in conventional ways of conducting the business of theater and demands instead a reflexive and appropriative relationship with hitherto established practices.

The question is, Whose practices? What does Lessing have in mind when he encourages attention to "our old dramatic plays"? After all, Gottsched certainly understood his own critical, translational, and poetic endeavors as the inheritance of a venerated past. Historiographical discrepancies between Gottsched and Lessing are especially evident in their differing approaches to cultural difference. Lessing objects to the servile dependence on French models that drives imposed improvement. His neologism "frenchifying" functions as a dismissal of the imitative mechanisms that formed the core of Gottsched's program. He objects not to imitation as such, but instead to a particular practice or method of imitation. So much is also clear from the fact that Lessing goes on to champion English drama—and Shakespeare in particular—as a more fitting model for German drama. In advancing the notion of progressive improvement, through a more avid interest in the English tradition, Lessing sings the opening line in what would become an epoch-making anthem, namely, the sense that Shakespeare—and not someone of the French neoclassical tradition—is the greatest modern dramatist.

The important thing for our purposes, however, is not the seesawing preference for the English or French, but rather the modification in the underlying logic of precedent. Note that in this passage, Lessing uses traditional rhetorical terminology of the paradigm case (*Muster, exemplum,* παράδειγμα), as was customary throughout the eighteenth century. In an argumentative move marking a break from the rule-governed reform program, Lessing

---

12. Goethe, FA I 9:32.

claims that what counts as an instance worthy of imitation depends on the imitative context.[13] Models remain an indispensable ingredient in improvement, as the humanistic recipe dictated; but henceforth genuine forward progress cannot take place in a cultural-historical vacuum, nor can it be measured against a uniform standard. Instead, autochthonous stage conventions are of a piece with more general features of a generalized and pervasive mentality (*Denkungsart*), and both together must inform the intermediary steps that reform should take. In lieu of a predetermined standard of perfection to aspire to, Lessing embeds the transformation process in a matrix of cultural comparison. In drawing out similarities as well as differences among the Germans, English, and French, Lessing rejects the possibility of a single standard that all should adhere to, thus introducing the notion of a local mentality.[14]

Although Lessing formulates the incompatibility in terms of a broad-based frame of mind or mental attitude, his remarks are part of what could be described as the cultural emplacement of the theater. However polyvalent and notoriously difficult to define, the concept of culture can provide a powerful heuristic. *Culture* may not have been the word used in all instances, and the paradigm at issue can be detected even in the decade or so before the word itself made inroads into German language.[15] After around 1750, discussion of theatrical practices and traditions, in fact,

---

13. It seems to me that Lessing's break with Gottsched becomes significantly stronger in the course of the 1750s; hence the difference between the view I am presenting here and my treatment of his introduction to the *Beyträge* in the opening of chapter 9.

14. There is a remarkable forerunner to Lessing's remarks—namely, Johann Elias Schlegel's "Gedanken zur Aufnahme des dänischen Theaters," reprinted in Johann Elias Schlegel, *Werke*, ed. Johann Elias Schlegel (Frankfurt am Main: Athenäum, 1971), 3:261–298. Although written in 1747, the more widely read edition of his collected works was not published until (tellingly!) 1764.

15. For a more focused history of the expansive use of the concept in the 1770s, particularly for historiographical purposes, see Michael G. Carhart, *The Science of Culture in Enlightenment Germany* (Cambridge, MA: Harvard University Press, 2007). My claim is that when the word "culture" entered the German lexicon in the 1770s some of its meanings were already at work, under different lexical markers. Indeed, the use of this loanword is perhaps best explained by its ability to describe a conceptual nexus that had gained a foothold over the preceding years.

became organized by a metalevel of substantive—in the view of some, irreducible—difference. This level of difference is the platform upon which comparison takes place between the English, French, and German. These group terms do not operate primarily as political distinctions. Instead, they function as an instrument for identifying a prejuridical and uncodified mode of mutual belonging. In the theatrical context, comparisons among the English, French, and Germans served to undermine the possibility of a set of universal, canonical rules. The rise of German literary drama was closely tied to a novel investment in the regional boundedness of all literatures.

Speaking of culture should not evoke the picture of a unified and internally coherent Englishness, Frenchness, or Germanness. It should, rather, allow for the articulation of a twofold concern: with the distinctiveness of a given theatrical tradition and with the proper procedure for normative assessment of such distinctiveness. Of course, the concept of culture functions in a number of other important ways—in opposition to nature, for example, or in the contrast between cultured and uncultured—but these are not the senses that are at work in Lessing, Nicolai, Herder, and Goethe.[16] In their texts, culture serves as a gauge for comparative difference and internal coalescence. As such, culture further develops the theme that first emerged at the beginning of part 3, namely, the relationship between theater and life. The introduction of cultural comparison, in fact, amounted to the inclusion of ever more quotidian features as relevant to the constitution of the theater. To step back for a moment and notice our place in the larger dialectic, we might say that, beyond the division between labor and restoration or earnestness and levity, we now stand on an additional level of mediation that deserves being called cultural life.

Looking at things in terms of cultural life draws out the difference between, for example, the meaning of "German theater" in 1730 and the meaning of the same terminology approximately

---

16. See Albrecht Koschorke, "Zur Epistemologie der Natur/Kultur-Grenze und zu ihren disziplinären Folgen," *Deutsche Vierteljahrsschrift für Literaturwissenschaft und Geistesgeschichte* 83, no. 1 (2009): 9–25.

thirty years later. The idea of a German theater changes once habitual and conventional features of day-to-day existence in a regionally bound social group become relevant to discursive construction of the theater.[17] The claim that German theater should be assessed according to its own measuring-stick made sense only because of the logically antecedent belief in the irreducibility of culture-specific traits. To give an example, cultural difference provides a key premise of Friedrich Just Riedel's *Theory of the Beautiful Arts and Sciences* (*Theorie der schönen Künste und Wissenschaften*, 1767/1774). He argues that aesthetic taste is relative to "the national character (*Nationalcharakter*) and, in general, the circumstances."[18] And why? Because "every people has national sources (*Nationalquellen*) out of which the judgments flow that it [the people] makes about the good and the beautiful."[19] Riedel (1742–1785) includes among the culturally specific domains of life "religion, conventions, traditions, prejudices, . . . their pride, their character, their language, their form of government, their knowledge (*Kenntnisse*), and a hundred other points."[20] This passage makes the claim that all domains of life, including literature, are colored by the regionally dominant culture, and for this reason Riedel issues the following proviso: "The character of a nation and its form of thought must be taken as foundational and be compared with the character of other nations. By these means, the true temperament (*Temperatur*) can be determined according

---

17. My claim is not that all of these differences are always indicated by the concept of culture, but rather that these differences become salient at this historical juncture, and that the rise of such differences is best described as the invention of cultural difference as a key discursive axis. A good example of this is the controversy over how to translate the English term "humor" into the German language, particularly in the large scale (English humor, German humor, French humor, and so on).

18. Friedrich Just Riedel, *Theorie der schönen Künste und Wissenschaften* (Vienna/Jena: Christian Heinrich Cuno, 1774), 22. This passage is taken from the epistles on aesthetic issues included as addenda in the revised version of Riedel's treatise. The passages I quote are taken from the second letter, which is addressed to Karl Friedrich Flögel.

19. Riedel, *Theorie der schönen Künste*, 22–23.

20. Ibid., 25.

to which the German muse must sing German."[21] It is noteworthy that Riedel uses the metaphor of temperament, which refers to the intentional deviation from a pure tonal interval in music, not to a set of general dispositions or a collective mood. Yet the metaphor contains an ambiguity that reveals the conceptual difficulties intrinsic to the redefinition of literary art in terms of culture. Speaking of musical temperament makes sense only if pure intervals exist, and it is exactly the possibility of such purity that his remarks call into question. Much like Lessing, with his simultaneous accusations of "frenchifying" and elevating the English, Riedel struggles to find the words to describe the tissue connecting cultural life and theater, including what makes German theater German.

Given the equivocality of the quoted passages from Lessing and Riedel, it may seem an exaggeration to label this a watershed moment. In order to see this transition more perspicuously, it is helpful to distinguish between two different ways in which group markers such as English, French, and German become attached to the theater—in other words, two different ways in which English, French, and German name species of the higher-order genus theater.[22] Recall that one of the founding gestures of the early Enlightenment reforms was the integration of the theater into a rule-governed poetics with universal applicability. The preference among early Enlightenment critics for the hybrid term "theatrical poetry" (*theatralische Poesie*) testifies to a specific method for harnessing the theater to a conception of poetry oriented toward universally valid guidelines. According to this scheme, then, among the kinds of poetry, one is theatrical poetry, which itself falls out into a variety of different

---

21. Ibid., 26: "Der Charakter der Nation und ihre Denkart müste zum Grunde gelegt, mit dem Charakter, andrer poetischen Völker verglichen und daraus die wahre Temperatur bestimmt werden, nach welcher die deutsche Muse deutsch singen muß." *Temperatur* here is a musical metaphor, referring to the deviation from pure tonal intervals to fulfill specific purposes.

22. I learned of the logical structure of this difference through the study of Anton Ford, "Action and Generality," in *Essays in Honor of Anscombe's Intention*, ed. Anton Ford, Jennifer Hornsby, and Frederick Stoutland (Cambridge, MA: Harvard University Press, 2011), 76–104. In my terminological decisions, I follow Ford's lead.

species (French, Italian, etc.). Each of these theaters adheres to a canon of rules required of theatrical poetry, yet these rules exist and operate entirely independently of what makes the French theater distinctively French or the Italian theater distinctively Italian. (The same holds, *mutatis mutandis,* for other species of poetry.) In more traditional philosophical vocabulary, we might say that the constituent species of the genus differ by virtue of their accidents. From a modern vantage point, theatrical poetry looks here much like the genus of mammals, who share the marker of nourishing offspring with milk and are differentiated among themselves by a host of additional, inessential markers. Even if bumblebee bats and baboons differ in so many respects that their association would seem nothing more than an alliterative ploy, they both belong to the genus of mammals because they share a way of supplying their young with nourishment. The parallel between biological and poetic classification accurately represents the early Enlightenment conviction that the rules that group together poetic kinds reflect the structure of the world and its underlying principle of reason.

But there is another genus-species relation, which can be called categorical, that is organized differently. In this second genus-species relation, it is not possible to separate differentiae from the qualities of a genus. A canonical example in philosophy relies on the fact that red and blue can intuitively be thought of as species of the genus color.[23] But there are no features of redness that are accidental to the genus color, such that they can function as the distinguishing features of red from blue without simultaneously undoing red's belonging to the genus of colors. In simpler terms, we cannot break off the features that make red different from blue and still end up with the properties that make red into a color in the first place. Each species that belongs to the genus color forms, so to speak, a category unto itself; put differently, the species belong to a single genus but are categorically different.

Unpacking this contrast with all of its nuance would take a good deal of additional argument, but even this skeletal contrast can

---

23. The example of color, cited in Ford's essay, is taken from Arthur N. Prior, "Determinables, Determinates, and Determinants (I)," *Mind 58* (1949): 1–20.

throw light on the functioning of the concept of culture after 1760. Assuming that English, French, and German theater are members of a more general class called theater, how should we think of the features that make them respectively distinct? What sort of a genus is the theater, such that it consists of English, French, and German species? Are culturally distinct theaters accidentally different or categorically different? The passages from Lessing and Riedel seem to pivot between these two conceptions.

Again, an example will help make these abstract considerations more concrete. Consider the remarks that Herder wrote in response to the *Letters Concerning Most Recent Literature.* Long recognized as a galvanizing force behind the explosion of German literature in the late eighteenth century, in his early career Herder was urgently concerned with the way different cultures inflect their literary creations.[24] A characteristic instance of this comes in a passage where he refers to the ancient Greeks as the "fathers of all literature in Europe."[25] The phrase seems standard enough and, with its invocation of progenitor-progeny relation, seems to map on well to a genus-species classification. Fatherhood here alludes to a reproductive pattern—the father's features and characteristics being passed down to the child. But the father-child relationship can also be understood, not in terms of the common traits, but instead according to the differentiae, the traits that are *not* bequeathed from parent to child, instead marking each

---

24. Within the abundant literature on Herder's relationship to nation and culture, see Sonia Sikka, *Herder on Humanity and Cultural Difference: Enlightened Relativism* (Cambridge: Cambridge University Press, 2011). See also Vicki A. Spencer, *Herder's Political Thought: A Study of Language, Culture, and Community* (Toronto: University of Toronto Press, 2012). On Herder's conception of national literature, including his notion of *Volk*, see Ulrich Gaier, "Volkspoesie, Nationalliteratur, Weltliteratur bei Herder," in *Die europäische République des lettres in der Zeit der Weimarer Klassik,* ed. Michael Knoche and Lea Ritter-Santini (Göttingen: Wallstein Verlag, 2007), 101–115; and Hans Adler, "Weltliteratur—Nationalliteratur—Volksliteratur: Johann Gottfried Herders Vermittlungsversuch als kulturpolitische Idee," in *Nationen und Kulturen: Zum 250 Geburtstag Johann Gottfried Herders,* ed. Regine Otto (Würzburg: Königshauses & Neumann, 1996), 271–284.

25. Herder, *Werke,* 1:213.

as an individual. If the Greeks are sponsors of German literature along these lines, then Herder is conceiving of literatures according to the first (accidental) model of genus-species relation.

Yet Herder's genetic picture of the Greeks' position in literary history and theory actually functions differently. He encourages the reader of his text to imagine the following transport:

> Take off from a literature to which the Greeks first gave form once and for all; become a reborn contemporary of a bygone history, a bard of past times—and then judge! Which people, which century has ever made itself anything but a literature of the age and nation? The Greeks did not, and neither did we.

> Setze dich aus einer Literatur hinaus, welcher einmal für alle die Griechen erste Form gaben: werde ein wiedergeborner Zeitgenosse einer abgelebten Geschichte, ein Barde vergangener Zeiten—so urteile! Welches Volk, welches Jahrhundert hat sich je eine andre als Sekular- und National-Literatur gebauet? Die Griechen nicht, und wir auch nicht.[26]

It is easy to miss the subtlety of Herder's lines, which deftly avoid paradox. The opening gambit suggests that the Greeks cast the mold for all literatures to come. And yet it is not clear what sort of priority this mold possesses after it had been cast "once and for all." Are there subsequent molds that follow temporally (i.e., historically) on this first mold? If so, then what the Greeks created "once and for all" seems to lead a double existence—once as the ancient Greek form and once as the form open to further iterations. But Herder is not entangling himself in such a paradox; he is gesturing toward a conception of literature as a genus that falls out along the lines of a categorical species. Evidence of this can be found in the latter half of the quoted passage where Herder insists on the *per se* historical and cultural distinctness of all literatures. Even in the case of the ancient Greeks, the constitutive qualities of their literature cannot be broken down into those that are specifically Greek and those specific to a literary genus. Instead, they are a literature only insofar as their distinctive attributes, their cultural and national qualities, are definitive of their status as literature.

---

26. Ibid., 1:219.

The Greeks first gave form to literature, and in this respect they are its parent. But this primacy is temporal; the Greek form of literature, by 1760, stands alongside other literatures, each with different cultural qualities. The qualities that qualify German literature as a literature cannot be separated from those qualities that make it German, just as the qualities that made Greek literature into the first literature cannot be separated from the qualities that made it Greek. The most straightforward way to distinguish these two varieties of genus-species relation is to say that Herder is advocating the birth of German as a national literature, insofar as to be a literature is to be national. Indeed, Herder is saying something along those lines, and doing so at the same time that he denies the existence of poetry in a universal rule-governed sense.

Talk of national literature flows with particular ease concerning the theater. Around the same time when Lessing, Riedel, and Herder were make these statements, municipal authorities, sometimes in collaboration with private enterprise, adorned local institutions with the name "national theater." Among these, the most prominent is undoubtedly the effort in Hamburg between 1764 and 1767 known as the Hamburg Enterprise, which enjoyed Lessing's active engagement. Despite the appellation *national*, two-thirds of the plays performed at the Hamburg national theater (80 of 120) were not originally written in German—a statistic that fits with the broader trend in theaters across Germany.[27] In addition, during the latter half of the eighteenth century, a number of courts also appended "national" to their residential theater.[28] The word "national" appeared, for instance, in the names Hamburger Nationaltheater, Mannheim Hof- und Nationaltheater, Das Königliche Hof- und

---

27. See H. B. Nisbet, *Gotthold Ephraim Lessing: His Life, Works, and Thought* (Oxford: Oxford University Press, 2013), 359–389, here 369. On the general context, see Reinhart Meyer, "Der Anteil des Singspiels und der Oper am Repertoire der deutschen Bühnen in der zweiten Hälfte des 18. Jahrhunderts," in *Das deutsche Singspiel im 18. Jahrhundert* (Heidelberg: Winter Universitätsverlag, 1981), 27–76.

28. Reinhart Meyer, "Das Nationaltheater in Deutschland als höfisches Institut: Versuch einer Begriffs- und Funtionsbestimmung," in *Das Ende des Stegreifspiels, die Geburt des Nationaltheaters*, ed. Roger Bauer and Jürgen Wertheimer (Munich: Wilhelm Fink Verlag, 1983), 124–152.

Nationaltheater München, and more—so many more, in fact, that it would be absurd to suppose that each was intended as the announcement of the sort of political representation as would the same nomenclature today. At the time of the surge in national theaters, the Germans, unlike the two predominant axes of comparison (English and French), were not territorially unified, nor did they possess a capital city. The absence of a sovereign nation-state with a single, unified governmental bureaucracy and rule of law provides a good hint that speaking of the birth of national literature here does not settle the matter. For nation does not function, at this historical moment, as a purely political signifier. One possibility is to say that nation means in these instances cultural nation (*Kulturnation*), but this just displaces the need for clarification onto a further term.[29] As chapter 12 will draw out in closer detail, the concept of nation, as it is used in the late eighteenth and early nineteenth centuries, is essentially a synonym for culture. To say cultural nation is, in fact, to say cultural culture—in other words, to say nothing at all. In order to avoid this confusion, it makes sense to understand national literature and national theater as primarily cultural denominations.

The notion of cultural-national literature is best understood, so the basic claim of this chapter, according to the model of a categorical genus-species relation. This is not to say that texts by Lessing and Herder ever aspired to the classificatory precision—or explicitness and formality—that a philosopher might demand. But there is a positive, more historically instructive reason underlying the incomplete or inchoate descriptions of German as a national literature. To wit, becoming a nationally distinct theater is something that, according to the self-descriptions of eighteenth-century authors, the Germans had thus far failed at. Again and again, authors such as Lessing and Herder complained that Gottsched's reform movement had inhibited the German theater from properly differentiating itself and instead relegated it to a dreadfully mongrel existence.

The question of whether the German stage had achieved a sufficiently idiosyncratic (*eigentümulich*) or original (*original*) status

---

29. Friedrich Meinecke, *Cosmopolitanism and the National State*, trans. Robert B. Kimber (Princeton: Princeton University Press, 1970).

constitutes a recurring theme beginning around 1760.[30] Herder, for one, brought together the developmental and cultural dimensions of improvement in his claim that the "German stage was . . . abandoned at birth; that instead of developing its *idiosyncrasy* (*ihr Eigentümliches*) the stage was made into a servile imitator."[31] Herder's remark indicates that overreliance on external models inhibited the cultivation of a German theater. It is not at all difficult to hear echoes of Lessing's condemnation of the "frenchifying" reform tendencies. The absent idiosyncrasy, meanwhile, is defined in terms of the German national character (*Nationalcharakter*), national spirit (*Nationalgeist*), national taste (*Nationalgeschmack*), and German practical life (*deutsche Sitten*). While these terms remain vague at this point, a series of installments in the *Letters Concerning Most Recent Literature* written by Friedrich Nicolai claim that a theater in German-speaking lands that performs "almost nothing but foreign pieces" (*fast lauter fremde Stücke*), cannot rightly be called a German theater.[32] He provides the following diagnosis of the current state of affairs and prognosis for potential improvement:

> So long as it is not yet possible to abolish the bad original compositions and still more miserable translations which are already on our stages; so long as we slavishly adhere to the rules in our original compositions and do not think to give our German stage an idiosyncratic character; so long these and various other conditions cannot yet be fulfilled; for that long we will not be able to boast that we have a German stage rightly deserving of the name.

---

30. I consistently translate the word *eigentümlich* as "idiosyncratic." Although the lines of filiation are not entirely clear to me, I suspect that the term actually gained traction as a translation of the Latin *genius*, particularly in formulations such as *genius saeculi* and *genius loci*. While we would now render these terms as *Zeitgeist* and *Ortsgeist*, at least in texts from the middle third of the eighteenth century, there was apprehension about using the term *Geist* in this context, since it still carried strong religious and genuinely spectral connotations. I return to this theme in chapter 12.

31. Herder, *Werke*, 1:337.

32. Friedrich Nicolai, "Beurtheilung der zufälligen Gedancken über die deutsche Schaubühne zu Wien," *Briefe, die neuste Literatur betreffend* 11 (1761): 307–316, here 314.

So lange es noch nicht möglich ist die schlechten Originale und noch
elendere Uebersetzungen, welche bereits auf unsern Schaubühnen sind,
abzuschaffen; so lange wir uns in unsern Originalen noch sclavisch an
die Regeln halten, und nicht daran denken, der deutschen Bühne einen
eigenthümlichen Charakter zu geben; so lange diese und verschiedene
andere Bedingungen noch nicht können erfüllt werden; so lange werden
wir uns nicht rühmen können, daß wir eine deutsche Schaubühne hätten, die diesen Nahmen mit Recht verdiente.[33]

Servile imitation and boundedness to rules had to be excluded
for German literature to take hold. This passage is a reiteration
of what could be called the the distinction between endogenous
and exogenous varieties of improvement. Cultural specificity is the
product of a self-appropriative generative process, a dominance of
endogamy over exogamy. What is most striking in light of the earlier remarks about genus-species relations is Nicolai's identification
of an "idiosyncratic character" with the denomination "German
stage." Everything else would render the stage unworthy of the
national moniker. This is congruous with the opening of the very
same sequence of epistles where Nicolai doubts that "we can say in
the genuine sense (*im eigentlichen Verstande*) that we have a German stage as the French and English can boast that they have their
own stages."[34] The concept of German literature, then, is coined
to mark a shortcoming, as the placeholder for a still absent form.
Universally valid rules are disavowed not to make a place for an
emphatic notion of creativity without precedence, but rather in the
aspiration to give a distinctive cultural flavor to the German theater. In the latter half of the eighteenth century, there was a prevalent dismissal of the desire to "go to market by the Greeks, the
Latins, and the French, and borrow or buy from foreigners what
we could have at home."[35]

---

33. Nicolai, "Von den Ursachen, warum die deutsche Schaubühne immer in
der Kindheit geblieben," 304–305.

34. Ibid., 299.

35. Justus Möser, *Ueber die deutsche Sprache und Litteratur* (Hamburg: Benjamin Gottlob Hoffmann, 1781), 6.

12

NATIONAL LITERATURE II

Custom

Just because the theater should "orient itself according to the taste of the spectators"[1] did not mean that advocates of theatrical reform wanted to hand things over to public opinion. Instead, it lent some precision to the widely circulating notion of *improvement*, encouraging the playwright and the critic to each behave much like a doctor whose relief comes not by way of "all violent means, but instead supports nature in order that it should help itself progressively."[2] The mention of doctoring brings us back, once again, to the thread that has guided us through the previous chapters, namely, the relationship between the theater and life (now construed as the life of an entire culture). The project of literary improvement that emerges in the latter half of the eighteenth

---

1. Heinrich Georg Koch, *Antwort auf das Sendschreiben an Herrn K- in Z- die Leipziger Schaubühne betreffend* (Leipzig: Adam Kießling, 1753), 7.
2 Ibid., 8.

century was organized around a teleological structure that sought to accomplish more than simply the imposition of abrupt change. Improvement functioned, according to this alternative model, as a process of step-by-step, self-appropriative transformation—of, in more readily recognizable terminology, *Bildung*.[3] The concept of *Bildung* underscores that improvement consisted of the realization of potential in preexisting structures, in the augmentation of already established conventions, thoughts, feelings, desires, and inclinations. Reformers did not want to sever all traffic with external cultural-historical forms; they rather sought to use what they regarded as foreign elements to exploit still unrealized artistic potential within the autochthonous German theater. Or, as Justus Möser would have it, in a less abstract formulation: "In my opinion we must get more from ourselves and from our soil than we have hitherto done, and use the art of our neighbors, at the most, insofar as it serves our idiosyncratic products and their culture."[4]

Before moving forward, a word of general orientation is in order. The fool, it may seem, has vanished from the story line as higher-order, more encompassing concepts, such as culture, literature, and nation, have become the protagonists. The reason for opening the aperture in this way has to do with the intimate relationship that these very same concepts entertain with the comic. These big-picture concepts provide the context that supported the surprising promotion, in the 1760s and beyond, of the fool as an inchoate local form with strong potential for making the German stage worthy of its name. During these years, the comic became

---

3. The structural transformation I outline in this and the previous chapter shows a basic analogy to the novelistic developments of the same era. My approach has been shaped by the incisive and far-reaching study of David E. Wellbery, "Die Enden des Menschen: Anthropologie und Einbildungskraft im Bildungsroman (Wieland, Novalis, Goethe)," in *Das Ende, ed.* Karlheinz Stierle and Rainer Warning (Munich: Wilhelm Fink Verlag, 1996), 600–639.

4. The passage in its original: "Meiner Meynung nach müssen wir also durchaus mehr aus uns selbst und aus unserm Boden ziehen, als wir bisher gethan haben, und die Kunst unsrer Nachbaren höchstens nur in so weit nutzen, als sie zur Verbesserung unsrer eigenthümlichen Güter und ihrer Kultur dienet." Justus Möser, *Ueber die deutsche Sprache und Litteratur* (Hamburg: Benjamin Gottlob Hoffmann, 1781), 33–34.

closely interwoven with concepts like culture and nature, and, in this process, the fool began to appear to a number of major writers as an underutilized resource for furnishing the Germans with a dramatic literature of rank. Before returning to the fool, however, a more precise sense of the historical predicaments faced by the notion of a German culture generally and a German theater more specifically is needed.

With this road map in mind, let us return to the lines quoted at the outset, written by the prominent acting troupe leader Heinrich Gottfried Koch (1703–1775). These lines could very well solicit a very simple question: to wit, is it really that remarkable for the leader of a troupe to insist on attentiveness to what a paying audience might want? Obviously not. But there is more at work in Koch's remark: it encapsulates the distinction from chapter 11 between endogenous and exogenous models of improvement. Authors such as Koch approach literary improvement as emerging from the conspiracy of two forces: on one side, the local conventions for making theater and, on the other, the distinct culture in which the theater is produced. In order for doctoring to do its healing, both forces have to be at work.

The discourse on cultural distinctness in the eighteenth century was remarkably vast, but its basic contours can be readily sketched out. There is good reason to suspect that the cultural inflection of the theater, including the emphasis on endogenous improvement, drew essential energies from a sudden explosion of disagreement over the question of whether the Germans possessed a "national character" or "national spirit," two concepts that migrated into the German language around 1760. These very same terms took center stage in the discourse on political and territorial independence beginning around 1800, but their earlier entrance into the German language was more troubled. Long before the jingoistic stridency among German intellectuals in response to Napoleon's invasion, and before the philosophical interest in the grounding of the nation-state among major philosophers from Kant to Hegel, the concern with a national character had a significant role to play in a less recondite discourse comparing different nations. One trigger of the interest in the concept of nation was surely the Pan-European conflicts of the Seven Years' War (1756–1763), while another was the immense resonance of the French philosopher Baron de Montesquieu's (1689–1755) massive tome *The Spirit of the Laws* (*De l'esprit des lois*, 1748), which itself was part of a much larger discussion of these issues taking place in France.[5] But the years after around 1760 witnessed a huge increase in the practice of delineating the relative advantages and shortfalls of the European peoples, including in their rules of positive law and their forms of government, but also their literatures.[6] This is the broader discursive pool from which the texts of Lessing, Nicolai, and Herder that I discussed in chapter 11 emerged.

As notions of national spirit and national character attracted interest across the German-speaking world, a common argumentative pattern took form. Convinced that the German people must possess a distinctive identity, political thinkers felt the need to describe its core attributes. The necessity of such fundamental properties of a nation rested on an argument by Montesquieu: that national identity was a result of its topography and regional climate.[7] The characteristic features of a people, we might say, are derivative of naturally given and immutable features of the world. Arguing along these lines posed a problem for German writers, who were haunted by the sense that their own identity was contaminated by an overreliance on foreign input. Thus it seemed that their own national spirit was both necessary and contingent, manifest and obscure. This dilemma was resolved by the realization that although nature imbues a people with unique elements

5. See David A. Bell, *The Cult of the Nation in France: Inventing Nationalism, 1680–1800* (Cambridge, MA: Harvard University Press, 2003), 140–168.

6. The emphasis on the Seven Years' War has been argued in Hans-Martin Blitz, *Aus Liebe zum Vaterland: Die deutsche Nation im 18. Jahrhundert* (Hamburg: Hamburger Edition, 2000), and reiterated in Dorothea E. von Mücke, *The Practices of the Enlightenment: Aesthetics, Authorship, and the Public* (New York: Columbia University Press, 2015). On the influence of Montesquieu, see Rudolf Vierhaus, "Montesquieu in Deutschland," in *Deutschland im 18. Jahrhundert* (Göttingen: Vandenhoeck und Ruprecht, 1987), 9–32.

7. By causal, I do not mean the single result. For most authors it was an exceedingly important factor in the formation of national character, but not the sole one. The strength of the causality assigned to climate differed from author to author, but the basic premise of an immutable foundation remained widespread.

and features, they may not be obvious to the empirical world. German writers located their own national identity along a historical timeline. Because their current reality seemed to belie the necessity of national specificity, the solution was to integrate the status quo into narratives of earlier Germanic peoples and the promise of a more glorious future. In particular, the picture of the Germanic tribes presented by the Roman historian Tacitus (ca. 56–120), and, more rarely, premodern feudalism, provide the scaffolding for the analysis and construction of the German nation of 1760.[8] This narrative structure had a clear purpose: it turned the discussion of national identity into a recovery of a time when the German spirit aligned with the German nature. Because this moment of pristine cultural coherence was long past, the path forward to the origin had to be charted.[9]

This abstract pattern helps make sense of some of the uneasiness evident when national character and national spirit become topics of learned debate. Take the first German translation of Montesquieu, which appeared just a few years after the original publication under the altered title *Des Herrn von Montesquiou Werk von den Gesetzen* (*Mr. Montesquieu's Work on the Laws*, 1753).[10] A few years later the word *Geist* was in fact used as a translation for the French *esprit* in a related publication, so the avoidance of this key word in the first translation is noteworthy.[11] The prefatory remarks to the first German edition of Montesquieu's work observe that the translator would have introduced *Geist* in the title if he did not "have to fear that it would be unintelligible to a large number of

---

8. It has long been noticed that a number of literary texts—Klopstock's is the most famous—appeared with Herrmann's battle as their primary theme. Goethe's early tragedy *Götz von Berchlingen* was also understood in a similar fashion, and for this reason generated lively debate, among whose main protagonists King Friedrich II of Prussia and Justus Möser were counted.

9. See Albrecht Koschorke, *Wahrheit und Erfindung: Grundzüge einer allgemeinen Erzähltheorie* (Frankfurt am Main: S. Fischer Verlag, 2012), esp. pt. 4.

10. Abraham Gotthold Kästner, *Des Herrn von Montesquiou Werk von den Gesetzen* (Frankfurt/ Leipzig, 1753).

11. Johann Heumann, *Der Geist der Geseze der Teutschen* (Nuremberg: Johann Georg Lochner, 1761); see, in particular, 89–91. Unlike the other texts I discuss in this context, Heumann's expresses comfort with the current sense of co-belonging as well as the political composition of the German people.

German readers."[12] Uneasiness with *Geist* may seem odd to the modern reader more familiar with nineteenth-century trends, but at this earlier historical juncture "character" was a more comfortable term in German than "spirit" for describing what makes a nation distinct. We can see this skittishness at work, for instance, in the final section of the aesthetic treatise Kant wrote in 1764, during the precritical phase of his career, concerning "the national characters insofar as they bear on the sublime and the beautiful."[13] The philosopher from Königsberg betrays his allegiance to the modern parlance in his use of "national spirit" (*Nationalgeist*) as a synonym for "national character." Consonant with contemporary preoccupations, he claims that differences among nations restrict the validity of aesthetic experience. Yet Kant, whose prose seems to today's reader to exude hypotactic Germanness, also has difficulty defining what makes his people unique. At one point, he even goes so far as to claim they are made up of a sort of hybrid feeling between that of a Frenchman and that of an Englishman, a claim that seems to undermine their specificity not just as a nation, but also as aesthetic subjects.[14]

Beyond strictly philosophical expositions of the German personality, there was a further corpus of texts articulating the steps necessary to make German culture more distinct. One work that hews closely to Montesquieu's terminology, Friedrich Carl von Moser's (1723–1798) *Von dem deutschen National-Geist* (*On the German National Spirit*, 1765), moves quickly from an analysis of the titular concept to its primary focus: the intermediate steps needed to forge a sense of fellowship.[15] While his point of departure in this treatise is the absence of a unified legal code, its real concern is an underlying "separatist way of thinking" among the Germans.[16] The fractured juridical-political situation is merely the

---

12. Heumann, *Der Geist der Gesetze der Teutschen*, penultimate page of unpaginated preface.

13. Immanuel Kant, *Werkausgabe*, ed. Wilhelm Weischedel (Frankfurt am Main: Suhrkamp Taschenbuch Wissenschaft, 1996), 2:868–884.

14. Ibid., 874.

15. See the illuminating presentation in Nicholas Vaszonyi, "Montesquieu, Friedrich Carl von Moser, and the 'National Spirit Debate' in Germany, 1765–1767," *German Studies Review* 22, no. 2 (1999): 225–246.

16. Friedrich Carl von Moser, *Von dem deutschen National-Geist* (Frankfurt, 1765), 36.

most striking piece of evidence that, as Moser writes, "Our spirit has left us" (*Unser Geist ist von uns gewichen*).[17] The task set before the German-speaking peoples is to find remedies that will fix this lack across all age groups, from the earliest youth to adulthood. Recovering naturally given attributes will require developing techniques to alter the German "practical way of thinking" (*praktische Gedenkungs-Art*)—the forms of quotidian and conventional conduct that shape the way a people thinks of itself in contrast to other nations.[18] In particular, Moser tries to uncover practical routines that will inculcate behaviors fostering mutual association and coresponsibility, which thereby restore the depleted nation to its original plentitude and wholeness. For the argumentative path we are following, the decisive feature of this text lies beneath the diatribe against the juridical-political fragmentation in the call for a transformation in practical thought.

Moser's text offers the indication of a more general tendency to anthropomorphize and atomize questions of communal belonging. To be more exact, when the problem of national unity came into focus, its source and solution could be found at the level of individual psychology and affect. Making the nation hang together properly was not a matter of grasping some piece of information or recognizing some intrinsic attribute. It had to be accomplished, instead, through the acquisition of more affectively charged qualities, such as patriotism (*Patriotismus/patriotisch*), national pride (*Nationalstolz*), national interest (*Nationalinteresse*), and love of the fatherland (*Liebe für das Vaterland*).[19] Each of these concepts had the capacity to address the individual's own sense of investment and participation in an encompassing nation. The functional advantage of locating the source of the national bond in the individual's affective disposition, rather than in a more encompassing concept such as character and spirit, is the avenue of redress it opens up. If, for

---

17. Ibid., 10 and 76–77.

18. Ibid., 24.

19. It would be a fool's errand to refer to specific uses of these concepts. To the attuned reader they jump out of the pages of Thomas Abbt, Justus Möser, and Herder, as well as almost all of the many, less well-known authors I have cited throughout part 3.

instance, national unity is composed of the "sum of self-love (*Ei-genliebe*) of each specific person,"[20] then the mechanisms for creating a shared sense of identity will lie in each individual's "feeling of the specific merits" that she possesses in contrast to individuals from other nations.[21] This proposal, from a text devoted to the theme of national pride, which appeared in four versions between 1758 and 1768 and was then reprinted again in 1793, recommends using the imagination to encourage collective self-identification. In a particularly instructive passage, the author, Johann Georg von Zimmermann (1728–1795), points to a mechanism for fostering cultural unity that his own people might learn from the ancient Romans. In particular, the Germans should develop a reservoir of stories addressing "famous deeds shining forth from the history of the fatherland."[22] Such stories should be sacrosanct, and serve as collective reminders much like the devotional scapular and rosary carried by Catholics.[23] Such a battery, forged in the imagination, could equip the Germans with a sense of the value of belonging to the German nation.

The reference to the inspiriting power of the imagination is not unique. A more or less contemporary text written by the Austrian jurist Johann von Sonnenfels (1732–1817), who published widely on *policey* and the theater, similarly identifies the "example for imitation" as the essential ingredient for "arousing self-love even among the multitude (*Haufen*)" and thereby "making an entire people into patriots."[24] "Dependency" or *Anhänglichkeit* is one of Sonnenfel's preferred terms to describe an ideal relationship; the term bears more strongly on the affectionate attachment among persons than on needs relevant for survival or on pecuniary reliance.[25] Much like pride, an awareness of mutual reliance among

---

20. Johann Georg von Zimmermann, *Vom Nationalstolze* (Zurich: Heidegger und Compagnie, 1758), 12.

21. Ibid., 3.

22. Ibid., 106.

23. Ibid., 138.

24. Johann von Sonnenfels, *Ueber die Liebe des Vaterlands* (Vienna: Joseph Kurzböck, 1771), 14.

25. See the definition on Sonnenfels, *Ueber die Liebe des Vaterlands*, 11.

the members of a nation equips them with motivations conducive to communal fellowship. Perhaps the most powerful manifesto for a subjective investment in the nation was Thomas Abbt's *Vom Tode für das Vaterland* (*On Death for the Fatherland*, 1761), a zealous call for bravery in the middle of the Seven Years' War. It explicitly names the imagination (again, *Einbildungskraft*) as the foundation of mutual affective investment. Abbt predicts that if even a small number of men sacrifice themselves on behalf of the nation, they will provide enough images (his word is *Gemälde*) that the "entire nation should soon follow suit, by virtue of which its entire way of thought will necessarily become new and sublime."[26] In addition to the pursuit of noble deeds, then, a nation is made out of a secondary layer of representations that can "be passed on through unbroken transmission to grandchildren."[27] It should perhaps not surprise us that, amid a flurry of citations from the contemporary poet Ewald Christian von Kleist (1715–1759) and from ancient Roman lyric, Abbt adverts in the final pages of his treatise to a concept we have already seen on a number of occasions, namely, to *Muster*, paradigmatic instances or examples.[28] The national bond that interests Abbt—a bond worthy of self-sacrifice—should be formed through the crafting, reproduction, circulation, and emulation of a culture-specific storehouse of examples. The notion of endogenous improvement, in short, provides the overarching design for nation building as well as national-literature building. Only with such internal improvement will the German nation and its literature achieve a timelessness akin to the timelessness embodied in the modern veneration of ancient Greek and Roman poetry.[29]

For each of the above mentioned authors, the campaign for the cultivation of a collective identity has a favored device. Each expresses the desire for a particular model of heroism, namely, that of the great man—and especially one drawn from the annals of

---

26. Thomas Abbt, *Vom Tod für das Vaterland* (Berlin: Friedrich Nicolai, 1761), 34–35.

27. Ibid., 51.

28. Ibid., 94.

29. The parallel is hinted at in the discussion of immortality at Abbt, *Vom Tod für das Vaterland*, 50–52.

history—whose virtue and valor should serve as benchmarks for an entire nation. Each, furthermore, associates this model of virile masculinity with the tragic genre. Consider the elaboration of this compositional recipe in a journal article concerning the use of national history on the stage, published in the 1787. Culture-internal resources, the anonymous author claims, have a distinct advantage for the spectators: "When we see the heroes, the heroes of the fatherland, as well as warm, soulful, upstanding burghers themselves acting in the true brilliance of their dignity, we can take to heart their deed[s] and by means of imitation also achieve the very same merit."[30] According to this scheme, erstwhile acts of greatness can provide a model for imitation to the entire people, thereby supplying them with a sense of their nation's own worth and value. The uncomplicated and zealous advocacy for greater provincialism in thematic choices testifies to the fervor, among German writers, surrounding the call for a national personality.

But what about comedy and the comic? Does it too foster a nation's sense of co-belonging and positive self-regard? Herder, for one, thought so. He believed—and he was not alone in this belief—that comedy could tell us more about human beings in their concrete historical and political existence than tragedy. Moreover, he claimed, comedy's proper deployment would more effectively foster cultural unity. Comedy, as he says at one point, is the genre with "life and lived experience (*das Leben und lebendige Erfahrung*) as its subject."[31] In the course of a series of remarks on the state of contemporary German letters, he argues that comedy should be understood more elastically than just as a rule-governed form inherited from antiquity. He says that even though "tragedy has more power for beholding the human separated from his political trappings (*politischen Hüllen*), only comedy can allow itself greater liberty, which one gladly grants it, in those cases when it does not laugh at the trappings, but instead at he who hides

---

30. Anonymous, "Ist nicht die Schaubühne das tauglichste Mittel, Volksgeschichte gemeinnütziger zu machen," in *Theaterkalender auf das Jahr 1787* (Gotha: Carl Wilhelm Ettinger, 1778), 33–40, here 34.

31. Johann Gottfried Herder, *Werke*, ed. *Wolfgang Pross* (Munich: Hanser Verlag, 1984–2002), 1:352.

beneath them."[32] We must note that in this passage, Herder's reference to the political is meant in an unusually capacious sense. The basic claim is that comedy can disclose with unique effectiveness the often discrepant relationship between the human being in an abstract and universal sense, on one side, and the human being as a determinate cultural and historical subject, on the other. Much more effectively than its sister genre, tragedy, comedy and comic theater more generally draw out mundane features of human life and expose them as laughable.

Is it possible to achieve a more well-defined sense of the contingent social-historical factors that the comic evidently exposes? In the case of German theater this question had no straightforward answer. To see why, it is helpful to consider a further example. Direction can be found in a passage from a little-known text on the relationship between national character and national theater composed in 1794 by Wilhelm Friedrich August Mackensen (1768–1798):

> The Swabian, the Austrian, the Silesian, the Westphalian, the resident of Lausatia, the one from Lower Saxony are all representatives of so many distinct nations, each with its own customs, own constitution, even its own particular language. Nonetheless, as soon as one views them as Germans, they have shared customs, shared constitution, shared language.

> Der Schwabe, der Oesterreicher, der Schlesier, der Westphälinger, der Bewohner der Lausitz, der Niedersachse, sind eigentlich Repräsentanten von so viel eigenen Nationen, deren jede besondere Sitten, besondere Verfassung, ja, ihre besondere Sprache hat, und die dennoch, sobald man sie als Deutsche betrachtet, gemeinschaftliche Sitten, gemeinschaftliche Verfassung, gemeinschaftliche Sprache haben.[33]

The passage specifies the concept of national culture at play in the case of Germany. Mackensen compares different kinds of regionally

---

32. The passage in the original German: "Ich weiß, daß die Tragödie mehr Gewalt hat, den Mesnchen, so wie er ist, abgesondert von seinen politischen Hüllen zu betrachten: allein die Comödie kann sich mehr Freiheit nehmen, die man ihr gerne zugibt, wenn sie nicht über die Hüllen lacht, sondern über den, der unter ihnen steckt." Herder, *Werke*, 1:347.

33. Wilhelm Friedrich August Mackensen, *Untersuchung über den deutschen Nationalcharakter in Beziehung auf die Frage: Warum gibt es kein deutsches Nationaltheater?* (Wolfenbüttel: Heinrich Georg Albrecht, 1794), 2.

bound groups in order to show that cultural difference is not absolute. It depends instead on the sort of similarities at issue. If the goal is to establish differences among municipalities, the sorts of similarities that appear salient will not be the same as the similarities that would appear in contrast to diverse provincial areas or entire nations. The scale of comparison is decisive.

One feature of the translation I have just presented might very well rankle speakers of English and German. "Custom" is not a standard translation of the word *Sitte*. Notoriously resistant to translation and often simply left as a calque, the concept of *Sitte* stands somewhere between a convention and a moral, inflected with more value than the former, but lacking in the absoluteness of the latter. In the mid-eighteenth century, it is often used as the equivalent of the French concept *moeurs*, an idiom that presents English translation with the very same difficulty. In the above passage, as in many of the texts at issue in this chapter, the plural *Sitten* is the salient usage, especially when accompanied by a national modifier (*deutsche Sitten, französische Sitten*, and so on). In this construction, the term refers to an array of (usually uncodified) behavioral conventions and manners that are held in high esteem, are imbued with a belief in their rightness, and yet differ from culture to culture. Given the generality of this definition, as well as an ineluctable imprecision in any English translation of the concept, the term *custom* provides a more than adequate fit. It is important to note, however, that there is a normative dimension to the references to *deutsche Sitten*, German customs. The phrase does not refer to all the German customs, irrespective of socioeconomic considerations. It instead implies the interactive patterns evident in day-to-day life that are especially well embodied by a select slice of society.[34]

---

34. I have the strong impression that in the latter half of the eighteenth century the concept *Sitte* functions differently than the cognate participial forms *gesittet* and the abstract noun *Sittlichkeit*. These two terms were often used, for instance, as translations of the English concept of morality, whereas *Sitte* allows for comparison among moral groups. Particularly instructive is the widely read and cited translation of Henry Home's 1751 *Essays on the Principles of Morality and Natural Religion*, which appeared in German as Heinrich Home, *Versuche über die*

What do these challenges to translating the concept of *Sitte* tells us about German comic theater? If we return to the sentences quoted above, we notice that the author claims that the comparison among nations allows the Germans to appear unified. This is not just straightforward, but plausible. It would, in fact, be both if not for the fact that over the following pages the argument repeatedly calls attention to the forces that have inhibited the formation of a genuine German national character and set of customs. Toward the end of his opening gambit and before moving into an in-depth discussion of the theater, Mackensen castigates his compatriots with the words "We seek to inject ourselves with foreign customs without asking if they will be able to grow on our trunk."[35] The distinction between a native and a foreign array of conventions amounts to the distinction between a stunted and a fecund growth. The Germans have failed to end up on the right side of this divide, thereby inhibiting the development of a unified character as well as a genuinely German theater. Mackensen returns to imitation—in particular, imitation of customs—as the crucial contribution of the stage to a consolidated nation. Much like the other texts we have been considering, Mackensen does not advocate a top-down imposition of legal or political infrastructure to foster unity, but instead recommends the stage as a bottom-up mechanism to create communal belonging. As a public forum, the theater has the capacity to alter, in Mackensen's turbid formulation, "the occult connections among ideas, according to which it [the nation] represents the

---

ersten Gründe der Sittlichkeit und der natürlichen Religion, trans. Christian Günther Rautenberg (Braunschweig: Johann Christoph Meyer, 1768). In the translation of Home's text, as in general, *Sittlichkeit* is used as the equivalent for the general concept of morality, and the terms *moralisch* and *Moral* describe the individual words or deeds. It is also important to note that *gesittet/ungesittet* also functions as a way of drawing hierarchical social distinctions—in order to claim that a privileged social group fully embodies the relevant *Sitten*, while a derided group is identified as *ungesittet*. *Deutsche Sitten*, we might say in a German idiom, are embodied in *die vornehmen Stände*. The customs worth having are those realized among the noble classes. In this respect, the German *Sitte* functions much like the French *moeurs*.

35. Mackensen, *Untersuchung über den deutschen Nationalcharakter*, 16. See also Möser, *Ueber die deutsche Sprache und Litteratur*, 15–16.

world and its objects; the idiosyncratic vantage points, which particularly determine its way of acting (*Handlungsweise*)."[36] Taken together, the Germans do not yet have an "idiosyncratic way of acting" because they have shown, over the course of their history, such "receptiveness to foreign customs."[37] Indeed, one of the chief tasks of the stage is to disseminate authentically German customs, thereby communicating to the nation its own exceptionality and uniqueness.[38]

Now it is possible to grasp the unique role of comic theater in the nation-building project of the latter half of the eighteenth century. The fundamental claim, propounded by a number of different writers, is that laughter feeds off of—but can also help spread—culture-specific customs. In this respect, though pathos-laden plays can depict "noble, sublime, and heroic" deeds, tragic figures are "not nearly as well suited" as those from comedy for the "depiction of a national ethical life" (*Schilderung der National-Sitten*). Theater where spectators go to laugh, meanwhile, depends on "middling people and the types of characters whose customs correspond to their spectators."[39] According to this line of thought, the mode of exemplarity that is the greatest strength of the tragic genre is also its greatest weakness. By depicting towering figures of human excellence—often from a bygone heroic age or from rarified social strata—tragedy introduces models that spectators cannot, by and large, identify with. To borrow Herder's terminology, it abstracts from the trappings of lived experience and addresses the human being in a fashion transcendent of time and space. The comic,

---

36. Mackensen, *Untersuchung über den deutschen Nationalcharakter*, 4.

37. Ibid., 5–6.

38. See in particular the remarks in Mackensen, *Untersuchung über den deutschen Nationalcharakter*, 7.

39. Jean Lois Castilhon, *Betrachtungen über die physicalischen und moralischen Ursachen der Verschiedenheit des Genie, der Sitten und Regierungsformen der Nationen* (Leipzig: Adam Heinrich Hollens Wittwe, 1770), 430. This text is an anonymous and very loose translation of the 1770 edition of Castilhon's *Considerations sur les causes physiques et morales de la diversité du genie, des moeurs, et du gouvernement des nations*, a text that plagiarizes François-Ignace d'Espiard de la Borde's 1752 *L'esprit des nations*. See Bell, *The Cult of the Nation in France*, 140–141.

meanwhile, has as its element familiar speech and relatable deeds. A basic tenet organizing the literary genres, according to the historian and theorist of the comic Karl Friedrich Flögel (1729–1788), is that "man sees himself in comedy and satire as in a mirror."[40] Accordingly, to write a history of the comic is to write a history of the "customs of the time and their alteration."[41] Unlike the timeless and placeless picture of human virtue often provided in tragedy, comic theater is closely bound together with the "idiosyncratic character of a nation and the specific characteristics of the age" or, in another formulation that shows the equivalence of the terms, with "the idiosyncratic customs and specific way of thinking of a nation."[42] As Flögel puts it in a final formulation, "As one can recognize a type of metal by the tone it makes, so too one can recognize the customs and way of thinking of a man by the jokes he makes."[43]

At the outset of this chapter, I claimed that endogenous improvement required the conspiracy of both local theatrical forms and a unique, surrounding culture. And, as we have just seen, comic practices are particularly revealing of a culture's defining customs. But the conclusion is not, and could not have been, that German comic theater could now simply begin portraying distinctively German customs, nor was there a storehouse of venerated forms to draw on. Autochthonous theatrical conventions appeared scarce to so many critics and playwrights because German writers had, at least since the early Enlightenment reforms, "despised indigenous fruits and instead preferred to reap Italian and French ones of middling quality" and consequently ignored the possibility of a "refinement of indigenous products."[44] In a kindred formulation, "For a long time now, we have seemed highly uninteresting to ourselves."[45] The

---

40. Carl Friedrich Flögel, *Geschichte der komischen Literatur* (Liegnitz/Leipzig: David Sieger, 1784), 1:28.

41. Ibid., 1:253.

42. Ibid., 1:130 and 134.

43. Ibid., 1:219.

44. Möser, *Ueber die deutsche Sprache und Litteratur*, 16–17.

45. Helfrich Peter Sturz, "Julie, ein Trauerspiel in fünf Aufzügen mit einem Brief über das deutsche Theater an die Freude und Beschützer desselben in Hamburg," in *Schriften* (Munich: Johann Baptist Strohl, 1785), 2:119–222, here 124. The tragedy with attached letter was originally published in 1767.

project of improving the stage has thus far produced only "boring or artificial" results "spun of French silk."[46] A German theater worthy of the name would be one emancipated of the servile dependence on external forms—one that appropriates already existing local conventions and works step-by-step to improve them. The domain of the comic would seem the natural candidate for such endogenous improvement, with its particularly close relationship to local customs. But the turn to German culture was imperiled by the internal diversity of the German peoples and lands. Lessing famously remarked upon the failure of a national theater in Hamburg that it was caused not by a diversity of "political constitution," but instead by a lack of coherence in "the character of customs" (*dem sittlichen Character*).[47] Customs could not form the foundation of an idiosyncratically German comic theater so long as authors had to ask, as another observer of the Hamburg enterprise put it, "Which customs shall we imitate? The customs of a single province?"[48] There was a broad-based sense that the Germans lacked a preestablished national unity—a coherence of customs—that a potentially improved comic theater could even draw on. The project of using the comic as a medium to reflect or even help fabricate national unity came to seem, in light of the internal diversity of German life, a hopeless dead-end.

Faced with this dilemma, an alternative had to be found. Given the proximity of the comic to local customs, the question became whether it was possible to use this theatrical form as an instrument for furnishing culture with unity. By way of imitation, the comic stage could potentially provide the vehicle for bringing forth a unified set of specifically German customs. The problem was identifying a theatrical form that cut across the internal heterogeneity of the German people and that could be readily appropriated and improved upon. Herder, among others, proposed that the faint

---

46. Sturz, "Julie, ein Trauerspiel in fünf Aufzügen," 125–126.

47. Gotthold Ephraim Lessing, *Werke und Briefe*, ed. Jürgen Stenzel (Frankfurt am Main: Deutscher Klassiker Verlag, 1989), 6:684.

48. Sturz, "Julie, ein Trauerspiel in fünf Aufzügen," 124–125. In the next sentence of his letter, written in 1767, Sturz goes on to say that all the clamoring about national spirit in recent treatises had done nothing to supply the nation with one.

hints of an unrealized national distinctness could be found in what he called "coarse humor" and "base laughter."[49] "A theater in its infancy must go through these paths [because] every nation in the world, which loves comedies according to their own nature, portrays this form of the comic—according to their own nature."[50] Strikingly, he further points to a particular preliterary resource, namely, the "old-German Hans-Wurst," as a touchstone for a stage culture yet to be invented. In his view, those pursuing the improvement of the German stage needed to realize that this ignoble figure provided a form that could become the motor for the dissemination of a national culture. In his view, no theatrical form but the comic could relate with the same vividness the "life and lived experience" of the people. Since the internal coherence of this German life had been compromised by its dependency on other cultures, the fool constituted a particularly promising mechanism for shaping the nation. As Herder remarks, crystallizing a widespread sentiment, if authors would only set about refining this theatrical form, they will "give birth slowly, with difficulty, but then ultimately," to a distinctively German form of literary theater.[51]

---

49. See Herder, *Werke*, 1:336 and 346. See also Sturz, "Julie, ein Trauerspiel in fünf Aufzügen," 2:125 and the suggestive remarks in Möser, *Ueber die deutsche Sprache und Litteratur*, 39–40.

50. The passage in the original: "Jede Nation in der Welt, die Comödien nach ihrer Art liebt, zeichnet dies Lächerliche—nach ihrer Art." Herder, *Werke*, 1:346–347.

51. Herder, *Werke*, 1:348.

Part IV

The Vitality of Folly in Goethe's *Faust* and Kleist's *Jug*

Und wenn der Narr durch alle Scenen läuft,
So ist das Stück genug verbunden.

And if the fool runs through all the scenes
Then the piece is tied together enough.

—Johann Wolfgang von Goethe,
Paralipomena to *Faust I*

Was du ererbt von deinen Vätern hast
Erwirb es um es zu besitzen.

What you have inherited from your fathers
Acquire it to possess it.

—Johann Wolfgang von Goethe,
Faust I, lines 682–683

13

FAUST I

Setting the Stage

In the midst of his scathing disavowal of the "frenchifying" tendencies of the reform movement, Gotthold Ephraim Lessing makes mention of the tale of Doctor Faustus as a promising theme for a genuinely German play.[1] It was an idea that Lessing entertained for much of his adult life—from about 1755 to 1775—but which never came to more than a handful of fragments. Lessing's idea for a German tragedy was, in truth, a single moment in a centuries-long tradition of enthusiasm for the Faust legend. English traveling players had first made a theatrical hit of the story, freely adapting a tragedy written by the English playwright Christopher Marlowe (1564–1593) that had itself been inspired by the German chapbook *Historia von D. Johann Fausten*, anonymously published in 1587. Lessing's turn to the Faust story was historically pivotal. It

---

1. Gotthold Ephraim Lessing, *Werke und Briefe*, ed. Jürgen Stenzel (Frankfurt am Main: Deutscher Klassiker Verlag, 1989), 4:501.

served the strategic purpose of establishing a counterweight to the emphasis that had been placed on the cultivation of culturally alien dramatic themes and forms. Lessing had the hunch that the Faust featured in marketplace puppet shows and theatrical spectacles could also become a German hero.

There can be no doubt that the apogee of the Faust fascination was Goethe's play of the same name, a project he put into print in 1808 but had embarked upon approximately ten years after Lessing's literary campaign against the French.[2] Given the historical proximity of these two authors' interest in Faust, it seems only natural to explore the relationship between Goethe's *Faust I* and the project of literary improvement from the latter half of the eighteenth century. Such a line of inquiry must confront a few points of resistance. Even though it is normal to speak of Goethe's tragedy as a high point in German national literature, this conventional locution does not tell us just how deep the affiliation cuts. Essentially any informed reader would have to admit that Goethe's tragedy is not the expression of narrow-minded provincialism. On the contrary, much of the scholarship over the last two centuries has sought to demonstrate the artistic rank of *Faust* by pointing out how it appropriates and integrates literary traditions extending from ancient Greek tragedy and the Bible to Golden Age Spain and Shakespeare's England.[3] Claims concerning the local specificity of

---

2. Throughout part 4, I provide the original German in parentheses as well as line numbers from the Deutscher Klassiker Verlag edition, which is cited in the notes as FA I 7/1. Since I support my argument concerning *Faust* with evidence from across Goethe's vast oeuvre, my references include the title of the relevant text as well as the volume of the Deutscher Klassiker Verlag Edition (FA) in which the text appears. Translations longer quotations from Goethe's *Faust* are taken from Johann Wolfgang von Goethe, *Faust: A Tragedy; Interpretive Notes, Contexts, Modern Criticism*, trans. Walter Arndt and ed. Cyrus Hamlin (New York: W.W. Norton, 2001).

3. On this point, I recommend Albrecht Schöne's introductory notes to FA I 7/2: esp. 11–26. See also Joachim Müller, "Goethes Dramentheorie," in *Deutsche Dramentheorien*, ed. Reinhold Grimm (Frankfurt am Main: Athenäum Verlag, 1971), 1:167–213, esp. 175–176. Jane Brown's comprehensive and insightful study of Goethe's *Faust* argues that the play should be seen as an attempt to establish a new form of (distinctively worldly and not narrowly German) literature. I have learned much from Brown's book as well as her other essays on Goethe, but do not feel compelled to take such an either-or stance. I also suspect that Brown

the plot seem equally out of place: the eponymous hero, for example, displays no interest in questions of nationhood. His desires head in the direction of the "forces of nature" (*Kräfte der Natur*, line 438); one of his chief ambitions is "to bear the earth's woe and the earth's joy" (*Der Erde Weh, der Erde Glück zu tragen*, line 465). From the opening dialogue in heaven up through the final scene of the tragedy's first part, when words of redemption are spoken by a disembodied divine voice, there is no denying the cosmic scale of Goethe's tragedy. Ultimately, the universalizing impulse evident in the adjective "Faustian"—common to a number of European languages—has a solid thematic basis in Goethe's tragedy.

But there is a more visceral objection to meet. Arguing in terms of national literature risks sounding hopelessly antiquated. Since its publication, the play's protagonist has often been construed as the embodiment of the German "mythological main character" (*mythologische Hauptperson*), as the philosopher Friedrich Schelling (1775–1854) once put it.[4] Along the same lines, the venerated poet Heinrich Heine once (1797–1856) declared that "the German people is itself that learned Doctor Faust."[5] Throughout the nineteenth and twentieth centuries, the hero's tortured quest made him the quintessential embodiment of the German nation's philosophical earnestness.[6] And for the last half century, it has not taken much to associate this sort of identificatory reading with the Faust figure, motivated by a sense of national pride, with the horrific excesses of the twentieth century. For many, it is difficult to celebrate Faust as a German hero without recalling the National Socialist appropriation of the very same figure.[7]

---

ultimately intended to make *Faust* appealing to a larger audience of European literature scholars, not to deny the legitimacy of an argument such as the one I advance here. See Jane Brown, *Goethe's Faust: The German Tragedy* (Ithaca: Cornell University Press, 1986).

4. Friedrich Schelling, *Philosophie der Kunst*, in *Schellings Werke*, ed. Manfred Schröter (Munich: C.H. Beck, 1927), 5:458; quoted in FA I 7/2:37.

5. Heinrich Heine, *Sämtliche Werke in zwölf Bänden*, ed. Klaus Briegleb (Munich: Hanser Verlag, 1976), 5:402.

6. For an abundance of references to this theme, see FA I 7/2:39–41.

7. Inez Hedges, *Framing Faust: Twentieth-Century Cultural Struggles* (Carbondale: Southern Illinois University Press, 2005), 44–71.

In suggesting a kinship between Goethe's *Faust* and the project of literary improvement, my goal is, ultimately, not to assert some (pernicious or anodyne) nationalistic core to Goethe's literary project. But it is undeniable that the Faust story first began to interest Goethe as he was writing about themes specific to German culture and its history. Among Goethe's prolific writings from the 1770s, the first decade of his literary career, we find a number of texts that, in one way or other, draw on culture-internal resources: *Götz von Berchlingen mit der eisernen Hand* (*Götz von Berchlingen with the Iron Hand*, 1773), which he referred to as "the story of a most noble German"; the famous essay *Von deutscher Baukunst* (*On German Architecture*, 1773); two plays based on the early modern tradition of carnival fairs; and a fragmentary farce entitled *Hanswursts Hochzeit oder der Lauf der Welt: Ein microkosmisches Drama* (*Hanswursts Wedding or the Way of the World: A Microcosmic Drama*, posthumous).[8] Goethe referred later in his life to his earliest work on the Faust story, together with the wildly vulgar Hanswurst farce, as part of a "secret archive" of texts with strong connections to popular theatrical traditions.[9] Even though Goethe's interest in literary drama is most often approached in terms of its universal scope—its potential to mirror the "history of the world," as he noticed in Shakespeare—there are also traces, well into the final decades of his career, of a more circumscribed interest in developing strategies for making art and literature appeal to and improve the entire German nation.[10] For instance, a number of pivotal essays from the time in the 1790s, when he was intensely working on *Faust*, cast cultural differences, founded on regional and climate-based characteristics, as the touchstone for all forms

---

8. Discussion of *Götz* in letter from 11/28/1771, FA II 1:247.

9. This connection was originally made in the searching essay by Thomas Mann, "Über Goethe's *Faust*," in *Gesammelte Werke* (Frankfurt am Main: S. Fischer Verlag, 1991), 9:581–621. See also FA I 15:923–924. There are striking acoustic and semantic echoes between the farce's incipit and Faust's monologue at the start of the tragedy.

10. Quotation from "Zum Schakespeares Tag," FA I 18:11. Especially interesting in this context is chapter 20 of *Wilhelm Meisters Theatralische Sendung*, FA I 9:53–55. See also "Zusätze zu Meyers Aufsatz 'Chalkographische Gesellschaft zu Dessau,'" FA I 18:635–637.

of aesthetic production and for the normative assessment of taste in general.[11] At one point, he even goes so far as to claim that the reliance on "alien custom and foreign literature" (*fremde Sitte und ausländische Literatur*), particularly within the educated elite, had inhibited the "German from developing himself as a German."[12]

Of course, none of this evidence supports the view of Goethe as a jingoist. It does, however, give us a sense of the framework within which Goethe developed a fascination with the "puppet-show tale" (*Puppenspielfabel*) of Faust's pact with the devil.[13] Already in his earliest sketches of the play, Goethe seized on the comic form that had established itself around the same time that the Faust story first became a theatrical hit: the fool. That the Faust story provided the occasion for Goethe's most wide-ranging and probing exploration of the fool as a theatrical form is, from a certain point of view, not surprising. For instance, the Jewish philosopher Moses Mendelssohn (1729–1786) responded to his friend Lessing's proposal of a Faust tragedy by skeptically noting that the theatergoing public so strongly associated the Faust story with a comic spectacle that "a single exclamation, o Faustus! Faustus! could make the entire parterre laugh."[14] Up to Goethe's own time, the story was as well known for its insatiably curious alchemist as for the parodic tone of the pieces he appeared in, often alongside an instantiation of the fool. And yet, unlike Mendelssohn, the modern reader rarely points to the comic as the definitive element of the Faust play.

It risks seeming at best exaggerated or at worst preposterous to assert that the tragedy's participation in the project of creating a distinctly German national literature was dependent on its comic

---

11. Particularly interesting in this respect is "Einleitung in die 'Propyläen,'" which Goethe published in 1798. The paralipomena make clear that he assigned critical importance to the comparison of what he calls "national physiognomies." See FA I 18:457–488, esp. 467 and 476.

12. From the essay he wrote under the title "Literarischer Sansculottismus," FA I 18:319–324, here 322.

13. See his remarks from his autobiography *Dichtung und Wahrheit*, FA I 15:451.

14. Moses Mendelssohn, *Gesammelte Schriften*, ed. Bruno Strauss (Stuttgart: Friedrich Frommann Verlag, 1974), 11/1:20.

dimension. Some of this issues from the tendency, among casual readers as well as scholars, to focus attention on the eponymous hero at the expense of his idiosyncratically diabolical sidekick. It also issues from the persistent unwillingness among literary historians to acknowledge the resolute persistence of the fool figure, who, as we saw in part 3, figured centrally in the national literature effort. But in order to grasp Goethe's understanding of the theatrical enterprise—an understanding that encouraged his appropriation and transformation of the stage fool within a new dramatic context—it is crucial to acknowledge that he remained a staunch opponent of the schoolmasterly classicizing approach of early Enlightenment reformers, particularly their failure to acknowledge the artistic potential borne by the fool. While the place of Faust within the tradition of German national literature is, admittedly, an almost insurmountably vast topic, the following chapters pick up on the thread that runs through part 3, namely, the claim that the fool proved integral to the literarization projects in the latter half of the nineteenth century. The guiding claim shall be that Goethe constructs the figure Mephistopheles as the projection of the theatrical form of the fool into a new artistic context that at once integrates preexisting aspects of the form and alters them to accommodate the particular literary context of *Faust I*. Not Faust the German hero, but Mephistopheles.

The term *hero* is, of course, not entirely accurate. While Goethe reworks the tradition of stage fool in Mephistopheles into much more than a comic ornament or addendum, allowing facets of the comic form to penetrate to the core of the tragedy's structure, the modifier *heroic* would grossly oversimplify the multiple layers of significance Goethe assigns its diabolical protagonist.[15] An adequate interpretation must attend closely to the nuanced and innovative manner in which the form appears in Goethe's singular literary text, and thus must abandon the synoptic approach that has organized the other chapters of this study. The following

---

15. Mann, "Über Goethe's *Faust*," 583.

discussion concentrates on a crucial and underappreciated strand that runs through the tragedy that Goethe published in 1808.[16]

Among the fault lines extending from the tradition of the stage fool to the form of *Faust*, perhaps the most underappreciated pertains to the drama-theater dyad. The historically contentious status of the fool in the establishment of a theatrical culture organized around literary drama comes to the fore in Goethe's unusual multiplication of framing devices. Famously, the play opens with the poem "Zueignung," which is typically translated as "Dedication" but bears the connotation of appropriation, or taking possession (of the Faust legend itself, as the poem suggests), followed by two mini-dialogues, *Vorspiel auf dem Theater* (*Prelude on the Theater*) and *Prolog im Himmel* (*Prologue in Heaven*). The *Prelude*, composed in the latter half of 1798, during a phase of Goethe's concentrated work on the tragedy, is as much a preparatory skit *about* the theater as it is a skit performed *on* the theater (i.e., the stage).[17] It is, at once, a self-reflexive statement about how to approach the play and a structurally integral element in it.

The dialogue presents a theater director (*Direktor*) and a poet (*Dichter*), in addition to a third figure whose identity has caused widespread confusion. In English translations, the figure Goethe calls the Lustige Person has been referred to as the Clown (Walter Kaufmann), Player of Comic Roles (Stuart Atkins), Merry Person

---

16. In addition to Jane Brown's study, which I have already mentioned, I wish to call attention to two excellent studies from recent years that attempt a unified interpretation of the tragedy's two parts: Karl Eibl, *Das monumentale Ich: Wege zu Goethe's "Faust"* (Frankfurt am Main/Leipzig: Insel Verlag, 2000); and Johannes Anderegg, *Transformationen: Über Himmlisches und Teuflisches in Goethes "Faust"* (Bielefeld: Aisthesis Verlag, 2011).

17. It has been speculated that even though Goethe published the playlet as part of *Faust* in 1808, it was composed either as part of his never-completed project of a second part to *The Magic Flute* or on the occasion of the 1798 opening of the theater in Weimar. See Oskar Seidlin, "Ist das 'Vorspiel auf dem Theater' ein Vorspiel zum 'Faust'?," in *Von Goethe zu Thomas Mann* (Göttingen: Vandenhock & Ruprecht, 1969), 56–64. See also Jost Schillemeit, "Das 'Vorspiel auf dem Theater' zu Goethe's *Faust*: Entstehungszusammenhänge und Folgerungen für sein Verständnis," *Euphorion* 80 (1986): 149–166. Both genetic arguments fail, in my view, to see the far-reaching repercussions of the *Vorspiel auf dem Theater* within the work as a whole.

(Walter Arndt), and Comedian (Randall Jarrell). "Clown" comes closest to the pedigree alluded to in the German nomenclature, but only works on the basis of the term's (now antiquated) association with a standard figure from Jacobean and Elizabethan English theater. Each of these translations fails to recognize that Goethe is offering an onomastic wink to the most controversial figure in eighteenth-century German theater, the fool. Gottsched first solidified the locution Lustige Person as a category in the 1730s. He subsumed the many Hanswursts, Pickelherings, Harlequins, Killian Brustflecks, Grobians, and others under the general term Lustige Person, a blanket term that I have translated consistently over the foregoing chapters as "the fool." Despite its initially defamatory connotations, Gottsched's terminology had, by Goethe's time, become common currency, losing some of its critical bite. The historical ambivalences inscribed in the term are important because, beginning already in his earliest youth, Goethe identified the fool as the crux on which the fate of eighteenth-century theater turned. In his autobiography, for instance, he looks back at the decades leading up to his first literary experiments and identifies an utterly simplistic logic at the heart of the reform movement. Making the theater useful (*nützlich*) demanded the imposition of moral rectitude, a standard that supposedly could be achieved only if "the fool (*lustige Person*) was banished."[18] Reform-minded critics and playwrights failed to heed the pleas of the wise few (*geistreiche Köpfe*) who spoke up in the fool's favor, condemning the German theater for the middle third of the eighteenth century—with the major exception of Lessing—to a deplorable existence. More than a late-in-life reminiscence celebrating the author's own redemptive arrival on the literary scene, this passage speaks to Goethe's core convictions about the decisive position of the fool for German theater—both its historical course of development and its present possibilities for improvement.

Goethe's choice to cast the fool in the *Prelude on the Theater* must be understood as a response to the general historical quagmire in which he believed the theater was stuck. For him, the abolishment of the fool demonstrated a misunderstanding of the heterogeneous

---

18. Goethe, *Dichtung und Wahrheit*, FA I 14:619.

and internally differentiated composition he identified as essential to a successful theater. The following passage from his novel *Wilhelm Meisters Theatralische Sendung* (*Wilhelm Meister's Theatrical Mission*, posthumous), which he worked on between 1775 and 1782 but abandoned incomplete, epitomizes a fundamental feature of Goethe's approach to the theatrical enterprise and can help us grasp the repercussions of the fool's reinsertion. In the novel's rich narrative tapestry, with its many images from and discussions of the contemporary theatrical world, we find the following remark by the protagonist:

> And I even claim that the more the theater is purified, the more it must become pleasing to people of reason and taste, but the more it must always lose of its original effect and purpose. It seems to me, if I may use a metaphor, like a pond, which needs to contain not only clear water, but also a certain portion of mud, weed, and insects, if fish and water-fowl should fare well there.

> Und ich behaupte sogar, daß je mehr das Theater gereinigt wird, es zwar verständigen und geschmackvollen Menschen angenehmer werden muß, allein von seiner ursprünglichen Wirkung und Bestimmung immer mehr verliert. Es scheint mir wenn ich ein Gleichnis brauchen darf wie ein Teich zu sein, der nicht allein klares Wasser, sondern auch eine gewisse Portion von Schlamm, Seegras, und Insekten enthalten muß, wenn Fische und Wasservögel sich darin wohl befinden sollen.[19]

According to this suggestive parallel between the theatrical enterprise and a muddy ecosystem, the entire project of theatrical ennoblement stands on an ill-conceived sanitary logic. The hard-and-fast division between pure and impure fails to do justice to the interdependency of multiple different elements needed for a flourishing theatrical culture. The deft subtlety of this metaphor lies in its replacement of a logic defined by the binary division between two classes with one defined by a diversified array of elements, within which no clear rank or privilege can be made out. One crucial result of the faulty binary division, Goethe here suggests, is that the supposedly purified stage can appeal only to the select segment of

---

19. Goethe, *Wilhelm Meisters Theatralische Sendung*, FA I 9:100–101.

the population with equally purified values and preferences. The vitality of the stage, however, depends on attracting diverse spectators and arresting everyone's attention. To create this more inclusive audience requires abandoning the entire purified/contaminated division and restoring the less culturally ennobled elements that had, at least in the past, made the theater into a widely appreciated spectacle.

With this inclusive structure in view, let us return to the *Prelude*, with its avowed concern with the fate of the stage "in the German lands" (line 35). The playlet's triangulated configuration—Director, Poet, Fool—allows for the articulation of differing stances toward the drama-theater dyad without installing an internal hierarchy or asserting a definitive viewpoint. It encourages an approach to the play much like the pond from *Wilhem Meister*, a heterogeneous habitat of mutually interacting elements, which cannot be arranged according to the distinction between the pure and impure. With unique conceptual intensity, the *Prelude* addresses what should, by now, be familiar issues concerning the drama-theater dyad, including (1) the nature of the audience as a collective and (2) the relationship between text and performance.

The dialogue shows that attempts to assign a purpose to either text or performance cannot be decided independently of the addressee. The Director, whose primary interest is in securing the play's commercial success, emphasizes the prosaic motivations and unsophisticated expectations that underlie the typical spectator's decision to visit the theater. On the most basic level, his remarks are entreaties to the Poet and the Fool that they ensure the engagement and satisfaction of the audience, but the limitation of his position is indicated by the complete absence of any ethical, epistemic, or metaphysical significance in the theater he envisions. His remarks indicate, rather, that the theater is emphatically for the sake of the collective that experiences it. In the opening gambit of the *Prelude*, he refers twice to the throng (*Menge*, lines 37 and 49), and once to "anyone" (*jedermann*, line 40) and the "people" (*Volk*, line 43). The use of these terms brings three points to the fore. First, the Director establishes an equivalence between the two lexemes *Volk* and *Menge*, in order to describe the constitution of the audience.

Although these terms had historically carried socially pejorative connotations, the Director employs them in an egalitarian sense. His definition fits within the same historical-semantic framework as the following definition from Kant's *Vorlesungen über Anthropologie in pragmatischer Absicht* (*Lectures on Anthropology from a Pragmatic Point of View*), delivered in 1800 and published posthumously, in which I leave the crucial terms untranslated: "Under the word *Volk* (populus) one understands a unified *Menge* of persons, insofar as it [the *Menge*] makes up a *totality*."[20] Kant defines a *Volk* as an entirety of a national-cultural people, made up of a *Menge* or a multiplicity of discrete individuals; in much the same spirit, the Director in the *Prelude* envisions spectatorship as a collective experience, as a ritual that coalesces individuals into a unified group. The theater functions as a space for a collective en masse, devoid of distinctions of education, vocation, or estate, where the group comes together and experiences itself as a unified whole. Since the theater should appeal to the entire group, not a select subset from among it, he calls a performance that is "fresh and new / and with significance, pleasing too" (lines 47–48). He turns to the Poet and the Fool to accomplish the principal charge of a theatrical performance, namely, to please the audience and capture their engaged attention.

The Director's assertion that the spectator's enjoyment is foundational for theater's success stands in clear opposition to the Poet's derision of the crowd and the theatrical setting. He decries the "motley throng" (*jener bunten Menge*, line 59), "the surging crowd" (*das wogende Gedränge*, line 61), which pulls him into a maelstrom and robs him of his "spirit" or *Geist* (line 60). The poet appropriates and denigrates the form of co-belonging celebrated by the Director; for him, a group means absorption into an uncontrolled and undifferentiated medium. Instead of the mundane world of performance before an audience, he seeks the "narrows of heaven" (line 63), confines that are at once sheltered and celestial. The expression of favor for solitary refuge over collective exposure,

---

20. Immanuel Kant, *Gesammelte Schriften/Akademieausgabe* (Berlin: Königlich Preußische Akademie der Wissenschaften, 1917), 7:311.

and in turn for the supermundane over the mundane, condenses a deep conceptual difference. The text here delineates a boundary between the dramatic text and the theatrical performance according to their respective functions and temporal constitutions. The Poet's labor consists in creating a singular and unchanging dramatic text associated primarily with an escape from the terrestrial sphere to the divine heavens. The dramatic product is, in his view, autarkic; it need not feed into a theatrical performance and does not depend upon one for its legitimacy. Whereas the Director solicits the Poet's text for the express purpose of its theatrical realization, the Poet imposes an unbridgeable hiatus between the fixed dramatic text and the ephemeral performance. This privilege of the text over performance is solidified in the Poet's use of one of the key terms in Goethe's lexicon in general and in *Faust* in particular: namely, the *Augenblick*, the fleeting moment as quick as the glance of the eye. Here a polarity emerges between the consuming "violence of the wild instant" (*des wilden Augenblicks Gewalt*, line 70) and the realm of "posterity" (*Nachwelt*, line 74), where the unalloyed truth perdures. The Poet regards fleeting experience as at best nugatory and at worst harmful in comparison with the ecstatic temporality of the celestial sphere. The crowd may coalesce around the fleeting instant, but the Poet seeks refuge in a domain immune to the vagaries of time and the violent impositions of the crowd.

The Fool, finally, appropriates the problem of temporality, but in order to elevate the present moment—the experience of the now within theatrical performance—to utmost importance. If he were to speak of the *Nachwelt*—literally the after-world, the world of posterity—who, he asks in a rejoinder to the Poet, would amuse the shared world of the now, the *Mitwelt* (lines 76–77). The domain of theatrical address is the domain of the present or *Gegenwart* (line 79), a term he invests with a double significance. With this term, he indicates the rapport between performer and spectator within the face-to-face setting, the mutual belonging within the live context of performance. But the term also points to the temporal experience shared by all audience members. Hewing close to the Director's emphasis on theatrical realization as the governing term in the drama-theater dyad, the Fool asserts that the spectators' collective mode of receptivity intensifies their sensory experience. His own powers are similarly enhanced within the communal theatrical setting, for no human response is so contagious as laughter. The fool "desires a big circle, in order to make it shake with laughter all the surer" (*wünscht sich einen großen Kreis, / Um ihn gewisser zu erschüttern*, lines 83–84).

At this juncture, an initial set of opposing and overlapping opinions pertaining to the status of the audience can be made out. Collective co-belonging stands against the forfeiture of individuality; publicness against seclusion; true lasting poetic value against risible folly in the present; the ethereal against the mundane; and the fleeting performance against the eternal text. With these antinomies in hand, let us turn to a second thematic complex found in the *Prelude*. The playlet also introduces a question that, as I argued in part 2, stands at the center of eighteenth-century debates: What exactly is a dramatic text or a theatrical performance? Again, the text sets up a system of oppositions pertaining to the rapport between stage and audience. The Director elevates the abundance of visual spectacle to paramount importance, asserting that sheer plenty will ensure the satisfaction of each member of the multitude. The following passage gives a fuller sense of the Director's vantage point:

> They like to look, so let them see a lot.
> You give the audience a solid eyeful,
> So they can gape and marvel all the time,
> You'll grip them by sheer quantity of trifle,
> Your popularity will climb.
> Mass calls for mass in order to be won,
> Each ends up choosing something for his own.
>
> Man kommt zu schaun, man will am liebsten sehn.
> Wird Vieles vor den Augen abgesponnen,
> So daß die Menge staunend gaffen kann,
> Da habt ihr in der Breite gleich gewonnen,
> Ihr seid ein vielgeliebter Mann.
> Die Masse könnt ihr nur durch Masse zwingen,
> Ein jeder sucht sich endlich selbst was aus.

(lines 90–96)

Theater is a spectacle; its purpose is to overpower the visual sense and throw the audience into a state of rapture. The Director assigns the Poet and Fool the responsibility of providing a sufficient quantity of visual elements, for amassing a diversity of elements, a sequence of beads that need not coalesce into a consistent stream. The theatrical object should aim for a multifariousness that accords with, indeed accommodates itself to, the multiplicity of spectators. A welter before the stage calls for a welter on the stage.

The Poet, by contrast, extols an opposing cluster of criteria oriented around his own writerly practice. For him, the audience is not the crucible of the theatrical object, but rather a consideration downstream from the author's production of the dramatic text. The poet enjoys the "highest privilege" (line 135), the "human right, granted him by nature" (line 136). This highly abstract claim achieves its full significance in light of what immediately follows. In a passage that warrants quoting at length, he spells out a conception of the poetic vocation laden with metaphysical implications:

The while indifferent nature helter-skelter
Twists the eternal thread upon her spindle,
When all created things' discordant welter
Would coalesce into a graceless brindle,
Who parts the sequence, changeless and perpetual,
Enlivening into rhythmic ease,
Who calls the single to the common ritual,
Where it resounds in glorious harmonies?
Who lets the tempest's passions rage their maddest
Imparts grave meaning to the sunset glow?
Who strews the bloom of springtime at its gladdest
Where the beloved is wont to go?
Who braids the insignificant green laurels
To every merit's honorific wreaths?
Who firms Olympus? unifies Immortals?
The might of man, which in the poet breathes.

Wenn die Natur des Fadens ew'ge Länge,
Gleichgültig drehend, auf die Spindel zwingt,
Wenn aller Wesen unharmon'sche Menge
Verdrießlich durch einander klingt:
Wer teilt die fließend immer gleiche Reihe
Belebend ab, daß sie sich rhythmisch regt?

Wer ruft das Einzelne zur allgemeinen Weihe?
Wo es in herrlichen Akkorden schlägt,
Wer läßt den Sturm zu Leidenschaften wüten?
Das Abendrot im ernsten Sinne glühn?
Wer schüttet alle schönen Frühlingsblüten
Auf der Geliebten Pfade hin?
Wer flicht die unbedeutend grünen Blätter
Zum Ehrenkranz Verdiensten jeder Art?
Wer sichert den Olymp, vereinet Götter?
Des Menschen Kraft im Dichter offenbart.

(lines 142–157)

Among the many features of this suggestive passage deserving of commentary, I wish to isolate one in particular. The Poet introduces here a symbolic position that also informs Faust's own monologues in the main body of the tragedy. The Poet imagines nature as a prediscursive and internally undifferentiated flow of appearances, a confused mass not unlike the crowd. He asserts his primordial access to a nature that first must be divided up and then enlivened. Nature, to him, is not the object of his imitation or emulation, but rather a domain that comes to intelligibility under his control. The task of the poet is to assign meaning to all that passes before him, including the gods. He imagines himself in a position above ordinary experience, at the point where the chaotic manifold of appearances becomes a world of meaningful particulars. The product of his labor, the dramatic text, provides the indispensable substrate for theatrical performance in a double sense: it is the basis of the discrete entities perceptible on the stage as well as their meaning. The poet thus outlines what one might call an absolute standpoint—one cut off and separated from the world of appearances and by virtue of which each becomes fully concrete and particular. Note also that the nomothetic poet, as the above passage goes on to indicate, reveals a primordial and universal human power (*des Menschen Kraft*, line 157), a power present only derivatively and partially in concrete individuals. It belongs, then, to the symbolic vantage point imagined in these lines that the Poet divides nature up in order to make it meaningful in the first place and that, in doing so, he discloses in unadulterated form a distinctively human vital power. Thus the Poet claims for himself a universal human capacity or power, by virtue of his elevation to a supermundane vantage point, from which the manifestations of nature achieve order and meaning. The poet's activity is world-disclosing.

The final remarks on the drama-theater dyad are put forth by the Fool. He assumes an intermediary stance, between the metaphysically laden and divinely isolated dramatic text championed by the Poet, and the Director's complete subordination of dramatic design to the audience experience. Appropriating and amending the Director's petition for an internally diverse theatrical object, the Fool pleads for a totalizing representation, a play that draws its resources from human life in its entirety. At the same time, the Fool robs the absolute standpoint outlined in the Poet's remarks of its metaphysical implications. The epigrammatic imperative—"Just reach into the whole of human life!" (*Greift nur hinein ins volle Menschenleben!* line 167)—calls for a portrayal of life in its fullness and diversity, a life devoid of distorting embellishments and false proprieties. Of course, this demand stands in stark contrast to the distilled subjectivity that, as the Poet claims, creates poetry. For the Fool, human life achieves visibility on the stage as a totalizing "revelation" that displays to "each and every person what he bears in his heart" (line 179). Such a complete play transects traditional generic boundaries, proving equally adept at provoking tears as laughter (line 180). To appeal to every person, to be as much a divine manifestation as a visual display, is to encompass the extremes of both folly and sobriety, levity and gravity.

The competing notions of human life that take shape in the exchange between the three figures encourage us to approach *Faust* much like the internally diversified ecosystem described in *Wilhelm Meisters Theatralische Sendung*. On the one hand, we have a vision of the Poet as the exclusive source of all meaningful divisions, as the sole possessor of a universal form-giving capacity. What reveals itself in the Poet's statements is a creative energy that is both absolute and universal. By contrast, the Fool advances a vision of the internally diverse theatrical object, in accordance with the diversity of its spectators. Human life must be presented in its mundane completeness, avoiding all sanitary efforts that seek to block what is regarded as prosaic or unsavory. Theater, on the Fool's view, does not have its roots in an abstract humanity or an absolute subjectivity, but instead in the plural dimensions of human life as it is manifested in the *Menge* and *Volk*.

The dialogue thus contains elements that will concern us in the next two chapters. In schematic form these are the following:

1. eternity vs. the present
2. enduring value vs. passing amusement
3. divine vs. mundane
4. fixed dramatic textuality vs. live theatrical performance

The *Prelude on the Theater* is a *prelude about the theater*, which offers up contrasting views of the good of the theater for life and for society; of the dose of seriousness or levity appropriate to the stage; and of the relationship between the poetic and the theatrical vocation. The mythic banishment of the fool in favor of seriousness, dramatic unity, and moral univocity has no place in Goethe's *Faust* project. Instead, his tragedy, as the *Prelude* emphasizes, contains both the high and the low, the earnest and the jesting, oppositions that, moreover, stand in a dynamic, dialogical relationship.

Goethe's belief that such oppositions should not be viewed in terms of a strict either/or, but instead as interdependent poles, emerges forcefully from a little-noticed passage in his essay "Weimarisches Hoftheater" ("The Weimar Court Theater," 1802). According to the essay, treating the theatergoing public as if they were the fickle and impetuous rabble (*Pöbel*) is a pedagogically and theatrically ineffective form of cultural elitism. The genuine task that the theater must confront, he argues, is to progressively improve the standard of taste among audiences, and to work to increase what

Goethe calls their multifariousness (*Vielseitigkeit*).[21] Improvement comes only by way of a collaboration of text and performance, of drama and theater. A flourishing theatergoing public would be one where these two stand in a reciprocal relationship—where the public reads texts before seeing a performance and where spectators feel inspired to go home and consult the text after seeing a staging. In the constellation of the *Prelude on the Theater*, the business of the Director can succeed only with the participation of both the Poet and the Fool. Eternal truths fall on deaf ears unless the audience is kept alert to the present with jests and entertainment. An unorthodox and socially inclusive methodology underlies Goethe's attempt to make a recursive loop out of the theater-drama dyad. The spectator should recognize that the "the entirety of the theater is nothing but play" (*das ganze theatralische Wesen nur ein Spiel sei*), but should not "for that reason take less pleasure in it" (*deshalb weniger Genuß daran zu finden*).[22] Rather, Goethe's *Faust* includes just as much of the Poet's metaphysical grandeur as the Fool's mundane folly. It is, in a formulation from a few months before his death, one of Goethe's "very serious jokes."[23]

---

21. I am simplifying Goethe's statements in the course of his essay "Weimarisches Hoftheater," where he makes the astonishing remark that the great accomplishment of his directorship in Weimar has been to not treat the theatergoing public (*Publikum*) like the rabble (*Pöbel*). It is important that Goethe does not say here that the rabble does not come to his theater or that he excludes them purposefully, but rather that he has done his best to avoid treating the diverse public according to the basest expectations. His proof of this is that there is an interdependency between theatergoing qua spectacle and reading. FA I 6:846.

22. FA I 6:849.

23. Letter, 3/17/1832, FA II 11:555. Jane Brown uses this phrase in her study, particularly to explain the position of the stage fool, though she neither attributes it to Goethe nor provides a full explication of its significance. See Brown, *Goethe's Faust*, 37ff.

14

Faust II

Mirroring and Framing in the Form of Faust

What is *Faust I*? The previous chapter used terminology that would, at first blush, seem to have supplied a ready-made answer to this question. The distinction between the frames and the main body of the tragedy presupposes knowledge both of what a tragic drama is and how it differs from its frames. The latter distinction prioritizes essence over accident, the thing itself over its supporting structures. The foregoing chapter would seem to have assumed that the frames are external to the tragic story of Faust's deal with the devil and the ensuing corruption, condemnation, and redemption of Margarete (Gretchen). This intuitive approach is worth analyzing in closer detail and revising.

One of the most prevalent ways of grappling with the curious design of Goethe's tragedy—its inclusion of multiple frames, its disconnected scenic structure, its intermingling of tragic gravitas and comic levity—is to invoke Shakespeare, whom Goethe deeply revered from his early youth to the end of his life. Indeed, the impact of Shakespeare's major plays can be felt in the formal construction of individual scenes as well as in the selection of plot elements in Goethe's tragedy; and, on a deeper level, Goethe's conception of tragic conflict owed a significant debt to his English forebear.[1] Despite the obvious merit to reading the form of *Faust* through a Shakespearean lens and thus as a riposte to the strictures of classicism, one of the most intensive periods of Goethe's work on *Faust*, 1797–1806, actually coincided with his concerted effort to work out "general poetic laws."[2] Remarkably, Goethe's attempt to draw categorical distinctions among types of poetry did not rely on any of the moderns, including Shakespeare. The famous epistolary exchange between Friedrich Schiller and Goethe during these years focused, instead, on the distinction between epic and drama that was first laid down in Aristotle's *Poetics*. In their back-and-forth, Goethe and Schiller took liberty with the classical categories, perhaps in no small part because the generic system did not, by this point in time and for Goethe in particular, have binding force. By this, I mean that Goethe did not feel beholden to traditional nomenclature or even to the necessity for a complete generic order; he relished experimental possibilities afforded by classical and non-classical forms alike, and even worked on both simultaneously.[3] This does not deny the deep meditation on the nature of the tragic in *Faust*, or the artful, often very subtle methods Goethe employs to inscribe his play within the lineage of European tragedy. In fact, the unobligatory status of genre in Goethe's hand actually makes the use of the denomination "tragedy" in the case of *Faust* all the more remarkable. Goethe's awareness of the contingency of generic systems—of their regional and temporal rootedness—invests the willful reproduction of their terms with increased significance.

The principal emphasis in the Goethe-Schiller correspondence is not on the classification of genres like comedy and tragedy, however, but on a higher-order distinction between the different modes

---

1. David E. Wellbery, *Goethes Faust I: Reflexion der tragischen Form* (Munich: Carl Friedrich von Siemens Stiftung, 2016), 69–70.

2. "Über Epische und Dramatische Dichtung," FA I 18:445.

3. Schiller's loyalty to the generic system is more thoroughgoing than Goethe's, as evidenced in particular by the emphasis he places on the conformity of his *Wallenstein* (1799) to the classical conception of tragedy.

of presentation in epic and dramatic literature. In 1797, the very same year that, after a seven-year dormancy, he resumed work on *Faust*, Goethe instigated a protracted discussion with Schiller on this very topic.[4] Their focus on Aristotle's *Poetics* dictated that Homer's *Odyssey* and Sophocles's *Oedipus Rex* stand in as paradigmatic examples of epic and drama. The best-known fruit of their exchange is the brief essay Goethe composed and, after Schiller's death, published under both their names: "On Epic and Dramatic Poetry."[5] Four points crystallize in their discussion and this compact but far-reaching essay:

1. Goethe rereads Homer in an attempt to uncover the fundamental principle upon which epic is founded, and applies this principle to his own already completed poem *Hermann und Dorothea*. He discovers that "one of the chief qualities of the epic poem" is that it is capable of moving "backwards and forwards" in time, thus rendering "all retarding motives epic."[6] Everything that happens within an epic has already happened; the events are "completely past." This, it bears emphasizing, is a principle of formal organization, not a thematic one. In other words, Goethe pays no mind to the traditional idea that epic poetry recounts the adventurous deeds of hero and nation. In fact, in an earlier letter to Schiller, he goes so far as to say that what determines a genuine epic is the "*how* and not the *what*."[7] Distinctions among kinds of poetry, in short, are distinctions among ways of

---

4. The poetological principles of the letters have been incisively discussed in Georg Lukács, "Der Briefwechsel zwischen Goethe und Schiller," in *Deutsche Literatur* (Berlin: Aisthesis, 1964), 89–124. For a discussion of the letters in relationship to *Faust*, see Wolfgang Binder, "Goethes klassische Faust-Konzeption," *Deutsche Vierteljahrsschrift* 42 (1968): 55–88; and Johannes Anderegg, " 'Grenzsteine der Kunst': Goethes Gattungspoetik und die Arbeit an Faust," *Monatshefte* 102 (2010): 441–457.

5. The essay has been reprinted in FA I 18:445–447. For the sake of simplicity over the next four paragraphs, I only indicate the reference for those quotations lifted from the letter exchange. The other quotations are taken from the three-page essay that was written by Goethe and shared with Schiller.

6. Letter, 4/19/1797, FA II 4:320.

7. Letter, 4/22/1797, FA II 4:322.

configuring time; drama and epic can be thought of as the arrangement of events into one of two forms, distinguished by their respective temporalities.

2. If epic is defined by the capacity to move freely across time, reaching back into the past and stretching forward to the future, drama is defined by its "complete presentness." Every word or deed of a drama unfolds as it is happening, and every instant in a drama occurs at the moment of its portrayal. Again, this is not a thematic distinction, but one that bears on the distinct way—the *how*—a drama creates a fiction. It is this absolute, formal inhabitation of the present that makes drama distinct.

3. When Goethe resumes work on *Faust*, he refers to the play as a "barbaric composition."[8] Given the prevailing interest in the poetic forms of classical antiquity during this period, he can mean by this only that *Faust* aspires to accomplish something quite different from what he had achieved in classicizing plays such as *Iphigenia in Tauris* (1787) and *Torquato Tasso* (1790), which were the fruit of his travels in Italy. Goethe goes so far as to refer to *Faust* as one of his "farces" or *Possen*, a genre-concept often used to describe the fool's antics.[9] This work, he suggests, does not proceed seamlessly and uniformly from start to finish, as was characteristic of the classical paradigm, but instead consists of "different parts" that can be "dealt with in different ways."[10] Goethe suggestively calls his internally heterogeneous work a "tragelaph," a mythological creature that is half goat and half stag.[11] *Faust* is a play marked by an unclassical, distinctly northern doubleness; it is a monstrous, hybrid creature that "will always remain a fragment."[12] It would not be a stretch to say that Goethe thinks of *Faust* as a play of *pieces and patches*, much like those that had their home on the itinerant stage.[13]

---

8. Letter, 6/27/1797, FA II 4:357.
9. Letter, 7/1/1797, FA II 4:362.
10. Letter, 6/22/1797, FA II 4:354.
11. Letters, 6/10/1795 and 6/18/1795, FA II 4:82 and 84.
12. FA II 4:357.
13. For this terminology, see chapter 2.

4. Schiller objected to the *Faust* fragment published in 1790 that he had encountered "great difficulty" in "happily get[ting] through the jest and earnestness" (*zwischen dem Spaß und dem Ernst glücklich durchzukommen*).[14] Ever protective of classificatory divisions, which predominate in his own poetological treatises, Schiller is perturbed by a drama that, in his own view, intermingles comic levity and tragic gravitas. In response to this challenge, Goethe merely responds that his goal was not so much to "fulfill" as to "touch upon" the "highest demands."[15] Goethe sees his play as the exploration of preexisting generic standards, as their productive appropriation and transformation, not their wholesale application. One might speculate that Goethe is here alluding to the comic as a countervailing force to tragic dimensions of the play.

Although the letter exchange between Goethe and Schiller never takes on the comic, comedy, or the tradition of the stage fool, these four distilled points chart provisional coordinates for identifying the structure of *Faust*. In particular, they point to the fact that Goethe defines drama by its immersion in the now; that the play satisfies this formal principle in a barbaric, that is, anticlassicizing, way; and that interference between comic and tragic elements shapes the final horizon of meaning in the play. Concerning the final item in this list, Schiller was not the only one to find the hybridity of *Faust* disturbing. No one less than the philosopher Friedrich Schelling (1775–1854) remarked of *Faust: A Fragment* (1790) that Goethe had written a "modern comedy of the highest style,"[16] a remark all the more baffling because this earlier version did not include the (then not-yet-written) *Prelude on the Theater*. Similarly, the first extensive commentary on the play in Madame de Staël's *De l'Allemagne* (*On Germany,*

---

14. For unclear reasons, Schiller's letter of 6/27/1797 is not included in the Frankfurter Ausgabe. See Emil Staiger and Hans-Georg Dewitz, eds., *Der Briefwechsel zwischen Goethe und Schiller* (Frankfurt am Main: Insel Verlag, 2005), 408.

15. FA II 4:357.

16. See Friedrich W. J. von Schelling, *Philosophie der Kunst* (Darmstadt: Wissenschaftliche Buchgesellschaft, 1960), 375–377.

1810/1813) devoted significant energy to understanding what she regarded as Goethe's bewildering figuration of the devil.[17] This very same figure has led some modern commentators to refer to the tragedy as a "disguised comedy" (*verkappte Komödie*).[18] In their puzzlement over this generic duplicity, some modern directors have even gone so far as to excise large sections of Mephistopheles's lines.[19] But what if such an emendation amounted to an amputation of an indispensable element in the tragedy? And what if the prevalence of the comic is not meant to indicate a hidden genre identity, but instead must be understood as immanent to the tragic as it is realized in *Faust*?

If *Faust I* amounted to a mongrel in Goethe's own eyes, then all the more reason to wonder whether the division between the frame and the main body of the tragedy, which I used in a naive fashion in chapter 13, provides an adequate vocabulary. According to the ordinary scheme, we might suppose that the tragedy begins with the scholar's monologue in the Night scene and concludes in the prison cell when Mephistopheles steals Faust away. The framing sections, according to this logic, are defined in terms of their job of presenting a separate entity, to which they are ultimately subordinate. Taken to the extreme, it would even seem that, by virtue of their detachability, the frames could be replaced with alternative ones, without modifying the self-identical core of the drama. The text actually seems to encourage this line of thought. In the 1808 publication as well as the 1828 final, authorized edition, Goethe interleaved a title page after the three framing units (fig. 3), indicating that the scenes

---

17. Quoted in Johannes Anderegg, *Transformationen: Über Himmlisches und Teuflisches in Goethes "Faust"* (Bielefeld: Aisthesis Verlag, 2011), 56–57.

18. The desire to grasp Mephistopheles's comic presence has led some critics to make a genre-based argument. My own approach is to analyze Mephistopheles's appropriation of the (genre-independent) role of the fool. Dieter Borchmeyer, "*Faust*—Goethes verkappte Komödie," in *Die großen Komödien Europas*, ed. Franz Norbert Mennemeier (Tübingen: A. Francke Verlag, 2000), 199–225; Walter Müller-Seidel, "Komik und Komödie in Goethes *Faust*," in *Die Geschichtlichkeit der deutschen Klassik: Literatur und Denkformen um 1800* (Stuttgart: J. B. Metzler Verlag, 1983), 173–188.

19. Jörg Hienger, "Mephistos Witz," in *J. W. Goethe: Fünf Studien zum Werk*, ed. Anselm Meier (New York: Peter Lang, 1983), 30–49.

Figure 3. Interleaved title page in first printing of Goethe's *Faust*
(1808)

thereafter constitute the first part of the tragedy. Although in many cases, we might treat this textual caesura as mere ornament or happenstance, Goethe's letters to his publisher, Cotta, indicate that he felt very strongly about the layout of the tragedy and sought to eliminate, insofar as possible, deviations from the (now lost) manuscript.[20] There is good reason to ask, then, whether the division in plain sight is a hermeneutic clue, a piece of material evidence pertinent to an investigation of the form of Goethe's play. The insertion of this page can be taken as a signal that the scenes thereafter really make up the tragedy. Accordingly, the three preceding framing units prop up but do not properly belong to the tragedy's first part.

A specific concept underlies this intuitive approach to the relationship between frame and work. Its basic contours can be drawn according to Aristotle's seemingly unimpeachable definition of tragic form in terms of three parts: a beginning, a middle, and an end.[21] The tragic process, it seems patently obvious, consists of the utterances, actions, and events that transpire in between the first and final scenes. These parameters render the frames extrinsic supplements that stand alongside, but do not properly belong to, the tragedy itself. In a more technical cant, they are parerga or paratexts. Such an understanding resonates with the Horatian verdict, foundational for the eighteenth-century conception of drama, that a poetic work must be *simplex et unum*: one story, recounted in sequential parts. Even if one does not wed tragedy to the classical unities (time, place, plot)—which the young Goethe jettisoned in his 1771 encomium for Shakespeare and ignores entirely in his essay "Epic and Dramatic Poetry"—it seems difficult to imagine what it means to refer to a tragedy, in the singular, if not to identify it as unified in its possession of a narrative beginning, middle, and end.[22] And, of course, the main body of the tragedy is held together by, among other things, the internal consistency of figures, the causal relationship among events, and the existence of a recognizable plotline. The function of the prefatory texts, according to this line of thought, consists in their disclosure of the "play character" of the tragedy that follows.[23] In the crudest summary, the *Zueignung* introduces what follows as a poetic song, as a verbal

---

20. See Goethe's letter of 9/30/1805 to his publisher, FA I 7/2:64.

21. Aristotle, *Poetics* 1450b–1451a.

22. For Goethe's earliest disavowal of the three unities, see "Zum Shakespears Tag," FA I 18:9–14.

23. For an influential discussion of framing under this heading, see Gregory Bateson, *Steps to an Ecology of Mind* (Chicago: University of Chicago Press, 1999), especially pt. 4.

configuration brought to life through live, lyric performance; the *Vorspiel auf dem Theater* portrays an object caught in the tension between drama and theater; and the *Prolog im Himmel* reveals the tragedy as the product of a deal between the devil Mephistopheles and the Lord.[24] Each in its own way, these three frames indicate the literary character of the tragedy.

Before contenting ourselves with this conventional stance, it is worth considering two further pieces of evidence. First, what are we to make of the fact that there is another title page that precedes the prefatory poem and playlets (fig. 4), and that seems to mark another sort of beginning? This title page, with its indication of generic affiliation (tragedy), supports the belief that the poem and two plays are not external signals of the fiction, but included within it. But what do we learn about the form of the work by taking the work-internal status of the frames seriously?

A partial answer can be found in one of the jottings among the paralipomena, the collection of drafts and notes that Goethe accumulated over decades of work on both parts of the tragedy. The verse text titled *Abkündigung*, a jocose send-off that Goethe composed as a bookend, asserts a concept of form, in line with the principle of narrative continuity but, at the same time, challenging the idea of completeness. The second half of the poem reads:

> The life of man is a similar poem
> it has its beginning and its end.
> But a whole it is not.
> Sirs, be so good and clap your hands at once.

> Des Menschen Leben ist ein ähnliches Gedicht
> Es hat wohl seinen Anfang und sein Ende.
> Allein ein Ganzes ist es nicht.
> Ihr Herren seyd so gut und klatscht nun in die Hände.[25]

---

24. I describe the *Prolog im Himmel* as the source of the deal because the dialogue leaves it ambiguous, in my view, as to whether it is the Lord who wants to test his servant Faust (lines 296ff.), or whether it is Mephistopheles who wishes to demonstrate his ability to corrupt him. It seems to me that one of the great accomplishments of the *Prolog* is to leave it uncertain whether the tragedy that follows is a demonstration of creation's goodness by the Lord (i.e., a theodicy) or a demonstration of an intrinsic failing of the human being.

25. FA I 7/1:573.

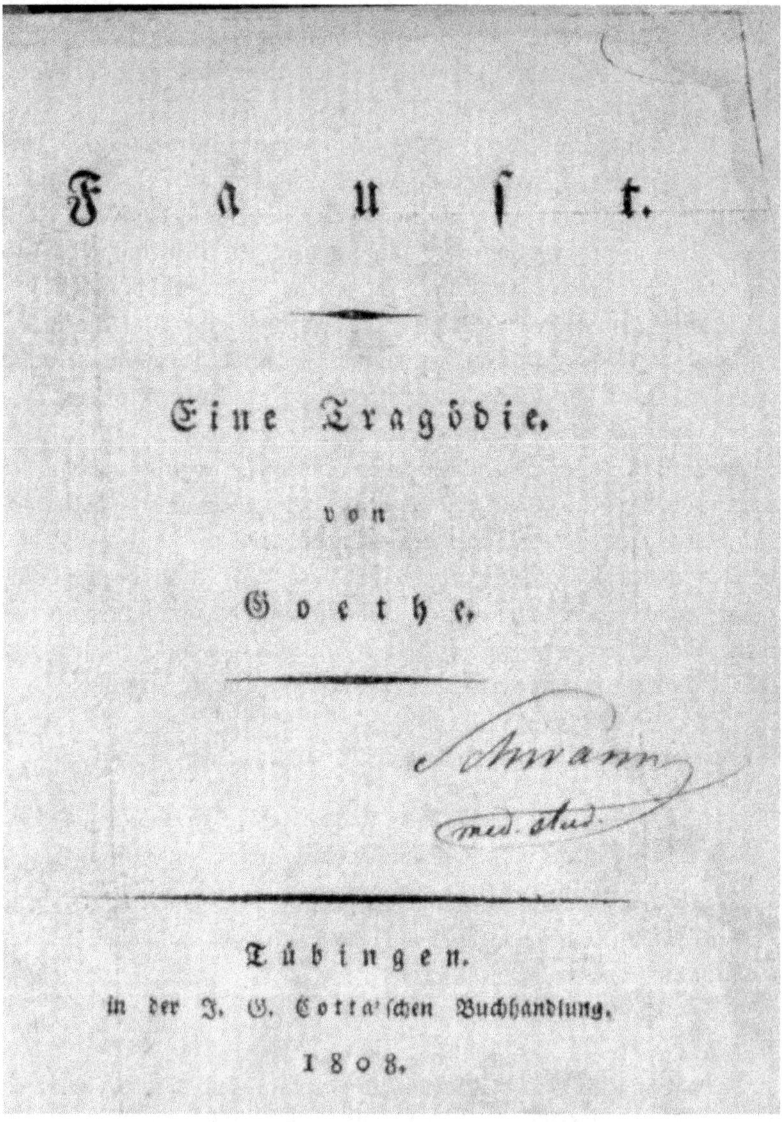

Fauſt.

———

Eine Tragödie.

von

Goethe.

Schwann
med. stud.

Tübingen.
in der J. G. Cotta'ſchen Buchhandlung.
1808.

Figure 4. Title page in first printing of Goethe's _Faust_ (1808)

The passage is revealing in three respects. For present purposes, it is crucial to note that these lines would have likely been delivered by the same fool who spoke in the *Prelude*.[26] In addition, the German title *Abkündigung* indicates an abrupt and willful quitting or discontinuation, rather than a consummation or progressive arrival at a terminal point. Finally, at the same time that the fool cites the Aristotelian narrative parameters of beginning and end, he discourages the perception of the play as an entity of perfectly interlocking parts and seamless transitions.

The fool's role in the coda is meant to echo his function in the prelude of the play. The envisioned parallelism between these two utterances hints at the echoing technique that, as scholars have noted, links together other discrete utterances, figures, and even scenes. Goethe indicated elsewhere in his aesthetic reflections that a procedure he called "repeated mirrorings" (*wiederholte Spiegelungen*) possesses programmatic importance for his literary activity in general.[27] He claims that his literary works are structured by the paratactic accumulation of related items that "work one upon the other, but are of little concern to one another" (*auf einander wirken, aber doch einander wenig angehen*).[28] The structural principle of "repeated mirrorings" can be illustrated by an example that builds on our discussion in chapter 13. The dedicatory poem uses the very same vocabulary (*Gedränge*, line 19; *der unbekannten Menge*, line 21) to describe its ambivalent

---

26. Goethe composed two concluding poems, neither of which was included in the publication of *Faust I* or in the final version of *Faust II* that Goethe completed before his death in 1832. He entitled the penultimate concluding unit *Abkündigung* and the final one *Abschied*. They evince thematic parallels with the *Vorspiel auf dem Theater* and *Zueignung*, respectively. As Schöne points out in his commentary, these were written long before the first part of *Faust* was completed, but after it was divided into two parts. Given the framing techniques associated with the fool and carried on by Mephistopheles in the course of the tragedy, we can comfortably ascribe these lines to the fool. I see no evidence in support of Schöne's conjecture that the lines could also have been spoken by the Director. See FA I 7/2:152 and 954–956.

27. In addition to the famous 9/27/1827 letter to Carl Iken, see the short jotting "Wiederholte Spiegelungen," FA I 17:371–372. There is also a good discussion in the editor's notes to the final volumes of *Kunst und Altertum*, FA I 40:1128–1132.

28. Letter, 2/13/1831, FA II 12:403.

relationship to its audience as later occurs in the *Vorspiel* dialogue and then again in the discussion between Faust and Wagner in the later scene *Vor dem Tor* (*Before the Gate*: e.g., lines 929, 1012, 1030). Each of these sections is characterized by a concern with insularity from the vagaries of the social world. These repetitions do not just lend increased emphasis to a single thematic element, but further establish a kinship among a group of figures in the play, including the Poet, Faust, and his amanuensis Wagner. Each of them expresses the desire for transcendence of the mundane sphere, a rejection of the bare facticity of experience, and discontent with the mere materiality of the object world. The serial arrangement of different but undeniably affine figures brings into view what appears like a class or type. That being said, the Poet, Faust, and Wagner are not all manifestations of a uniform type; they are, rather, independent figures making up a similar but nonidentical array. That they should not be treated uniformly is also evident from one of the most brilliant comic scenes in the tragedy's first part, in which Mephistopheles masquerades as Faust, speaking to an aspiring student. The recurrence of the similar is meant to create oppositions and differences, not eliminate them in favor of an overarching type.[29]

In addition to narrative coherence (beginning, middle, end), *Faust I* is held together by processes of serial configuration. As is evident from Goethe's methodological essay "Der Versuch als Vermittler zwischen Subjekt und Objekt" ("Experiment as Mediator between Subject and Object," 1793), the concept of the series is foundational for scientific work beginning in the early 1790s. Although the essay has recently commanded significant scholarly attention, all indications are that Goethe regarded it as a minor, even dated, account of the proper conduct of science. In the present context, it has the advantage of clarifying Goethe's belief that scientific observations cannot be made individually but rather through the "unification and connection" (*Vereinigung und Verbindung*)[30] of

---

29. Nor is this serial arrangement reducible to the sort of double plot structure found in Elizabethan drama. For the contrary view, see Jane Brown, *Goethe's Faust: The German Tragedy* (Ithaca: Cornell University Press, 1986), 64.

30. LA I 8:309.

an array of closely related experiments. The task of the scientist is to craft a succession of experiments that approach a single phenomenon or closely related phenomena from a plurality of perspectives and that, through their aggregation, capture regularities in natural processes of change.[31] Serial experimentation has the capacity to furnish natural phenomena with a structural relationship where none existed beforehand, thereby enabling the observer to recognize the relationships among natural entities. Although the concept of the series is most strongly affiliated with Goethe's scientific endeavors, it is relevant to his literary projects as well. In an exceedingly complex letter from 1797, Goethe remarks to Schiller that at the origin of his writing stands the study of certain sorts of objects, namely, ones that "call for a series, excite similar and different things in my mind, and that therefore make a claim to unity and allness" (eine gewisse Reihe fordern, ähnliches und fremdes in meinem Geiste aufregen und so von außen wie von innen an eine gewisse Einheit und Allheit Anspruch machen).[32] Goethe claims that the "auspicious subject for the poet" is not one that can be captured individually, but rather one that is articulated in a series of related but distinct terms. We might extrapolate from this oblique formulation that the activity of reading one of Goethe's literary works demands a comparative back-and-forth among distinct elements (figures, lexemes, images) in order to reconstruct their serial structure.

This methodological framework opens up an avenue to understanding the complex form of Faust I, without relying on narrative modes of compositional unity or for a classical dramatic whole. In particular, acknowledging the importance of serial constructions provides an alternative to the opposition introduced at the outset of this chapter, namely, the opposition between the extrinsic frame and the tragedy itself. By searching for related constellations throughout the entirety of Faust I, from the frames up through the rest of the play, an attentive reader of Goethe's play begins to

31. For a recent discussion, with references to further literature, see Eva Geulen, "Serialization in Goethe's Morphology," in Compar(a)ison (Bern: Peter Lang, 2013), 53–70.

32. Letter, 8/16–17/1797, FA II 4:389.

notice the repetition of shapes such as circles, objects such as mirrors, images such as the alpine hut, activities such as weaving, and properties such as liquidity. But the present discussion has a more limited purview: the "repeated mirrorings" between the Fool of the *Prelude* and the *Prologue* and, in turn, the irrepressibly funny devil Mephistopheles, as he appears throughout the remainder of the tragedy, opposite the austere scholar Faust. The formal principle of "repeated mirrorings" provides a starting point to understand the comic elements that have so puzzled readers since Schiller and Schelling. Of course, the unity that shall come into view will not be one defined simply in terms of beginning, middle, and end, nor a unity of seamlessly connected and causally interrelated plot episodes, but rather one constituted by the serial arrangement of related and mutually informing elements.

For the analysis of the fool in Goethe's tragedy, then, it is crucial to recognize that the triangular structure of the *Prelude*—Poet, Fool, Director, as we saw in chapter 13—reappears under altered guise in the second prefatory playlet, the *Prologue in Heaven*. Many interpreters see the dialogue between Mephistopheles, the Angels, and the Lord as the proper frame of the tragedy, the threshold that launches the plot trajectory and introduces the core thematic concerns of the play.[33] But there are also patterns of reflection that extend across such divisions. The contrast between the thrall of the present moment championed by the Fool, associated with the earthly domain of human cohabitation, and the Poet's emphasis on the gravity of the eternal, sought in the heavenly province, reappears here under altered guise.

The *Prologue* provides an array of details about Mephistopheles that extend back to the *Prelude* and forward into the rest of the tragedy. Unlike the rough-hewn Satan or adversary from the book of Job, upon which the *Prologue* is famously based, Goethe's devil is introduced as a playful, even comical, showman. After an initial round of statements from the three archangels Raphael, Gabriel, and Michael, celebrating creation for its pristine glory and

---

33. See Karl Eibl, *Das monumentale Ich: Wege zu Goethe's "Faust"* (Frankfurt am Main/Leipzig: Insel Verlag, 2000), 69; Brown, *Goethe's Faust*, 66.

its violent force, Mephistopheles greets the Lord with an address that strongly dissociates him from religious embodiments of the devil: "Fine speeches are, beg pardon, not my forte. / Though all this round may mock me; but I know, / My rhetoric you would laugh it out of court, / Had you not cast off laughter long ago" (*Vezeih, ich kann nicht hohe Worte machen, / Und wenn der ganze Kreis verhöhnt; / Mein Pathos brächte dich gewiß zum Lachen, / Hätt'st du dir nicht das Lachen abgewöhnt*) (lines 275–278). Mephistopheles offers more than a *captatio benevolentiae* to solicit the Lord's goodwill. He begins by distinguishing himself and the Lord along the lines of earnestness and folly, much like the Poet and the Fool of the previous playlet: the Lord is incapable of laughter, Mephistopheles of seriousness.[34] And this distinction is coordinated with a second one that comes immediately on its heels. Mephistopheles knows nothing of the cosmological glory that the angels have been extolling; he feels out of place in the ethereal and timeless domain of the Lord. His proper station is within the mundane sphere inhabited by humankind, for whom he bears far less ill will than one might expect. This devil is remarkably sympathetic with the suffering of man: he "feels for mankind" in their "wretchedness" so much that he "wants to plague them less" (lines 297–298):

Earth's little god runs true to his old way
And is as weird as on the primal day.
He might be living somewhat better
Had you not given him of Heaven's light a glitter;
He calls it reason and, ordained its priest,
Becomes more bestial than any beast.

Der kleine Gott der Welt bleibt stets von gleichem Schlag,
Und ist so wunderlich als wie am ersten Tag.
Ein wenig besser würd' er leben,

---

34. The suggestion that the Lord does not laugh may be the appropriation of a topos associated, at least in the Middle Ages and early modern period, with Jesus Christ. See Karl-Heinz Bareiß, *Comoedia: Die Entwicklung der Komödiendiskussion von Aristoteles bis Ben Johnson* (Frankfurt am Main: Peter Lang, 1982), 122.

Hättest du ihm nicht den Schein des Himmelslichts gegeben;
Er nennt's Vernunft und braucht's allein
Nur tierischer als jedes Tier zu sein.

(lines 281–286)

Mephistopheles inverts a commonplace theologeme, which would have it that reason constitutes the presence of the divine in man and that, as a consequence, sets him apart from the rest of creation. By the devil's account, however, it is the intrusion of the celestial light (*Himmelslicht*) into the mundane sphere that diminishes human happiness in life and condemns mankind to a rude existence. The source of human dissatisfaction is not vice or guile, but the aspiration to the inbuilt element of the divine.

At this point, Mephistopheles has already emerged in association with three elements connected to the Fool of the *Prelude*: laughter, the earthly domain, and antipathy toward reason. And yet just as the dynamic interplay among the three figures of the *Prelude* sets up a tension between the Fool's, the Poet's, and the Director's perspectives, so too does the *Prologue* set up a contrast between the Lord and Mephistopheles. There is also a parallel between the Director and the Angels.[35] For now, it is important to take note of the deal made in this final framing playlet that sets up the remainder of *Faust I*. The Lord hands his "servant" Faust (line 299) over to Mephistopheles "for as long as he lives on earth" (line 315). Although it is not made explicit, the Lord here introduces a division between Faust's earthly existence and his heavenly salvation in death. At first blush, this appears a mere consequence of the relationship between the devil and the mundane sphere. But the citation of this spatial division is also one that recurs as an internal fissure in Faust himself; he is a figure suspended between the mundane and supermundane, a figure tortured by the faculty of reason that Mephistopheles denounces. The details of Mephistopheles's initial description of Faust—the first contours the doctor achieves

---

35. We might say that the Director and the Angels share an encompassing viewpoint within which the opposing viewpoints of the Lord and Mephistopheles, the Poet and Fool, coexist.

in this play—tell us quite a bit about the dynamic interplay of these two spheres at the heart of the tragedy:

> Not of this earth the madman's drink or ration,
> He's driven far afield by some strange leaven,
> He's half aware of his demented quest,
> He claims the most resplendent stars from heaven,
> And from the earth each pleasure's highest zest,
> Yet near or far, he finds no haven
> Of solace for his deeply troubled breast.

> Nicht irdisch ist des Toren Trank noch Speise.
> Ihn treibt die Gärung in die Ferne,
> Er ist sich seiner Tollheit halb bewußt;
> Vom Himmel fordert er die schönsten Sterne,
> Und von der Erde jede höchste Lust,
> Und alle Näh und alle Ferne
> Befriedigt nicht die tiefbewegte Brust.

(lines 301–307)

The distinction between Mephistopheles and the Lord reappears as the structure of Faust's desire and the cause of his dissatisfaction. Particularly striking is the reference to the fact that Faust's unhappiness comes from a source "not from the earth" (*nicht irdisch*). This unearthliness is manifest on both sides of Faust's internal division: he is torn between the desire to possess heavenly bodies associated with the beautiful (*die schönsten Sterne*) and to satisfy the most extreme corporeal pleasures (*jede höchste Lust*). On a linguistic level, the superlative adjectival forms describing Faust's pursuit of the stars and pleasures underscore the extreme, constitutionally self-undermining nature of Faust's aspiration. Mephistopheles thereby names the foundation of the overpowering dissatisfaction that Faust obsessively laments in the first scenes of the tragedy and that he seeks to escape through conjuration or imaginative projection. Although the dialogue hints at the traditional notion that the devil shall supply Faust with a period of sinful indulgence, Goethe imbues their pairing, through the Lord's remarks, with a novel purpose. The Lord entrusts his servant to

the devil under the explicit premise that their relationship will encourage Faust's overreaching of earthly boundaries, not in order to
facilitate their overcoming, but instead to perpetuate the pursuit of,
their limits. The key passage follows:

> Man all too easily grows lax and mellow,
> He soon elects repose at any price;
> And so I like to pair him with a fellow
> To play the deuce, to stir, and to entice.

> Des Menschen Tätigkeit kann allzuleicht erschlaffen,
> Er liebt sich bald die ungedingte Ruh;
> Drum geb' ich gern ihm den Gesellen zu,
> Der reizt und wirkt, und muß, als Teufel, schaffen.

(lines 340–343)

The Lord assigns Mephistopheles to Faust as a provocateur, as a
spur driving Faust forward indefatigably.[36] If this partnership entails
a Job-like test of faith, its measure is untraditional. Mephistopheles,
as one of "the spirits who negates" (linr 338), pricks and prods Faust
in such a way that, in the end, is generative (the key word here is
schaffen). The famous formula—"Man errs as long as he strives" or
Es irrt der Mensch so lang er strebt (linr 317)—is transformed from
an abstract apothegm into a genuine description of the period in
Faust's human life overseen by Mephistopheles. Mephistopheles does
not lead Faust toward a determinate goal, neither toward moral perfection nor toward destruction, but instead ensures that his stretching
beyond the limits of his own finitude will not abate. And it is this
unabated overreaching that the Lord calls "creating" (*schaffen*).

At this point it is worth recalling the temporal and spatial opposition between the Fool and the Poet introduced in the previous

---

36. David Wellbery reads this passage, following Max Kommerell, as the signal
that apathy (*Trägheit*) constitutes the mortal pitfall that the partnership with Mephistopheles is meant to test. Our interpretations diverge in the assessment of the
danger's source. In the *Prologue*, the Lord expresses confidence that Mephistopheles cannot pull Faust from his *Urquell* (line 324), and goes on to say that the devil's accompaniment shall provide an antidote to the desire for the *unbedingte Ruh*
(line 341). I address this theme at greater length in chapter 15.

playlet. The guiding distinction there was between the here and now of the *Mitwelt* and the eternity of the *Nachwelt*. It is not difficult to feel the reverberations of this opposition in the lines I have just quoted. Mephistopheles assumes his place alongside Faust to ensure that he goes on inhabiting the world of the now, his *Mitwelt*, and that his unhappiness at his inability to escape from his delimited sphere is productive rather than destructive. The Lord assigns, in a seeming paradox, Mephistopheles as Faust's accompaniment, with the injunction that the devil should encourage the mortal's striving. Mephistopheles counters Faust's search for "unconditional peace," for possession of the most beautiful object and satisfaction of the most intense desire, with ever new experiences of the present moment that, ultimately, perpetuate this search. Rather than feeding into satisfaction or the disavowal of unremitting pursuit, the devil plays an enabling role. In the terms laid out in the essay "On Epic and Dramatic Poetry," Mephistopheles's association with the present instant makes him not just the orchestrator of this dramatic process, but of the tragic drama as such.

After Mephistopheles emerges as the advocate of the embodied here and now of human experience, a position that aligns him with that of the Fool in the playlet, he goes on to play this role scenically as well. In a two-step process, the heavens close and the archangels disperse, severing the earthly domain in which the ensuing drama will take place from the heaven of the *Prologue*. And then, left in his mundane element, Mephistopheles performs a scenic operation—which is to say, he makes a move within the orchestrated sequence of speech and gesture—that evokes the comic practices of the fool. Closing the frame in a double sense, Mephistopheles provides a final commentary on the foregoing scene. He not only announces the end of the scene, but also provides hermeneutic information on how it should be understood. His concludes the playlet: "It is quite swell of such a grand lord / To speak so humanely with the devil himself" (*Es ist gar hübsch von einem großen Herrn, / So menschlich mit dem Teufel selbst zu sprechen*) (lines 352–353). These lines do more than express gratitude for the creator's kind bearing. As one would again expect from a fool, they break out of the intrafictional space and humorously underscore the simulated status of what has just transpired, neutralizing the effect of the Lord's imposing presence. In having the last word, Mephistopheles steps to the fore, orchestrating the events of the drama in two ways: theatrically and cosmically. For his task is not only to ensure Faust's endless striving, but also to serve as the comic commentator of his divine-like aspirations. And this double role depends upon Mephistopheles's ability to stand both inside and outside the fiction in the drama, treading the line, traditionally reserved for the fool, between extrafictional and intrafictional modes of address.

15

FAUST III

The Diabolical Comic

In an 1850 essay, Ralph Waldo Emerson (1803–1882) claims that Goethe's central literary achievement is his "habitual reference to interior truth."[1] Perhaps more than any other work from Goethe's vast oeuvre, *Faust I* has appeared as the preeminent exploration of a titanic and solitary individual, restlessly discontent with the available dimensions of worldly experience. Projected onto the system of oppositions that have come into view over the previous two chapters, we might say that for Emerson the core message of Goethe's *Faust I* is manifest in the titular hero's repeated expressions of desire to abandon the earthly sphere and to ascend to the celestial precinct affiliated with the Lord and the Poet. However appealing this line of thought may be, it tells at best half the story. Half, that is, because it does not account for Mephistopheles's

---

1. Ralph Waldo Emerson, "Goethe; or, the Writer," in *Essays and Lectures* (New York: Library of America, 1983), 746–761.

comic presence, without which the play as we know it would not exist. Only by ignoring the traces of the fool is it possible to find the scholar's sublime ministrations, pathos-laden attempts at transcendence, and lethal enchantment with Gretchen constitutionally necessary ways of coping with the human predicament. Ultimately, Emerson is but a single installment in a tradition of readers who have understood Goethe's *Faust* as the elaboration of an emphatic notion of subjectivity, founded upon the incessant striving for self-overcoming, utterly incompatible with the comic tradition of concern in this study. The question that must be posed is, Does Mephistopheles's presence, particularly as a comic force, inveigh against reading *Faust* as a "philosophical testament" to the supposedly ineluctable need, in human knowing and willing, to pass beyond the finite bounds of existence?[2]

An alternative path of interpretation begins with a remark Goethe made to Schiller during the course of his work on Faust: that literary works, and in particular tragedies, are "founded on the depiction of the empirically pathological state of man" (*auf die Darstellung des empirisch pathologischen Zustandes des Menschen gegründet*).[3] In general, Goethe rejected the view that the infinite depths of the individual's interiority provided a worthy subject for literary art, in fact claiming such a focus should be regarded as the symptom of a declining literary culture.[4] If *Faust I* takes its start from a preexisting psychic deformation, rather than from an intact psyche vulnerable to seduction and corruption, then the entire purpose of Mephistopheles's inclusion in the tragedy requires further scrutiny. Indeed, the form of the tragedy that unfolds between beginning and end must be understood as a dramatic

---

2. George Santayana, *Three Philosophical Poets: Lucretius, Dante, and Goethe* (Cambridge, MA: Harvard University Press, 1910), 152.

3. Letter, 11/25/1797, FA II 4:455. For the emphasis on tragedy, see letter, 12/9/1797, FA II 4:461.

4. This becomes a more prominent theme later in Goethe's life. See the observations on poetry in the collection *Maximen und Reflectionen,* FA I 13:139–140, as well as the famous remarks on the difference between the romantic and the classical on 239 of the same volume. There are also pointed remarks in conversation with Eckermann in FA I 39:169–170.

process, facilitated by Mephistopheles, shaped by a pathological state already present at the outset. It will stand to questioning, over the pages that follow, whether Mephistopheles's strategies for countering Faust's pathological desires do not themselves evince a parallel but different deficiency.

Something along these lines is evident in Mephistopheles's words from the *Prologue*: Faust's "unearthly" pursuits preclude him from ever finding satisfaction (lines 300–307). While superficially compatible with the traditional story line, casting Faust as an apostate occultist, a theme that is artfully exploited in the conjurations of the Night scene, Mephistopheles's characterization also serves to lay out the intrinsically pathogenic nature of Faust's desires. Rather than viewing the mortal-devil coupling as some permutation, however refined, of good versus evil, it is worth asking, in line with the formal principle of "repeated mirrorings," if Mephistopheles's interactions with Faust evince structures that align him with the stage fool. It is, further, worth asking what consequences Mephistopheles's fool-like interventions have for the overarching patterns of significance in the play.

The role of Mephistopheles as a challenge to Faust's "interior truth" is already present in the oldest strata of Goethe's text, the scenes Goethe composed between 1772 and 1775, and becomes only more clearly distilled during later phases of work on the tragedy. In what follows, I begin with the two central Study scenes that introduce the famous pact between mortal and devil and provide a diabolical parody of Faust's pursuit of knowledge.[5] I shall then turn to the portrait of Mephistopheles that emerges in "Auerbachs Keller in Leipzig," a carefully choreographed scene that establishes essential, but little understood, linkages between Mephistopheles and the stage fool. It is only natural that these scenes should open a window onto Goethe's interest in the tradition of the stage fool, since, at least in part, they belong to the kernel of

---

5. It makes sense that I would focus in particular on these scenes, as they are among the earliest that Goethe wrote—initially composed in the 1770s and returned to periodically in the ensuing decade, in other words in the immediate aftermath of the material we examined in part 3.

the tragedy composed in the first half of the 1770s as part of his youthful "secret archive."[6]

It is common to use the locution "scholar's tragedy" to refer to the failed attempts at transcendence laid out at the start of the play, especially in the Night and Before the Gate scenes. Two distinct aspirations can be gathered from Faust's extensive speeches and repeated conjurations. The first pertains to the overcoming of the epistemic bounds of human finitude and is typically depicted as freedom from the terrestrial sphere of bodily circumscription, liberation from the shackles of mundane time, and transport to a disembodied spiritual realm. The tragedy's famous opening scene, for instance, contains three related but distinct attempts to break out of and surpass what Faust perceives as his pitifully limited knowledge and experience. Each involves the seizure of the status of a god, through an impulse that "drives upwards and forwards" (line 1093) and that yearns to escape to "a new colorful life" (line 1121).[7] Both movements are essential: the removal from the domain of terrestrial limitation and the passage to a life distinct from and beyond this one. The act of corporeal elevation is associated with the assumption of an epistemic standpoint above the ordinary human "sea of error" (line 1065). Thus, Faust envisages more than an enhancement of his ordinary existence, more than the dawning of some knowledge or even wisdom. In fact, he desires to leave behind human terrestrial existence and inhabit the status of a demiurge, thereby assuming a divine vantage point on creation.

Faust's manic-depressive oscillation drives him to the point of suicide at the end of "Night," only to be rescued by the Easter chorus. This semantically condensed peripeteia has at its core a redemptive moment of anamnesis (*Erinnerung*, line 781), as the sound of the chorus effects an affective (*mit kindlichem Gefühle*, line 781) and

---

6. The discussion between Mephistopheles and the visiting student can be found in the earliest draft, the so-called *Urfaust* or *Frühe Fassung*. See FA I 7/1:477–484. It is evident that already at this point, Goethe envisioned a comic parallel between Mephistopheles's conversation with the student and Faust's conversation with Wagner.

7. See David E. Wellbery, *Goethes Faust I: Reflexion der tragischen Form* (Munich: Carl Friedrich von Siemens Stiftung, 2016), 73–81.

imaginative restoration to Faust's own youth (*Jugend*, lines 769, 779). Although on one level the scene thereby associates Faust's return to life after near suicide with the passion and resurrection of Christ, it has the more subtle and dramatically significant purpose of revealing the second dimension of Faust's desire to escape human finitude. Beyond his desire to achieve the standpoint of a god, Faust also longs for an escape from what can be called the finitude of a biographical career. He is imbued with a deep sense of diminished possibility—a sense of the fundamental inadequacy of his own individual and therefore limited life-trajectory. He regards his accomplishments as nugatory and, more importantly, his future as lacking any meaningful potential. Faust tragically aspires to overcome the intrinsic limitation of human subjectivity to a single biological life and trajectory through time. His redemption through the recollection of youth points to his desire—crucially reiterated in the Study scenes—to escape from the facticity of *this* life as his *own* and *only* life.

Such a schematic understanding of the opening sequence allows us to recognize Mephistopheles as an all-too-earthly counterweight to Faust. This opposition should not be construed in Mephistopheles's favor; his corrective to Faust's discontent with his this-worldly existence is not purely anodyne. Just as Faust presents a pathological variant of the desire for transcendence of human finitude, so too Mephistopheles one-sidedly advocates the preeminence of the material world and the limitations of human life. It is worth recalling that the separation between the mundane and supermundane spheres plays a structuring role both in the *Prelude on the Theater* and the *Prologue in Heaven*; the relationship between Faust and Mephistopheles presents a further, more nuanced variant of the same opposition.

Whereas the extensive monologues of the opening scenes bring Faust into the clear light of the stage, Mephistopheles's appearance in the main body of the tragedy proceeds by way of an indirect, shadowy, and indeterminate route.[8] When he makes his first appearance

---

8. Juliane Vogel, " 'Nebulistische Zeichnungen': Figur und Grund in Goethes Weimarer Dramen," in *Der Grund: Das Feld des Sichtbaren*, ed. Gottfried Boehm and Matteo Burioni (Munich: Wilhelm Fink Verlag, 2012), 317–328.

opposite Faust, after a spectacle of shape-shifting from dog to hip-popotamus to elephant, he finally appears in the garb of an "itiner-ant scholar" (*fahrender Scholasticus*). The costume is remarkable for two reasons: on the one hand, the itinerant scholar is nothing more than the prototypical swindler or confidence man of the early mod-ern period, a cousin to the quack and mountebank; on the other, the outfit makes Mephistopheles into a doppelgänger, albeit a distorted one, of the melancholic scholar opposite him.[9] But Mephistopheles's role as country-fair hustler also sets up a paradigm echoed later in "Auerbachs Keller," when the young drunk men identify Faust and Mephistopheles as carnival barkers (line 2178). Much like the many instantiations of the fool before him, Mephistopheles repeatedly ob-scures his identity, leaving in place a core indeterminacy that he can cover over with the many masks and costumes he assumes. His first appearance, in particular, shows him not just as a protean master of disguises, but also as a skillful improvisor and dissembler, with strong associative links to the town-square performance environ-ment within which the fool originally flourished.

The closest he comes to exposing his identity takes place by way of a functional explanation. He defines himself in terms of a force that "always wants evil and always does good" (*stets das Böse will und stets das Gute schafft*) (line 1336). This apothegmatic line can be read within a theological paradigm, dictating that the devil Mephistopheles is so malevolent and malfeasant—the proponent of "absolute nothingness" and "enemy of being, the beautiful and the good," as one interpreter put it—that any action he considers worthy of approbation falls, according to ordinary human under-standing, into the category of evil.[10] Indeed, the first Study scene

9. Edward Beever, *The Realities of Witchcraft and Popular Magic in Early Modern Europe: Culture Cognition and Everyday Life* (New York: Palgrave Mac-millan, 2008), 190–192.

10. These quotes are translations from Oskar Seidlin, "Das Etwas und das Nichts: Versuch einer Neuinterpretation einer 'Faust'-Stelle," *Germanic Review* 19 (1944): 170–175. The same view is echoed in Peter Michelsen, "Mephistos 'ei-gentliches Element': Vom Bösen in Goethes *Faust*," in *Das Böse: Eine historische Phänomenologie*, ed. Carsten Colpe and Wilhelm Schmidt-Biggemann (Frankfurt am Main: Suhrkamp Taschenbuch Wissenschaft, 1993), 229–255. Schöne reads the passage similarly in his commentary, FA I 7/2:251.

paints a distinctively negative picture of Mephistopheles's actions, as he identifies himself, echoing the Lord's words from the *Prologue*, as the "spirit that ever negates!" (Ich bin der Geist der stets verneint!) (lines 338–339 and 1338). The repetition of the same description across the two sections of the play, including the use of the almost technical verb *verneinen*, casts this theatrical figure as an agent defined in terms of a distinctive activity. The negating function realized through Mephistopheles is, however, only one half of an opposition, a denial that depends, in essence, on its affirmative complement. This devil displays a keen awareness of his place within an encompassing pulse of growth and decay that, ultimately, limits his impact. Despite all his destructive effort aimed against humanity, he must admit that "not much is done by it" (line 1362) and that "a new, fresh blood always circulates" (line 1372). The discrepancy between Mephistopheles's professedly "negating" nature and his admission of its ultimate futility deserves emphasis, as it complicates one of the most convincing lines of interpretation that the play has attracted over recent decades. Prominent scholars have claimed that Goethe integrates the Job story, beginning with the *Prologue*, in order to render Faust's tragic experience into a test of the goodness of creation.[11] If the play should be read as a dramatic theodicy, however, it is striking that the figure putatively responsible for challenging the divinity of creation, Mephistopheles, coyly hints at his own ineffectuality, acknowledging his limited place in a circular movement of creation and destruction.

Mephistopheles's attenuated, structurally integrated destruction fits together with the purpose he repeatedly avows he will fulfill for Faust. Perhaps the single most important recurring theme in Mephistopheles's speeches is his promise that he will show Faust "what life is" (line 1543). The second Study scene is shot through with Mephistopheles's pledges to show Faust "the joy of life" (line 1819), "the wild life" (line 1860), the "joys of the earth" (line 1859); he vows to take him out into the "world" (line 1829) and help him see what "to lead a life" really means (line 1836), and

---

11. See David Wellbery's study, which I have already repeat cited.

to lead him on a "new course of life" (*Lebenslauf*) (line 2072). In this profusion of statements on earthly life, Mephistopheles draws a line between his own purpose and Faust's melancholic yearning. Paradoxical though it may sound, his negative and destructive activity actually involves making a display of life—the life of the human here and now, of immanence and finitude—that Faust has sought to escape through his magical ministrations. Mephistopheles's emphasis on life is ambivalent. On the positive side, it counters Faust's morbid fixation on an escape from the limitations of his human existence—both his existence as a distinctively mortal (that is, not divine) human knower and doer and his aspiration to escape from the determinate trajectory of his *own* and *only* life. Mephistopheles offers him an escape from his individual biographical career, but in such a way that ultimately denies all possibility for transcending what is materially given.

In an 1818 court masque, a decade after *Faust I* had become a literary hit, Goethe reiterated the life-exhibiting purpose of the devil's guidance. Recounting the events of the tragedy in compressed form, Mephistopheles challenges the idea that his own penchant for disguise and dissimulation (*Verstellung*) makes him "an evil spirit."[12] Instead, his accompaniment has the purpose of showing the scholar that he should not waste time on "lunacies, / fantasies and idiocies," but instead embrace the view that "life / is actually given for living" and that "as long as one lives, one should be lively."[13] The relationship between Faust and Mephistopheles is organized by the tension between the devil's positive purpose of breaking through Faust's life-negating fixation on overcoming the limitations of his mundane existence, on the one hand, and his radical denial of all manifestations of Faust's desire for transcendence, on the other.

---

12. From a masque entitled *Dichterische Landes-Erzeugnisse, darauf aber Künste und Wissenschaften vorführend*. For the relevant passage, see FA I 6:848–849.

13. The crucial passage in the original: "Gequält war er [Faust] sein Lebelang; / Da fand er mich auf seinem Gang. / Ich macht' ihm deutlich, daß das Leben / Zum Leben eigentlich gegeben, / Nicht sollt' in Grillen, Phantasien / Und Spintisiererei entfliehen. / So lang man lebt, sei man lebendig! Das fand mein Doctor ganz verständig." FA I 6:850.

The opposition between Mephistopheles's vitality and Faust's immobility fits within a systematic opposition that is reflected repeatedly throughout the entire text. Recall that the Fool in the *Prelude* first insists on the need to speak to his contemporaneous world (*Mitwelt*), while it is the Poet who seeks the refuge of heavens and eternity (*Nachwelt*). In the *Prologue*, Mephistopheles expresses his affinity with the earth of mortals and his unease with the heavenly sphere. In much the same way, Mephistopheles vows to disabuse Faust of his fixation on the "pain of narrow earthly life" (lines 1544–1545). Faust's sense that "existence is a burden" (line 1570) will be alleviated if he "takes his steps through life" with Mephistopheles as his "companion" (*Geselle*) (line 1646), "servant" (*Diener*), and "vassal" (*Knecht*) (line 1648). Of course, on an immediate level, this affiliation mimics that of the traditional Faust story, in which the devil agrees to serve Faust in this world in exchange for Faust's obedience in the next. However, the pleonastic list of vocations indicates Mephistopheles's dual role as both accomplice and menial, partner and subaltern. In guiding Faust through life, Mephistopheles aims "to rid of lunacies" (*die Grillen zu verjagen*) (line 1534) the melancholic scholar who sees in the present world nothing but deficiency and privation. There are, then, two dimensions to Mephistopheles's activity as Faust's "companion": he asserts his ability to expose the illusions underlying his malcontent, and, perhaps more importantly, he promises to recuse Faust from his suicidal denial of life's worth. Of course, the exact nature of the life the devil offers will still require clarification, but it should be uncontroversial to claim that the Study scenes portray the devil's destructive capacities as yielding salubrious effects. At the heart of the joking relationship between master and servant in Goethe's tragedy lies the promise to disenchant Faust's "unearthly" desires and thereby to restore his sense of life's worth.

Famously, one of the many liberties Goethe took when crafting his own version of the tragedy is the addition of a wager between devil and mortal. It comes about in response to Mephistopheles's vow to give Faust "what no man has ever seen" (line 1674) while "taking the steps through life" (line 1643). One must see that Faust's understanding of this offer is shaped fundamentally by the "pathological state" of despair, instability, and sense of ontological lack emphasized repeatedly across the opening scenes of the tragedy. It is not forbidden knowledge, but instead the desire to surpass finite human experience that shapes the conditions under which Faust enters into an alliance with the devil. Perhaps the best-known passage of the play begins:

> Should ever I take ease upon a bed of leisure,
> May the same moment mark my end!
> When first by flattery you lull me
> Into a smug complacency,
> When with indulgence you can gull me,
> Let that day be the last for me!

> Werd' ich beruhigt je mich auf ein Faulbett legen:
> So sei es gleich um mich getan!
> Kannst du mich schmeichelnd je belügen,
> Daß ich mir selbst gefallen mag,
> Kannst du mich mit Genuß betrügen:
> Das sei für mich der letzte Tag!

(lines 1692–1697)

And then he goes on:

> If the swift moment I entreat:
> Tarry a while! You are so fair!
> Then forge shackles to my feet,
> Then I will gladly perish there!
> Then let them toll the passing-bell.
> Then of your servitude be free,
> The clock may stop, its hands fall still,
> And time be over then for me!

> Werd ich zum Augenblicke sagen:
> Verweile doch! du bist so schön!
> Dann magst du mich in Fesseln schlagen,
> Dann will ich gern zu Grunde gehn!
> Dann mag die Totenglocke schallen,
> Dann bist du deines Dienstes frei,
> Die Uhr mag stehn, der Zeiger fallen,
> Es sei die Zeit für mich vorbei!

(lines 1699–1706)

These lines have attracted a vast body of critical literature, inciting controversy over the uniformity of the wager (is there one or multiple?), its implications for the play's overarching themes (how does this fit together with the frame wager between the Lord and Mephistopheles?), and its provenance (does Goethe here appropriate Rousseauean or Christological ideas?).[14] For present purposes, it is crucial to notice the extent to which these passages are founded in an acute sense of desperation, which Faust believes cannot be relieved even by Mephistopheles's accompaniment. His proposal presumes, on the most straightforward level, that there can be no passing moment worth holding on to. For Faust, human experience of the here and now constitutes a homogeneous and interminable series of valueless moments, each one identical to the next, and none of genuine worth. He suffers from the sense that time is stale, that its products endure after they have lost their validity, but also from the senselessness of the future.[15] Indeed, the passages in which he foreswears hope (*Hoffnung*, line 1505) and, with surprising emphasis, patience (*Geduld*, line 1506) indicate that Faust's sense of the vacuity of time has robbed him of his ability to project his desires into the future, to see his present activity as a link within a larger causal chain, potentially eventuating in a worthwhile accomplishment. If Faust did not believe it impossible for a human experience to provide him with satisfaction and that his undertakings could achieve valuable results, he would not assert that Mephistopheles cannot show an instant worth holding fast. The overwhelming wish for an absolute experience—one affording insight into the totality of nature and the totality of human experiences—has so consumed Faust that he gambles the devil cannot supply him with any experience that would quell it.

With this framework in place, the contrast to Mephistopheles's avowed purpose comes clearly into view. In all the devil's

---

14. See Jane Brown, *Goethe's Faust: The German Tragedy* (Ithaca: Cornell University Press, 1986), 66–84; Karl Eibl, "Zur Bedeutung der Wette in 'Faust,'" *Goethe Jahrbuch* 116 (1999): 271–280; and Gerrit Brüning, "Die Wette in Goethe's *Faust*," *Goethe Yearbook* 17 (2010): 31–54.

15. The relationship to the past is insightfully discussed in Harold Jantz, "The Structure of Time in Faust," *MLN* 92, no. 3 (1977): 494–508.

statements, he promises nothing beyond a trip through life—which is to say, a trip through human life, absent the lofty metaphysical requirements Faust places on experience. The pact sets up an imbalance of expectations, and guarantees that this asymmetry will afford Mephistopheles the role of comic check on Faust's uncompromising desire. After Faust exits the stage to prepare for his peregrinations, Mephistopheles reflects on the aspirations his "companion" projects on their quest. He does so in a way that mixes baleful malice with a good measure of cold realism:

> Fate has endowed him with a forward-driving
> Impetuousness that reaches past all sights,
> And which precipitately striving,
> Would overleap the earth's delights.
> Through dissipation I will drag him,
> Through shallow insignificance,
> I'll have him sticking, writhing, flagging,
> And for his parched incontinence
> Have food and drink suspended at lip level;
> In vain will he be yearning for relief,
> And had he not surrendered to the devil,
> He still must needs have come to grief!

> Ihm hat das Schicksal einen Geist gegeben,
> Der ungebändigt immer vorwärts dringt,
> Und dessen übereiltes Streben
> Der Erde Freuden überspringt.
> Den schleppe ich durch das wilde Leben,
> Durch flache Unbedeutenheit,
> Er soll mir zappeln, starren, kleben,
> Und seiner Unersättlichkeit
> Soll Speis' und Trank vor gier'gen Lippen schweben;
> Er wird Erquickung sich umsonst erflehn,
> Und hätt' er sich auch nicht dem Teufel übergeben,
> Er müßte doch zu Grunde gehn!

(lines 1856–1857)

On its surface, this passage is a statement of seditious intent and of the ineluctable dissatisfaction their partnership will entail.

Mephistopheles's words reek of malice, to be sure, but also of a sober and accurate estimation of Faust's obsessive striving for an unavailable experience. In this respect, the key juncture in the passage is the final two lines. They state that Faust's ultimate demise, the bondage of biological finitude, is not at all the product of his pact with the devil, but rather issues from the "pathological state" of his desires. Mephistopheles promises to redeem Faust from his suicidal desperation by allowing him to feel what he repeatedly refers to as his most basic humanity. Given that Mephistopheles's vision of the human being focuses particularly on the immanent gratifications of the here and now (*der Erde Freuden*, line 1859), the life he can show Faust is intrinsically partial and deficient. His presence may provide an antidote to the almost monomaniacal focus on the absolute that destroys Faust's capacity to envisage the worth of his own experience, but remains nonetheless limited by Mephistopheles's disavowal of the human being's aspiration to surpass the bounds of the given and finite. In this respect, the fulfillment he can offer Faust expresses Mephistopheles's own "pathological state."

Beyond its thematic content, the above monologue also possesses signal dramaturgical function. Uttered on an otherwise empty stage, immediately after Faust's departure, the quoted lines offer commentary on what has just happened and a forecast of what will subsequently occur. Their function thus differs fundamentally from, for instance, the rapturous monologue at the start of the drama, which provides information pertaining directly to the past and present internal state of the speaker. There is no "inner truth" disclosed in Mephistopheles's remarks: he does not profess anything, and we learn little of his psychological processes or motivational structures. These lines function, rather, much like the closing lines of the *Prologue in Heaven*, when Mephistopheles stands in front of the closed gates of heaven and offers words of praise for the Lord's goodwill. Breaking free from the concatenated sequence of statements that constitutes the ordinary structure of dialogue, Mephistopheles here reframes the dramatic action with information unknown to other characters in the story. The speech is *ad spectatores*, fiction-external for readers or audience members. Such framing operations, which Mephistopheles repeatedly executes throughout the play, have, as we saw in detail in chapter 3, historically been reserved for the stage fool. Thus two dimensions of Mephistopheles are here drawn into close proximity with the stage fool: his functional role as commentator and his emphatic opposition to metaphysical investments.

The connection between the Fool in the *Prelude* and Mephistopheles surpasses thematic concerns and impacts the interweaving of utterances and gestures in dialogue. The final segment of the second Study scene, as the devil dons Faust's frock and engages an aspiring student who has come to solicit the scholar's services, utilizes this linkage to great dramaturgical effect. In a sequence that clearly parallels and parodies Faust's opening monologue as well as his earlier conversation with Wagner, Mephistopheles uses his facility for thespian simulation to confuse and manipulate his unsuspecting interlocutor. Once again, Mephistopheles appears as a distorted reflection of the scholar Faust; once again, the real significance of this scene can be grasped only if one abandons the search for coherent epistemological or metaphysical positions and instead views Mephistopheles as a comic improviser. Mephistopheles's role is defined by his distinctive linguistic act: negation. In his lengthy back-and-forth with the naive student, Mephistopheles's real accomplishment consists in the way he interlaces plausible recommendations and sententiae with parodic statements that draw on Faust's own previous, sincere avowals. His negation comes in the form of reiteration and distortion. Each discipline that Mephistopheles touches on—logic, metaphysics, theology, medicine—is discounted as a potential source of genuine knowledge. Whereas Faust's desperation regarding the futility of traditional learning stems from his persistent and earnest pursuit of its fruits, Mephistopheles pretends to encourage the student while simultaneously denying the fruitfulness of such an endeavor. Logic, he says, can be useful for developing rigorous classificatory knowledge, but ultimately dismembers and mortifies living things: "Then he has the parts in his hand, / Absent only the spirit that holds them together!" (lines 1938–1939). Metaphysics, meanwhile, offers deep insight into "those things that don't fit into man's brain" (line 1951), and in theology it is most important to "hold fast to words" (line 1990) rather than overly concerning oneself with concepts and referents. Medicine costs intensive study, but in the end leaves the world "as it pleases God" (line 2014). Disguised as Faust, Mephistopheles playfully evacuates all his scholarly pursuits of significance. In a linguistic tour-de-force, he reiterates Faust's lamentations concerning the futility of language, his inability to assist others medically, and so on, robbing them of their pathos. This scene, in short, offers a comic double, a caricature, of Faust's tragic desperation.

The strategy at work in this scene, by means of which Mephistopheles supplies an unvarnished and thoroughly caustic assessment of Faust, could be called *comic redoubling*. And so it is only fitting that, after the comic reiteration of past events, Mephistopheles offers an anticipatory frame for what is yet to come. In contrast to Faust's conviction that no moment can capture the exorbitant demand he seeks in experience, Mephistopheles encourages the student to "seize the instant" (line 2017), to grab hold of the *Augenblick*. In so doing, he calls attention to the genuine source of Faust's dissatisfaction: his valuation of the impermanent instant. The vacuity of the moment is not an intrinsic feature of time, but a function of Faust's estimation of it. Faust assumes a fundamentally life-negating stance when he presupposes that the temporal unfolding of experience lacks any potential significance. The emptiness of experience, the melancholic sense of valuelessness, issues from Faust's own unstable comportment toward the world. Mephistopheles's parodic redoubling, meanwhile, points out that a single moment can serve as either a source of desperation or a springboard to action.

Comic reversals like these illustrate an especially important dimension of Mephistopheles's role in dialogue. Throughout the play but particularly in this scene, his speech evinces an unnerving coincidence of accuracy and impropriety. His mockery of academic disciplines, just like the insistence on the subjective utilization of the instant, does not lack for plausibility. Mephistopheles echoes prominent Enlightenment views and advocates epistemic positions at the center of Goethe's own scientific investigations in morphology and the theory of color.[16] But it is important to notice that his form of

---

16. See my essay, Joel Lande, "Acquaintance with Color: Prolegomena to a Study of Goethe's *Zur Farbenlehre*," *Goethe Yearbook* 23 (2016): 143–169.

articulation, this parodic ruthlessness, betrays a "cynicism" driven by "being right at the cost of shame."[17] In his overt commentaries and extended dramatizations, like his conversation with the student, Mephistopheles recasts—which is to say, renders intelligible for a second time, within an altered framework—subjective viewpoints and dramatic events, in a manner devoid of all social pretense.

The profound comic effect of such social impropriety depends on the transgression of communicative expectations.[18] In general, the content and linguistic register of a face-to-face exchange is conditioned by the speaker's and the listener's respective sense of what one's interlocutor anticipates hearing, including the tone and word choice. In order to avoid ruptures in dialogue or, worse, offense, speakers generally accommodate themselves to the speech conventions that they, by means of habituation as well as route imaginative projection, believe the interlocutor expects. Such a conversational approach assumes that one wishes to avoid the uncomfortable feeling of shame that generally follows a breach of decorum—the shame of not having lived up to what one believes the situation, as understood by others, demands. Not so Mephistopheles. Establishing a precedent that recurs again and again in the play, particularly in the seduction of Gretchen, Mephistopheles achieves comic effect by infringing on propriety, particularly sexual propriety, but bereft of the social response of shame. A key instance of this, which previews the seduction episode Faust will soon engage in, is the rather lewd courtship advice Mephistopheles shares with the student:

> Especially the women learn to guide;
> Their everlasting ahs and ohs,
> Their myriad woes,
> Can all be cured at one divide.

---

17. Max Kommerell, "Faust zweiter Teil: Zum Verständnis der Form," in *Geist und Buchstabe der Dichtung* (Frankfurt am Main: Vittorio Klostermann, 1956), 9–74, here 26.

18. My remarks here have their foundation in ideas first developed by Talcott Parsons and theorized most thoroughly by Niklas Luhmann. The "double contingency" of communication receives its fullest treatment in Niklas Luhmann, *Soziale Systeme: Grundriß einer allgemeinen Theorie* (Frankfurt am Main: Suhrkamp Taschenbuch Wissenschaft, 1984), 148–190.

If you adopt a halfway decent air,
You'll lure them all into your lair.

Besonders lernt die Weiber führen;
Es ist ihr ewig Weh und Ach,
So tausendfach
Aus einem Punkte zu kurieren,
Und wenn ihr halbweg ehrbar tut,
Dann habt ihr sie all' unter'm Hut.

(lines 2023–2028)

As before, the comic force of these lines can be gleaned only if one reads them as more than a travesty of romantic love. The relevant backdrop here is the subsequent events in the tragedy—that is, the story of Gretchen's seduction. Mephistopheles is preempting the metaphysical scaffolding Faust will erect around his courtship of Gretchen, reducing love to a matter of erotic prowess and self-presentation. Of course, this contravenes Faust's own belief that Gretchen is a maiden of immaculate beauty, capable of satisfying the very same desires that motivated his dabbling in magic. As the above passage already indicates, his companion Mephistopheles will here too serve as his all-too-earthly antithesis, stressing the corporeal underpinning of their courtship. Perhaps the most caustic comic challenge to the supreme significance Faust assigns to his love for Gretchen comes in the scene "Forest and Cavern," itself a turning point in the tragedy.[19] Mephistopheles appropriates the language and pathos Faust first introduced in the Night scene, with his longing to encompass all of earth and heaven, to penetrate to the inner force driving the eternal renewal of being, and to completely abandon his merely mortal existence (lines 3282–3289). But Mephistopheles's comic redoubling of Faust's spiritual desperation closes with a reference to a climactic moment of "high intuition" that he accompanies with what the stage instruction refers to as just a "gesture," but that one can justifiably suppose should indicate a crude grab of his phallus (lines

---

19. See Harold Jantz, *The Form of Faust: The Work of Art and Its Intrinsic Structures* (Baltimore: Johns Hopkins University Press, 1978), 92ff.

3291–3292). If Gretchen's love is pure, Mephistopheles introduces the possibility that ulterior motives, particularly the need for libidinal release, underlie Faust's claims to transcendent experience. Indeed, Mephistopheles's absence of shame, here manifest in his reduction of love to the most fleeting corporeal satisfaction, raises a specter of responsibility that hangs over the remainder of the play. For he introduces the claim that Faust himself, deluded by inhuman desires, infects Gretchen with a love that, as subsequent scenes will bear out, has catastrophic consequences. There is an undeniable truth to Mephistopheles's assertion that Faust "poured into her heart" a "rage of love" that robs her of her innocence and drives her to commit what would have previously seemed to her unimaginably heinous acts.

The purpose of Mephistopheles's comic redoubling is to disclose an alternative comic viewpoint, to switch the frame from serious counsel to subtly licentious ribbing. Accordingly, the alliance between Faust and Mephistopheles supplies the dramatic action with a bifocal lens, with each half shaped by a distinct "pathological state": investment in significance is coupled with divestment of significance, gravity with levity. The consequences of this programmatic duplicity are far-reaching, even after the seduction of Gretchen. In this section, too, Mephistopheles's presence splits everything that transpires into two irreconcilable registers of value, one weighty with significance, the other a parasitic parody robbing it of meaning. Once Faust projects his hypertrophic desires onto Gretchen—and the agency of projection is essential—Mephistopheles employs his role as guide, as the arranger of the events, to expose Faust to comic deflation. In so doing, Mephistopheles preserves two dramaturgical privileges of the stage fool: first, the ability to deliver utterances and gestures that are manifest to the audience but not to Faust; and, second, to stand equally inside and outside the fictional universe, to play guide for Faust and (in his commentaries) for the audience. For this reason, Mephistopheles violates an expectation of theatrical representation: his position within dialogue, indeed within the narrative trajectory, should not be understood in terms of a consistent set of beliefs or desires. That is, his patterns of stage integration are better understood as reactive than active.[20] His utterances are fundamentally situational; they are oriented toward his interlocutor and therefore depend more strongly on the beliefs or desires of his opposite than any core convictions of his own.

A moment before Faust encounters Gretchen, the first stop of the journey through life, "Auerbachs Keller in Leipzig," can help lend more contour to Mephistopheles's parasitic relationship to tragic pathos. Although the scene belongs to the earliest strata of *Faust*, Goethe rewrote it in the course of his final phase of work on the play, introducing a subtle and profound meditation on the relationship between Mephistopheles and the encompassing tragedy. The scene can be read as addressing a question that has, by and large, been ignored by the scholarship: to wit, how does Mephistopheles, as Faust's comic guide, fit with the tradition of the tragic genre that Goethe inscribes his play within? According to the framing remarks made by the devil upon their arrival, the scene has a definite purpose. It should show Faust the conviviality and festivities enjoyed by the *Volk*, helping him to see the potential ease of life (lines 2158–2161). It thereby picks up on themes already introduced in Before the Gate, especially Faust's desire for reprieve from the misery of his isolation. Beyond what we might call the psychological import of the scene, it also provides valuable instruction concerning Mephistopheles's role.

In keeping with the tradition of the stage fool, Mephistopheles emerges here as not just the playful trickster, but also the advocate of the play and indeed of tragedy itself. It is worth considering, in a schematic fashion, what happens during the second half of the scene, after Faust and Mephistopheles arrive. The scene contains a song sung by Mephistopheles and a jubilant chorus (lines 2211–2240); the conjuration of wine that is collectively enjoyed (lines 2284–2295); and the promise of the revelation of "bestiality" (2297–2298); and finally a moment of collective near dismemberment in a state of delirium (lines 2316–2321). The scene concludes with Mephistopheles saying that the entire foregoing action had

20. Martin Seel, "Drei Formen des Humors," *Deutsche Vierteljahrsschrift für Literaturwissenschaft und Geistesgeschichte* 76 (2002): 300–305.

the purpose of demonstrating "how the devil jests" (line 2321). Within the tradition of European tragedy, there is one play that evinces astonishing structural affinities with this scene, namely, Euripides's *Bacchae*, a play of which Goethe produced a partial translation and that he revered until the end of his life.[21] Euripides's tragedy has at its core the arrival of Dionysus—the god of wine and tragedy—and his effort to make a display of his divinity to the city of Thebes. It concerns an episode of collective festivity that culminates in the dismemberment of the king of Thebes, Pentheus, who had displayed profound skepticism toward the god and his rites. The play reaches its high point as the god takes possession of the Theban women, sending them into revelries that confuse the boundary between human and brute.

The structural similarities between "Auerbach's Keller" and the *Bacchae* are, indeed, striking and can illuminate certain verbal anomalies within the scene. To give one important example, Mephistopheles conjures wine from the table with the words "The vine bears grapes! / The goat horns" (lines 2284–2285). Unless one reads the scene as amassing traces of the tragic genre's chief avatar, Dionysus, there is no contextual evidence to support the collocation of wine and the goat. But if the scene plays out, in highly compressed form, the plot of the *Bacchae*, then the invocation of traditional elements from tragic and Dionysian iconography makes perfect sense. It should be emphasized that Mephistopheles is far from a Greek god, and his role lacks the gravity of Euripides's Dionysus. As he says himself, he is making a display of his diabolic jest, not his divinity (line 2321). One of the supreme accomplishments of this scene, particularly of the distorted resemblance between Dionysus and Mephistopheles, is to compel the reader or spectator to question the contribution of Mephistopheles's comic role to the overarching design of the tragedy, to ask how Mephistopheles's particular brand of comic destruction fits within the encompassing tragic unity.

---

21. See Goethe's letter to Göttling of March 3, 1832. The scene he translated and then published in 1827 in *Kunst und Altertum* concerns the moment when Queen Agave awakens from her possession to realize that she has decapitated her own son.

If we see Mephistopheles as contributing something essential to Faust's tragedy, indeed as a quasi-Dionysian guide through and exponent of the tragic, we can lend a more precise shape to the Manichaeism often associated with Goethe and, in particular, with this tragedy.[22] Throughout his vast oeuvre, we find a great number of remarks on a fundamental duplicity of the natural world. In a revealing phrase he describes humans as the "spawn of two worlds." In some instances, Goethe depicts this suspension between two domains as a coevality of good and evil.[23] But in others, he asserts that the human being is essentially torn between the real and ideal, between a material existence and an aspiration to the divine. Perhaps the most poignant illustration of this duplicity comes in his autobiography, where Goethe elaborates on a cosmological "myth" of the origin of humankind.[24] The story is remarkable because it deals directly with a Lucifer figure, but lacks a straightforward account of the fall. I wish to call attention to five features of this exceedingly complex passage. The first, which has to the best of my knowledge escaped commentators, concerns the context in which Goethe introduces his cosmological myth. His remarks are meant to illustrate his youthful fascination with the "hermetic, mystical, kabbalistic," which he prefaces with the general principle "The spirit of contradiction and the pleasure of the paradoxical is in each of us" (*Der Geist des Widerspruchs und die Lust zum Paradoxen steckt in uns allen*). The phrase "spirit of contradiction" should ring familiar; it is a phrase that Faust, too, uses to describe Mephistopheles (line 4030). There as here, the phrase has surprisingly neutral connotations. As Goethe moves into the myth itself, then, he seeks to lay the foundation for this universal

---

22. See Karl Eibl, *Das monumentale Ich: Wege zu Goethe's "Faust"* (Frankfurt am Main/Leipzig: Insel Verlag, 2000), 107–112. With a strong emphasis on potential sources, see also Rolf Christian Zimmermann, *Das Weltbild des jungen Goethe: Studien zur hermetischen Tradition des deutschen 18. Jahrhunderts* (Munich: Wilhelm Fink Verlag, 2002), 1:111–144.

23. The duplicity has been discussed in Jantz, *Form of Faust*, 60–75. *See the discussion of the Lucifer myth in Eibl, Das monumentale Ich, 99–101.*

24. From the end of the eighth book of *Dichtung und Wahrheit*, FA I 13:382–385. All the remaining quotations in this chapter are taken from this brief but spectacularly dense myth.

anthropological proclivity. The background positive valuation of contradiction and paradox explains the second crucial feature of the myth, namely, that the "entire power of creation" (*ganze Schöpfungskraft*) behind the material world belongs to the "infinite activity" (*unendliche Tätigkeit*) of Lucifer. Because Lucifer is himself born of the original divinity, he maintains a divine potential through various stages of creation. Third, Goethe asserts that humankind was created as a means to restore "the original connection with divinity." Finally, because humankind is the product of the original divinity, it is "at once the most perfect and imperfect, the most felicitous and infelicitous creation" (*das Vollkommenste und Unvollkommenste, das glücklichste und unglücklichste Geschöpf*). The human being is a mirror image of Lucifer: both bear an inbuilt potential and remnant of divinity; they are, in Goethe's recondite vocabulary, "unconditioned" (*unbedingt*). Both, however, are also "limited" (*beschränkt*), because they are derivatives of divinity rather than the divine itself.

The importance of this passage in the context of the mortal-devil relationship in *Faust* is counterintuitive. The myth makes vivid that Mephistopheles cannot be merely reduced to a principle for evil nor indeed a figure with any set of determinate beliefs. Nor should he be identified with Lucifer himself.[25] More convincing is to see Mephistopheles as the dramatic agent that brings the "limited" character of the human being to the surface. But he does not illuminate these limitations by way of clear avowals or consistent arguments. Instead, as a theatrical figure following in the tradition of the stage fool, his labor is one of comic distortion and reduplication, of masquerade and parody. His role exposing the "limited" dimension of the human, the hic et nunc of bald materiality, makes him the perfect counterpart to a figure whose "pathology" consists in the relentless pursuit of an escape from the very conditions Mephistopheles uses his comic interventions to expose. Far from the embodiment of evil, Mephistopheles is a stage practitioner whose

---

25. Goethe did consider writing a scene about Satan, though there is no indication that he wanted this figure to be identified with the Lucifer discussed in his autobiography. See Eibl, *Das monumentale Ich*, 117–120; and Albrecht Schöne, *Götterzeichen, Liebeszauber, Satanskult* (Munich: C. H. Beck, 1993).

strategic interventions do more than point out this or that illusion, this or that peccadillo. They are the practice of revealing the vulnerability of the grandest aspirations to radical diminution. Mephistopheles, to borrow a phrase from Goethe's contemporary Jean Paul, inverts the sublime.[26] And yet one must be careful not to paint an overly celebratory picture of the comic devil. Inverting the sublime does not restore a sober-minded view on the world, but rather installs a perspective with its own constitutive distortions. There can be little doubt that Mephistopheles's comic interventions offer a painfully icy reckoning with Faust's most ardent and highest aspirations. They betray a cynicism, to return again to Max Kommerell's term, that offers a deficient insistence on the human being's "limited" nature, failing to recognize that the human also possesses the capacity for being "unconditioned." The devil's jest, the life he shows Faust, is one of codependence between the aspiration to the heavens and the crash down to earth. The possibility that our grandest wishes can be revealed as mere folly is not just a definitive part of Goethe's tragedy, but of his vision of the human being. As he put it, "We attribute our states sometimes to God and sometimes to the devil, and err both times: in ourselves lies the puzzle, we who are the spawn of two worlds."[27]

---

26. I believe there is a close relationship between Mephistopheles and Jean Paul's notion of humor as the "inverted sublime" or *das umgekehrte Erhabene*. See Jean Paul, *Werke* (Munich: Carl Hanser Verlag, 1973), 5:125ff.

27. "Unsere Zustände schreiben wir bald Gott, bald dem Teufel zu und fehlen ein- wie das andere Mal: in uns selbst liegt das Rätsel, die wir Ausgeburt zweier Welten sind." From among the aphorisms collected under the title *Älteres, Beinahe Veraltetes* in Goethe's *Hefte zur Naturwissenschaft überhaupt*, LA I 8:361.

16

Antinomies of the Classical

On Kleist's Broken Jug

Around 1800, Goethe's only peer in the literary deployment of the stage fool was Heinrich von Kleist. Although his plays never achieved the theatrical success of the third great dramatist of the age, Friedrich Schiller, there is, by now, little doubt that Kleist's singular oeuvre of plays testifies to a literary imagination as subtle as it is profound, as hermetic as it is rewarding. With microscopic precision, his comedy *Der zerbrochne Krug* (*The Broken Jug*, 1811) grapples with and innovates on the themes that have stood at the center of the foregoing chapters.[1] Although the play was first performed in 1808, the very same year that Goethe's *Faust I* finally appeared in print, its form reflects the major developments in eighteenth-century theater with unique formal energy.

---

1. All the following references are to the version of the play found in Heinrich von Kleist, *Sämtliche Werke und Briefe* (Munich: Carl Hanser Verlag, 2010), 1:163–276. I recommend the use of this edition, as the detail I focus on has often been elided by editors. References to the play are given parenthetically by line number.

The point of departure in this final chapter will be an anomalous detail from this play, not simply because it reveals much about Kleist's incisive manipulation of literary form, but because it explores the conditions of dramatic composition and theatrical visibility that played out so controversially in the course of the eighteenth century. The anomaly that provides the cornerstone of this chapter stands at the cusp of the nineteenth century in two respects: it looks back and reflects upon the mechanisms underlying the emergence of eighteenth-century dramatic literature, and it also leaves open the question of whether these mechanisms should be perpetuated or set to rest.

One of the chief accomplishments in dramatic composition around 1800, evident in Kleist's works just as much as in Goethe's, is the acute awareness of the historicity of literary forms—the awareness, that is, of their plurality, their roots in particular periods and places, their connection to concrete social-historical constellations, and their varying assignments of strategic import. In the literary universe that Goethe and Kleist inhabited—better yet, helped create—the multiplicity of historical forms, lacking an obligatory force, imbued the selection and redeployment of any particular form with heightened significance. Under the aegis of historical contingency, the use of a traditional form is not merely the affirmation of an outmoded compositional standard or technical scaffolding, or even of the values that the form may have stood for. Within the modern literary ecosystem, the use of a traditional form is itself a heightened mode of expression, an embedded semantic feature of the text that requires decipherment. Kleist's playful appropriation in *The Broken Jug* of forms that had been passed down since antiquity, with varying degrees of binding force, has not escaped the attention of scholarship.

Over recent decades, critics have shed considerable light on the reworking of tragic form, especially Sophocles's *Oedipus Rex*, in a play its author named a comedy.[2] As is well known, Kleist prefaced the manuscript version of his play with a description of an

---

2. See the pioneering essay by Wolfgang Schadewaldt, "*Der zerbrochen Krug von Heinrich von Kleist und Sophokles' König Ödipus*," in *Heinrich von Kleist: Aufsätze und Essays*, ed. Walter Müller-Seidel (Darmstadt: Wissenschaftliche Buchgesellschaft, 1967), 317–325.

engraving by Jean-Jacques Le Veau, in the course of which he establishes parallels in Sophocles's tragedy. Moreover, Kleist's play appropriates the analytic structure for which *Oedipus Rex* is so famous—namely, the progressive disclosure—through a process of investigation and inquiry of the protagonist's culpability for an antecedent wrongdoing. The envelopment of perhaps the quintessential tragic form within a comedy stands in striking contrast to *Faust*, in which Goethe renders the comic a crucial structural element of tragedy. But before considering the repercussions of Kleist's reverse approach, we must examine his artful appropriation of a formal standard that stood at the very center of the eighteenth-century effort to create a dramatic literature of rank—a formal standard that belonged as much to one genre as to the other and that figured centrally in the effort to furnish drama with a standard of internal coherence, which left no place for the fool's interjections and interruptions.

The anomaly that provides orientation for the following chapter does not, at first sight, appear to be one at all. It comes in the penultimate scene, scene 12, of *The Broken Jug*, which begins with the inconspicuous stage direction "The previous figures (without Adam.—They move to the front of the stage)" (*Die Vorigen, [ohne Adam.—Sie begeben sich alle in den Vordergrund der Bühne]*).[3] The guiding claim of this chapter is that this parsimonious stage direction is tightly interlaced with the controversies organizing debate over drama and theater in the eighteenth century. In particular, it replays the early Enlightenment wager that a culturally ennobled drama and theater demanded the expulsion of the fool, and it also responds to the late eighteenth-century endeavor to restore his presence. For this reason, the scene instantiates the tendency in comedy, at least since the New Comedy of Hellenistic Greece, to "reflect its own phylogenesis."[4] Comedy, in the course of its long history, has regularly employed standardized scenic structures and

---

3. See Kleist, *Sämtliche Werke und Briefe*, 1:253.
4. Peter von Matt, "Das letzte Lachen: Zur finalen Szene in der Komödie," in *Theorie der Komödie—Poetik der Komödie*, ed. Ralf Simon (Bielefeld: Aisthesis Verlag, 2001), 127.

plot events to realize its participation in a preestablished generic order. In Kleist's case, however, belonging to the comedic genre amounts to more than falling within a time-transcendent category; it means responding to the time-and-place-specific question of whether the fool deserves a place in German literary drama.

To be sure, such an emphatic reading of a single stage direction can seem rather far-fetched in isolation. The scene break and stage direction can bear such interpretive weight because, considered in context, they stand out as an anomaly in Kleist's play, in which most of the scenes are woven together according to a convention indebted to the French neoclassical tradition, known as *liaison des scenes*. And yet the subtle deviation in this scene from the established convention of coordinating scene breaks with comings and goings should be read as a clue, as a strategically aberrant trace, in Kleist's anachronistic appropriation of a form. Crucially, the scene comes at a pivotal juncture in the plot, immediately after Adam, the village judge, has suddenly disappeared for good. It is anomalous because, unlike all the other exits in the play, this one does not have an accompanying stage direction; ordinarily the author includes, as one would expect, the abridged directive *ab* or "off" to indicate the event of departure. But Adam absconds without a textual marker, and the scene break is occasioned by a different choreographed movement. As we shall see, the scene farcically replays the most controversial episode in eighteenth-century theater and the founding myth of eighteenth-century drama: the banishing of the stage fool.[5]

To grasp the exceptional significance of this stage instruction, we must first take a step back. Here is what is happening in the play on a very general level.[6] It has just become clear that a judge named Adam from the fictional Dutch village Huisium is a shifty

---

5. See above, chapter 5.

6. For the interpretation of the major themes of the play that has been foundational to the research over recent years, see David E. Wellbery, "*Der zerbrochne Krug*: Das Spiel der Geschlechterdifferenz," in *Kleists Dramen*, ed. Walter Hinderer (Stuttgart: Reclam, 1997), 11–32. Wellbery also takes note of the relationship between Adam and the tradition of the stage fool, referring to Kleist's comic judge as a reincarnation of the Hanswurst.

representative of the law who broke the jug that provides, at least ostensibly, the centerpiece of the comedy. It is also clear that the entire foregoing court case, played out over the previous scenes, has been, from the perspective of plot development, a charade of dissemblance and evasion.[7] Adam broke Frau Marthe's most prized jug the night before while escaping out the window after visiting her daughter Eve, whom he hoped to steal away from her beloved, Ruprecht. All of this has come to light in the previous eleven scenes, which take place over court proceedings that Adam is judging, but that are also being overseen by a visiting district judge, Walter, who is a state representative meant to ensure the soundness of Huisium's court procedures. The end of the court proceedings—and the near end of the play—is not a verdict is-sued on Adam's guilt, but rather his abrupt flight. The visiting judge and Licht, Adam's scribe and deputy, spend much of the play confused by Adam's repeated prevarications and impropri-eties. Just before this scene, it has come to light that the judge is also the culprit—the breaker of the prized jug. It would not be far-fetched to suppose that with this revelation and the judge's flight, the comedy should come to a close: the mystery has been resolved, the fraud revealed, and the clandestine attempt to drive a wedge between Eve and Rupreht thwarted. But, importantly, the comedy does not end with the banishment of the villain. Instead, Kleist introduces a scene break and calls the dramatis personae to the front of the stage.

The seemingly unspectacular stage direction that begins scene 12 reflects, with breathtaking density, the historical vicissitudes of dramatic form that have been our focus in this study. Kleist, in

---

7. My characterization does not account for the profound meditation on law and its offices in the play. On this subject, I recommend Cornelia Vismann, *Medien der Rechtsprechung* (Frankfurt am Main: S. Fischer Verlag, 2011), 38–71. See also the insightful essay by Ethel Matala de Mazza, "Hintertüren, Gartenpforten und Tümpel: Über Kleists krumme Wege," in *Ausnahmezustand der Literatur: Neue Lektüren zu Heinrich von Kleist*, ed. Nicolas Pethes (Göttingen: Wallstein Verlag, 2011), 185–207. Both texts make much of the relationship between Kleist's play and Sophocles's *Oedipus Rex*. De Mazza closes her essay with incisive observa-tions on the contentious status of Gottsched's conception of literary comedy, in-cluding the banishment of the stage fool, in Kleist's comedy.

fact, poignantly identifies the forces responsible for the significant alterations to the dramatic form in Germany, from its first emergence in the 1730s to the early decades of the nineteenth century. In order to unearth the stage instruction's embedded semantic content, I shall adduce three familiar analytic dimensions. Kleist's text, I claim, positions itself within the contentious and variable relationship between the fixed, written text and the immediate unfolding of live performance, the drama-theater dyad. It is concerned, too, with the way the dramatic text relates to the audience, through its two constitutive axes, the fiction-internal axis and the fiction-external axis. The third and final analytic dimension of concern is that of comic temporality. In other words, Kleist's dramatic text, especially this anomalous scene break, responds to the difference between the controlled temporality of text and the potentially explosive temporality of theatrical presence. Kleist's text provides a particularly powerful means for addressing these issues, for its form draws out an aporetic moment in the attempt to install a literary embodiment of the fool on the stage. Considering the play from these three analytic dimensions will, further, allow us to reframe the form-semantic question that has most preoccupied interpreters, namely, the importance of analytic tragedy to Kleist's comedy.

The stage direction itself will be a guide in this chapter. The following pages begin with the question, Who are "the previous figures"? Then the analysis turns to the question, Who or what is Adam? And finally the discussion of Kleist's comedy responds to the question, What does this movement to the "front of the stage" mean?

The Previous Figures   Scene 12 diverges, as suggested above, from the formal parameters that otherwise govern the transition from scene to scene. Kleist's comedy is divided into thirteen scenes, each of which—except for this one—is distinguished from the ones on either side by the entrance or exit of a single figure. The stage in *The Broken Jug* is never empty, and the curtain never falls; each scene surges forcefully into the next. For this reason, nearly every scene, including this one, begins with the stage direction "The previous figures," underscoring the continuity of persons across scene divisions. Perhaps it is for this reason that Goethe remarked, upon first encountering

Kleist's play in draft form, that the formal presentation of the play proceeds with "violent presence" (*mit gewaltsamer Gegenwart*).[8] Within this unbroken, onward-pressing movement, however, the twelfth scene marks a subtle deviation, which opens up this drama into one of the central debates of eighteenth-century poetics.

Even though it was a flop when Goethe first staged it in 1808 in the court theater in Weimar, this comedy, more than any of Kleist's other plays, treats the relationship of the dramatic text to theatrical embodiment as one of its central themes. A significant indication of this is the coordination in every scene (except this one) of the textual demarcation of a scene break, of textual segment, with the entrance of a figure into or an exit out of the field of theatrical visibility. The inclusion of thirteen junctures of arrival and/or departure was particularly attractive, we might conjecture, because the prime integer challenges the partition of the play into symmetrical parts. The absence of acts, in addition, makes large-scale subdivision difficult—or is itself, at least, already an interpretive gesture. While the play does admit of division according to a 6–1–6 structure, with the middle scene as the turning point, where, among other things, the history of the jug is explained, this partitioning can assist only a close reader and interpreter, not a stage director. The play, one might say, possesses an abstract, textual symmetry that transforms to its opposite the moment it is rendered theatrically concrete. The scenic construction is dramatically regular and theatrically irregular—and from both perspectives impregnably sealed.

The organization of the drama into thirteen internally contiguous scenes locates it within a particular historical constellation. The strategy of seamless concatenation, of supplying the stage with uninterrupted visual continuity, was codified in seventeenth-century French classicism as *liaison des scenes*.[9] It gained traction within

---

8. Letter, 8/28/1807, FA II 6:229.

9. See Jacques Scherer, *La dramaturgie classique en France* (Paris: Nizet, 1950), esp. 201–208. I have also discussed this phenomenon in Joel Lande, "Auftritt und Interaktion: Zu Lessings *Minna von Barnhelm*," in *Auftreten: Wege auf die Bühne*, ed. Juliane Vogel and Christopher Wild (Berlin: Theater der Zeit, 2014), 233–246. I owe my alertness to this phenomenon in eighteenth-century drama to Juliane Vogel, as well as the other members of the research group on entrances.

the German context in the course of Gottsched's theatrical reforms. Nearly every dramatic text published from approximately 1730 to 1775 in the German language adheres to this structuring principle. This was, to be sure, a belated, and in many respects piecemeal, appropriation of a principle that had been codified earlier in France. Nonetheless, the principle of *liaison des scenes* is, paradoxically, both fulfilled and violated in the scene under scrutiny here. This duplicity is the crux of Kleist's intense reflection on dramatic form. Because the French neoclassical notion, as it gained traction in eighteenth-century Germany, amounts to more than a stylistic preference, it bears on the ontology of the dramatic text and its relationship to theatrical performance.

The implications of this formal device for eighteenth-century drama are evident already in Gottsched's 1730 *Critische Dichtkunst*. Gottsched asserts in his treatise that "the entrances within the scenes of a plot must always be connected with one another, in order that the stage is never totally empty until an entire act is over. One person from the previous scene must always remain present, when a new one comes, in order that the entire act hangs together (*Zusammenhang*). The Ancients, as well as Corneille and Racine, have adhered to this principle dutifully."[10] The weaving together of a fabric of scenes, entirely without ruptures, is for Gottsched the textual precondition for the theatrical simulation of a verisimilar fictional world. *Liaison des scenes* is the formal principle Gottsched uses in order to secure metaphysically coherent intraworld relations in drama. It is the mechanism for ensuring the interlinking of the narrative from beginning to middle to end, for ensuring a play hangs together in a way deserving of being called *simplex et unum*. Throughout the eighteenth century, *liaison des scenes* provides the ordering principle that guarantees a play is, in Johann Georg Sulzer's terms, a "whole work" (*ein ganzes Werk*), which is to say, "an indivisible whole" (*ein unzertrennliches Ganzes*).[11] Within the rule-governed regime that took hold in the early

---

10. Johann Christoph Gottsched, *Versuch einer critischen Dichtkunst vor die Deutschen* (Leipzig: Bernhard Christoph Breitkopf, 1730), 585.

11. Johann Georg Sulzer, "Anordnung," in *Allgemeine Theorie der Schönen Künste* (Leipzig: Wiedemanns Erben und Reich, 1771), 1:57–59, here 57.

Enlightenment, a play can make a "vivid impression" on a spectator only through the "order according to which everything follows
one after the other."[12] The concatenation of entrances and exits
becomes, within this formal paradigm, a mechanism for keeping
at bay potential lacunae, for ensuring the internal coherence of
persons and events on the stage, and for avoiding the intrusions
of the fool. The concept of *liaison des scenes* binds together the
drama-theater dyad in the belief that the plausibility of a fictional
world on the stage depends on the maintenance, within the text, of
a distinct, but parallel form of temporal continuity the spectators
experience while watching. The text is not just a work to be read,
studied, or understood; it is, in the traditional Aristotelian terminology, the formal cause of theatrical verisimilitude. A key piece
of textual evidence for this text-performance sequential arrangement is the fact that, beginning around the time of Gottsched in
the 1730s, scenes are called *Auftritte* (entrances) and acts, *Aufzüge*
(raisings of the curtain). Textual segmentation, in other words,
draws not just its nomenclature, but also the justification for its
divisions, from its causal connection to the spectator's perception
of a theatrical performance.

Scene 12 in *The Broken Jug* reflects this relationship between
text and performance, drama and theater on multiple levels. Even
though this scene does not begin with an entrance or an exit, it
preserves the continuity of the fictional fabric by leaving all of the
characters from the previous scene on stage. If there is an action
that occasions the scene break, then it is the anomalous directions
that call the ensemble to the front of the stage. For a spectator ac-
customed to regarding entrances and exits as the ordering device,
this anomaly would remain inconspicuous; it is only scrutable on
a textual level. The textual anomaly of this scene break is a difference that makes a difference—one that reflects, however subtly,
Kleist's critical distance from the eighteenth-century conception of
the dramatic text. To unfold the implications of this textual clue,
we must consider, first, who Adam is, and second, what the group's
approach to the foreground means.

---

12. Ibid., 65.

Without Adam   So who is this Adam? A full answer to this question must include, among other things, the importance of his biblical namesake and his erotic adventuring, as well as his juridical stratagems. I wish to isolate a dimension of the play that has received sporadic mention in the abundant literary scholarship, but the significance of which has remained underappreciated: Adam is a literary incarnation of the most controversial stage figure of the eighteenth century, the funnyman whose persistence has been our focus, and whose banishment coincided with the institution of the formal principle of *liaison des scenes*. Four aspects, sketched below in compressed form, reveal Kleist's awareness of the comic practice of the early modern stage fool.

1. Adam is a figure of mundane corporeality. References to his grotesquely porous and misshapen body pervade this drama. From the repeated references to two orifices of his body—"one in front and one in back" (line 1467)—to his curse of his own phallus—"be damned my midriff" (line 1774)—Adam is symbolically associated with the nether regions of the body in his person and in his humor. The play begins with the scribe Licht's remarking on Adam's gaping wounds and closes with others attempting to thrash him. Adam is the sole figure whose body becomes the subject of discourse and, indeed, of dramatic consequence. Moreover, his office as court judge is contaminated by his base somatic existence. In the cabinet meant for documents and transcripts, he keeps food. This veritable pantry is stuffed with everything from a "Braunschweiger Wurst" (line 216) to "Cheese, Ham, Butter, Sausages, and Bottles" (line 194), as well as the fool's classic moniker, Hanswurst. And it is only fitting that his humor often hews closely to the rude, sexual register.

2. Adam is an intractable rascal. The courtroom proceedings, which make up the major action of the comedy, are repeatedly derailed by Adam's outbursts and digressions. Much to the alarm of the visiting district judge, Walter, Adam does not respect the juridical protocol of question and response, but instead interjects and misdirects at every turn. In this

way, Adam embodies the fool's interruptive relationship to the continuity of plot-driving dialogue. His distinct mode of derailing the court proceedings is profoundly improvisatory. Accounts of past events often spin off a word or phrase in a previous statement, without regard for internal consistency or the avoidance of contradictory reports. In virtue of his desire to elude the appearance of guilt for the broken jug, his utterances all have the character of role-playing, of a spontaneous reaction to his interlocutor and an unforeseen attempt to keep the illusion of innocence alive. The parallel between court proceedings and plot—in German, *Prozess* and *Handlung*—that shapes the entire drama means that Adam's interruptions are both irruptive moments in the courtroom procedure and digressions from the continuous unfolding of the plot. They can even be understood as attempts to forestall the unfurling of a coherent plot and to hinder the revelation of truth.

3.   Adam's participation in the patterns of dialogue is characteristic of the fool's comic practice that gained a foothold first in the 1590s. For instance, Adam delivers eight of the comedy's ten asides.[13] One notable instance of an aside comes at the beginning of the seventh scene, when he frames the ensuing events before the scene gets under way.[14] In general, much of the humor in this comedy is produced by Adam's verbal lapses, which inadvertently reveal his guilt but which go unnoticed by the other characters in the fiction. His tergiversations create a division between the internal axis of communication and the external actor-spectator axis of communication. The comedy's humor, in other words, is based upon the audience's knowledge, achieved via the fiction-external axis of communication, of Adam's strategic but clumsy obfuscations, about which the other members of the fiction remain largely ignorant. The visiting district judge, Walter, reprimands him on three occasions

---

13. Explicitly named in scenes 2, 4, 7, 8, 10, 11, 12, and 13—but equally true in scenes 3, 5, 6, and 9.
14. Kleist, *Sämtliche Werke*, 1:190.

for his duplicity of speech—the key word, which always appears in the same metrical abbreviation, is *zweideut'g* (lines 542, 805, and 20 of Variant), a term that refers here as much to his evasiveness as to his comedic toeing of the line between inside and outside the fiction.

4. Adam's heterodox and highly improvised management of the courtroom is associated with oral speech and set in contradistinction to the written law. He even goes so far as to claim that he is proceeding according to local statutes, "idiosyncratic ones" (*eigentümliche*), which are "not the written ones, but instead ones transmitted through proven tradition" (lines 627–629). He describes his shifty, inconsistent, and self-interested management of the court case as strictly adhering to a juridical "form" (line 630), just one distinct from the rigorous procedure practiced elsewhere in the realm. Adam's unscripted participation as judge of the court case demonstrates the very same temporality of extemporized theatrical presence that the Enlightenment insistence upon the static text had sought to control.

These four points throw Adam's departure just before the beginning of the twelfth scene into sharp relief. His flight replays what we have identified as the founding myth of eighteenth-century theater: the banishment of the fool from the stage.

Before returning to the relationship between the scene break and Adam's disappearance from the stage, it is worth recalling a few details from the broader historical framework. The Enlightenment reforms had altered the importance assigned to the textual configuration of a play by making it into a vehicle for the transformation of the existing stage culture. The notion that textual continuity would produce theatrical verisimilitude, as part 2 showed, went hand in hand with the banishment of the fool, whose incessant interruptions, spontaneous improvisation, and corporeal jest made him the pariah of the reform project. The structure of *liaison des scenes* provided the formal strategy for ensuring that there would never be a pause in the performance in which the fool might burst onto the stage, and that the play would achieve the requisite internal continuity.[15] A rupture in the principle of *liaison des scenes* amounts, in other words, to a rupture in the Enlightenment attempt to yoke together performance and text.

It further bears pointing out that the constellation of figures in Kleist's play reflects the historical forces that have stood at the center of this study. There is Adam, who is an intractable improviser; his secretary, Licht, who transcribes the events of the trial in the instant of their occurrence; and the visiting district judge, Walter, whose visit to Huisium aims to ensure conformity of court proceedings with the generally applicable written rules. Put more abstractly, Kleist writes into his play a figure of improvisational theatricality, an author of texts, and a regulatory instance. The comedy establishes a triangulated structure among three forces responsible for the genesis of the literary drama: poetological regulation, fixed textuality, and the unforeseeable presence of live theater. Once the conceptual-historical associations underpinning the constellation of figures come into view, the commencement of the twelfth scene emerges as the immediate aftermath of the fool's departure. We are left at the beginning of this scene with Walter (regulatory instance) and Licht (scribe), who step, together with the other dramatis personae, to the front of the stage.

How, though, are we to make sense of the fact that at the moment that Adam has departed, the pattern of coordinating textual segmentation with theatrical entrances and exits becomes irregular? How are we to make sense of this sudden interruption of a crucial formal instrument for the reform imposition of dramatic unity? Simply put: through Adam's disappearance in the middle of the foregoing scene. Here Kleist's literary maneuvers are as subtle as they are instructive. In keeping with the parallel between Adam and the fool, his comings and goings cannot be regulated by those figures who represent textual fixity in the play. That is, once it has come to light that Adam broke the jug during his clumsy attempts to seduce the young maiden Eve, he scurries off the stage, but his departure is not marked as such. His departure breaks the formal convention and textual regulation that all the other figures dutifully obey. Readers learn of his flight only obliquely by way of Ruprecht

---

15. See chapter 7.

(Eve's beloved), who exclaims as he evidently reaches for Adam: "It is just his cloak" (*Es ist sein Mantel bloß*) (line 1902). Adam's actual exit from the stage is never textually registered in a stage direction. All that the representatives of the ordered text can grasp is an outer garment, a surface shell or covering, detached from the figure himself. Within this analogy, we might say that the text can hold onto only the surface semblance, the textual signifier, while the thing itself, the performed referent, remains forever unpredictable and elusive. Once Adam has fled, theatrical performance and dramatic text are thrown out of sync; the textual segment is not able to keep a firm hold on the entrances or exits. In the absence of Adam, the "previous figures" have lost their principle of theatricality and assume an exclusively textual shape. And for this reason, his departure coincides with the jettisoning of *liaison des scenes* as the instrument of regulating theatrical performance. It becomes clear that this compositional principle, this attempt to form a strict drama-theater dyad, had always been an exclusively textual endeavor, an attempt to place the theater under textual control, without attending properly to the preexisting conditions of theatrical performance. It is perfectly fitting, then, that within the formalized context of drama, this aberration is textually legible but not theatrically visible.

They Move to the Front of the Stage   The absence of Adam and the introduction of an anomalous scene division render the final element in the stage direction all the more mysterious. Why does Kleist emphasize the collective movement to the front of the stage upon Adam's disappearance? With the fool gone, Kleist's comedy inaugurates its own principle of textual segmentation, built not around the passage into theatrical presence or absence, but rather around the formation of a collective. At first glance, it seems that, with this scene, Kleist introduces a tableau of social cohesion, much as conventions in the comedic tradition dictate. The comedic finale often portrays the pacification of social conflict through the act of social cohesion par excellence, the betrothal.[16] And with Adam gone, all obstacles to the marriage between Eve and Ruprecht are removed, clearing the way for a paradigmatic happily-ever-after. In

---

16. Matt, "Das letzte Lachen," 128–140.

accord with a second comedic convention, after Adam has left the stage, Ruprecht goes on to violently and repeatedly beat the cloak he has left behind. Such a scene of corporal punishment strongly resembles slapstick, with Adam (just dispatched) embodying the symbolic role of the scapegoat.[17]

And yet the finale of Kleist's comedy adheres to conventions only insofar as it redoubles and thereby denudes them. There is no scapegoat to beat, only the trace of abandonment, and beating this hollow surrogate with such alacrity is in and of itself laughable. Kleist provides here a simulacrum of the ritualized scapegoat punishment, allowing for an explosion of violence on Adam's judicial livery, but also one that fails to touch his real body. If one of the purposes of generic conventions is to signal, however subtly, participation in an overarching generic pattern, Kleist here reveals the act of scapegoat violence as irreducibly symbolic—which is to say, that it aims less at the execution of violence on a specific individual than at the ritual-like execution of a predetermined and unalterable sequence of actions. It suits Adam's status as an improvisatory fool figure, then, that his unscripted departure reveals the scripted nature of the scapegoat ritual and, one might speculate, thereby exposes the perils of ossified generic conventions.

So what is the significance of this synchronous collective movement to the front of the stage? Why does it occasion a scene break? On the most basic level, the scene presents here a putatively harmonious unity fostered by the banishing of a figure of illicit sexuality, irreverence to juridical norms, comic improvisation, and procedural intractability. In keeping with the scapegoat structure, the act of violent exclusion has a community-binding force, furnishing the play with a tableau of social cohesion. But Kleist accomplishes more than a harmonious ending to his play with the banishment of the fool.

The choreographic arrangement of this scene is breathtaking in its subtlety. First, by moving to the front of the stage, the collective inhabits a space typically reserved for the fool—in particular for his speech *ad spectatores*—at the very threshold in between the inside and outside of the fiction. The scene enacts, in other

---

17. Northrop Frye, *Anatomy of Criticism: Four Essays* (Princeton: Princeton University Press, 2000), 163ff.

words, the symbolic usurpation of the fool's liminal space, which allows him—and only him—to operate both inside and outside the fictional world. In this moment of collective formation, the group embodiment of dramatic fixity closes off the porous zone within which the fool had his home. A key piece of evidence for this interpretive line is what happens next in the scene. It is not long before Licht, the scribe and, by metonymy, the instantiation of the literary author, calls everyone over to a window where they watch Adam flee. It is not at all far-fetched to suppose that this window is a reference to a widespread motif in painting since the Renaissance. The window typically functions as a pictorial device, which demarcates a separation between the internal, imaginary space of the painting and external reality beyond it.[18] The window, in other words, operates as the symbolic boundary point within the fiction that indicates the self-enclosed status of the fiction itself. Kleist's scene is, therefore, organized around a twofold movement: on the one hand, there is the occlusion and appropriation of the fool's liminal space, and, on the other, there is the spatial identification with a symbol of perfect fictional continence. The closing of the former is the precondition for the full establishment of the latter.

Once everyone gathers in front of the window, the group cries out in in unison, "Look! Look! / he is being whipped by his own wig!" (lines 1958–1959). Together, the group delights in a theatrical prop lashing the scapegoat fool. The function of comedy, Kleist points out in this scene, lies not simply in stories that reinforce social cohesion, but in ones that unite through the shared spectating of the self-inflicted perils of human folly. The ever-skeptical Kleist grapples with the fragile and always fleeting identity of the collective by insisting upon a founding moment of violent exclusion. Immediately thereafter, the district judge, Walter, sends Licht to bring him back. Kleist makes evident, in the ensemble's approach to the front of the stage and ensuing operatic *unisono*, that the act of social inclusion is nothing more than spectatorial enjoyment

---

18. See Victor Stoichita, *La instauration du tableau: Métapeinture à l'aube des temps modernes* (Paris: Méridiens Klincksieck, 1993). In addition to Foucault's famous analysis in *The Order of Things*, see Svetlana Alpers, "Interpretation without Representation, or, The Viewing of *Las Meninas*," *Representations* 1 (1983): 30–42.

at violent exclusion. As Kleist himself wrote in 1809, soon after completing *The Broken Jug*, "Every great and encompassing danger affords, if it is well met, the state, for an instant, a democratic appearance."[19] The concluding scene is just such a fleeting, democratic instance of collective formation.

This moment of collective coalescence, in the aftermath of the fool's expulsion and his symbolic thrashing, introduces a conventional comedic conclusion to a court trial that, in principle, had aimed for a different sort of resolution. The scene break, that is, marks the unexpected conclusion to the proceedings of a cultural institution that functions as a mediating instance between parties in conflict and thereby avoids open physical confrontation.[20] Channeling and thereby limiting conflict, court proceedings, in general, circumscribe the scope of disagreement and, at least in principle, afford a means for its resolution. Structured conflict should, within this institutional context, obviate the need for direct violence. Meanwhile, the court proceedings that make up the plot of Kleist's play fail to provide a structure within which conflict can be played out, without the threat of physical violence repeatedly bubbling to the surface. Evidence of this failure can be found in Frau Marthe's repeated expressions of desire to exact physical revenge on the party responsible—in her mind, Ruprecht—for the broken jug. Her first appearance before the court is punctuated by a speech in which she equates the judge with a henchman and imagines the culprit receiving a sound whipping (lines 493–497). Her protracted description of the broken jug includes the demand that Ruprecht be broken on the wheel (line 767); she interrupts Ruprecht's account of the past evening's events with threats of inflicting harm on him once the court proceedings are over (lines 951–953); and she even threatens to break Eve's bones for refusing to say who broke the jug (line 1199). Perhaps the most striking explosion of potential violence comes from Eve, when her silence about Adam's responsibility for the broken jug eventually breaks down and she instructs her betrothed, Ruprecht, to grab hold of and

19. Heinrich von Kleist, "Über die Rettung Österreichs" in *Sämtliche Werke*, 2:337.

20. See the subtle observations in Niklas Luhmann, *Legitimation durch Verfahren* (Frankfurt am Main: Surhkamp Verlag, 1983), esp. 100–106.

bash the judge without restraint (lines 1894–1896). Despite these repeated verbal calls for brutality, the thrashing of Adam's cloak, upon his escape from the stage, is its sole physical manifestation. Adam's inability to maintain his role as judge—to establish, that is, a division between his self-presentation as an officer of the court and the rest of his person—means that the court proceedings do little to suppress the potential for physical violence. And, of course, since that failure ultimately reveals his own culpability, he becomes the intended object of abuse. In place, then, of a juridical resolution and the suppression of violence, the transition from the eleventh to the twelfth scene of Kleist's comedy introduces a moment of what one might call generic self-identification—a moment, that is, when the play asserts its participation in the conventions of the comedic genre. Compared with tragedy, comedy has an unusually high tolerance for both verbal descriptions of and optical displays of physical violence.

And yet this is a play that draws much of its comedic energy from its close proximity to tragedy. As scholars have often noted, the court proceedings in Kleist's play reprise the analytic structure of Sophocles's canonical tragedy, *Oedipus Rex*. One of the chief differences between the two plays pertains to the question of self-knowledge. Whereas Oedipus progressively uncovers his responsibility for a patricidal crime that had necessarily escaped his knowledge up to that point, Adam works throughout the comedy to obscure his wrongdoings. His various attempts at articulating his whereabouts on the previous evening and explaining the multiple wounds covering his body and his mysteriously absent wig ultimately disclose his responsibility. Whereas the tragic process confronts Oedipus with the limits of his self-knowledge due to circumstances beyond his experience, the comedic process exposes Adam's self-knowledge, despite his best attempts to obscure his unscrupulous machinations. Ultimately, his inability to provide a consistent testimonial account *expresses* his culpability, even as he repeatedly *avows* his innocence.[21] In the perilous

---

21. On the distinction between expression and avowal, with reference to Wittgenstein and the unconscious, see David Finkelstein, *Expression and the Inner* (Cambridge, MA: Harvard University Press, 2003).

discrepancy between his expressions and avowals, Adam lives up to the anthropological claim that he introduces at the outset of the play: "Everyone carries the woeful stumbling block in himself" (*Denn jeder trägt / den leidig'n Stein zum Anstoß in sich selbst*) (lines 5–6). Adam's fall is not a transgressive act of the will, nor an encounter with an inhospitable fate, but rather an internalized *lapsus* that leads him to stumble over his own two feet. It is his own failure to produce consistent untruths, to serve as a reliably false witness, that ultimately costs him. Like the many fools before him, his utterances are fundamentally situational responses. But as Kleist makes a protagonist out of the fool, installing him as the central figure of his literary comedy, improvisatory comic prevarications run up against the consistency of self-presentation demanded from a full-blooded character. Returning to the idiom I introduced in my discussion of the early Enlightenment reforms, one might even speculate that Adam trips over the inconsistencies of character that come to expression in a drama composed under the aegis of syntagmatic unity.

At its conclusion, then, *The Broken Jug* insists upon its own status as a literary drama, including its media-historical foundation in textuality. After all, even though the group takes pleasure in the fool's humiliation, Walter, the regulatory instance in the play, ultimately sends Licht after him. The play comes to a close with the poetological imperative for the fool's reinclusion in the aftermath of his expulsion, and it is the embodiment of fixed textuality who is assigned the responsibility of bringing the fool back to the stage. Kleist's attempt to restore the fool takes place not on the stage but on paper. And yet *The Broken Jug* withholds a final verdict on the viability of a theatrical fool under the aegis of the literary text, with its emphasis on character. The question of whether or not the fool ever returns, and under what conditions he does so, remains unsettled. This finale, which replays the founding myth of eighteenth-century German comedy, holds in abeyance the question of whether the project of instituting literary drama, launched in the early decades of the eighteenth century, can overcome its founding act of violent exclusion.

POSTLUDE

In perhaps the most technically astute aesthetic treatise from the turn of the nineteenth century, *Preschool of Aesthetics* (*Vorschule der Aesthetik*, 1804/1812) by Jean Paul, we find the claim that the stage fool is the "chorus of comedy."[1] It is a straightforward-enough, but also very surprising, assertion. The statement comes in a lament over the declining state of the contemporary German-speaking theatrical world. The author blames the current situation on the suppression of the figure whom he calls the "true god of laughter, the personification of humor." Reflecting on the major transformations in eighteenth-century theater, Jean Paul (1763–1825) identifies the disappearance of the fool from the stage as the event that robbed the German theater of its vitality and hindered the development of a literature of rank. In passing this judgment, Jean Paul

---

1. Jean Paul, *Werke* (Munich: Carl Hanser Verlag, 1973), 5:160–161. All quotations are from §40, a short section entitled "Der Hanswurst."

takes a place in an impressive lineage of writers around 1800, including Goethe and Kleist, who shared the conviction that the fool, either through his presence or absence, determined the fate and phases of German theater. Jean Paul makes the fool into the center-piece of his discussion of comic theater, well aware that the theatrical figure had been a lightning rod for critical energies, attracting vituperative attacks as well as passionate support. Looking back at the eighteenth century, there was little doubt in Jean Paul's mind that the stage fool had consistently provided a medium for disputing the conditions of dramatic composition and theatrical performance.

In his assessment, Jean Paul avoids commonplace definitions of the fool in terms of a specific linguistic register, a particular garb, or even an individual actor. Instead, he introduces the strange equivalence between the fool and the chorus. But what does the group song and dance from the most vaunted genre of classical antiquity share with the figure whose mutations since his first appearance in the German-speaking lands have been the focus of the foregoing sixteen chapters? Jean Paul's analogy, which makes the fool into a more ennobled figure than many of his predecessors would have countenanced, relies on a pattern of formal similarity between two far-removed theatrical cultures. Moreover, the analogy urges us to approach the notion of role in an emphatic sense: much like the chorus, the fool does not possess a "character of his own," but instead "hovers above the dramatis personae without being one." The two are united in a *how*, not a *what*. To be more precise, their connection lies in a practice of interaction, in a particular way of conducting dialogue. What is more, the reference to the chorus invokes a distinctive rapport between performer and spectator, as the ancient Greek chorus is a voice of retrospection and anticipation on behalf of the audience.

It is helpful to think of Jean Paul's analogy within the context of other major statements about the ancient Greek chorus from around 1800. Friedrich Schiller authored perhaps the most influential one, when he introduced the claim that the chorus separates "reflection" from "plot."[2]

---

2. Jean Paul was clearly familiar with Schiller's text, as is evident in Jean Paul, *Werke*, 5:396. For the relevant passage from Schiller, see *Friedrich Schiller*, "Über den Gebrauch des Chors in der Tragödie," in Friedrich Schiller, *Werke und Briefe in zwölf Bänden* (Frankfurt am Main: Deutscher Klassiker Verlag, 1996), 5:281–291, here 288.

According to this division of responsibilities, the chorus is not an agent in the forward march of deeds and events, but is instead the source of interspersed commentary, which effects a pause and brief respite for the audience, a step back from the events on stage, and a remark on what has transpired or a preview of what is still to come. The chorus is a full-fledged member of the dramatic fiction, observing events as they transpire and even engaging in back-and-forths with the other participants in the play. But the chorus also enjoys a special ability to step outside of the story and communicate with the spectators watching it. Often enough, the commentary by the chorus seems more directed toward the spectators than the other members of the dramatic fiction, whom the chorus "hovers above." This special communicative arrangement imbues the chorus with its civic function: its odes ensure that the audience members from the polis have clarity about the meaning of the tragedy.

The theoretical accomplishment of the parallel between chorus and fool lies in the mode of explanation it encourages us to assume. It tells us to look at the stage fool primarily in terms of his function within the fabric of the fiction, to consider his distinctive way of relating to other figures and the theatrical environment. Upon this basis, Jean Paul feels justified in following what had become standard practice since Gottsched's early Enlightenment reforms, gathering together under a single heading a genuine grab bag of seemingly distinct personae. In fact, it is also the justification for the disputable translation with which I began, but have not yet acknowledged, namely, my statement that Jean Paul is here talking about the fool. For Jean Paul entitles the section "The Hanswurst," and I have implicitly claimed that, with this moniker, he is not talking about one specific actor or persona, but rather about the fool as a single category. I find the translation convincing given that Jean Paul goes on to list a number of other names, including Pickelhäring, Kasperl, Harlequin, and Lipperl, as all falling under the same category. The litany of distinct names is not evidence of just as many full-fledged individuals—the fool does not have a "character of his own"—but rather conventional ways of referring to a single theatrical and dramatic function. While a microhistorical disposition might take offense at gathering together such an array of titles under a general heading, Jean Paul is doing much the same, as when the chorus of enslaved Trojan women from Euripides's *Hecuba* and the chorus of male Theban elders in Sophocles's *Antigone* appear as cognate theatrical devices. Jean Paul's bold analogy, ultimately, rests on two assertions. First, the German fool and the Greek chorus play a similar function in dialogue and dramatic action. Second, the fool is capable of passing under variable guises across a variety of plays, much as all Greek tragedies feature a chorus whose identity changes from case to case.

Jean Paul's discussion of the fool, composed at a watershed moment in the history of German theater, led to the heart of the issues that have stood at the center of this study. The foregoing chapters have sought to understand the confluence of cultural forces that made a renaissance of the fool in German literature around 1800 not only possible, but probable. Around the same time that the *Preschool of Aesthetics* appeared in print, Goethe was putting the finishing touches on the first part of his *Faust* tragedy, and Kleist *The Broken Jug*. As the foregoing chapters have argued, these plays lent literary prominence to a figure who had for nearly two centuries been a vehicle for testing and revising the fundamental categories of literary drama and performed theater. The fool—who had made his first appearance in the German-speaking lands in the age of Shakespeare and quickly become a fixture on the stage of the early modern period, had stood at the center of intense controversy among reform-minded Enlightenment thinkers seeking to endow the theater with moral and aesthetic legitimacy, and had provided a cornerstone of the late eighteenth-century effort to furnish the Germans with a distinctive literary tradition—became, in the years around 1800, a figure redolent with artistic possibility and a valuable instrument in the effort to put German dramatic literature on the world stage.

Jean Paul, Goethe, and Kleist were not alone in their sense that a rejuvenation of comic theater in Germany could draw powerful energies from the tradition of the stage fool. In fact, the magnetic pull of the fool could be felt across lines separating the multiple different literary centers that took shape in the years around 1800. Indeed, there emerged broad consensus among what one might call the literary avant-garde around 1800 that Enlightenment reform efforts had misunderstood the relationship between the theater and comic play. The Romantics, for instance, also recognized that a genuine artistic resource had been lost with the fool's banishment. One the movement's leading figures in the 1790s, and a pillar of German literary culture in the early decades of the nineteenth century, Ludwig Tieck (1773–1853), brings a Hanswurst onto the stage in his satire *Der gestiefelte Kater* (*Puss in Boots*, 1797), in order to decry the degradation of all forms of "play" (*Spaß*) into something "common, raffish, abject" (*gemein, pöbelhaft, niederträchtig*).[3] A literary satire that portrays all the constitutive elements of the theatrical enterprise, including audience and author, Tieck's play has Hanswurst denounce the suggestion that the absence of the fool enhances the spectator's absorption in a fictional universe, and expresses skepticism about the worth of a theater without a funnyman to solicit the audience's laughter. The fool, in this play, is split between two roles: on the one side, he is a standard court jester, and, on the other, he functions as a sort of rival to the fictional Poet, who repeatedly appears to express his displeasure with the staging.[4] Beyond his standard role as commentator, Tieck's fool further claims authority over the play-within-the-play. While the Poet tries, in vain, to control the play from behind the curtain, the fool figure functions as a compère with privileged access to the other members of the fictional world and to the audience. The Poet's domain ends where the Fool's begins—in the field of theatrical visibility.

Tieck's portrayal of the fool, within a play that satirizes multiple dimensions of eighteenth-century theater, inhabits familiar conceptual terrain. The fool operates in this play—as in the writings of Herder, Lenz, Goethe, Kleist, and Jean Paul—as the paradigmatic exponent of theatrical presence, with a uniquely powerful and immediate rapport with audiences. The plot-driven serious drama of the Enlightenment, which assigned a preeminent role to the author and to fixed textuality, according to this epochal line of thought,

---

3. Ludwig Tieck, *Der gestiefelte Kater*, in *Schriften in zwölf Bänden* (Frankfurt am Main: Deutscher Klassiker Verlag, 1985), 6:492–566, here 524.

4. See, in particular, Tieck, *Der gestiefelte Kater*, 6:538–542.

had not fulfilled its avowed purpose of ennobling comic theater, but instead destroyed its very essence. The recrudescence of the fool around 1800 was built on the belief that this form lies at the origin of comic theater, the indispensable essence required for the comic to achieve its theatrical purpose. The Romantics, in general, were possessed of the belief that the fool is, in the words of August Wilhelm Schlegel (1767–1845), "immortal," reappearing again and again "even when one believes so confidently to have buried him." For Schlegel, the fool is an "allegorical person" representing and thus persisting along with the comic itself.[5] The great virtue of the fool is to recognize that, in the words August Klingemann (1777–1831), another writer loosely associated with the Romantic movement, "he does not take the farce as anything higher than as a farce."[6] In other words, the power of the fool issues from his wholehearted endorsement of the audience's thrall as the highest possible theatrical achievement.

Jean Paul's analogy between the fool and the ancient Greek chorus—a notion Klingemann similarly champions—is founded on the attempt to trace comic theater back to an original rapport between stage and audience.[7] The "immortal" fool, whose multiple rebirths run across the second half of the eighteenth century and the early decades of the nineteenth, persists as the demand for the experience of a theatrical performance that, with speech and gesture, holds attention in steady thrall and, in the corporeal experience of laughter, provides explosive moments of playful joy.

---

5. August Wilhelm Schlegel, *Vorlesungen über die dramatische Kunst und Litteratur* (Heidelberg: Mohr und Zimmer, 1811), 2:383.

6. August Klingemann, *Nachtwachen von Bonaventura: Freimüthigkeiten* (Göttingen: Wallstein Verlag, 2012), 39.

7. See Klingemann, *Nachtwachen von Bonaventura*, 69.

BIBLIOGRAPHY

Primary Sources

Abbt, Thomas. *Vom Tod für das Vaterland*. Berlin: Friedrich Nicolai, 1761.

Adelung, Johann Christoph. *Über den Deutschen Styl: Zweiter und Dritter Teil*. Berlin: Christian Friedrich Voß, 1785.

Anonymous. "Des berühmten französischen Paters Poree Rede von den Schauspielen: Ob sie eine Schule guter Sitten sind, oder seyn Können? übersetzt. Nebst einer Abhandlung von der Schaubühne, heraus gegeben von Joh. Friedrich Meyer." *Beyträge zur Critischen Historie* 9 (1734): 3–29.

———. *Comoedia, Bitittult Der Flüchtige Virenus, Oder Die Getreue Olympia*. Regensburg: Johann Georg Hofmann, 1686.

———. "Harlekin, oder Vertheidigung des Groteskekomischen." *Bibliothek der schönen Wissenschaften und der freyen Künste* 7, no. 2 (1762): 334–351.

———. "Ist nicht die Schaubühne das tauglichste Mittel, Volksgeschichte gemeinnütziger zu machen." In *Theaterkalender auf das Jahr 1787*, 33–40. Gotha: Carl Wilhelm Ettinger, 1778.

———. "Nachricht von der unter der Presse befindlichen deutschen Schaubühne." *Beyträge zur critischen Historie der deutschen Sprache, Poesie und Beredsamkeit* 23 (1740): 521–526.

————. *Pickelhärings Hochzeit Oder Der Lustig-singende Harlequin.* Fröhlichshaussen, 1794.

————. "Versuch eines Beweises, daß eine gereimte Comödie nicht gut seyn könne." *Beyträge zur critischen Historie der deutschen Sprache, Poesie und Beredsamkeit* 23 (1740): 466–485.

Ayrer, Jakob, and Adelbert von Keller. *Ayrers Dramen.* Stuttgart: Litterarischer verein, 1865.

Bodmer, Johann Jakob. *Critische Betrachtungen und freye Untersuchungen zum Aufnehmen und zur Verbesserung der deutschen Schau-bühne.* Bern, 1743.

Bolte, Johannes. *Die Singspiele der englischen Komödianten und ihrer Nachfolger in Deutschland, Holland und Skandinavien.* Hamburg/Leipzig: Leopold Voss, 1893.

Brandt, George W., ed. *German and Dutch Theater, 1600–1848.* Cambridge: Cambridge University Press, 1993.

Brauneck, Manfred, and Alfred Noe. *Spieltexte der Wanderbühne.* Berlin: De Gruyter, 1970.

Brennecke, Ernest. *Shakespeare in Germany, 1590–1700, with Translations of Five Early Plays.* Chicago: University of Chicago Press, 1964.

Brück, Heinrich Samuel von. "Gedanken von der Dichtkunst überhaupt." In *Der deutschen Gesellschaft in Leipzig eigene Schriften und Uebersetzungen,* 1:2–31. Leipzig: Bernhard Christoph Breitkopff, 1735.

Castilhon, Jean Lois. *Betrachtungen über die physicalischen und moralischen Ursachen der Verschiedenheit des Genie, der Sitten und Regierungsformen der Natione.* Leipzig: Adam Heinrich Hollens Wittwe, 1770.

Cohn, Albert. *Shakespeare in Germany in the Sixteenth and Seventeenth Centuries: An Account of English Actors in Germany and the Netherlands and of the Plays Performed by Them during the Same Period.* London: Asher & Co, 1865.

Conradus, Hektor. *Necrobaptista: Die Historia von Johanne dem Teufer/Wie er von Herode Gefangen/vnd wie er jm endlich das Heubt abschlagen Lassen.* Uelzen: Michael Kröner, 1600.

Darjes, Joachim Georg. *Erste Gründe der Cameral-Wissenschaften.* Leipzig: Bernhard Christoph Breitkopf, 1768.

Eschenburg, Johann Joachim. *Entwurf einer Theorie und Literatur der schönen Wissenschaften.* Berlin: Friedrich Nicolai, 1789.

Fischer, Heinrich August. *Von der Polizei und Sittengesetz.* Zittau/Görlitz: Adam Jacob Spielermann, 1767.

Flemming, Willi. *Deutsche Literatur: Sammlung literarischer Kunst- und Kulturdenkmäler in Entwicklungsreihen.* 6 vols. Weimar: Böhlau, 1931.

Flögel, Carl Friedrich. *Geschichte der komischen Litteratur.* Vols. 1, 4. Liegnitz/Leipzig: David Sieger, 1784, 1787.

Gellert, Christian Fürchtegott. *Gesammelte Schriften: Kritische, Kommentierte Ausgabe.* Edited by Bernd Witte. Vol. 5. Berlin/New York: De Gruyter, 1988.

Goethe, Johann Wolfgang von. *Faust: A Tragedy; Interpretive Notes, Contexts, Modern Criticism.* Translated by Walter Arndt and edited by Cyrus Hamlin. New York: W.W. Norton, 2001.

———. *Sämtliche Werke: Briefe Tagebücher und Gespräche.* Frankfurt am Main: Deutscher Klassiker Verlag, 1985–1999. [Abbreviated as FA in citations, with part number (I for works or II for letters), followed by the volume and page number.]

———. *Die Schriften zur Naturwissenschaft.* Weimar: Böhlau Verlag, 1947–. [Commonly referred to as the Leopoldina Ausgabe, this authoritative edition of Goethe's scientific writings is abbreviated as LA in citations, with part number (I for works or II for commentary), followed by the volume and page number.]

Gottsched, Johann Christoph. *Der Biedermann.* Edited by Wolfgang Martens. Stuttgart: Metzler, 1975. Originally published 1728.

———. *Der deutschen Gesellschaft in Leipzig gesammlete Reden und Gedichte.* Leipzig: Breitkopf, 1732.

———. *Die deutsche Schaubühne nach den Regeln der Griechen und Römer.* Vols. 1–6. Leipzig: Bernhard Christoph Breitkopf, 1741–1750.

———. *Erste Gründe der gesamten Weltweisheit, Praktischer Teil.* Leipzig: Bernhard Christoph Breitkopf, 1762.

———. *Gesammlete Reden.* Leipzig: Bernhard Christoph Breitkopf, 1749.

———. *Die Vernünfftigen Tadlerinnen: Erster Jahr-Theil.* Frankfurt/Leipzig: Brandmüller, 1725.

———. *Versuch einer critischen Dichtkunst vor die Deutschen.* Leipzig: Bernhard Christoph Breitkopf, 1730.

———. *Versuch einer critischen Dichtkunst vor die Deutschen.* 4th ed. Leipzig: Bernhard Christoph Breitkopf, 1751.

Grimmelshausen, Hans Jacob Christoffel von. *Simplicissimus Teutsch.* Frankfurt am Main: Deutscher Klassiker Verlag, 2005.

Gryphius, Andreas. *Dramen.* Edited by Eberhard Mannack. Frankfurt am Main: Deutscher Klassiker Verlag, 1991.

Hafner, Philipp. *Burlesken und Prosa.* Edited by Johann Sonnleitner. Vienna: Lehner Verlag, 2007.

Harsdörffer, Georg Philipp. *Poetischer Trichter: Die Teutsche Dicht- und Reimkunst, ohne Behuf der lateinischen Sprache, in VI. Stunden Einzugiessen.* Vol. 2. Hildesheim/New York: G. Olms, 1971.

Heine, Heinrich. *Sämtliche Werke in zwölf Bänden.* Vol. 5, edited by Klaus Briegleb. Munich: Hanser Verlag, 1976.

Heinrich, Julius, *Die Schauspiele des Herzogs Heinrich Julius von Braunschweig, nach alten Drucken und Handschriften.* Edited by Wilhelm Ludwig Holland. Stuttgart: Litterarischer Verein, 1855.

Herder, Johann Gottfried. *Werke.* Edited by Wolfgang Pross. 3 vols. Munich: Hanser Verlag, 1984–2002.

Heumann, Johann. *Der Geist der Geseze der Teutschen.* Nuremberg: Johann Georg Lochner, 1761.

Himberger, Johann Franz Philipp von. *System der Polizeywissenschaft und dem Erkenntnißgrundsatze der Staatsklugheit und ihrer Zweige.* Freiburg im Breisgau: Johann Andreas Satron, 1779.

Home, Heinrich. *Versuche über die ersten Gründe der Sittlichkeit und der natürlichen Religion.* Translated by Christian Günther Rautenberg. Braunschweig: Johann Christoph Meyer, 1768.

Horace. *Satires, Epistles, and Ars Poetica, with an English Translation.* Edited by H. Rushton Fairclough. Cambridge, MA: Harvard University Press, 1932.

Justi, Johann Heinrich Gottlob von. *Deutsche Memoires, oder Sammlung verschiedener Anmerkungen.* Parts 1 and 2. Vienna: Jean Paul Krauss, 1751.

———. *Grundfeste der Macht und Glückseligkeit der Staaten.* Vol. 2. Königsberg/Leipzig: Verlag Woltersdorfs Wittwe, 1761.

———. *Grundriß aller Oeconomischen und Cameral-Wissenschaften.* Frankfurt, 1759.

Kant, Immanuel. *Gesammelte Schriften/Akademieausgabe.* Vol. 7. Berlin: Königlich Preußische Akademie der Wissenschaften, 1917.

———. *Werkausgabe.* Vol. 2. Edited by Wilhelm Weischedel. Frankfurt am Main: Surhkamp Taschenbuch Wissenschaft, 1996.

Kästner, Abraham Gottholf. *Des Herrn von Montesquiou Werk von den Gesetzen.* Frankfurt/Leipzig, 1753.

Kelchner, Ernst. "Sechs Gedichte über die Frankfurter Messe." *Mittheilungen des Vereins für Geschichte und Althertumskunde in Frankfurt am Main* 6 (1881): 317–396.

Kleist, Heinrich von. *Sämtliche Werke und Briefe.* Munich: Carl Hanser Verlag, 2010.

Klingeman, August. *Nachtwachen von Bonaventura: Freimüthigkeiten.* Göttingen: Wallstein Verlag, 2012.

Koch, Heinrich Georg. *Antwort auf das Sendschreiben an Herrn K- in Z- die Leipziger Schaubühne betreffend.* Leipzig: Adam Kießling, 1753.

Krüger, Johann Christian. *Werke: Kritische Gesamtausgabe.* Edited by David G. John. Tübingen: Niemeyer, 1986.

Langemack, Lucas Friedrich. *Abbildung der volkommenen Policei.* Berlin: Johann Jacob Schütze, 1747.

Lau, Theodor Ludwig. *Entwurff einer wohl-eingerichteten Policey.* Frankfurt am Main: Friedrich Wilhelm Förster, 1717.

Lenz, Jakob Michael Reinhold. *Werke und Briefe in drei Bänden.* Edited by Sigrid Damm. 3 vols. Frankfurt am Main: Insel Verlag, 2005.

Lessing, Gotthold Ephraim. *Schreiben an das Publicum, die Schaubühne betreffend.* Frankfurt/Leipzig, 1753.

———. *Werke und Briefe.* Edited by Wilfried Barner. 12 vols. Frankfurt am Main: Deutscher Klassiker Verlag, 1989.

Lessing, Gotthold Ephraim, and Christlob Mylius. *Beyträge zur Historie und Aufnahme des Theaters.* Vols. 1–4. Stuttgart: Johann Benedict Metzler, 1750.

Löwen, Johann Friedrich. *Geschichte des deutschen Theaters*. Edited by Heinrich Stümcke. Berlin: Ernst Frensdorff, 1905.

Mackensen, Wilhelm Friedrich August. *Untersuchung über den deutschen Nationalcharakter in Beziehung auf die Frage: Warum gibt es kein deutsches Nationaltheater?* Wolfenbüttel: Heinrich Georg Albrecht, 1794.

Marperger, Paul Jacob. *Beschreibung der Messen und Jahr-Märkte*. Leipzig: Johann Friedrich Gleditsch and Son, 1710.

May, Franz. *Vermischte Schriften*. Mannheim: Neue Hof- und akademische Buchhandlung, 1786.

Meier, Georg Friedrich. *Abbildung eines Kunstrichters*. Halle: Carl Hermann Hemmerde, 1745.

———. *Gedancken von Schertzen*. Halle: Carl Herrmann Hemmerde, 1744.

Mendelssohn, Moses. *Gesammelte Schriften*. Vol. 11/1, edited by Bruno Strauss. Stuttgart: Friedrich Frommann Verlag, 1974.

Meyer, Reinhart. *Das deutsche Drama des 18. Jahrhunderts in Einzeldrucken*. Vol. 4. Munich: Kraus, 1983.

Moryson, Fynes, and Charles Hughes. *Shakespeare's Europe; Unpublished Chapters of Fynes Moryson's Itinerary, Being a Survey of the Condition of Europe at the End of the 16th Century*. London: Sherratt & Hughes, 1903.

Moser, Friedrich Carl von. *Von dem deutschen National-Geist*. Frankfurt, 1765.

Möser, Justus. *Harlekin: Texte und Materialien mit einem Nachwort*. Edited by Henning Boetius. Bad Homburg: Max Gehlen, 1968.

———. *Patriotische Phantasien*. Vol. 4. Berlin: Verlag der Nicolai'schen Buchhandlung, 1858.

———. *Ueber die deutsche Sprache und Litteratur*. Hamburg: Benjamin Gottlob Hoffmann, 1781.

Mylius, Christlob. "Eine Abhandlung, worinnen erwiesen wird: Daß die Wahrscheinlichkeit der Vorstellung, bey den Schauspielen eben so nötig ist, als die innere Wahrscheinlichkeit derselben." *Beyträge zur critischen Historie der deutschen Sprache, Poesie und Beredsamkeit* 29 (1742): 297–322.

Neuber, Friederike Carolina. *Poetische Urkunden*. Vol. 1, edited by Bärbel Rudin and Marion Schulz. Reichenbach: Neuberin Museum, 1997.

Neudorf, Johann. *Asotvs Das ist COMOEDIA vom verlohrnen Sohn, auß dem 15. Capitel S. Lucae*. Goslar: Geschichts- und Heimatschutzverein Goslar, 1958. Originally published 1608.

Nicolai, Friedrich. "Von den Ursachen, warum die deutsche Schaubühne immer in der Kindheit geblieben." *Briefe, die neuste Litteratur betreffend* 11 (1761): 299–306.

Niessen, Carl, ed. *Frau Magister Velten verteidigt die Schaubühne: Schriften aus der Kampfzeit des deutschen Nationaltheaters*. Emsdetten: H. & J. Lechte Verlag, 1940.

Nietzsche, Friedrich. *Zur Genealogie der Moral*. In *Sämtliche Werke: Kritische Studienausgabe in 15 Bänden*, edited by Giorgio Colli and Mazzino Montinari. Berlin: De Gruyter, 1999.

Omeis, Magnus Daniel. *Gründliche Anleitung zur teutschen accuraten Reim- und Dichtkunst.* Nuremberg: Wolfgang Michahelles and Johann Adolph, 1704.

Opitz, Martin. *Buch von der deutschen Poeterey.* Edited by Wilhelm Braune and Richard Alewyn. Tübingen: M. Niemeyer, 1963.

Paul, Jean. *Werke.* Vol. 5. Munich: Carl Hanser Verlag, 1973.

Platner, Ernst. *Neue Anthropologie für Aerzte und Weltweise.* Vol. 1. Leipzig: Siegfried Lebrecht Crusius, 1790.

Quintilian. *The Orator's Education.* Translated by Donald A. Russell. 5 vols. Cambridge, MA: Harvard University Press, 2001.

Reuters, Christian. *Werke in einem Band.* Edited by Günter Jäckel. Berlin: Aufbau Verlag, 1965.

Riedel, Friedrich Just. *Theorie der schönen Künste und Wissenschaften.* Vienna/Jena: Christian Heinrich Cuno, 1774.

Riemer, Johannes. *Der Regenten bester Hoff-Meister oder lustiger Hoff-Parnassus.* Leipzig: Weißenfels, 1681.

Rist, Johannes. *Depositio Cornuti Typographici, D.i. Lust-Oder Freuden-Spiel.* Lüneberg: Stern, 1654.

Schelling, Friedrich. *Philosophie der Kunst.* Vol. 3 of *Schellings Werke,* edited by Manfred Schröter. Munich: C. H. Beck, 1927.

———. *Philosophie der Kunst.* Darmstadt: Wissenschaftliche Buchgesellschaft, 1960.

Schenk, Christian Ernst. *Komisches Theater.* Breslau: Carl Gottfried Meyer, 1759.

Schiller, Friedrich. *Werke und Briefe in zwölf Bänden. Edited by Matthias Luserke. Vol. 5.* Frankfurt am Main: Deutscher Klassiker Verlag, 1996.

Schlegel, August Wilhelm. *Vorlesungen über dramatische Kunst und Litteratur.* Vol 2. Heidelberg: Mohr und Zimmer, 1811.

Schlegel, Johann Elias. *Werke.* Edited by Johann Heinrich Schlegel. Vol. 3. Frankfurt am Main: Athenäum, 1971.

Schoch, Johann Georg. *Comoedia Vom Studenten-Leben.* Leipzig: Johann Wittigauen, 1658.

Schottelius, Justus Georgius. *Neu Erfundenes Freuden Spiel Genandt Friedens Sieg.* Wolfenbüttel: Conrad Buno, 1648.

Seckendorff, Veit Ludwig von. *Teutscher Fürstenstaat.* Frankfurt am Main: Thomas Mathias Götzens, 1660.

Sidney, Sir Philip. *The Prose Works of Sir Philip Sidney.* Edited by Albert Feuillerat. Vol. 3. Cambridge: Cambridge University Press, 1968.

Sonnenfels, Johann von. *Ueber die Liebe des Vaterlands.* Vienna: Joseph Kurzböck, 1771.

Stieler, Kaspar von. *Ernelinde oder Die Viermahl Braut.* Rudolstadt: Caspar Freyschmidt, 1665.

Sturz, Helfrich Peter. "Julie, ein Trauerspiel in fünf Aufzügen mit einem Brief über das deutsche Theater an die Freude und Beschützer desselben in Hamburg." In *Schriften,* 2:119–222. Munich: Johann Baptist Strohl, 1785.

Sulzer, Johann Georg. *Allgemeine Theorie der Schönen Künste*. Vol. 1. Leipzig: Wiedemanns Erben und Reich, 1771.

Tieck, Ludwig. *Schriften in zwölf Bänden*. Edited by Manfred Frank. Vol. 6. Frankfurt am Main: Deutscher Klassiker Verlag, 1985.

Weise, Christian. *Sämtliche Werke*. Edited by Hans-Gert Roloff. 21 vols. Berlin: De Gruyter, 1991.

Zimmermann, Johann Georg von. *Vom Nationalstolze*. Zurich: Heidegger und Compagnie, 1758.

Secondary and Other Sources

Adler, Hans. "Weltliteratur—Nationalliteratur—Volksliteratur." In *Nationen und Kulturen: Zum 250. Geburtstag Johann Gottfried Herders*, edited by Regine Otto, 271–284. Würzburg: Königshausen & Neumann, 1996.

Alewyn, Richard. "Schauspieler und Stegreifbühne des Barock." In *Mimus und Logos: Eine Festgabe für Carl Niessen*, 1–18. Esdetten: Verlag echte, 1952.

Alexander, John. "Will Kemp, Thomas Sacheville, and Pickelhering: A Consanguinity and Confluence of Three Early Modern Clown Personas." *Daphnis-Zeitschrift* 3, no. 4 (2007): 463–486.

Alexander, Robert J. "George Jolly [Joris Joliphus], Der wandernde Player und Manager." *Kleine Schriften der Gesellschaft für Theatergeschichte* 29/30 (1978): 31–48.

Alpers, Svetlana. "Interpretation without Representation, or, The Viewing of *Las Meninas*." *Representations* 1 (1983): 30–42.

Anderegg, Johannes. "'Grenzsteine der Kunst': Goethes Gattungspoetik und die Arbeit an Faust." *Monatshefte* 102 (2010): 441–457.

———. *Transformationen: Über Himmlisches und Teuflisches in Goethes "Faust."* Bielefeld: Aisthesis Verlag, 2011.

Antonsen-Resch, Andrea. *Von Gnathon zu Saturio: Die Parasitenfigur und das Verhältnis der römischen Komödie zur griechischen*. Berlin/New York: De Gruyter, 2004.

Asper, Helmut G. *Hanswurst: Studien zum Lustigmacher auf der Berufsschauspielerbühne in Deutschland im 17. und 18. Jahrhundert*. Emsdetten: Lechte, 1980.

Bakhtin, M. M. *Rabelais and His World*. Bloomington: Indiana University Press, 1984.

Bareiß, Karl-Heinz. *Comoedia: Die Entwicklung der Komödiendiskussion von Aristoteles bis Ben Johnson*. Frankfurt am Main: Peter Lang, 1982.

Barish, Jonas A. "The Double Plot in 'Volpone.'" *Modern Philology* 51, no. 2 (1953): 83–92.

Barner, Wilfried. "Der Jurist als Märtyrer: Andreas Gryphius' Papinianus." In *Literatur und Recht: Literarische Rechtsfälle von der Antike bis in die Gegenwart*, edited by Ulrich Mölk, 229–242. Göttingen: Wallstein Verlag, 1996.

———. "Über das Negieren von Tradition: Zur Typologie literaturprogrammatischer Epochenwenden in Deutschland." In *Epochenschwelle und Epochenbewußtsein*, edited by Reinhart Herzog and Reinhart Koselleck, 3–52. Munich: Wilhelm Fink Verlag, 1987.

Barwig, Edgar, and Ralf Schmitz. "Narren, Geisteskranke und Hofleute." In *Randgruppen der Spätmittelalterlichen Gesellschaft*, edited by Bernd-Ulrich Hergemöller, 239–269. Warendorf: Fahlbusch Verlag, 2001.

Baskervill, Charles Read. *The Elizabethan Jig and Related Song Drama*. Chicago: University of Chicago Press, 1929.

Bateson, Gregory. *Steps to an Ecology of Mind*. Chicago: University of Chicago Press, 1999.

Beard, Mary. *Laughter in Ancient Rome: On Joking, Tickling, and Cracking Up*. Berkeley: University of California Press, 2014.

Beecroft, Alexander. *An Ecology of World Literature: From Antiquity to the Present Day*. London: Verso, 2015.

Beever, Edward. *The Realities of Witchcraft and Popular Magic in Early Modern Europe: Culture Cognition and Everyday Life*. New York: Palgrave Macmillan, 2008.

Bell, David A. *The Cult of the Nation in France: Inventing Nationalism, 1680–1800*. Cambridge, MA: Harvard University Press, 2003.

Berghahn, Klaus. "Von der klassizistischen zur klassischen Literaturkritik 1730–1806." In *Geschichte der deutschen Literaturkritik*, edited by Peter Uwe Hohendahl, 10–75. Stuttgart: J. B. Metzlersche Verlagsbuchhandlung, 1985.

Binder, Wolfgang. "Goethes klassische Faust-Konzeption." *Deutsche Vierteljahrsschrift* 42 (1968): 55–88.

Blitz, Hans-Martin. *Aus Liebe zum Vaterland: Die deutsche Nation im 18. Jahrhundert*. Hamburg: Hamburger Edition, 2000.

Blumenberg, Hans. " 'Nachahmung der Natur': Zur Vorgeschichte des schöpferischen Menschen." In *Ästhetische und metaphorologische Schriften*, edited by Anselm Haverkamp, 9–46. Frankfurt am Main: Suhrkamp, 2001.

Böckmann, Ralph. *Die Commedia dell'arte und das deutsche Drama des 17. Jahrhunderts*. Nordhausen: Verlag Traugott Baut, 2010.

Bolte, Johannes. *Die Singspiele der englischen Komödianten und ihrer Nachfolger in Deutschland, Holland und Skandinavien*. Hamburg: Voss, 1893.

Borchmeyer, Dieter. "*Faust*—Goethes verkappte Komödie." In *Die großen Komödien Europas*, edited by Franz Norbert Mennemeier, 199–225. Tübingen: A. Francke Verlag, 2000.

Brand, Peter, and Bärbel Rudin. "Der englische Komödiant Robert Browne." *Daphnis* 39 (2010): 1–134.

Breuer, Ingo. "Wi(e)der die falschen Possen? Zur Rezeption von Luigi Riccobonis theatertheoretischen Schriften bei Gottsched und Lessing." In *Deutsche Aufklärung und Italien*, edited by Italo Michele Battafarano, 67–86. Bern: Peter Lang Verlag, 1992.

Brink, C. O. *Horace on Poetry: The "Ars Poetica."* Cambridge: Cambridge University Press, 2011.

Brooks, Douglas A. *From Playhouse to Printing House: Drama and Authorship in Early Modern England.* Cambridge: Cambridge University Press, 2000.

Brown, Jane. *Goethe's Faust: The German Tragedy.* Ithaca: Cornell University Press, 1986.

Brüning, Gerrit. "Die Wette in Goethe's *Faust.*" *Goethe Yearbook* 17 (2010): 31–54.

Caillois, Roger. *Man, Play, and Games.* Urbana: University of Illinois Press, 2001.

Campe, Rüdiger. *Affekt und Ausdruck: Zur Umwandlung der literarischen Rede im 17. und 18. Jahrhundert.* Tübingen: Max Niemeyer Verlag, 1990.

———. "Theater der Institution." In *Konfigurationen der Macht in der frühen Neuzeit,* edited by Rudolf Behrens and Roland Galle, 258–287. Heidelberg: Universitätsverlag, 2000.

Carhart, Michael G. *The Science of Culture in Enlightenment Germany.* Cambridge, MA: Harvard University Press, 2007.

Creizenach, Wilhelm Michael Anton. *Die Schauspiele der englischen Komödianten.* Berlin/Stuttgart: W. Spemann, 1889.

de Mazza, Ethel Matala. "Hintertüren, Gartenpforten und Tümpel: Über Kleists krumme Wege." In *Ausnahmezustand der Literatur: Neue Lektüren zu Heinrich von Kleist,* edited by Nicolas Pethes, 185–207. Göttingen: Wallstein Verlag, 2011.

Devrient, Eduard. *Geschichte der deutschen Schauspielkunst.* Leipzig: J.J. Weber Verlag, 1848.

Dimock, Wai Chee. "Genre as World System." *Narrative* 14, no. 1 (2006): 85–101.

Döring, Detlef. "Die Anfänge der literatur- und sprachwissenschaftlichen Studien an der Leipziger Universität bis zur Mitte des 18. Jahrhunderts." *Jahrbuch für Internationale Germanistik* 44 (2012): 103–138.

———. *Die Geschichte der Deutschen Gesellschaft in Leipzig: Von der Gründung bis in die ersten Jahre des Seniorats Johann Christoph Gottscheds.* Tübingen: Max Niemeyer Verlag, 2002.

Douglas, Mary. "Jokes." In *Collected Works,* 5:146–164. New York: Routledge, 2010.

Eibl, Karl. *Das monumentale Ich: Wege zu Goethe's "Faust."* Frankfurt am Main/Leipzig: Insel Verlag, 2000.

———. "Zur Bedeutung der Wette in 'Faust'." *Goethe Jahrbuch* 116 (1999): 271–280.

Emerson, Ralph Waldo. "Goethe; or, the Writer." In *Essays and Lectures,* 746–761. New York: Library of America, 1983.

Finkelstein, David. *Expression and the Inner.* Cambridge, MA: Harvard University Press, 2003.

Fischer, Ludwig. *Gebundene Rede; Dichtung und Rhetorik in der literarischen Theorie des Barock in Deutschland*. Tübingen: M. Niemeyer, 1968.

Fleming, Paul. *The Pleasures of Abandonment: Jean Paul and the Life of Humor*. Würzburg: Königshausen und Neumann, 2006.

Föcking, Marc. "'Qui habitat in caelis irrideibit eos': Paradiesisches und irdisches Lachen in Dantes *Divina Commedia*." In *Paradies: Topographien der Sehnsucht*, edited by Claudia Benthien and Manuela Gerlof, 77–98. Cologne: Böhlau Verlag.

Ford, Anton. "Action and Generality." In *Essays in Honor of Anscombe's Intention*, edited by Anton Ford, Jennifer Hornsby, and Frederick Stoutland, 76–104. Cambridge, MA: Harvard University Press, 2011.

Foucault, Michel. "'Omnes et singulatim': Toward a Critique of Political Reason." In *Power*, edited by James D. Faubion, 298–325. New York: The New Press, 2000.

———. *The Order of Things*. Translated by Alan Sheridan. New York: Pantheon, 1970.

———. *Security, Territory, Population: Lectures at the Collège de France, 1977–1978*. Translated by Graham Burchell. New York: Picador, 2007.

Fraenkel, Eduard. *Plautine Elements in Plautus*. Translated by Tomas Drevikovksy and Frances Muecke. Cambridge: Cambridge University Press, 2007.

Freud, Sigmund. *Der Witz und seine Beziehung zum Unbewussten*. Vienna: F. Deuticke, 1905.

Frye, Northrop. *Anatomy of Criticism: Four Essays*. Princeton: Princeton University Press, 2000.

Gaier, Ulrich. "Volkspoesie, Nationalliteratur, Weltliteratur bei Herder." In *Die europäische République des lettres in der Zeit der Weimarer Klassik*, edited by Michael Knoche and Lea Ritter-Santini, 101–115. Göttingen: Wallstein Verlag, 2007.

Geulen, Eva. "Serialization in Goethe's Morphology." In *Compar(a)ison*, 53–70. Bern: Peter Lang, 2013.

Giesen, Bernhard, and Kay Junge. "Vom Patriotismus zum Nationalismus." In *Nationale und kulturelle Identität: Studien zur Entwicklung des kollektiven Bewußtseins in der Neuzeit*, 255–303. Frankfurt am Main: Suhrkamp Taschenbuch Wissenschaft, 1991.

Girard, Rene. *Violence and the Sacred*. Translated by Patrick Gregory. Baltimore: Johns Hopkins University Press, 1979.

Graf, Ruedi. *Theater im Literaturstaat*. Tübingen: Max Niemeyer Verlag, 1992.

Grote, Simon. "Review-Essay: Religion and Enlightenment." *Journal of the History of Ideas* 75, no. 1 (2014): 137–160.

Gumbrecht, Hans-Ulrich. "Literarische Gegenwelten, Karnevalskultur und die Epochenschwelle vom Spätmittelalter zur Renaissance." In *Literatur in der Gesellschaft des Spätmittelalters*, 95–144. Heidelberg: Universitätsverlag Winter Universitätsverlag, 1980.

Gurr, Andrew. *Playgoing in Shakespeare's London*. Cambridge: Cambridge University Press, 1987.

———. *The Shakespearian Playing Companies*. Oxford: Clarendon Press; New York: Oxford University Press, 1996.

Habersetzer, Karl-Heinz. *Politische Typologie und dramatisches Exemplum: Studien zum historisch-ästhetischen Horizont des barocken Trauerspiels am Beispiel von Andreas Gryphius' Carolus Stuardus und Papinianus*. Stuttgart: Metzler, 1985.

Haekel, Ralf. *Die englischen Komödianten in Deutschland: Eine Einführung in die Ursprünge des deutschen Berufsschauspiels*. Heidelberg: Winter Universitätsverlag, 2004.

Halliwell, Stephen. *Greek Laughter: A Study of Cultural Psychology from Homer to Early Christianity*. Cambridge: Cambridge University Press, 2008.

Hänsel, Johann Richard. "Die Geschichte des Theaterzettels und seine Wirkung in der Öffentlichkeit." PhD diss., Freie Universität Berlin, 1962.

Hedges, Inez. *Framing Faust: Twentieth-Century Cultural Struggles*. Carbondale: Southern Illinois University Press, 2005.

Hienger, Jörg. "Mephistos Witz." In *J. W. Goethe: Fünf Studien zum Werk*, edited by Anselm Meier, 30–49. New York: Peter Lang, 1983.

Hinck, Walter. *Das deutsche Lustspiel des 17. und 18. Jahrhunderts und die italienische Komödie: Commedia dell'arte und Théâtre italien*. Stuttgart: Metzler, 1965.

Hügli, Anton. "Lachen, das Lächerliche." In *Historisches Wörterbuch der Rhetorik*. Tübingen: Max Niemeyer Verlag, 2001.

Huizinga, Johan. *Homo Ludens: A Study of the Play-Element in Culture*. London: Routledge, 1949.

Jakobson, Roman. *On Language*. Edited by Linda R. Wauh and Monique Monville-Burston. Cambridge, MA: Harvard University Press, 1995.

Jantz, Harold. *The Form of Faust*. Baltimore: Johns Hopkins University Press, 1978.

———. "The Structure of Time in Faust." *MLN* 92, no. 3 (1977): 494–508.

Kinser, Samuel. "Presentation and Representation: Carnival at Nuremberg, 1450–1550." *Representations* 13 (1986): 1–41.

Klotz, Victor. *Geschlossene und offene Form im Drama*. Munich: Hanser Verlag, 1960.

Köhler, Anette. "Das neuzeitliche Fastnachtspiel (1600–1800)." In *Fastnachtspiel—Commedia dell'arte: Gemeinsamkeiten—Gegensätze*, 103–117. Innsbruck: Universitätsverlag Wagner, 1992.

Kommerell, Max. "Faust zweiter Teil: Zum Verständnis der Form." In *Geist und Buchstabe der Schrift*, 9–74. Frankfurt am Main: Vittorio Klostermann, 2009.

Koschorke, Albrecht. *Körperströme und Schriftverkehr*. Munich: Wilhelm Fink Verlag, 2003.

————. *Wahrheit und Erfindung: Grundzüge einer allgemeinen Erzähltheorie.* Frankfurt am Main: S. Fischer Verlag, 2012.

————. "Zur Epistemologie der Natur/Kultur-Grenze und zu ihren disziplinären Folgen." *Deutsche Vierteljahrsschrift für Literaturwissenschaft und Geistesgeschichte* 83, no. 1 (2009): 9–25.

Koselleck, Reinhart. "Historia Magistra Vitae: Über die Auflösung des Topos im Horizont neuzeitlich bewegter Geschichte." In *Vergangene Zukunft: Zur Semantik geschichtlicher Zeiten*, 38–66. Frankfurt am Main: Suhrkamp Taschenbuch Wissenschaft, 1989.

Kosenina, Alexander. *Anthropologie und Schauspielkunst*. Tübingen: Max Niemeyer Verlag, 1995.

Kühlmann, Wilhelm. *Martin Opitz: Deutsche Literatur und Deutsche Nation.* Heidelberg: Manutius, 2001.

Lande, Joel. "Acquaintance with Color: Prolegomena to a Study of Goethe's *Zur Farbenlehre.*" *Goethe Yearbook* 23 (2016): 143–169.

————. "Auftritt und Interaktion: Zu Lessings *Minna von Barnhelm.*" In *Auftreten: Wege auf die Bühne*, edited by Juliane Vogel and Christopher Wild, 233–246. Berlin: Theater der Zeit, 2014.

Levin, Richard. "Elizabethan Clown Subplots." *Essays in Criticism* 16, no. 1 (1966): 84–91.

Limon, Jerzy. *Gentlemen of a Company: English Players in Central and Eastern Europe, 1590–1660.* Cambridge: Cambridge University Press, 1985.

Link, Jürgen. "Was heißt: 'Es hat sich nichts geändert'? Ein Reproduktionsmodell literarischer Evolution mit Blick auf Geibel." In *Epochenschwellen und Epochenstrukturen im Diskurs der Literatur- und Sprachhistorie*, edited by Hans Ulrich Gumbrecht and Ursula Link-Heer, 234–250. Frankfurt am Main: Suhrkamp, 1985.

Luhmann, Niklas. "Kultur als historischer Begriff." In *Gesellschaftstruktur und Semantik*, 4:31–54. Frankfurt am Main: Suhrkamp, 1995.

————. *Legitimation durch Verfahren.* Frankfurt am Main: Suhrkamp Taschenbuch Wissenschaft, 1983.

————. *Soziale Systeme: Grundriß einer allgemeinen Theorie.* Frankfurt am Main: Suhrkamp Taschenbuch Wissenschaft, 1984.

Lukács, Georg. "Der Briefwechsel zwischen Goethe und Schiller." In *Deutsche Literatur*, 89–124. Berlin: Aisthesis, 1964.

————. "Zur Soziologie des modernen Dramas." *Archiv für Sozialwissenschaft und Sozialpolitik* 38 (1914): 303–345 and 662–706.

Lyons, John D. *Exemplum: The Rhetoric of Example in Early Modern France and Italy.* Princeton: Princeton University Press, 1989.

Malinowski, Bronislaw. "The Problem of Meaning in Primitive Languages." In *The Meaning of Meaning: A Study in the Influence of Language upon Thought and of the Science of Symbolism*, edited by Charles Kay Ogden and Ivor Armstrong Richards, 296–336. London: Kegan Paul, 1946.

Mann, Thomas. "Über Goethe's *Faust.*" In *Gesammelte Werke*, 9:581–621. Frankfurt am Main: S. Fischer Verlag, 1991.

Martens, Wolfgang. "Obrigkeitliche Sicht: Das Bühnenwesen in den Lehr-büchern der Policey und Camerialistik des 18. Jahrhunderts." *Internationales Archiv für Sozialgeschichte der deutschen Literatur* 6 (1981): 19–51.

Martus, Steffen. "Negativität im literarischen Diskurs um 1700." In *Kulturelle Orientierung um 1700*, edited by Sylvia Heudecker, Dirk Niefanger, and Jörg Weschke, 47–66. Tübingen: Max Niemeyer Verlag, 2004.

———. *Werkpolitik: Zur Literaturgeschichte kritischer Kommunikation vom 17. bis ins 20. Jahrhundert.* Berlin: De Gruyter, 2007.

Matt, Peter von. "Das letzte Lachen: Zur finalen Szene in der Komödie." In *Theorie der Komödie—Poetik der Komödie*, edited by Ralf Simon, 128–140. Bielefeld: Aisthesis Verlag, 2001.

Meier, Hans. *Die ältere deutsche Staats- und Verwaltungslehre: Ein Beitrag zu der politischen Wissenschaft in Deutschland.* Neuwied am Rhein: Luchterhand, 1966.

Meinecke, Friedrich. *Cosmopolitanism and the National State.* Translated by Robert B. Kimber. Princeton: Princeton University Press, 1970.

Meise, Helga. "Narrheit in den Dramen Heinrich Julius' von Braunschweig-Wolfenbüttel und Lüneberg." In *Der Narr in der deutschen Literatur im Mittelalter und in der frühen Neuzeit*, edited by Jean Schillinger, 171–180. Bern: Peter Lang, 2008.

Meyer, Reinhart. "Der Anteil des Singspiels und der Oper am Repertoire der deutschen Bühnen in der zweiten Hälfte des 18. Jahrhunderts." In *Das deutsche Singspiel im 18. Jahrhundert*, edited by Rainer Gruenter, 27–76. Heidelberg: Winter Universitätsverlag, 1981.

———. "Hanswurst und Harlekin, oder: Der Narr als Gattungsschöpfer: Versuch einer Analyse des komischen Spiels in den Staatsaktionen des Musik- und Sprechtheaters im 17. und 18. Jahrhundert." In *Schriften zur Theater- und Kulturgeschichte des 18. Jahrhunderts*, 289–318. Vienna: Hollitzer, 2012.

———. "Das Nationaltheater in Deutschland als höfisches Institut: Versuch einer Begriffs- und Funtionsbestimmung." In *Das Ende des Stegreifspiels, die Geburt des Nationaltheaters*, edited by Roger Bauer and Jürgen Wertheimer, 124–152. Munich: Wilhelm Fink Verlag, 1983.

Michelsen, Peter. "Mephistos 'eigentliches Element': Vom Bösen in Goethes *Faust*." In *Das Böse: Eine historische Phänomenologie*, edited by Carsten Colpe and Wilhelm Schmidt-Biggemann, 229–255. Frankfurt am Main: Suhrkamp Taschenbuch Wissenschaft, 1993.

Milden, Ursula, and Ian Rutherford. "Decorum." In *Historisches Wörterbuch der Rhetorik*, edited by Gert Ueding, 2:423–452. Tübingen: Max Niemeyer Verlag, 1994.

Mücke, Dorothea E. von. *The Practices of the Enlightenment: Aesthetics, Authorship, and the Public.* New York: Columbia University Press, 2015.

Mukařovský, Jan. *The Word and Verbal Art: Selected Essays.* Translated by John Burbank and Peter Steiner. New Haven: Yale University Press, 1977.

Müller, Joachim. "Goethes Dramentheorie." In *Deutsche Dramentheorien*, edited by Reinhold Grimm, 1:167–213. Frankfurt am Main: Athenäum Verlag, 1971.

Müller-Seidel, Walter. "Komik und Komödie in Goethes *Faust*." In *Die Geschichtlichkeit der deutschen Klassik: Literatur und Denkformen um 1800*, 173–188. Stuttgart: J. B. Metzler Verlag, 1983.

Nagy, Gregory. *The Best of the Achaeans: Concepts of the Hero in Ancient Greek Poetry*. Baltimore: Johns Hopkins University Press, 1999.

Neuhuber, Christian. "Der Vormund des Hanswurst: Der Eggenbergische Hofkomödiant Johann Valentin Petzold und sein Killian Brustfleck." *Daphnis* 35 (2006): 263–299.

Nisbet, H. B. *Gotthold Ephraim Lessing: His Life, Works, and Thought*. Oxford: Oxford University Press, 2013.

Oestreich, Gerhard. "Policey und Prudentia civilis in der barocken Gesellschaft von Stadt und Staat." In *Strukturprobleme der frühen Neuzeit*, 367–379. Berlin: Dunker & Humblot, 1980.

Paul, Markus. *Reichsstadt und Schauspiel: Theatrale Kunst in Nürnberg des 17. Jahrhunderts*. Tübingen: Max Niemeyer Verlag, 2002.

Peters, Julie Stone. *Theatre of the Book, 1480–1880: Print, Text, and Performance in Europe*. Oxford/New York: Oxford University Press, 2000.

Plessner, Helmuth. *Laughing and Crying: A Study of the Limits of Human Behavior*. Translated by James Spencer Churchill and Marjorie Grene. Evanston, IL: Northwestern University Press, 1970.

Preiss, Richard. *Clowning and Authorship in Early Modern Theatre*. Cambridge: Cambridge University Press, 2014.

Prior, Arthur N. "Determinables, Determinates, and Determinants (I)." *Mind* 58 (1949): 1–20. 1949.

Propp, Vladimir. *Morphology of the Folktale*. Translated by Laurence Scott. Austin: University of Texas Press, 1968.

Raabe, Paul. "Gelehrtenbibliotheken im Zeitalter der Aufklärung." In *Bibliotheken und Aufklärung*, edited by Werner Arnold and Peter Vodosek, 103–122. Wiesbaden: Otto Harrassowitz, 1988.

Radcliffe-Browne, A. R. "On Joking Relationships." In *Structure and Function in Primitive Society*, 90–104. New York: The Free Press, 1965.

Reden-Esbeck, Friedrich Johann. *Caroline Neuber und ihre Zeitgenossen: Ein Beitrag zur deutschen Kultur- und Theatergeschichte*. Leipzig: J. A. Barth, 1881.

Riewald, J. G. "The English Actors in the Low Countries, 1585–c. 1650: An Annotated Bibliography." In *Studies in Seventeenth-Century English Literature, History, and Bibliography*, edited by G. A. M. Janssens and G. A. M. Aarts, 157–178. Amsterdam: Rodopi, 1984.

Rudin, Bärbel. "Pickelhering, rechte Frauenzimmer, berühmte Autoren: Zur Ankündigungspraxis der Wanderbühne im 17. Jahrhundert." *Kleine Schriften der Gesellschaft für Theatergeschichte* 34/35 (1988): 29–60.

――――. "Der Prinzipal Heinrich Wilhelm Benecke und seine 'Wienerische' und 'Hochfürstlich Bayreuthische' Schauspielergesellschaft: Zur Geschichte des deutschen, insbesondere des Nürnberger Theaterwesens im ersten Viertel des 18. Jahrhunderts." *Mitteilungen des Vereins für Geschichte der Stadt Nürnberg* 62 (1975): 179–233.

――――. "Von Alexanders Mord-Banquet bis zur Kindheit Mosis: Eine unbekannte Kollektion von Theaterzetteln der Wanderbühne." *Daphnis* 35 (2006): 193–261.

Santayana, George. *Three Philosophical Poets: Lucretius, Dante, and Goethe.* Cambridge, MA: Harvard University Press, 1910.

Schadewaldt, Wolfgang. "*Der zerbrochene Krug* von Heinrich von Kleist und Sophokles' *König Ödipus.*" In *Heinrich von Kleist: Aufsätze und Essays,* edited by Walter Müller-Seidel, 317–325. Darmstadt: Wissenscahftliche Buchgesellschaft, 1967.

Scherer, Jacques. *La dramaturgie classique en France.* Paris: Nizet, 1950.

Schillemeit, Jost. "Das 'Vorspiel auf dem Theater' zu Goethe's *Faust*: Entstehungszusammenhänge und Folgerungen für sein Verständnis." *Euphorion* 80 (1986): 149–166.

Schletterer, Daniela. "Die Verbannung des Harlekin—programmatischer Akt oder komödiantische Invektive?" *Frühneuzeit Info* 8, no. 2 (1997): 161–169.

Schmidt, Erich. *Lessing: Geschichte seines Lebens und seiner Schriften.* Berlin: Weidmann, 1923.

Schmidt, Jochen. *Die Geschichte des Genie-Gedankens in der deutschen Literatur, Philosophie und Politik.* 2 vols. Darmstadt: Wissenschaftliche Buchgesellschaft, 1985.

Schöne, Albrecht. *Götterzeichen, Liebeszauber, Satanskult.* Munich: C. H. Beck, 1983.

Schrickx, Willem. "English Actors at the Courts of Wolfenbüttel, Brussels, and Graz during the Lifetime of Shakespeare." *Shakespeare Survey* 33 (2007): 153–168.

――――. "'Pickelherring' and English Actors in Germany." *Shakespeare Survey* 36 (1983): 135–147.

Schubert, Ernst. *Arme Leute, Bettler und Gauner im Franken des 18. Jahrhunderts.* Neustadt an der Aisch: Gegner & Co., 1983.

――――. *Fahrendes Volk im Mittelalter.* Bielefeld: Verlag für Regionalgeschichte, 1995.

Schwanitz, Dietrich. "Zeit und Geschichte im Roman—Interaktion im Drama: Zur wechselseitigen Erhellung von Systemtheorie und Literatur." In *Theorie als Passion,* edited by Jürgen Markowitz, Rudolf Stichweh, and Dieter Baecker, 181–213. Frankfurt am Main: Suhrkamp, 1987.

Seel, Martin. "Drei Formen des Humors." *Deutsche Vierteljahrsschrift für Literaturwissenschaft und Geistesgeschichte* 76 (2202): 300–305.

Seidlin, Oskar. "Das Etwas und das Nichts: Versuch einer Neuinterpretation einer 'Faust'- Stelle." *Germanic Review* 19 (1944): 170–175.

———. "Ist das 'Vorspiel auf dem Theater' ein Vorspiel zum 'Faust'?" In *Von Goethe zu Thomas Mann*, 56–64. Göttingen: Vandenhock & Ruprecht, 1969.

Sikka, Sonia. *Herder on Humanity and Cultural Difference: Enlightened Relativism*. Cambridge: Cambridge University Press, 2011.

Somerset, Alan. "'How Chances It They Travel?' Provincial Touring, Playing Places, and the King's Men," *Shakespeare Survey* 47 (1994): 45–60.

Spencer, Vicki A. *Herder's Political Thought: A Study of Language, Culture, and Community*. Toronto: University of Toronto Press, 2012.

Sprengel, Peter. "Herr Pantalon und sein Knecht Zanni: Zur frühen Commedia dell'arte in Deutschland." In *Wanderbühne: Theaterkunst als fahrendes Gewerbe*, edited by Bärbel Rudin, 5–18. Berlin: Gesellschaft für Theatergeschichte, 1988.

Staiger, Emil, and Hans-Georg Dewitz, eds. *Der Briefwechsel zwischen Goethe und Schiller*. Frankfurt am Main: Insel Verlag, 2005.

Stern, Martin, and Thomas Wilhelmi. "Samuel Werenfels (1657–1740): Rede von den Schauspielen." *Daphnis* 22 (1993): 73–171.

———. "*Über die Schauspiele*: Eine vergessene Abhandlung zum Schultheater des Basler Theologen Samuel Werenfels (1657–1740) und ihre Spuren bei Gottsched, Lessing, Gellert, Hamann, und Nicolai." In *Théâtre, nation & société*, edited by Ronald Krebs and Jean-Marie Valentin, 167–192. Nancy: Presses Universitaires de Nancy, 1990.

Stoichita, Victor. *La instauration du tableau: Métapeinture à l'aube des temps modernes*. Paris: Méridiens Klincksieck, 1993.

Trappen, Stefan. *Gattungspoetik: Studien zur Poetik des 16. bis 19. Jahrhunderts und zur Geschichte der triadischen Gattungslehre*. Heidelberg: C. Winter, 2001.

Turner, Victor. *From Ritual to Theater: The Human Seriousness of Play*. New York: Performing Arts Journal Publications, 1982.

Unger, Thorston. "Das Klischee vom Mangel an deutschen Stücken: Ein Diskussionsbeitrag zur Internationalität des Hof- und Nationaltheaters." In *Theaterinstitution und Kulturtransfer*, vol. 1, edited by Anke Deten, Thorston Unger, Brigitte Schultze, and Horst Turk, 233–247. Tübingen: Gunter Narr Verlag, 1998.

Vandiver, E. P., Jr. "The Elizabethan Dramatic Parasite." *Studies in Philology* 32, no. 3 (1935): 411–427.

Vaszonyi, Nicholas. "Montesquieu, Friedrich Carl von Moser, and the 'National Spirit Debate' in Germany, 1765–1767." *German Studies Review* 22, no. 2 (1999): 225–246.

Vierhaus, Rudolf. "Montesquieu in Deutschland." In *Deutschland im 18. Jahrhundert*, 9–32. Göttingen: Vandenhoeck und Ruprecht, 1987.

Vismann, Cornelia. *Medien der Rechtsprechung*. Frankfurt am Main: S. Fischer Verlag, 2011.

Vogel, Juliane. "'Nebulistische Zeichnungen': Figur und Grund in Goethes Weimarer Dramen." In *Der Grund: Das Feld des Sichtbaren*, edited by Gottfried Boehm and Matteo Burioni, 317–328. Munich: Wilhelm Fink Verlag, 2012.

Vogl, Joseph. "Staatsbegehren: Zur Epoche der Policey." *Deutsche Vierteljahrsschrift für Literaturwissenschaft und Geistesgeschichte* 74 (2000): 600–626.

Voßkamp, Wilhelm. "Gattungen als literarisch-soziale Institutionen." In *Textsortenlehre—Gattungsgeschichte*, edited by Walter Hinck, 27–43. Heidelberg: Quelle & Meyer, 1977.

Warning, Rainer. "Elemente einer Pragmasemiotik der Komödie." In *Das Komische*, edited by Wolfgang Preisendanz and Rainer Warning, 279–333. Munich: Wilhelm Fink Verlag, 1976.

Wellbery, David E. "Die Enden des Menschen: Anthropologie und Einbildungskraft im Bildungsroman (Wieland, Novalis, Goethe)." In *Das Ende*, edited by Karlheinz Stierle and Rainer Warning, 600–639. Munich: Wilhelm Fink Verlag, 1996.

———. *Goethes Faust I: Reflexion der tragischen Form*. Munich: Carl Friedrich von Siemens Stiftung, 2016.

———. *The Specular Moment: Goethe's Early Lyric and the Beginnings of Romanticism*. Stanford: Stanford University Press, 1996.

———. "*Der zerbrochne Krug*: Das Spiel der Geschlechterdifferenz." In *Kleists Dramen*, edited by Walter Hinderer, 11–32. Stuttgart: Reclam, 1997.

Wiedemann, Conrad. "Andreas Gryphius." In *Andreas Gryphius*, edited by Harald Steinhagen and Benno von Wiese, 435–472. Berlin: Erich Schmidt Verlag, 1984.

Wild, Christopher J. *Theater der Keuschheit—Keuschheit des Theaters: Zu einer Geschichte der (Anti-)Theatralität von Gryphius bis Kleist*. Freiburg im Breisgau: Rombach, 2003.

Wölfel, Kurt. "Moralische Anstalt: Zur Dramaturgie von Gottsched bis Lessing." In *Deutsche Dramentheorien: Beiträge zu einer historischen Poetik des Dramas in Deutschland*, edited by Reinhold Grimm, 56–122. Frankfurt am Main: Athenäum Verlag, 1980.

Yaffee, Glenn. "The Figure of the Parasite in Renaissance Comedy." PhD diss., University of Toronto, 1983.

Zielske, Harald. "Die deutschen Höfe und das Wandertruppenwesen im 17. und frühen 18. Jahrhundert—Fragen ihres Verhältnisses." In *Europäische Hofkultur im 16. und 17. Jahrhundert: Vorträge und Referate*, edited by August Buck, 521–541. Hamburg: Hauswedell, 1981.

Zimmerman, Rolf Christian. "Die Devise der wahren Gelehrsamkeit: Zur satirischen Abischt von Lessings Komödie *Der junge Gelehrte*." *Deutsche Vierteljahrsschrift für Literaturwissenschaft und Geistesgeschichte* 66 (1992): 283–299.

———. *Das Weltbild des jungen Goethe: Studien zur hermetischen Tradition des deutschen 18. Jahrhunderts*, 1:111–144. Munich: Wilhelm Fink Verlag, 2002.

INDEX

Page numbers in *italics* indicate illustrations. Titles of authored works will be found under the author's name, unless otherwise indicated.